PEACE OR PARTITION,

The Habsburg Monarchy and British Policy
1914–1918

by
Wilfried Fest

ST. MARTIN'S PRESS / NEW YORK

FOREWORD

When, in 1961, Professor Fritz Fischer published his important study of *Germany's Aims in the First World War* (English trans.), historical attention turned again to examine a theme which had fascinated an earlier generation of scholars but which inevitably had been overshadowed by the events of the Second World War. After all, if a fierce debate was raging in German historical circles about their country's policies during the 1914–1918 conflict, it was felt to be incumbent upon other scholars to broaden the scope of that debate by investigating the war aims of the Allied governments too. Such investigations could not have been possible earlier, certainly in this country, because the operation of the fifty-year-rule kept the relevant files in the Public Record Office closed to public scrutiny; but by the mid-1960s, this was no longer the case. From that time onwards, scholars have been able to produce a considerable number of publications, based upon these official records, to show the policy of Great Britain (and, to a lesser extent, of France and Italy) during the First World War.

The present study offers a further contribution to this debate and is, quite clearly, a substantial and welcome one. Even granted that Germany always was, both subjectively and objectively, the most formidable enemy of the Allied powers, the position of Austria–Hungary remained of the highest significance. If Berlin and Vienna continued to fight as one united *bloc,* then the military and geopolitical task of conquering them would be formidable indeed. If, however, the Austro-Hungarians could be detached from their German allies by means of a separate peace, the Allies would have made a great diplomatic *coup* and the balance of power would have swung decisively in their favour. Hence, as Dr. Fest shows, the repeated attempts to negotiate such a secret arrangement with Austria–Hungary, especially after the accession of the Emperor Karl in 1916. Yet, despite the pressing reasons both in Vienna and in the Allied capitals for a separate peace, the obstacles were too great to be overcome. This left the decision-makers in London and Paris with little alternative but to bring their second 'card' out from their sleeve – that of the policy of national self-determination for the various peoples of east-central Europe.

If the principle of national self-determination was not as direct a blow against Germany as the proclamation of Austro-Hungarian neutrality, it was nevertheless a very effective stroke against the Central Powers. The 'splintering' or 'balkanisation' of east-central Europe into a cluster of small, ethnically-based countries would lead to a considerable reduction in Germany's eastern frontiers and to the creation of a set of buffer-states between Berlin and Constantinople. It would also mean, *nolens volens,* the complete disintegration of the Habsburg Empire, the multi-national state above all others. This consequence was by no means desired by all members of the Allied decision-makers, but it *was* welcomed by the Slav peoples themselves, their representatives in Allied capitals, and their many western supporters. For almost the entire duration of the war, the debate raged between 'Peace or Partition'. By 1918, the decision had been made in favour of partition; yet even this, as Dr. Fest suggests at the end of his study, did not eliminate the problems of eastern Europe. It simply replaced them with new ones.

If Dr. Fest's book is to be greeted as the most thorough treatment of Allied policy towards Austria–Hungary, it should also be seen as a significant contribution towards the larger theme of 'war aims' and decision-making during the First World War. Scholars interested in more general questions about Allied behaviour (especially Britain's) in those years – questions, for example, about the functioning of the War Cabinet, the role of the Foreign Office, the influence of individuals such as Cecil or Smuts, the part played by 'public opinion' and the press, the treatment of nationality problems – will find a mine of information in *Peace or Partition*. Here is a further reason, then, for historians to welcome the publication of Dr. Fest's work.

Paul M. Kennedy
Reader in History
School of English and American Studies
University of East Anglia

CONTENTS   *Page*

LIST OF ABBREVIATIONS

A.A.   *Auswärtiges Amt*
Add. MSS. Additional Manuscript
B.D.   British Documents on the Origin of the War
B.M.   British Museum
Cab.   Cabinet Office
C.I.G.S. Chief of the Imperial General Staff
D.D.   *Die Deutschen Dokumente zum Kriegsausbruch*
D.D.F.   *Documents Diplomatiques Français*
D.D.I.   *Documenti Diplomatici Italiani*
D.M.I.   Director of Military Intelligence
D.M.O. Director of Military Organization
F.O.   Foreign Office
For.Rel. Papers Relating to the Foreign Relations of the United States
Hansard Hansard's Parliamentary Debates (House of Commons)
H.H.St.A. *Haus-, Hof- und Staatsarchiv*
I.B.D.I. Intelligence Bureau of the Department of Information
Int.Bez. *Die Internationalen Beziehungen im Zeitalter des Imperialismus*
I.W.C.   Imperial War Cabinet
J.C.E.A. Journal of Central European Affairs
J.M.H.   Journal of Modern History
J.C.H.   Journal of Contemporary History
Min.Aff.Etr. *Archives du Ministère des Affaires Etrangères*
Ö.U.A.   *Österreich-Ungarische Aussenpolitik*
P.A.   *Politisches Archiv*
P.H.S.   Printing House Square
P.I.D.   Political Intelligence Department
P.R.O.   Public Record Office
R.A.M.C. Royal Auxiliary Medical Corps
R.D.M. *Revue des Deux Mondes*
S.E.E.R. Slavonic and East European Review
S.W.C. Supreme War Council
WC   War Cabinet
Wk.geh. *Weltkrieg geheim*

AUTHOR'S PREFACE

This study is mainly based upon original archival material, the recent release of which has made it possible to undertake a detailed study of the subject – with the first hand help of sources. The documents in the Public Record Office have constituted the largest amount of material for this study. But they have been supplemented by the private papers of British personalities involved in this aspect of First World War policy. Among them the papers of Lloyd George, Balfour, Cecil and Steed were particularly valuable.

Apart from these British records archives in other countries were examined. Of these the French documents in the Quai d'Orsay were essential in judging inter-Allied policy, although it was not possible to clarify all aspects of it, because the important series "La Paix" has not survived the turmoils of the Second World War. To set British and Allied policy in the right perspective on the international scene the records of the Austrian State Archives and the German Foreign Ministry were examined with special regard to the initiatives and reactions on the part of the Central Powers and also from the point of view of their own inter-alliance relationship.

Besides the wide range of manuscript sources available the printed collections still remain important. This is particularly the case for those countries where no archives could be searched such as Russia, Italy and the United States. Attention has also been devoted to publications of Austrian and German documents. In fact such editions have been referred to in preference to the location in the archives of an already published document.

Previous research on the topic of this thesis practically started with the involvement of Steed and Seton-Watson in Austro–Hungarian affairs. Yet it needed the passing of another war to enable a detached treatment of the many interesting questions raised by the outbreak of the First World War to take place. Not surprisingly the problem under consideration appealed to descendants of the former subject nationalities of the Habsburg Monarchy. One of them, Harry Hanak, wrote a painstakingly detailed study on the formation of public opinion (*Great Britain and Austria–Hungary during the First World War*, Oxford

1962), which covers this ground almost completely. Hence the author has not attempted to surpass Hanak in his field but has rather tried to examine more closely the relations between public opinion, pressure groups and the actual decision makers. The undertaking of this task was only made possible through the insights provided by new material. Hanak himself must have been aware of the deficiency inherent in his approach and has recently published the results of his latest research in an article, which appeared while this thesis was being completed ("The Government, The Foreign Office and Austria–Hungary, 1914–1918", *Slavonic and East European Review*, xlvii, Jan. 1969). In it Hanak provides a sound survey of official British attitudes which can be regarded as a competent introduction to the problem. However, the scope of his supplementary study is too limited to cover the full complexity of the subject. He restricts himself to giving an account from selected British records, which did not call for a detailed discussion throughout this thesis and therefore his contribution is only acknowledged here in its entirety.

Two more recent books touching the Austro-British issue within the wider context of the diplomacy of the First World War are V. H. Rothwell, *British War Aims and Peace Diplomacy 1914–1918*, Oxford 1971 and Z. A. B. Zeman, *A Diplomatic History of the First World War*, London 1971. K. J. Calder, *Britain and the Origins of the New Europe 1914–1918*, Cambridge 1976, approaches the Austrian problem from an alternative angle, i.e. the claims of the representatives of the subject nationalities and the recognition of their aims. This book appeared too late to be referred to in the text.

Other research on the Habsburg Monarchy in the period of the First World War could treat the subject under discussion only tentatively because of the lack of documentary evidence. Nevertheless some valuable information and criticism is provided in some other works. The first to be noted is A. J. May, *The Passing of the Hapsburg Monarchy, 1914–1918*, Philadelphia 1966, a comprehensive study which includes much detailed secondary evidence. Z. A. B. Zeman, *The Break-up of the Habsburg Empire*, London 1961, is largely concerned with the activities of the emigre politicians in Austria–Hungary itself but also deals with their representatives abroad and gives a first appreciation of Allied propaganda against the Monarchy.

The inter-Allied aspect is well treated by V. S. Mamatey, *The United States and East Central Europe*, Princeton 1957, which throws much light on the Anglo-American relationship. Italian policy has been put into an international perspective by L. Valiani, *La dissoluzione dell'Austria–Ungheria*, Milan 1966, to whom this author is much indebted as he was unable to consult official Italian records himself. Unfortunately there is not yet any modern study from the French point of view and due to the incompleteness of the French documents, the French edition of Beneš's Memoirs (*Souvenirs de guerre et de révolution*, Paris 1928), which is relatively reliable, has to be referred to.

The situation is much better on the Austrian side where the debate on the so-called "war guilt" question has stimulated a thorough search of the Austrian and German archives. The major works by German scholars, however, concentrate on the Austro–German policy-making and their background treatment of the British side is either lacking in sufficient documentation or suffers from the attempt to exculpate the German government. (Cf. G. A. Ritter, *Staatskunst und Kriegshandwerk*, vols. iii, iv; Munich 1966–68 and W. Steglich, *Die Friedenspolitik der Mittelmächte*, 1917–1918, Wiesbaden 1964.) In Austria itself a recent attempt to balance these studies is I. Meckling, *Die Aussenpolitik des Grafen Czernin*, Munich 1969, which gives a slightly biased Austrian version without too many new insights. Rather more original are the monographs by the Nestors of Austrian historiography, H. Benedikt and F. Engel-Janosi (Cf. bibliography). A concise but shrewd study of the peace question is R. Kann, *Die Sixtusaffaire*, Munich 1966, whereas G. Brook-Shepherd, *The Last Habsburg*, London 1969, despite the use of some interesting sources, cannot be regarded as a scholarly contribution to the problem.

The author, while trying to digest the research hitherto done, has concentrated on those aspects which have not yet been adequately covered or have been completely neglected so far. The main emphasis in this study is therefore on questions which are still controversial or have not been raised at all.

Wilfried Fest

ACKNOWLEDGEMENTS

This book evolved from a D.Phil. thesis submitted to the University of Oxford. Many people and institutions assisted me in the preparation of both the thesis and the book and I would like to express my gratitude to all of them.

Foremost among those whose counsel must be acknowledged is my tutor, Professor A. J. P. Taylor, who patiently presided over my labours for three academic years, gave invaluable hints, pointed out mistakes and suggested alterations and additions.

My thanks are also due to Professors Agnes Headlam-Morley, Agatha Ramm, C. A. Macartney and J. Joll who discussed the topic with me at various stages of the work. Professors Christopher and Hugh Seton-Watson supplied me with information about their father and permitted me to consult his correspondence in the School of Slavonic and East European Studies in London.

Of my fellow students who did research in related fields I have to thank in particular Dr. P. M. Kennedy who read a draft of the thesis and pointed out various errors and Germanisms in my English. He and Mr. Eino Lyttinen were most kind in introducing me to the archival technicalities of the Public Record Office.

I owe a debt of gratitude to St. Antony's College, Oxford, for its material support as well as congenial atmosphere which stimulated me during my research. My special thanks are due to my college tutor, Mr. A. J. Nicholls, for his assistance in many problems during my Oxford days.

I would like to express my appreciation to the Volkswagen Foundation for the financial assistance that made this project possible; to the officials and staff of the Public Record Office; the Bodleian Library; the British Museum; the Beaverbrook Library; *The Times* Archives; the State Archives in Vienna and the Archives of the French Foreign Ministry.

I wish to thank the Librarian of St. Antony's College, particularly for the procurement of extra microfilms from Vienna and from the files of the German Foreign Office. Quotations from the Crown copyright

Peace or Partition

records in the Public Record Office appear by permission of the Controller of H.M. Stationery Office, London. For permission to quote from copyright material I am indebted to the Beaverbrook Library and *The Times* Archives.

Free University of Berlin   *Wilfried Fest*

INTRODUCTION

The Pre-War Heritage of the Traditional Friendship

For centuries the relations between Great Britain and Austria were rather indifferent, because their interests seldom brought them into contact with each other. It was not before the evolution of the "Balance of Power" in Europe as the maxim of British foreign policy that the Habsburg Monarchy became a country which was taken into consideration by British statesmen who wanted to prevent any power from attaining continental supremacy. After the Napoleonic bid for hegemony the common interest of the two countries was realized by both Metternich and Castlereagh, and since the Congress of Vienna the Habsburg Empire was by and large appreciated by Britain as a useful factor to bar Russia from advancing to the Near East and the Balkans. So on the basis of this common interest there developed a "traditional friendship" which was described by Lord Palmerston in a speech in 1849:

> Austria stands in the centre of Europe, a barrier against encroachment on the one side and against invasion on the other. The political independence and liberties of Europe are bound up, in my opinion, with the maintenance and integrity of Austria as a great European Power, and therefore anything which tends by direct, or even remote contingency to wreck and to cripple Austria, but still more to reduce her from the position of a first-rate Power to that of a second state, must be a great calamity to Europe which every Englishman ought to deprecate and try to prevent.[1]

This view was confirmed later by Lord Salisbury, who believed that in the strength and independence of Austria lay the best hopes of European peace and stability.[2] The basically friendly attitude towards Austria–Hungary in England was expressed by the historian and philosopher Lord Acton, who thought that "the theory of nationality is a retrograde step in history" and "the co-existence of several nations under the same State is a test, as well as the best security of its

---

[1] A. F. Pribam: *Austria–Hungary and Great Britain, 1908–1914*, London 1951, p.43.
[2] A. May, *The Passing of the Habsburg Monarchy*, Philadelphia 1966, p.223.

1

freedom."[3] Despite such sympathies Great Britain did not take Austria's side in the war of 1859, but after the victory of the Italian liberation movement and the settlement of the Danish question the controversies that had affected Anglo-Austrian understanding were removed.

In the latter stage of the 19th century, the Balkans became the focus of discussion between Vienna and London. Here, where all the great powers had an increasing interest, the presuppositions for a common approach were more favourable, although the Austrians had the feeling that they were used by the British as their cat's-paw, a mistrust that was fostered by Britain's aversion to binding agreements. However, the Congress of Berlin ended satisfactorily for both countries. Despite the feelings of Gladstone, who regarded the Danubian Monarchy merely as a "brilliant second of the German Empire" and declared in 1880 that there was no spot on the world map on which you could lay a finger and say; "Here Austria did good", co-operation became even closer in 1887 with the conclusion of the Mediterranean agreements under Salisbury and in May 1893 Rosebery allowed his ambassador in Vienna to describe Austria-Hungary as "the natural ally" of Great Britain.[4]

The Bosnian crisis of 1908 led to a serious deterioration in the relations between London and Vienna, when the Austrian action met with the disapproval of Asquith and Grey. Possibly English indignation was increased by the fact that an attempt to detach Austria from the Triple Alliance had obviously failed, although such endeavours have later been denied by British diplomats. It seems certain that there was at least an attempt to stop German naval armament, but whether Edward VII made any offer to Francis Joseph during his sojourn in Ischl remains obscure.[5]

The Austrian court and government remained convinced of the equality of Austrian and British interests and the necessity of maintaining the traditionally friendly relations between the two countries. Aehrenthal was intelligent enough to see that after the Anglo-Russian entente of 1907 it had become even more necessary for Austria to be on good terms with England. When the British grudge over the annexation of Bosnia–Herzegovina was dying down, official circles in Vienna expressed a wish for the closest and friendliest relations. The British ambassador Cartwright did not believe that it was possible to detach Austria–Hungary from her alliance with Germany, but he thought that

---

[3] Lord Acton, *Essays on Church and State*, London (2), 1952.

[4] A. J. P. Taylor, *The Struggle for Mastery in Europe 1848–1918*, Oxford 1954, pp. 284, 342.

[5] Lord Hardinge, *Old Diplomacy*, London 1947, p.164, denies that any such attempt was made; apparently there is no record of it in the files, which the Foreign Office staff searched in vain after a war speech of the Emperor Charles hinting at an alleged British offer. F.O.371/3081, No. 215380/f.97807 of 11 Nov. 1917 – but cf. O.(sterreichisch)–U.(ngarische) A.(ussenpolitik), i, Nos. 36–38, 55; B.(ritish) D.(ocuments), v, App.IV. and ix, pt.1, No. 71.

We may succeed by rendering little services and by showing proofs of friendship to her to lay little ties between Austria–Hungary, ourselves, France and Italy, and perhaps finally Russia which, in a critical moment, may counteract the great pull from Berlin, and, paralysing Austria–Hungary, cause her to hesitate taking sides in a great European struggle until the issue has been practically decided. . . .[6]

In this combination an Austro-Russian reconciliation was indeed the most questionable, but a continuance of this opposition could be useful for Britain.[7] Tensions over Persia strained the new understanding with Russia, which was not comparable with the other agreements among the Triple Entente. Politicians continued to think in terms of a conservation of the Habsburg Empire as a counterweight to Russia's ambitions in Eastern Europe and Asia. On 13 March 1911 Grey declared in the House of Commons that Britain was anxious to restore her former friendly relations with Austria-Hungary. He explained that Britain had never desired that her ties with a third power should make friendly relations with Germany impossible.[8] This speech was received favourably by the Austrian press,[9] which interpreted it as a denial of the so-called policy of "encirclement" and an outspoken offer for good mutual relations between London and Vienna.

The Foreign Office regarded relations with Austria as "quite good", although they were insignificant insofar as Austrian policy was restricted to her own internal affairs and "her own immediate part of the world". Consequently Britain came into little direct contact with her, and this was perhaps the main reason why trouble between the two countries seldom arose. The dark clouds which covered the diplomatic horizon two to three years ago had vanished by 1911 and there was no discord left between the British and the Austrian government.[10]

As for Austria, she was in permanent financial difficulties. Her dependence on foreign capital aid was steadily increasing and leading her into a position of economic subservience to Germany. The centre of Central European policy was thus shifted from Vienna to Berlin. But while the danger of the German *"Weltpolitik"* was recognized in Whitehall, the situation of the Habsburg Empire met with little understanding there and the spokesmen of the subject nationalities critized the Triple Entente for its ignorance in this matter.[11]

It was the French who were most apprehensive of Germany's *Drang*

---

[6] B.D., ix(1), No. 19 of 9 July 1909.

[7] F. R. Bridge, *Great Britain and Austria-Hungary 1906–14*, London 1972, points out that Cartwright was unable to convince Grey that Austria could be encouraged to take a more independent line towards Germany and concludes that the breakdown of relations was due to the "iron logic of the balance of power" as Grey conceived it.

[8] *Hansard*, 5th Ser., xxii, 1972ff.

[9] B.D., vi, No. 452 of 16 Mar. 1911 (press summary).

[10] Minutes of a meeting of the Committee of Imperial Defence, 26 May 1911; B.D., vi, App.v.

[11] E.g. by Kramár in a Chamber speech, reported by Cartwright on 31 Jan, 1911; B.D., ix. No. 211.

nach Osten in the South Eastern direction. Before the conclusion of the *entente cordiale* the belief was widespread in France that Britain might come to an agreement with Germany giving her rival a *carte blanche* for the execution of her *Mitteleuropa* plans, and thus deflecting the Prussian ambition from the British imperial possessions.[12] This prospect had been sufficient reason for France to care for a viable Habsburg Empire, which would have opposed the above scheme. Now that France felt more secure with Russia and Britain as allies, her interest in a closer relation with the Monarchy dissipated. This became evident when Aehrenthal ventilated the possibility of a substantial Austrian loan in Paris. The French ambassador believed they were approaching a "crossroads", at which Austria would offer her hand to the Triple Entente in order to be able to detach herself gradually from Germany. His British colleague was not so sure whether Aehrenthal really contemplated the possibility of a secret agreement with France according to which Austria would be obliged to remain neutral in case Germany attacked France. Cartwright was convinced that Aehrenthal would keep to "the letter of the treaty" (with Germany), but he regretted that the French government might miss the chance of sounding out how far Austria was prepared to abandon Germany.[13] However, Poincaré disapproved of lending Austria 1 million francs, though French financial circles (*La société générale*) were in favour of it because of their manifold economic links with Austria.[14]

Britain also had economic links with Austria, although moderate. In the 19th century British capital and enterprise had helped the early railroad building and particularly in Bohemia the industrialization was almost exclusively based on British investment. Before the war British capital was mainly represented in state debentures and public loans, mortgages, railroad obligations, and the gas industry. A prominent sign of Britain's share in the economic life of the Monarchy was the Anglo-Austrian bank in Vienna.[15] But this economic interest of the City was not to influence political decisions in the direction of attempting an Anglo-Austrian entente. On the contrary English financiers were unfavourable to any part of an Austrian loan in England, as *The Times* found out in connection with the Aehrenthal offer, which was soon killed by leaks in the press.[16]

With Aerenthal's death Europe lost a kind of *chef d'orchestre* whom Edward VII had appreciated. The Austrian foreign minister had fostered good relations with England and her associate France in order to

---

[12] A. Chéradame, *L'Allemagne, la France et la question d'Autriche*, Paris 1902, pp.186–87.

[13] B.D., vii, Nos. 696 & 708, Nov. 1911.

[14] D(ocuments) D.(iplomatiques) F.(rançais), 3 Sér., i, No. 168; H. Feis, *Europe, the World's Banker*, New York repr. 1965, pp. 201–09.

[15] J. Křížek, *Die wirtschaftlichen Grundzüge des österreichisch-ungarischen Imperialismus in der Vorkriegszeit* (1900–1914), Prague 1963, p.54.

[16] H. W. Steed, *Through Thirty Years*, i, London 1929, pp.345–47.

facilitate a rapprochement with Russia, which was to have enabled him to oppose Germany's selfish exigencies. While the Germans naturally disliked the idea of an Austro-Russian understanding, Grey was in favour of it because from the British point of view a war between the Habsburg and the Tsarist Empires, in which they themselves had no interest, would have been most inconvenient.[17] Thus the heritage of the Anglo-Russian rivalry might have benefited Austria–Hungary and saved her from a "falling out" among the conquerors. The Habsburgs could at least count upon a benevolent British attitude towards them, because the maintenance of the Monarchy helped Britain's desire to block both German and Russian influence.

However, the existence of the Habsburg Empire was more and more threatened by the rise of nationalism among the Slavs. The grant of universal suffrage did much to improve the general position of the Slav nationalities in the Dual Monarchy, but there was now a resurgence of fear over German expansion and domination. The formation of a common front in the face of German aggression was propagated at the Slav conference which took place in St. Petersburg in July, 1908, the initiative having come mainly from the Czechs. The adoption of the new term "neo-Slavism" signified a break with Russian Panslavism and laid emphasis on the liberation of the Slav peoples of Austria–Hungary. The aim of Kramář and his supporters was a Slavization of the Monarchy – not her destruction. Their Russian sponsors thought along the same lines.[18] The principal adviser of the Foreign Minister, Prince G. Trubetzkoi, wrote in 1910 that an independent Austria, as long as she respected the *status quo* in the Balkans and the sovereignty of the small nations in that region, "was an absolute necessity for Russia as well as for Europe as a counterweight to Pan-Germanism".[19] But the rulers in Russia were not prepared to accept another humiliation as the one of 1908 and thus tried to prevent it by shaping the Balkan League. Russia's hostility against Austria and the desire to take revenge were regarded as the basic evil by H. Nicolson who praised Austria for acting with "great conciliation and dignity" and showing "great moderation and forbearance under considerable provocations".[20]

During the Balkan crisis of 1911/12 the Radical Party in Serbia looked increasingly for support to Tsarist Russia. Not only the activities of the secret Serb organizations, but also the official Serb policy, bore a marked anti-Habsburg character. Russian diplomacy tried to play down the aggressive character of the Serb pretentions by

---

[17] B.D., ix, (1), No. 557 (22 Feb. 1912) & No. 537 (9 Jan. 1912).
[18] J. Erickson, *Panslavism*, London 1964, pp.30–32.
[19] G. Trubetzkoi, *Russland als Grossmacht*, Stuttgart 1917 (2), p.147.
[20] B.D., ix (2), No. 238 of 19 Nov. 1912.

insinuating that "the Austrian Empire had only a few years more to run before it broke up".[21] According to a secretary of ambassador Hartwig – who "inspired" Serbia's policy – the mobilization in November 1912 was not directed against Serbia or Russia but to cover the danger of internal risings. The British representative in Belgrade, R. Paget, feared that there was little hope for a satisfactory settlement. Bad blood would probably be bred between Austria and Serbia until one of the following two things happened: either the Slav peoples detached themselves and, together with Serbia and Montenegro, formed a South Slav kingdom; or Serbia was absorbed by Austria. For Paget the outcome depended almost entirely upon which policy Austria was going to pursue in her Slav provinces. He had gathered from utterances of his Austrian colleague that the Austrian government intended to conciliate the Slavs as soon as possible by introducing much more liberal regimes in Croatia and Bosnia–Herzegovina.[22]

Yet in face of such vague promises, which did not sound as if Austria was going to reform the Dual structure of the Empire drastically in favour of the Slavs, the sceptical British observer excluded an Austro–Serbian compromise. A tripartite solution for the pacification of the South Slavs was conceived by the heir apparent. Francis Ferdinand must have realized that he needed support for his plans abroad also in case of German objections. Having been none too friendly towards Britain previously, he seemed convinced after his hearty welcome in London that his country would gain from mutually friendly relations.[23] But the impression evoked by him in London was deceptive. It never occurred to Francis Ferdinand that he might do anything to bring that "strange, perfidious, and above all Protestant" Empire into fruitful co-operation with his own.[24] His conservative mind was rather inclined towards Russia, where sympathies for the Habsburgs were still preserved among court circles. Francis Ferdinand, however, was soon viewed in St. Petersburg as the head of the military party in Austria whose policy found the support of Berlin.[25] The conflict over Skutari finally divided the Habsburgs and the Romanovs and set an end to the attempts to restore the cordial relations of the Mürzsteg times. Nicholas II was now embittered against Austria and refused to resume any personal contacts with the Habsburgs.[26] This definite decision against a renewal of the Three Emperors' Alliance led to second thoughts about the existence of the Habsburg Empire at all.

[21] *Ibid.*, No. 313 of 30 Nov. 1912.
[22] B.D., ix (2), No. 347 of 6 Dec. 1912.
[23] Annual report on Austria–Hungary, 1913, F.O.371/2241, f.20855.
[24] E. Crankshaw, *The Fall of the House of Habsburg*, London 1963, p.364.
[25] B.D., ix (2), No.576 (30 Jan. 1913).
[26] K. B. Vinogradov/J. A. Pissarev, "Die internationale Lage der ö.u. Monarchie in den Jahren 1900 bis 1918", in *Österreich-Ungarn in der Weltpolitik*, Berlin 1965, p.23.

They were expounded by Nicholas in an interview with ambassador Buchanan on 14 April 1913.[27] On this occasion the Tsar spoke about Austria without acrimony but called her "a source of weakness for Germany and a danger for peace", because Germany felt obliged to support her Balkan policy. The Emperor seemed to believe that the dissolution of the Austrian Empire was "merely a question of time" and envisaged the shaping of a Hungarian and a Bohemian kingdom, while the South Slavs would be absorbed by Serbia and the Transylvanians by Rumania and the remaining German provinces would be included in the German Empire.

Buchanan could not understand how the Tsar arrived at this conclusion. For the British ambassador and probably also his government it was impossible to imagine the disappearance of a political entity that had existed for centuries and played a prominent part in the concert of powers. So Buchanan contented himself in replying that "such a change on the map of Europe was not likely to be effected without a general war".

This dissolution was also undesirable for Russia, where the break-up of the monarchy was by no means taken for granted. Sazonov, in a memorandum which he submitted to the Tsar half a year after the latter's interview with Buchanan,[28] still left open two possible solutions: federalism for the various nationalities *or* a desperate struggle ending in war, for which Russia was not prepared. Therefore the Russian Foreign Minister disclaimed any direct interest in the fate of the Czechs at another Neo-Slav congress in May 1914.[29] Only Serbia could, in case of a war, count on Russia as a protector. She also reckoned – "rightly or wrongly" according to the undecided British *chargé d'affaires* in Belgrade – on the disaffection of the Austro-Hungarian Slavs.[30]

Did Britain favour the aspirations of Slav irredentism before the war? Joseph Redlich, the Austrian Liberal, who visited London after the Balkan wars, gained the following impression:

> Austria–Hungary ... is seen as being very weak, but even so as highly awkward: again above all in connection with Germany, whose satellite she appears to be. In London they would gladly see the Monarchy shattered: for the ideal of English policy is the formation of small states in Europe which can be played against each other.[31]

Only the first part of the judgment is true to some extent. The fact that

[27] B.D., ix (2), No. 849; the telegram, which was addressed to Grey, was also sent to the King, Asquith, the Cabinet and the D.M.O.
[28] *Int.(ernationale) Bez.(iehungen) im Zeitalter des Imperialismus*, II, i, p.48ff. (20 Jan. 1914).
[29] T. G. Masaryk, *The Making of a State*, p.13.
[30] B.D., x (1), No. 20 of 25 Sept. 1913 (Crackanthorpe to Grey).
[31] *Schicksalsjahre Österreichs* (The political diary of J. Redlich), Graz 1953, i, p.196 (entry of 15 April, 1913).

Austria was tied up with Germany was accepted by Britain as unalterable for the near future. In the last years before the war Grey therefore very definitely avoided attempting to detach Austria from Germany. His policy was based on a mutual and loyal recognition of the existence of the two alliances. There was, therefore, no question of undermining the position of the Habsburg Empire by promoting the balkanisation of Europe. On the contrary, British diplomatic actions in 1912/13 were directed against the rise of a strong South Slav state. Grey denied to Sazonov British support for a Serbian access to the Adriatic and it was intimated in Vienna that Britain's attitude in the question of the Straits remained unchanged and that basically there were no objections to the anti-Russian course of the foreign policy of the Habsburg Empire, which was still regarded as a useful counterweight against an advance of Russia's Slav brothers.

Cartwright even went so far as to make public declarations, in which he expressed his surprise about Berchtold's love of peace in the face of Serbia and Montenegro.[32] His councillor Theo. Russell was of the opinion that Berchtold had proved himself "as a friend of England and ardent admirer of Sir Edward's impartial policy". Since Albania, the object of dispute in the second Balkan war, was of no importance for Britain but "vital" for the Dual Monarchy, it would be a pity to give the other powers the pleasure of seeing Britain break with Austria.[33] Grey found the letter interesting, though he was not so convinced of Austria being an asset for Britain in the future:

> Austria will be of little use to us as a friend, if she falls to pieces. One cannot steer with confidence by a star that may dissolve.[34]

This remark shows that the belief in the viability of the Habsburg Empire was already shaken. This did not mean that London intended to promote the fall, but at least a certain measure of doubt had developed. Sir Maurice de Bunsen, Britain's last diplomatic representative at the Hofburg, after reading Steed's book,[35] wrote to Nicolson:[36]

> It is a standing marvel that the country still holds together. . .
> Logically it should fall to pieces, but it does not.

The centrifugal forces at work are recognized, but the underlying conservative admiration for the cohesion of the Monarchy is there at the same time.

The concern about the possible dissolution of the Habsburg Empire

---

[32] *O.U.A.*, iv, Nos. 3579, 3634, 3639, 3645, 3674; v, Nos. 4902, 5580.
[33] *B.D.*, x (1), No. 316 of 21 Nov. 1913.
[34] Grey's minute, *ibid.*
[35] Undated letter between 30 Mar. & 24 Apr. Cit. in E. T. S. Dugdale, *Maurice de Bunsen*, London 1934, pp.283–4.
[36] For H. W. Steed, *The Hapsburg Monarchy*, London 1913, cf. ch.I, 1.

was the greatest in the Wilhelmstrasse. It was intimated by Jagow[37] to ambassador Goschen, who did not share the then widespread argument that the Monarchy would break up with the death of Francis Joseph. But Jagow's fears had their origin in the rise of the "nationality-fever", which in his opinion had even infected the Austro-Germans and created a chaos that rendered Austria's value as an ally doubtful. Goschen believed that Jagow's remarks were simply the expression of a temporary depression. But should the German Austrians really cease to form a bulwark against the Slavs, this would preoccupy the leading German politicians.[38] From this Nicolson surmised that if Germany had started to doubt whether Austria deserved her support, she might prefer to shake hands with Russia.[39]

Meanwhile Britain tried to mitigate the tensions by keeping up contacts with the Central Powers. In early May 1914 Grey listened with great pleasure to Berchtold's discourse on British policy and its warm applause in the Austrian press, which also welcomed a visit of the Royal Navy.[40] Austro-British relations seemed cordial again and the general impression in Vienna was that Britain would not go beyond demonstrations in the case of Austrian military action against Serbia. After the assassination of Francis Ferdinand the predominant feeling at the Ballplatz was that Austria's cause was so just that the Great Powers would not intervene. Berchtold and Conrad counted upon Britain's restraining influence on Russia, which without British support would thus have to stand aside. The Austrians did not want to recognize, de Bunsen noted critically, "that their only chance of resisting the downward pressure of Germany upon them would lie in a broad policy of conciliation towards the South Slav elements . . ."[41]

The Foreign Office also did not think of war as a result of the incident. Nicolson wrote to Buchanan and de Bunsen that he hoped that the tragedy of Sarajevo would not lead to further complications.[42] The British Consul General in Budapest relieved his Foreign Secretary with a report about an opulent wedding ceremony which was celebrated by undisturbed Magyar magnates.[43] In the meantime Grey was anxious to win the Russian government for a conciliatory attitude towards Austria in case the Viennese Cabinet felt it necessary to take a stronger stand against Serbia because of the Sarajevo murder. Much of the British attitude depended, however, on the character of the meas-

---

[37] *B.D.*, x (2), No. 532 of 27 Mar. 1914.
[38] Jagow must have been confirmed in his pessimism by Tschirschky, who reported from Vienna on 22 May that the Monarchy was "creaking in all joints"; *Die Grosse Politik der europäischen Kabinette*, vol. 39, No. 15734.
[39] *B.D.*, x (2), No. 533 of 30 Mar. 1914.
[40] *Ibid.*, No. 506 of 6 May, 1914.
[41] De Bunsen to Nicolson, 3 July; cit. E. T. S. Dugdale, *op.cit.*, p.291.
[42] *B.D.*, xi, No. 19 of 30 June & No. 33 of 6 July.
[43] *Ibid.*, No. 70 of 14 July.

ures planned by Vienna and Berlin; and whether they would not arouse the Slav feeling in a way that made it impossible for Russia to remain passive. Grey was willing to exert his influence on Serbia in favour of the acceptance of the Austrian conditions, if they were "compatible with the sovereignty of the Serbian state".[44] On the other hand the British government made it quite clear that it could not tolerate policy which used Sarajevo as a pretext for the Austrian Balkan aspirations.

The Austro-Hungarian ultimatum suddenly made Grey (who called it "the most formidable document which has ever been addressed to an independent state")[45] fear serious consequences for the general peace. He remained disinterested in a mere Austro-Serbian dispute but was apprehensive of a conflict between Russia and Austria, which could not be localized.[46] M. de Bunsen summarized the tenor of British policy in his interpellations at the Ballplatz:

> I disclaimed any British lack of sympathy in the matter of her legitimate grievances against Serbia and pointed out that whereas Austria seemed to be making these a starting point of her policy, Her Majesty's Government were bound to look at the question primarily from the point of view of the maintenance of the peace of Europe. In this way the two countries might easily drift apart.[47]

The Foreign Office tried to hold back Austria by pointing out that the resistance of Serbia was underrated. At any rate, it would be a long-lasting, exasperating struggle, which would weaken Austria extraordinarily and in which she would lose much blood.[48] Thus as well as the Germans and Austrians, the British themselves were looking ahead and considering what effect a general war could have on the Habsburg Empire. But these warnings did not fall on fruitful ground, and London soon had to recognize that it was the declared intention in Berlin and Vienna to bring about a war.[49] The Austrian declaration of war upon Serbia on 28 July raised the question for the British government of whether Britain should participate, a question which was ultimately decided by Germany's conduct. The Foreign Office had been aware of the fact that in case of France and Russia considering it a bigger cause, the Serbian dispute would engage the Triple Alliance against the whole of the Triple Entente.[50] But while Grey, Nicolson, and Crowe regarded the Balkan issue as being inevitably linked with Britain's control of the European balance of power, it needed the pretext of the German

---

[44] *D.(eutsche) D.(okumente)*, No. 121 of 23 July.
[45] *B.D.*, xi, No. 91, Grey to de Bunsen, 24 July.
[46] *Ö.U.A.*, No. 10600 of 24 July (Mensdorff to Berchtold; *B.D.*, xi, No. 98, Grey to Bertie.
[47] *F.O.*371/1900, No. 48877 (final report of 1 Sept.).
[48] *D.D.*, No. 157, 24 July, Lichnowsky to Jagow; marginal note by Wilhelm II; "nonsense".
[49] *B.D.*, xi, No. 100 (minute by Crowe of 25 July) & No. 170 of 27 July.
[50] *Ibid.*, No. 101 (minutes by Crowe & Nicolson on Buchanan's telegram to Grey of 24 July).

invasion of Belgium to win over the majority of the Cabinet.[51]

On the day that Britain took up arms Grey wired to his ambassador Rennell Rodd in Rome: "I do not suppose we shall declare war upon Austria unless some direct provocation is given or she declares war upon us . . ."[52] Did this mean that Britain still wanted to leave the door open for Austria? The explanation is purely naval. The Admiralty did not want war with Austria till the French fleet was prepared. After Churchill had informed Grey that they were ready for action Britain, as well as France, declared war upon Austria–Hungary on 12 August.[53]

The Habsburg Empire had arbitrarily gambled away its credit in London during the July crisis. Once the Monarchy had agreed to play Germany's game she was treated alike and could not hope to be spared from British counteraction because of traditional sympathies. Albert Mensdorff, the last Habsburg ambassador at the Court of St. James, who was a relative of Queen Victoria(!), seemed to think that such feelings might still prevail. Even after the British declaration of war on Germany he repeatedly pressed upon Grey the desirability of avoiding war between Britain and Austria. The Foreign Secretary, who gathered that Mensdorff did this solely on his own initiative, told him that Britain did not want war with Austria but that he could hardly think that:

> we should fight with the French against the Germans in the North Sea and that at the same time in the Mediterranean British warships should look on and take no part.[54]

Nevertheless there remained much mutual sympathy, both personal and real, which could be an asset for a future understanding. Both sides believed that the parting was only temporary. When diplomatic relations were broken off, Nicolson wrote to Mensdorff: "I am so dreadfully sorry that we shall have to lose you for a time and I also deeply regret the cause".[55] Berchtold, when saying good-bye to de Bunsen, still could not understand the turn of events: "It seems absurd for good friends like England and Austria to be at war".[56]

[51] *Cab.*41, 35/25, letters by Asquith to George V of 2 & 3 Aug.
[52] *B.D.*, xi, No. 591.
[53] *F.O.*371/2167, No. 37762/f.36211 of 10 Aug. Cf. F. R. Bridge, "The British Declaration of War on Austria–Hungary in 1914", *Slav. & East Eur. Rev.*, xlvii, 1969, p.412 ff.
[54] *Ibid.*, No. 37172 of 7 Aug.
[55] *F.O.*800/375, 13 Aug.
[56] E. T. S. Dugdale, *op.cit.*, p.304.

CHAPTER I

First Actions and Reactions concerning the Monarchy

1. British Spokesmen of the Nationalities

The outbreak of the war served as a catalyst for the formation of opinion on the future of Austria–Hungary. This is especially true of those people who had hitherto taken a deeper interest in the intrinsic problems of the Habsburg Empire. Such extraordinary interest in Austro-Hungarian affairs was indeed limited to a handful of intellectuals, for, to the majority of Englishmen, the Habsburg Empire was just a political entity in the family of European nations like any other and general knowledge about it was very slight. More important for the moulding of public opinion was the attitude of the few recognized experts in the matter.

One of the most articulate authorities on Austria–Hungary was Henry Wickham Steed, who had been *The Times* correspondent in Vienna from 1902 to 1913. There he acquired an intimate knowledge about the internal and external problems of the Empire, after he had been stimulated to do research in connection with a request to prepare an obituary for Francis Joseph as early as 1905. The upshot of his studies was a book on *The Hapsburg Monarchy*.[1] His interpretation of the dynastic, economic, and racial factors of the Empire was not too friendly to the political system of the Habsburgs. Steed refused to accept the right of existence of the Dual Monarchy *per se* and brand-marked the exalted opportunism of the existing regime.

Steed had been particularly appalled by the Zagreb and Friedjung trials in 1908/09, which proved to him that the imperial judiciary was corrupt and the whole governmental machinery only served the purpose of keeping up the German–Magyar supremacy established after

---

[1] First edition, London 1913. P. Schuster, *Henry Wickham Steed und die Habsburgermonarchie*, Vienna 1970, informs about the manuscript of a second version. For details on Steed's career cf. H. Hanak, *Great Britain and Austria–Hungary during the First World War*. (A Study in the Formation of Public Opinion), London 1962, pp. 11–20.

the *Ausgleich*. This dual system appeared to him riveted more firmly together by the Austrian annexation of Bosnia–Herzegovina, which he also regarded as a step forward in Germany's *Mitteleuropa* scheme, in which the Habsburg Empire was a tool of Prussian militarism.

Steed's attitude towards Austria–Hungary was that of an Englishman whose view of the Empire was conditioned primarily by her political relations with Germany. As long as the Monarchy was allied to Germany, she was seen as a danger to Britain. This view of the continental balance was supplemented by ideological views. Steed had strong suspicions against the "conspiration" of international Jewry as well as Jesuit Catholicism, which he discovered as pillars supporting the Habsburg fabric.[2]

But although he was a severe critic of the shortcomings of the Austrian Empire, Steed basically retained pro-Austrian sentiments. He had many friends among leading Austro-Germans,[3] and he could boast of having done "more perhaps than any European writer to discredit the legend of the inevitable 'break-up' of Austria".[4] Until the war Steed remained a supporter of the territorial integrity of the Empire. He believed in its continued existence to the advantage of Europe and wished it to gather the strength to pursue a foreign policy independent of Germany. He also hoped that the Crown would finally be stronger than the Church, the Jews, the Germans and the Magyars.

The latter were his main concern. He sincerely hoped to see the "good Magyars" federating with the other nationalities of the Hungarian half on equal terms.[5] The whole of his attitude towards Hungary was inspired by the following consideration:

> The Magyars, if harmoniously united with the other Hungarian races, the Austrian Slavs, will be strong enough to act as a brake upon the House of Hapsburg, if it should ever wish to side with Germany against us in a European war. If, on the contrary, the Magyars are at loggerheads with one half of the Hungarian population, they will not only be reduced to impotence but will feel, as they now feel, all the enmity of the twenty-five million Austro-Hungarian Slavs who as anti-Germans are now on our side.[6]

Before the Balkan Wars Steed was still convinced that a reconciliation between the Magyars and the Slavs was possible. He was also ready to promote good feeling between Austria–Hungary and Britain, if there were signs of a diplomatic independence of Austria, which he post-

---

[2] Cf. his autobiography *Through Thirty Years*, 2 vols., London 1924.
[3] E.g. Joseph Redlich, cf. his diary *Schicksalsjahre Österreichs*, ed. F. Fellner, Vol. i (1908–1914), Graz 1953.
[4] In a conversation with Cartwright in Sept. 1910, quoted in *The History of The Times*, iii, London 1952, pp.688–89.
[5] Letter to L. S. Amery of 25 Feb. 1906, *ibid.*, p.478.
[6] Memorandum (undated, 1912?), Steed papers, P.H.S.

ulated as an essential condition for the improvement of Anglo-Austrian relations.[7] But as long as this existed only *in spe* he declined to support a policy which might have been interpreted as implying a tendency, on the part of Britain, "to draw near to Austria at the expense of our friendship with Russia."[8] For even if Austria emancipated herself from Germany this was likely to lead to the reestablishment of the *Dreikaiser-bündnis* with Vienna as its pivot and result in the detachment of Russia from Britain. Russia's assistance, however, was regarded as vital by Steed for the supreme goal of keeping Germany in check, a purpose for which she was certainly more valuable than the extremely vague prospect of an Austrian emancipation from Berlin.

To avoid any alienation of Russia from the western powers, Steed advised vigilance against "wantonly expansive tendencies" in the Balkans on the part of Austria, which he wanted "to remain a factor in European equilibrium while exercising her natural influence over the Southern Slavs".[9]

In late 1912 Steed found it still impossible to believe that Austria contemplated solving the South Slav question by war, but he began to scent that "the subterranean struggle ... between the Slav nationalities of the Monarchy and the German and Judaeo–Magyar elements that are the props of the Dual system (was) now reaching a turning point".[10] For the first time since he came to Vienna he felt

> that the existence of the Monarchy is really in danger and that only an (apparently impossible) series of brilliant victories or a difficult and patient policy of peace and internal reconstruction can avert this danger.[11]

When Austria nevertheless decided to use the Sarajevo assassination to quell the Serbs, Steed, who was approached by Mensdorff to influence British public opinion in Austria's favour, declined to intervene on her behalf and explained:

> I am a friend of Austria and have proved it by warning people for years that your policy has been fatally wrong. I can only say that I am too good a friend of Austria to help her to commit suicide.[12]

Steed went personally to the Foreign Office to convey his impression that Vienna was ready for a general war and *The Times* leader of 22 July 1914 hinted at the impossibility of localizing such a war, which bore little prospect of ending "without disaster to the Dual Monarchy".

---

[7] *The Times* leader of 30 Aug. 1909 and Steed's reply to the *Fremdenblatt*, *ibid.*, 7 Sept. 1909.
[8] Letter to Chirol, 9 Sept. 1909; *History of The Times*, iii, p.689.
[9] Letter to Chirol, 15 Sept. 1909, *ibid.*
[10] *Ibid.*, iv, pp.83, 104 (letters to Dawson of 28 Nov. 1912 and 25 Apr. 1913).
[11] *Through Thirty Years*, i, p.365 (extract from letter to Dawson of 5 Jan. 1913).
[12] *Ibid.*, i, p.404. Cf. also *The History of The Times*, iv, pp.188–89; O.U.A., viii, No. 10217.

Once hostilities had started Steed was convinced that there was no escape for the Habsburg Empire, of which he expected only fragments to remain at the end of the war, since he felt sure that Austria was not able to stand the strain of a prolonged war.[13]

Steed now openly rejected a "trialist" solution, calling it a stratagem for bringing the Serbs under Habsburg authority. To overcome arguments against the Balkanization of Central Europe he tried to persuade his readers that it would be in the British interest to erect an anti-German barrier consisting of new nation states. Specifically, he wanted a strong, united kingdom of the South Slavs, an autonomous Russian Poland, home-rule or independence for the Czechs and the Slovaks and the cession of preponderantly Rumanian-inhabited territory from Hungary.[14]

Steed was joined in his efforts by Robert W. Seton-Watson, an Oxford scholar who originally was an admirer of Hungarian parliamentarism, appreciating the Magyars as the true wardens of Hungarian liberty. Shocked by a journey to Hungary in 1905, he came to agree with Steed that the Habsburg Monarchy would bring disaster upon Europe unless means could be found to replace the dual system by some form of federal unity in which the South Slavs would find a place. Seton-Watson came into first contact with Masaryk in connection with the Friedjung trial, which increased his critical attitude towards the Magyar ascendancy, although Steed himself was not sure whether at that time Seton-Watson was not more attracted by the personality of the Czech leader than the problems of Bohemia in the Austrian part of the Empire.[15] Before the war Seton-Watson's attention was focussed on the Yugoslav question and he thought in terms of the "trialist" solution, which was the upshot of his argument in "The Future of Austria–Hungary".[16] Therein he anticipated the advent to the throne of Francis Ferdinand, whom he credited as the representative of "progressive" ideas and whom he later considered to have been the only man capable of undertaking a radical reform of the dual system.[17] With the death of the heir-apparent, all of Seton-Watson's hopes for a peaceful solution of the South Slav question crumbled. Reluctantly he abandoned his belief in a federal reconstruction of the Empire. He could not approve of the Austrian note to Serbia because like Steed he anticipated

---

[13] Letters to his last successor in Vienna, Loch, and to the Canada correspondent, J. Willison, of 18 Jan. & 31 Jan. 1914, Steed papers, P.H.S.

[14] *Edinburgh Review*, April 1916. Steed was forced to publish his "Programme for Peace" in a provincial periodical, because at that time he did not yet influence Dawson and Northcliffe. Cf. his letter to the leader writer Clutton Brock of 26 Jul. 1917 (P.H.S.).

[15] H. W. Steed, "Tributes to R. W. Seton-Watson: A Symposium", *Slavonic and East European Review*, June 1952, pp.333–34.

[16] London 1913. Cf. pp.43, 46, 50; cf. also H. Hanak, *op.cit.*, pp.20–35.

[17] Letters to Mme. Grujić of 21 July 1914, Seton-Watson papers, partly quoted in A. May, *op.cit.*, pp.27–28; cf. obituary in *Contemporary Review*, Aug. 1914, pp.165–74.

that it would bring about war. After its outbreak Seton-Watson not only became a passionate supporter of the South Slavs, for whom he had always seen a future in the long run, but also championed the other subject races, for whom the war, as he realised, was a unique chance for liberation. Were Austria to be successful through her ties with Germany, this would have so strengthened the ruling Germans and Magyars that they could have easily maintained their privileged position and continued the suppression of the subject races.

Thus Seton-Watson from now on became eager to rally support for a solution that would also satisfy Czech, Polish and Rumanian aspirations, although at the beginning of the struggle he did not seem to have been completely convinced of the realizability of full independence in each case.[18] This understandable scepticism of a drastic change in the structure of Central Europe did not prevent him propagating their case. As early as December 1914 he published a pamphlet in which he advised the erection of a *cordon sanitaire* of new states in the Danube basin.[19] Thereafter he called persistently for the dismemberment of the Habsburg Empire and the consequent liberation of its subject nationalities, whom he praised as Britain's natural allies.[20] Seton-Watson and Steed could quickly enlist the support of other academics and journalists in Britain. Sir Valentine Chirol, G. M. Trevelyan, and H. G. Wells were given space in *The Times* to express their confidence in the maturity of the Slav nations and emphasized the value of these peoples for the Entente in the struggle against Germany both in and after the war. Britain was called upon to sympathize with these movements,[21] and possible objections pointing to the danger of Russian expansionism into Central Europe as the consequence of the destruction of the Austro-Hungarian Empire was hastily dismissed.[22]

The conviction that the break-up of the Habsburg Empire was necessary was not confined to those who resented her closeness to Germany. The feeling that the Monarchy had forfeited her right of existence by giving reason for the outbreak of war also prevailed among Liberals who had not hailed the intervention of Britain on behalf of Russian interests. Once they were convinced that the problem could no longer be solved in a Habsburg sense, they tried to solve it scientifically, assuming that future frontiers on exactly ethnological lines would be an insurance against the repetition of European catastrophe.

Among these Radical Liberals one of the most renowned experts of the problems of the nationality question in South Eastern Europe was

[18] Cf. Seton-Watson's essay "The Future of Bohemia" in *Masaryk in England*, Cambridge 1943.
[19] Seton-Watson *et. al.*, *War and Democracy*, London 1914.
[20] Cf. his letter to *The Times* of 25 Apr. 1915, cit. H. Hanak, *op.cit.*, p.34.
[21] Cf. their letters to *The Times*, 18, 22 Sept., 29 Oct. 1914.
[22] E. J. Barker, "The Ultimate Disappearance of Austria–Hungary", *Nineteenth Century*, Nov. 1914, pp.1003–31.

Noel Buxton, who before the war had frequently visited the disputed areas. Together with his brother Charles Rhoden he published his conclusions in *The War and the Balkans*.[23] The authors agreed that it was hardly possible to draw boundaries in that area which corresponded with national claims, because absolute accuracy was unattainable due to the intermingled populations. Yet boundaries could be drawn which would be much more just than the existing ones. In the opinion of the Buxtons this could be done so well that "no injustices of sufficient magnitude to provide the basis of agitation or another war" would be left. Most desirable was the expansion of Serbia not only to a Greater Serbia but the larger ideal of a South Slav kingdom embracing the Croatian and the Slovene races. The Austro-Hungarian policy of *divide et impera* had evidently failed in its effect in the war, as the Buxtons deduced from the great proportion of "Ugoslavs" (sic) among the prisoners taken from Austria by the Serbs. They saw therein a striking demonstration "of the unnatural basis upon which the present Austro-Hungarian Empire is founded". But if the Austrian Empire was broken up, the Entente should define certain limits in their allowances to Serbia both with regard to the Italian claims and the economic necessities of the remaining part of the kingdom of Hungary, giving the latter an access to the sea through Fiume. For Italy the Quarnero line was supposed to be ideal and for some renunciations of the treaty of London she should be compensated with a portion of Turkey (Adalia). But all these were minor technical consequences deriving from the main conclusion of the Buxtons:

> The Austro-Hungarian Empire, as we have shown it, must come to an end if the causes of war in the future are to be effectively removed.

The Buxtons soon regretted their precipitate demand, but for the time being they had added their prominent backing to what seemed to be developing into an overwhelmingly anti-Habsurb feeling in British public opinion.

Another Liberal, but one ranging among the "never-endians" who wanted to see Britain achieve complete victory, was A. J. Toynbee. He analysed the possibilities for a future settlement in two books on *The New Europe* and *Nationality and the War*.[24] Toynbee recommended a politically and economically viable solution which would guarantee a permanent settlement. He saw the ideal set-up in a Balkan *Zollverein*, where economic collectivism would secure national self-realization. Compromises had to be made. The future Austria and Hungary both needed an outlet to the sea (Trieste, Fiume). The Czechs, Toynbee

---

[23] London 1915, pp.104–110.
[24] Both London 1915.

thought, were too small an entity to claim independence and should confine their aspirations to obtaining home-rule inside Germany.

Because he became preoccupied with the Near East, Toynbee's often very sound suggestions were not pressed upon the decision-makers with the same persistency as those by Steed and Seton-Watson who, contrary to Toynbee's approach, neglected the economic factor in their deliberations. They underestimated the fact that the Habsburg Empire had developed almost into a self-sufficient economic unit, in which the industry of Bohemia, the commerce of Vienna and the agriculture of Hungary were so well adapted to each other's needs. They also did not pay tribute to the fact that Austria–Hungary had grown as a bulwark of Christian civilisation against the Turks and the Russians and was the only alternative to a Slavisation of Central Europe, if this role was not to be assumed by a "Greater Germany". The dismissal of such economic and strategic facts was characteristic of Steed's and Seton-Watson's overrating of the racial strife in the Empire. They overlooked the fact that not only the great mass of the people but also many of their prominent representatives, some of them formerly belonging to Francis Ferdinand's circle (Skrzyński, Schober, Korošec, Vajda-Voevod and Hodza) were moderate in their demands and showed signs of willingness to compromise with the Monarchy.[25]

Although there was considerable sympathy in Britain for the small nationalities, many influential personalities continued to appreciate the values represented by the Habsburg Empire. So people like G. P. Gooch, C. P. Scott, M. Sykes, and Ph. Kerr refused to get actively involved in the anti-Austrian campaign of Steed and Seton-Watson.[26] But they certainly did not escape from their forceful arguments, which were anonymously propagated in the *Round Table* and appeared under the pseudonym of "Scotus Viator" in the *Spectator*.[27]

One prominent reader of these imperial journals who was captured by their theories was Lord Cromer, the former pro-consul in Egypt. In early 1914 he still believed that the Central Powers would be seriously defeated but he did not want them to be crushed out of existence, because the only result would have been an extreme predominance on the part of the Slavs, which Cromer regarded as "only one degree better than Pan-Germanism". He did not think it would be wise that the Allies, if victorious, should attempt to dictate changes in the internal government of Germany or Austria, a matter which in Cromer's view might be safely left to the Germans and Austrians themselves.[28]

---

[25] Cf. G. Franz, *Erzherzog Franz Ferdinand und die Pläne zur Reform der Habsburger Monarchie*, Brünn 1943; R. Kiszling, *Erzherzog Franz Ferdinand von Österreich-Este*, Graz 1953; M. Hodza, *Federation in Central Europe*, London 1942.

[26] Cf. A. May, *op.cit.*, i, p.242 and H. Hanak, *op.cit.*, p.193.

[27] No. xvii (Dec. 1914), p.83ff. & *Spectator* of 15 Aug. 1914.

[28] Cf. his correspondence with St. Loe. Strachey, Lady Alice Shaw Stewart and Sir Herbert Warren in Autumn 1914, Cromer papers, *F.O.633/23–24*.

But the questionability of the survival of the Habsburg Empire as a single political entity was soon instilled in Cromer's mind by Steed and Seton-Watson, whose publications he reviewed and combined with extensive musings of his own on the prospects of Austria.[29] Admitting a certain recuperative power of this "bundle of disconnected national units termed 'Austria' ", he argued that this strength had been operative at a time when the maintenance of the Balance of Power was regarded by all statesmen as the cornerstone of European policy. Now this principle had to be applied in a very different spirit.

Cromer observed that the "fire of nationalism" now burnt so strongly as to obscure all other interests, whether social or economic. He acknowledged that there was a certain nobility and idealism in the Austro-German programme of assimilation, because for him it was a fundamental fact that German civilisation was superior to Slav civilisation. Because of the lack of a true Pan-Slav movement in Austria and the vigilant opposition of the Pan-Germans, he did not expect any attempt to convert Austria–Hungary into a great Slav Empire. "Trialism" appeared statesmanlike to Cromer but he was inclined to concur with Seton-Watson[30] that it was now too late for that and nothing short of an independent South Slav state would meet the requirements of the situation.

The creation of a South Slav state would have automatically involved the granting of the same right to the Northern Slavs, in other words the cessation of the Habsburg Empire. In his conclusions Cromer was careful not to commit himself in that sense, but he visualized the problem ahead:

> The day of retribution for Austria seems to be at hand. The ultimate survival of Austria as a separate political entity is more than doubtful, but if she is to survive at all, she will certainly have to make a radical change in the principles of government which, under political and military influences, have so far guided her action.[31]

In 1916 Cromer agreed to become chairman of the Serbian Society which had written the cause of a Yugslav state on its banners.[32] Cromer had come to believe in its desirability for the same reasons as Steed. In a strong South Slav state he hoped to have found the panacea to thwart the German ambitions for world dominion, which were supposed to be barred by a solid block of anti-Teutonic races.[33] For members of the

---

[29] "Modern Austria", *Quarterly Review*, October 1915, p.463ff.

[30] Seton-Watson had impressed this view on Cromer in a letter of 15 Sept. 1915. Seton-Watson papers. Cf. also Cromer's letters to Seton-Watson of 10 Sept. 1915 and to Rodd of 19 Sept. 1915, in which he hesitates to approve of Italy's entry into the war, because of the danger to Trieste(!) and the South Slavs from an Italian victory. Cromer papers, *loc. cit.*

[31] *Quarterly review, loc. cit.*

[32] Cf. H. Hanak, *op.cit.*, pp.191–93.

[33] Cf. Cromer's inaugural speech to the Serbian Society, held on 24 Oct. 1916, printed in *New Europe*, 26 Oct. 1916.

government it was much more difficult to speak out publicly for the Yugoslav cause, especially in view of the Italian interests involved. Right at the beginning of the war Churchill, then First Lord of the Admiralty, tried to entice the Italians to join the Allies by hinting at Austria's military weakness. He implied that the inheritance of the Habsburg Empire was at stake and appealed to Italy to take advantage of this situation by helping to promote the cause of the nationalities and assist the Triple Entente in their fight against the suppression of irredentism by supporting them in their aim "to settle the map of Europe on national lines".[34] Churchill postulated "a natural and harmonious settlement which liberates races", but this should not be interpreted as identical with a demand for the complete dismemberment of the Habsburg Empire. The irredentism referred to by Churchill was solely the Italian minorities in Austria–Hungary. Even when he later urged that the Entente should press for "the liberation of the imprisoned nationalities in the grip of the Hapsburgs" and expressed his conviction that after the war Austria–Hungary would be dissolved into her component parts, he remained careful in the wording of his prediction:

> We may see a Poland united and in loyal and harmonious relations with the Crown of Russia. We may live to see a federation of the Christian states of the Balkans . . . We may see an Italy whose territory corresponds with the Italian population.[35]

Churchill not only put forward his view in the subjunctive but also restricted himself to calling only two of the peripheral races of the Monarchy by name. He did not say whether the federation of the Balkans was to be autonomous under the Habsburg Crown or completely independent of it and in his reflections there was no reference to either the Czechs or the Rumanians.

The Liberal politicians were even vaguer in their statements. Lloyd George scorned at Austria's weakness, praised the small nations and displayed a wholeheartedly pro-Serbian attitude, but he did not discuss the more intrinsic problems of the Empire.[36] Asquith in his Guildhall speech of 9 November[37] declared the doctrine of nationality to be a British war aim, when he said that Britain would go on fighting until the rights of the smaller nationalities were "placed upon an unassailable foundation". Of course, when speaking of small "nations" British statesmen at that time were thinking mainly, if not exclusively, of Belgium and Serbia, the restoration of which was what the Entente had

---

[34] *The Times*, 25 Sept. 1915.
[35] 24 October 1914, partly quoted in A. May, *op.cit.*, p.251.
[36] *The Times* of 20 Sept. 1914.
[37] *Ibid.*, 10 Nov. 1914.

been fighting for since their early occupation. The attack on these little states was successfully exploited for the purpose of propaganda to make the Allied cause appear just and honourable. The subject nationalities of the Habsburg Empire were not yet mentioned by name in any official pronouncements, but they profited from the acceptance of the principle of nationality as an idealistic Allied war aim, which created an atmosphere that should be favourable to their hopes in the later stages of the war.

Since there was not yet any binding statement from Britain concerning the fate of Austria, Britain's allies could only speculate about the war aims of the British government with regard to a settlement in Central and Eastern Europe. The Tsarist ambassador Count Benckendorff drew his conclusions from private conversations with ministers and influential Conservatives,[38] according to which it seemed to him that Russia would be welcome to annex the Galician districts and parts of the Bukovina. Furthermore, Austria would lose Transylvania, Bosnia–Herzegovina and the Adriatic coast (the latter to be divided among the "Slav states" and Italy) and the Trentino. All this presupposed that Italy and Rumania would take up arms against the Central Powers. Otherwise Benckendorff had doubts as to whether the British had definite ideas about Austria. But the whole of her influence would press "for a far-reaching rectification of the map of Europe on the basis of ethnology", a result which could only be achieved at Austria's expense. This conclusion, Benckendorff explained, was mainly derived from the aim or rather necessity to guarantee peace for the future by liquidating causes for conflict. But the British had arrived at this conclusion with a certain regret, since one generally regarded Austria "as an instrument, which was victimised by Germany".

2. The Russian Programme and Britain's Tacit Cognizance

While Britain and France had in practice only become nominal enemies of Austria–Hungary, the burden of fighting the Dual Monarchy on land rested solely with Tsarist Russia. It is therefore no surprise that the interest in the political future of the Habsburg Empire and Eastern Europe in general was much greater in the country concerned with the warfare in that area. This interest was eloquently expressed in the manifestoes which were issued in August and September, 1914, signed by the Supreme Commander, the Grand Duke Nicholas. The first of them summoned the Poles to reunite into one body under the sceptre of the Russian Emperor. This declaration, when transmitted to London, was received favourably in the Foreign Office. Lord Crewe called it a "statesmanlike move in the right direction" and Sir Arthur

---

[38] Benckendorff to Sazonov, 28 Sept. 1914, *Int. Bez.*, vi, No. 329, pp.253–54.

Nicolson agreed, because "it will win over the Poles".

However, Polish emigré leaders, who asked for British support of the manifesto, had to be told by Sir George Clerk that Britain "cannot guarantee Russian promises", although Sir Edward Grey assured them of the government's "thorough sympathy with the Russian manifesto and that it was welcomed by public feeling here".

Soon afterwards another proclamation was made to the Slavs in the German and Austrian territories, followed, in mid-September, by a manifesto addressed to the peoples of Austria–Hungary in nine languages, promising them the "re-establishment of rights and justice" and "liberty and realization of national dreams". Each nationality would preserve its own language and faith. The Russian troops should be welcomed, because they came to emancipate them from a foreign yoke.

Although on the surface this proclamation seemed to secure national freedoms, there was no concrete formulation of the future status of the nationalities. For a propaganda leaflet designed to encourage separatist sentiments it was not necessary for the Russians to commit themselves publicly to a definite scheme. Policy makers in Whitehall nevertheless took notice of this first appeal to the subject nationalities of Austria, but since they were not approached to give their opinion on this paper, it was filed without any commentary.[39]

The programme which the Russians intended to realize in the case of a military victory was expounded by the Russian Foreign Minister Sazonov in a "purely academic conversation" with Buchanan and Paléologue, the ambassadors of Britain and France respectively, on 13 September.[40] Sazonov proposed the destruction of German hegemony through territorial changes justifiable on the basis of the principle of nationality, but he avoided any extreme solution for the Danubian Monarchy. Austria would be converted from a Dual Monarchy into a Triple Monarchy and the crowns of Hungary and Bohemia would be vested in the Emperor under a personal union. Serbia would acquire Bosnia–Herzegovina and the part of Dalmatia giving her access to the sea. Whether Austria was to retain Transylvania and the Trentino would depend on the action of Rumania and Italy.

The demands put forward by Sazonov were quite extensive for such an early stage of the war, but obviously he was encouraged by the advance of the Russian armies, which were approaching the Bohemian–Moravian border, and regarded the Austrian army as a "*quantité négligeable*". A victorious outcome would certainly have allowed the

---

[39] *F.O.*371/2095, Nos. 39209, 43058, 46676, 55226.
[40] Buchanan to A. Nicolson, F.O.800/375 – cf. also Paléologues's partly differing report in *Int. Bez.*, Ser. II, vi, p.487 and its interpretation by M. Abrash, "War Aims toward Austria–Hungary", *Russian Diplomacy and Eastern Europe 1914–1917*, New York 1963, pp.80–82.

Russians to re-arrange Eastern Europe to their advantage. However, Sazonov emphasized that his sketch was "a tapestry the woof of which is not yet woven". At any rate, had it been carried out, it would not have implied the dismemberment of the Habsburg Empire. Despite the rigid amputations his scheme left it in possession of the great ports in the Adriatic, and a loss in territory would have been counterbalanced by a gain in cohesion.

The opinion of the British government on the Russian proposal is difficult to assess precisely. On 28 September, the Russian ambassador in London, Benckendorff, after "private conversations with ministers and influential Conservatives" reported their consent to the severing from Austria of her Polish and Ukrainian provinces and the addition of the Bukovina to Russia. Rumania might be given Transylvania, if she joined the side of the Entente; Italy in the same event would be given the Trentino, and part of Dalmatia which she had to share with Serbia. Benckendorff was sure that British sentiment desired a settlement based upon ethnography as essential for maintaining peace in the future, but he pointed out that the above outline was approved of "with a certain regret since Austria is fairly generally regarded as a victim of Germany".

Allied reservations were more openly expressed to ambassador Isvolski, who reported from Paris the "fear of too strong an advance of the Slavs to the Mediterranean". In his despatch the question of an eventual dissolution of the Monarchy is taken up for the first time in its full width. The French Foreign Minister, M. Delcassé, in spite of his assurances of French support to Russia for her claims in general, was very reserved about the Habsburg Monarchy. His interlocutor noticed

indubitable French sympathies for Austria–Hungary . . . (and) of a much higher degree in England.[41]

In all these more or less informal conversations the problem of Austria–Hungary was never discussed in isolation but as part of a European settlement. It was the French ambassador in St. Petersburg, Paléologue, who frequently broached the subject of peace conditions, while his colleague Buchanan always contended that it was useless to discuss terms of peace until the Allies were nearer Berlin. Grey and Nicolson called the Frenchman's initiative "unduly active" and refused to enter into a discussion on the ideas expressed by Nicholas II in an interview to Paléologue on 22 November. The Tsar assumed that the Austro-Hungarian "associates" would no longer continue to work together and that Bohemia at least would reclaim its autonomy.

---

[41] *Int. Bez*, pp.253–54 & 305.

Austria should be reduced to the Hereditary States, German Tyrol and Salzburg.[42]

This imperial statement in favour of a disintegration of Austria–Hungary is reminiscent of the view ventured by the Tsar to Buchanan more than a year before the war broke out.[43] It is, however, very questionable whether his opinion as communicated by Paléologue represented the attitude of his government. Certainly it embarrassed the British who simply ignored it.

One reason for the British reserve towards the Russian plans for Austria–Hungary was their desire not to exclude the chance of a diplomatic understanding with Germany's ally. The possibility of such a manoeuvre had already been discussed quite openly in the press. On 17 September, the *Daily Chronicle* published an article that had appeared in the Milan *Corriere della Sera* and reported on preliminary steps towards peace:

> It is asserted that the Emperor Francis Joseph cherishes the hope that Great Britain would offer no serious opposition, since, apart from the cordial traditional friendship that has marked Anglo-Austrian relations, there are strong grounds for believing that England really desires the preservation of Austria–Hungary.

France was also loth to deal Austria the death blow, the correspondent speculated, and even Russia was not unwilling to make up the quarrel with the Monarchy, while Viennese political circles would probably not be averse (should the Triple Entente be victorious) to obtaining compensations for Austria for likely losses through Russian and Serbian conquests by the fresh inclusion of Silesia, and even Bavaria, in a remodelled Austro-Hungarian Empire.

Although the matter was far from having been discussed in such detail, it was to be taken up soon. On 2 December Ambassador Bertie cabled from Bordeaux that the French Foreign Minister had heard that

> in certain quarters in Austria there is an inclination to try to make peace independently of Germany through mediation of Spain and this tendency is encouraged by the Vatican.[44]

On the same day Grey broached to the Russian amabassador the notion of a direct deal with Austria–Hungary, because Serbia's catastrophe appeared to him "an exceedingly grave matter". Grey acknowledged the Russian pledge for Serbia, which he compared with Britain's for Belgium, whereas the other Austro-Russian questions were of more direct concern to Russia.[45] In other words the Foreign Secretary, who

---

[42] F.O.371/2174, No. 79199 and *Int. Bez.* vol. *cit.*, p.468; cf. also M. Paléologue, *La Russie des Tsars pendant la Grande Guerre*, Paris 1921–22, i, p.199–201.

[43] G. W. Buchanan, *My Mission to Russia*, London 1922, i, p.182.

[44] F.O.371/2176, No. 79101.

[45] *Int. Bez.*, *loc. cit.*, p.506.

did not pursue this exchange of ideas, indicated that Britain sympathised with the Russian efforts in Serbia's behalf, but was far less interested in (if not actually opposed to) her further aims which should not be allowed to block a compromise peace. The British belief in the likelihood of an eventual approach by Vienna was strengthened by news from a Spanish source saying that the Austrians felt sacrificed by the Germans. According to this, the Austrians admitted that they were going to lose Galicia and Bosnia–Herzegovina and feared the formation of a separate Hungarian state. This pessimistic outlook was due to their fear of Russian military power and their assumption that Rumania was abandoning her neutrality and would shortly join the Allies, thereby aggravating the strategic position of the Dual Monarchy.[46]

Thereupon Grey instructed Buchanan that Britain and France would not object to a peace with Vienna, if she proposed terms acceptable to Sazonov.[47]

The idea of detaching Austria from Germany was brought forward more emphatically by France. Already in mid-December Isvolski reported the Quai d'Orsay's inquiry, whether Russia would insist on the complete fragmentation of Austria–Hungary or prefer "to isolate Germany by a separate peace".[48] On 1 January 1915, Paléologue – in the presence of his British colleague – argued to Sazonov that "the Czech and Yugoslav problems seemed to him secondary", but he met the stern opposition of the Foreign Minister who allegedly answered: "No, Austria–Hungary must be dismembered". Thereafter the ambassador was ordered by Paris to drop the matter.[49]

The British Foreign Office was more cautious before discussing this delicate issue so openly. Grey wanted first to find out whether the circulating reports about the Austrian anxiety for peace had any foundation, so he instructed H. Howard in Rome to sound out clerical circles.[50] When he failed to elicit any definite information, London drew the conclusion: "It is not likely that Austria will make a separate peace".[51] At this same time there were first signs that a possible dissolution of the Habsburg Monarchy was being envisaged by the Foreign Office:

It is appalling to think of the difficulties which will arise when the moment arrives for the discussion of peace terms. I cannot imagine any peace which would be more difficult to make. It will practically

---

[46] Report by Lord Derby in Lloyd George Papers, C/25/8/1, 21 Dec. 1914.
[47] Grey's tel. of 29 Dec., deciphered by the Russians, *Int. Bez.*, *loc. cit.*, p.567, n.3.
[48] *Int. Bez.*, II, vi, No. 668.
[49] M. Paléologue, i, pp.199–201. There is no record by Buchanan confirming this incident.
[50] Grey to Rodd for H. Howard, 4 Jan. 1915, *F.O.*371/2505, f.1500, No. 2520.
[51] Minute by A. Nicolson, *ibid*. (cf. the report by Murray of Elibank, 7 Jan. 1915, copy in Lloyd George papers, C/25/8/2).

amount to the remodelling of the whole map of Europe and (probably) we shall have to find some means of liquidating both the Dual Monarchy and the Turkish Empire. However, it is too early yet to discuss these problems, as I myself am convinced that this campaign will be a long one.[52]

3. Negotiations for the Treaty of London and the Yugoslav Question

The aspirations for an independent Yugoslav state were most ardently propagated in the Allied camp by the Croat leader Supilo, who during his first sojourn in London in autumn 1914, with the mediation of Steed and Seton-Watson, saw among others the Foreign Office officials William Tyrrell (Grey's Private Secretary), Arthur Nicolson and also Lloyd George.[53] On 7 January 1915 Supilo submitted a memorandum on the South Slav question to the Foreign Office.[54] In his paper he pleaded for British help in securing an independent existence for all the South Slavs, who were not satisfied with the autonomy promised by the Habsburgs, which would still allow the Germans to make use of the Slav parts of Austria–Hungary after the war. For Under-Secretary Sir George Clerk, who briefed his superiors on the matter, this was "a question of material importance to the Allies, who by helping to create a Greater Serbia would impose a solid barrier against the German advance". But Supilo was not thinking of a mere aggrandizement of Serbia; he rather wanted a federal Serbo–Croat state and asked his British interlocutors to prevent Serbia from coming as a conqueror instead of a liberator to Bosnia and Dalmatia. Furthermore, Supilo had also heard of the negotiations that were taking place between the Allies and Italy and he asked them to oppose the ill-founded Italian claims. On 11 January Supilo was received by Grey and Asquith, who apparently were sympathetic to him and his cause. Grey is reported to have said:

> That Croat, Supilo, is the most interesting and far-sighted politician that I have ever met in my dealings with the Middle Europeans.[55]

However, the British government was far from committing itself and Supilo departed to St. Petersburg to hear what view the Russians held – "the all important view", as Nicolson noted.[56] Russia was primarily opposed to a Serbo–Croat state, fearing Vatican influence on the Catholic Croatian population. On the other hand, Russia was unwil-

---

[52] Private letter from A. Nicolson to Buchanan, 8 Jan. 1915, *F.O.*800/377.
[53] Information derived from Supilo's private papers, cf. L. Valiani, *La dissoluzione dell'Austria–Ungheria*, Milan 1966, pp.153 and 179.
[54] *F.O.*371/2241, No. 4404.
[55] Quoted in Bonifacić-Mihanović, eds., *The Croatian Nation*, Chicago 1955, p.179.
[56] Minute on No. 4404, *F.O.*371/2241.

ling to agree with the far-reaching demands of Italian irredentism, which were for the first time revealed in full in St. Petersburg, where the Italian ambassador did not deny that his country aspired to areas where the Slavs were in a majority, i.e., Istria, the Southern portion of Croatia, parts of Dalmatia with the islands facing these shores and a borderline following the watershed of the Alps as far as the Quarnero.

Tsarist diplomacy was quick to spot the tendency of the Rome Cabinet to take Austria's place in the Balkans. Sazonov informed Benckendorff that "we have drawn the Italian ambassador's attention to the danger of creating an irredentism as the outcome of the war. We cannot consent to such an aim". The Russians were now opposed to an Italian intervention and explained this by the recently weakened position of Austria–Hungary, which made Italy's contribution "pretty well a matter of indifference" to them.[57]

London had little sympathy with Russia's sponsorship of her kindred races in the Balkans. Although the British also thought that the Italian claims were immoderate, they were prepared to meet them in order to secure their participation, which Grey regarded as important "to finish this war as quickly as possible on satisfactory terms".[58] Grey called Sazonov's objections "the height of folly",[59] but nevertheless tried to mediate on their behalf. In a memorandum to the Italian ambassador Imperiali he pointed out that their demand for Dalmatia left to Serbia restricted opportunities for her outlet to the sea and shut in the Yugoslav provinces, "which have with reason looked to this war to secure for them the legitimate aspirations of expansion and development". Grey therefore urged the Italians to find means of "satisfying Yugoslav aspiration".[60]

Since the eclipse of the Dual Monarchy was now coming into sight, the Consulta decided that "we cannot possibly change over to a Slav menace" and implied that a Yugoslav state was hardly acceptable.[61] From an Italian point of view Yugoslav unification involved an undesired increase of Russian influence, Rome rather counted on the survival of their arch-enemy Austria–Hungary in a thoroughly curbed and castigated form. For instance, they did not go so far as to demand the Hungarian Croat coast *around* Fiume in order to leave Hungary at least one major port. Moreover, this could become the precondition for negotiations with the anti-German Magyar forces led by Count Károlyi. In January 1915 the Italians were informed by the Foreign Office that a member of the Hungarian opposition, a Count Szapary,

[57] W. W. Gottlieb, *Studies in Secret Diplomacy during the First World War*, London 1957, pp.320–21.
[58] Grey to Bertie and Buchanan, 4 & 5 Mar. 1915; E. Grey, *Twenty Five Years*, ii. p.206–07 and *Int. Bez.*, vii, No. 303, p.282.
[59] W. W. Gottlieb, *op. cit.*, p.321.
[60] *Ibid.*, p.336. Cf. *Int. Bez.*, vii, No. 402, pp.374–75.
[61] R. Rodd, *Memoirs*, London 1935, iii, p.242.

"has made certain proposals concerning a peace with Hungary",[62] and while Italy was strictly opposed to making peace with Austria–Hungary, a separate peace with Hungary alone was seriously considered.

The Italian hints of common interest with Britain in checking the westward trend of Panslavism found their response in London. It was decided to satiate the appetite of Russian expansionism elsewhere by a complete recognition of Russia's claims to Constantinople "to remove Russian objections to the participation of other nations".[63] Thereupon Sazonov advised Frano Supilo to recognize some Italian claims. When the Croat leader complained in a message to the Foreign Office, the minutes on it speak for themselves:[64]

> We wish the war to be ended, as far as possible, on the basis of nationality, certainly, but we did not set out on a Nationality Crusade. (G. Clerk)
> We can but do our best for them – and it is impossible that all the hopes and aspirations will be fully realized (A. Nicolson)
> What we are doing is to take the best means to ensure that the Slavs get all but a fraction of their claims. If we were not to secure Italian co-operation the Slavs might get less than nothing. (Grey)

On 8 April Sazonov made a final attempt to convince the Entente of the advantage of a policy based on the principle of nationality. By having taken up arms with this doctrine the Entente had gained general sympathies and "made the oppressed peoples of Austria–Hungary turn their eyes on her saluting her as liberator". The desire to shorten the war made some sacrifices necessary, but these should be reduced as much as possible so "as not to lose the sympathies of the peoples of Austria–Hungary".[65]

The British government, however, only scrutinized the strategical justification of the Italian claims. The Admiralty was inclined to give Italy a *carte blanche* in the Adriatic. Churchill pointed out to Asquith:

> There is no reason why we should not acquiesce in the Adriatic becoming strategically an Italian lake. The advantages of preventing Austria from having a navy are overwhelming.[66]

Grey was also in favour of a formal convention to be concluded whereas Paul Cambon objected, because it was not desirable to give guarantees which would mean that the Allies had to continue the war,

[62] *F.O.*371/2505, f.1500.
[63] British *aide-mémoire* of 12 Mar. 1915, Cab. 42/2/1,5. The theory that the desire for an Italian entry brought about the Constantinople agreement has been advanced by C. J. Lowe, "Britain and the Italian Intervention, 1914–1915", *Historical Journal*, xii, pp.533–48. The conclusive evidence is, however, scarce and rests mainly on the timing of the agreement, from which at least a tactical connection can be inferred.
[64] *F.O.*371/2241, No. 41098/f.4404 (Buchanan's telegram of 31 March).
[65] *F.O.*371/2508, No. 41097/f.28275.
[66] *Ibid.*, No. 41174 (8 April).

e.g. to compel Austria to cede Pola to Italy.[67] The Italian Foreign Minister Sonnino, on 24 March, had tabled a draft according to which the destiny of the littoral not appertaining to Italy would be left to the decision of Europe, after the war. When Buchanan presented this formula to Sazonov, he insisted on adding the area between Istria and Fiume to Croatia "whatever the fate of the latter". Grey found fault with the idea of determining at this moment the question:

> Before the war is over it is conceivable that we may wish to make other dispositions as regards both Croatia and Montenegro, and may have cause to regret having tied our hands.[68]

Grey's unwillingness to commit himself is undoubtedly due to the fact that in 1915 no one really expected and few desired the complete collapse of Austria–Hungary. The utmost aim of the other powers was a "sensible diminuation of its strength".[69]

Another obstacle for British diplomacy arose when it became known that the Austrians were entertaining negotiations with the Italians with the aim of keeping her neutral at the expense of adequate concessions. Austria was urged by Germany to satisfy her neighbour and the Germans seriously considered compensating their ally with part of Prussian Silesia for the loss of the Trentino.[70] But Austria's decision to satisfy some of the Italian requirements came much too late. In April and May the negotiations were carried on rather half-heartedly, Burián, the Austrian Foreign Minister knowing through "confidential reports" about the conclusion of the London Pact.[71] A reversal of the treaty was only possible under a new Italian government and Grey and Nicolson were in fact worried about pro-German feeling in Italy.[72] The final Ballplatz terms of 9 May satisfied the moderate Italian opposition under Giolitti who had demanded a "*parecchio*" for neutrality.

However, the chance for an Austro-Italian agreement had lapsed and the only effect of these still-born negotiations was the impression gained in the Allied camp that Austria was prepared to make territorial concessions to Italy – a willingness which was already very limited at that time and would be further diminished by the sacrifices on the Alpine battlefield.

On the other hand, after Italy had entered the war on their side, the Allies lived in constant fear that on a subsequent occasion Rome might decide that a separate peace would be in her interest. To counteract this

---

[67] *Ibid.*, No. 428606 (10 April).

[68] Grey to Buchanan, 19 April, *F.O.* 371/2508, No. 45968/f.28275.

[69] R. Rodd, *op. cit.*, iii, p.243.

[70] *F.O.*371/2375, f.2113 and *Int. Bez.*, p.459; cf. also L. Valiani, "Italian-Austro-Hungarian Negotiations 1914–1915", in *Journal of Cont. Hist.*, i/3 (1966), p.127.

[71] St. Burián, *Austria in Dissolution*, p.56.

[72] Nicolson to Buchanan, 15 Mar. 1915, *F.O.*800/377; Grey to Rodd, 25 May in G. M. Trevelyan, *Grey of Falloden*, London 1937, p.29.

possibility the Allies thought it wise to bind Italy and thereby themselves not to conclude peace separately. This agreement reduced the possibilities of shortening the war diplomatically even further than the very terms of the Treaty of London as signed on 26 April 1915, which promised to Italy the Trentino, cisalpine Tyrol to the Brenner frontier, Trieste, Goricia, all of Istria as far as the Quarnero, North Dalmatia, a part of Albania (Valona) and the Dodecanese islands. In a special appendix to article V the sovereignty over the littoral between the bay of Volosca and the mouth of the Drina was allotted to Serbia, Croatia and Montenegro. If these became or remained independent states it would have meant that both Austria and Hungary were without access to the sea. This seemed "perfect madness" to Hardinge, "if Austria was to remain a power at all". He agreed with Nicolson that, if the terms of the treaty leaked out, "Austria would fight to the last gasp".[73]

The disappointment of the South Slav emigrés over the Treaty of London was shared by their British friends, who had already tried to mobilize public opinion against the proposed regulations while the negotiations were under way. Seton-Watson, G. M. Trevelyan and R. Muir wrote articles in the Socialist daily *Unità*, in which they approved of the Italian claim to the Trentino and Trieste, but simultaneously demanded the creation of an independent Yugoslav state comprising together with Serbia all the Austro-Hungarian territories inhabited by South Slavs.[74]

On 23 April Seton-Watson undertook a last minute attempt with a letter which Steed published in *The Times*. Seton-Watson's letter had the complete approval of "some very high people in the Foreign Office".[75] Arthur Nicolson was most apprehensive of the problem embodied in the Italian insistence that there be no union between Croatia and Serbia, for any Italian attempt to incorporate Austria's Southern Slavs would be utterly resented by them and "we will have a Southern Slav question with Italy in place of Austria".[76] The dilemma between idealistic principles and the necessity of a *Realpolitik* is fully transparent in George Clerk's remark to Seton-Watson that "unless Italy comes in at once and turns the scale decisively against Austria and Germany, Grey, Delcassé and Sazonov will deserve to be hanged".[77] However, when Rodd telegraphed from Rome that the articles in *The Times* (Evans had contributed one with a similar bias) continued to offend Italian susceptibilities and hinted "that their publication in the

---

[73] *F.O.* 800/378 of 25 May 1915.
[74] Quoted in L. Valiani, *op. cit.*, p.171.
[75] Steed to McClure, 24 Apr., Steed papers. See also A. J. May, "Seton-Watson and the Treaty of London", *Journal of Modern History*, 1957, pp.42–47.
[76] Minute on a telegram by Buchanan dating back to 7 Oct. 1914! *F.O.* 371/2008, No. 57095.
[77] Steed to Dawson, 29 Apr., Steed papers.

present circumstances can serve no useful purpose", *The Times* dropped the issue.[78]

Seton-Watson was convinced that he had to act openly, but his direct intervention with Grey bore no fruit. The Foreign Secretary repeated that British and French military authorities had given it as their opinion that Italy's entry would decide the outcome of the war and he could not ignore their advice. Grey used the interesting argument that "ragged fringes" were inevitable at any great territorial settlement:

> We shall have to make concessions to one another. Not one of us can get 100 per cent of the extreme national demands. The Serbs and the other Slavs, who are really going to gain more than anyone else, must not deny to those who are fighting for them the means of securing victory.[79]

The victory of the Allies, Grey told the Serbian minister in London, "would secure for Serbia Bosnia and Herzegovina wide access to the Adriatic (by which he meant a large part of the Adriatic coast), to say nothing of what Montenegro and Croatia would have".[80]

If this was realized, Serbia would practically double her size. Moreover, the very next day Grey held out to Pašić a federation between Serbia and Croatia, though this was naturally "a matter for the Croats themselves".[81] What Serbia was asked in return, was to give Macedonia to Bulgaria in order to induce the latter country to enter into the war on the side of the Entente. But the Serbian Premier hesitated to agree to such a bargain, apparently led by the conviction that it was better to insist on the retention of already acquired territory than to exchange this for the prospect of a South Slav union, in which the supremacy of the Serbs would be contested.

This unification remained the supreme goal of the South Slav leaders in exile. Their next move was the foundation of a Yugoslav Committee which came into being in London in May 1915. They addressed a letter "to the British Nation and Parliament" respecting the aspirations of the Southern Slavs, in which they said that Serbs, Croats and Slovenes prayed for an Entente victory and awaited the salvation of the Yugoslav nation. After reading this memorandum Sir G. Clerk advised that a reply "full of sympathy" should be given, but the Foreign Office ought to "convey the warning that none of us can win the war without some bitter sacrifices".[82]

The Yugoslav spokesmen, mainly of Croat stock, did not relax their

---

[78] *F.O.* 371/2376, No. 51340/f.45460 of 28 Apr.; cf. *History of The Times*, iv, p.237.
[79] G. M. Trevelyan, *op. cit.*, p.299.
[80] *F.O.* 438/6 (No. 56465) of 6 May 1915.
[81] *F.O.* 371/2241, f.249, Grey to Ch. des Graz, 7 May 1915.
[82] *F.O.* 371/2258, No. 90173/f.55031 of 27 June 1915.

31

solicitation. Unwilling to accept a half-way solution, they employed all sorts of propaganda to get their demands across. In late June of 1915, an exhibition of one of their members, Ivan Meštrović, a well-known sculptor, took place in London and was opened by Robert Cecil. Seton-Watson urged the Foreign Office to make use of the Committee by utilising it for intelligence purposes,[83] but the advice of their "new counsellors" was regarded with scepticism by the traditionally-minded Foreign Office staff. The attitude of the French ally had a more direct bearing on Foreign Office reactions. Since Delcassé had seen the Yugoslav delegation, the British agreed to do the same. On 2 July they were received by Lord Crewe, who expressed his sympathy, assured the South Slavs of the goodwill of the British government, but emphasized that in European history no people had been liberated entirely in one single war and that all had to pass through several stages of unity.[84] At this stage Steed could be placed at the general trend, for

> people in England are gradually understanding how direct and vital is our interest in the creation of a large and complete Jugoslavia. The foolish doctrine that it may be to our interest to spare Austria–Hungary as much as possible is giving way to the sounder doctrine that our vital interest is to aid in the creation of as many moderately strong states as possible in Europe that will be directly interested in preventing the establishment of any kind of hegemony, German or other.[85]

A further breakthrough for the South Slav case was the message from Pašić, according to which he seemed now to be willing to co-operate with the Croats. Thereupon Grey thought, provided that Serbia agreed, the Allies could say that

> after the war, Bosnia, and Herzegovina, South Dalmatia, Slavonia and Croatia will be free. They will be able to decide their own fate.[86]

Supilo was satisfied with this declaration by the Foreign Secretary. It clearly implied that the Yugoslavs would be granted a plebiscite before the settlement.

With the entry of Bulgaria into the ranks of the Central Powers, however, all the promises made to the South Slavs could be questioned again. Legally the British government was not obliged to anything beyond the restoration of Serbia's pre-war boundaries. In addition to that, Bosnia–Herzegovina were understood silently to become part of a Greater Serbia. The establishment of a South Slav state, comprising all

---

[83] *F.O.* 371/2241, No. 115057.
[84] P. D. Ostović, *The Truth about Yugoslavia*, New York 1952, p.61.
[85] Steed to McClure, 16 July, quoted in the *History of The Times*, iv, p.237.
[86] *F.O.* 371/2241, No. 123158/f.55031 (minute by Clerk of 31 Aug. 1915). The declaration was made by Grey on 15 Sept., cf. Lloyd George, *The Truth about the Peace Treaties*, i. p.37.

the Serbs, Croats, and Slovenes hitherto belonging to the Habsburg Empire, was not officially sponsored by the British government. Existing sympathies for the South Slav cause had to be suppressed for another reason. The Italians observed all the activities of the South Slavs with mixed feelings. For that reason the Yugoslav committee had not been allowed to publish its memorandum, because many passages denounced Italian claims. Later in 1916 the Serbian Society, which enjoyed the patronage of Lord Cromer, became the main target of the ultra-nationalist Italian press, which suggested that it was sponsored by Yugoslavs in the pay of Austria–Hungary with the object of creating dissensions among the Allies. Wickham Steed as the protagonist of Yugoslav propaganda became the bugbear in Italy, although the British looked very detached at these activities. Ambassador Rodd commented: "They do not realize . . . that even the chairmanship of Lord Cromer and active support of the editor of *The Times* do not necessarily imply that the Serbian Society is going to control the policy of His Majesty's Government".[87]

The policy of the latter was in fact controlled by the desire to avoid too far-reaching a commitment to the South Slavs, which it might be impossible to honour at a later time. On the other hand they were in a position in which their hands were still untied by any binding agreement with the Czechs. The door for a settlement was kept open, should a further chance arise to strengthen the war effort against Germany by a direct deal with Austria. The future course of events was to decide to which side the scales would weigh.

4. The Addition of the Rumanian Claim

The compliance with most of the Italian claims on the part of the Entente was due to the belief that the Italian entry would stimulate other powers to follow Italy's example. From the beginning of the war it had been the aim of the British to enclose Germany and Austria with a ring of states allied with the Entente.[88] The Allies had high hopes of creating a Balkan block consisting of Bulgaria, Rumania, and Greece in support of Serbia's struggle against Austria–Hungary. Grey was convinced that Italy's intervention would lead to that of the other nations, in particular Rumania.[89]

Already before the negotiations with Italy had materialised, Grey had promised his support for Rumanian territorial claims, to which he could not bind Britain while he had no objection if Russia succeeded in obtaining "those advantages from Rumania".[90]

---

[87] Rodd to Grey, rec. 17 Nov. 1916 (No. 231670), circulated in the Cabinet, *Cab.* 37/162 (23 Nov.).
[88] Cf. Eyre Crowe's memorandum of 5 Aug. 1914, *F.O.* 371/2162, No. 36542.
[89] E. Grey, *op. cit.*
[90] *F.O.* 371/2163, No. 17, Grey's telegram to Buchanan of 9 Aug. 1914.

Sazonov, however, entirely mismanaged the situation by assuring Rumania of Russia's support if the former invaded Transylvania.[91] Such a benevolent attitude towards Rumanian aspirations was meant to encourage her to come into the war but it only strengthened the bargaining position of Bratianu, who immediately stepped up his demands. To overcome possible Allied objections to his wishes he tried to act in harmony with the Italians, with whom he concluded an agreement promising mutual support of territorial claims.[92] This was to prove worthless than the paper on which it was written, once the Italians had secured their own *desiderata*, but this did not prevent the Rumanians from confronting the Allies with increasingly extensive demands as a price for their co-belligerency.

As a *sine qua non* for Rumania's participation in the war Bucharest insisted on the Theiss and the Pruth frontiers. To the Foreign Office these claims seemed colossal and A. Nicolson noted with resignation that the Rumanians had been influenced by Italy's example, when they asked for two-thirds of Hungary and the Bukovina. Nicolson found the former claim especially preposterous, as he was sure there were "but scattered portions of Rumanians in most of the districts which would be incorporated". He therefore warned:

> We should be careful as to meeting these exorbitant claims. We cannot blot Austria and Hungary out of the map and convert them into larger Switzerlands with no sea access. Promises hastily made now for an immediate object will be most embarrassing to realize when peace terms come to be discussed.[93]

Formerly only Transylvania and a fraction of the Bukovina had been contemplated as concessions to Rumania and it seemed to Nicolson that this was reasonable and could be granted. But when the Rumanian *desiderata* transmitted by the British minister in Bucharest, Barclay, remained the same, the Permanent Under-Secretary advised against accepting "these exaggerated claims":[94]

> We could not realize them and even if after a prolonged war Hungary was so crushed as to submit to any terms we should be sowing the seeds for future conflicts.

Nicolson was afraid that co-operation on the part of Rumania on the terms suggested by her was more likely to prolong than to shorten the war. The Entente wanted to achieve the latter by enlisting her as an ally, but if they had to dismember the kingdom of Hungary to such a

---

[91] A. Rieber, "Russian Diplomacy and Rumania", *Russian Diplomacy and Eastern Europe, op. cit.*, pp.243–54.
[92] *D.D.I.*, 5th Ser., pp.419–20 (17 Sept. 1914).
[93] *F.O.* 371/2244, No. 49484/f.214, minute of 24 Apr. 1915.
[94] *Ibid.*, No. 5326 of 1 May.

degree as Rumania asked for, they "should have to pulverize (their) enemies before they would subscribe to such conditions" and Nicolson was certain that this could not be expected within a few months.[95] Nicolson objected to the project of obtaining the co-operation of Rumania at the indicated price because he was of the opinion that it would be an "erroneous thing to do so". He wanted the Allies to act with foresight and avoid engagements which in all probability they could not fulfil, "apart from the question as to whether we should be justified in undertaking all the engagements desired of us".[96]

Apart from the fact that the Rumanian claims presupposed a complete defeat of Austria–Hungary or at least the surrender of the Hungarians, they also clashed with the interests of the Serbs. In order to gain the support of Bulgaria the Allies had previously offered her Serbian Macedonia and felt obliged to compensate Serbia with Austro-Hungarian territory in return: Bosnia–Herzegovina, a wide access to the Adriatic sea and parts of the Banat. The extent of the latter was still undefined but Grey had to point out to the Rumanian minister in London, Misu, "the absolute necessity of securing some territory to the North of Belgrade to give Serbia a strategic frontier".[97]

Grey approved of the agreements reached between Russia and Rumania regarding Transylvania and the Bukovina and added that this need not be all. But the rest of the Rumanian claims ought to be left for the general peace.[98] Grey promised to do all he could to promote an understanding but declined the extreme claims of Rumania, which he admonished to pursue a policy of give and take. Though Grey showed some inclination of accepting the idea of Rumania taking part of the Theiss frontier, he refused to tell the Rumanians what the Cabinet considered to be her appropriate share.[99]

The Rumanians had approached the British in the hope that they could get their backing against the Russians on the assumption that Britain was disinterested in the territorial settlement of the Balkans. Grey, however, made it quite clear that Britain was not indifferent to the fate of Serbia, whose rights he ranked equal to those of Belgium, emphasizing that it was mainly for these two cases that Britain was waging war. This did not exclude that Britain and her Allies would consider Rumanian wishes as long as they were in accordance with Serbian interests.[100]

Thus the matter was left alone until a loophole could be found out of

---

[95] *Ibid.*, cf. also Nicolson's letter to Hardinge of 21 July 1915, *F.O.* 800/378.

[96] Minute on Barclay's telegram of 5 May, *F.O.* 371/2258, No. 55734/f.55100.

[97] Cf. Grey's telegram to des Graz of 6 May (No. 56465), copy in *F.O.* 438/6 and British *aide-mémoire* submitted by Buchanan to Sazonov on 4 May, *Int. Bez.*, vii, No. 676, pp.664–65.

[98] *Ibid.*

[99] *Ibid.*, No. 741, Benckendorff to Sazonov, 12 May.

[100] *Ibid.*, No. 805, Benckendorff to Sazonov, 21 May.

the Rumanian impasse. The deadlock was tackled by Delcassé at an Anglo-French conference at Calais on 6 July, when the French Foreign Minister presented Asquith with his idea of compensating Serbia with Croatia.[101] What initially sounded like the hour of birth of Yugoslavia was immediately reviewed unfavourably by the Italians. Sonnino objected to the new scheme, because, if Rumania finally failed, such a pledge could hinder the Allies from detaching Hungary from the Central Powers.[102] The Russians were also sceptical about the prospect of realizing the French proposals. They feared that the Rumanians would always find a pretext not to march and in that event the Entente would be exposed to reproach from Serbia for interfering with her interests.[103]

Nicolson thought it was "impossible to attempt to ride more than one horse"[104] and while Grey allowed the matter to drift the strategic situation at the Eastern front developed so negatively that for the time being all idea of drawing Rumania into the war had to be abandoned. The Allies had to recognize that under these circumstances and after having witnessed the fate of Serbia, Rumania could not be expected to intervene on the side of the Allies until the military situation had improved.

Only in summer 1916, in connection with the preparations for the Brusilov offensive, the Russians resumed negotiations with Bucharest. When Bratianu started to shuffle again, the British military attaché, O'Beirne, alluded to the possibility of a separate peace between the Entente and Austria–Hungary. But the Rumanians were not intimidated by such unfounded threats. They were convinced that the Austro-German partnership was unbreakable and counted on the eventual dismemberment of the Habsburg Empire as a result of the war.[105] So the Rumanians succeeded in extracting most of the territorial promises they had asked for: Transylvania, the Banat of Temesvar and the Bukovina to the Pruth river.

When the military convention was drafted, Bratianu also managed to overcome Russian reservations according to which the promised territories could only be guaranteed by the other powers as long as the general results of the war would allow it.[106] The Rumanian counterdraft demanded from all the governments which were party to the treaty "not to conclude a separate peace or the general peace without the Austro-Hungarian territories . . . being annexed to the Rumanian Crown".[107] The British, who did not want to continue the war for the

---

[101] A. Pingaud, "L'Entente et la Roumanie en 1915", *Revue des Deux Mondes*, May 1930, p.155.
[102] Rodd to Grey, 3 July 1915, *F.O.* 371/2259, No. 88943.
[103] *Ibid.*, No. 91744 (8 July).
[104] *Ibid.*, No. 88997 (minute on French memorandum of 29 June).
[105] *F.O.* 371/2606, No. 119584/f.761 (20 June 1916).
[106] *F.O.* 371/2607, No. 156012.
[107] *Ibid.*, No. 146750.

sake of Rumania alone, suggested the addition of a provision accepting the Rumanian formula on condition that all the Allies realized their territorial aspirations.[108] While this was tacitly understood afterwards and secretly laid down between Russia and France, the Entente felt compelled to accept the Rumanian text, which put Rumania on an equal footing with Italy, in order not to delay her entry any longer. [109] The territories promised to Rumania, if amputated from the Habsburg Empire, would have weighed heavily on the destiny of the Monarchy. The territorial losses of Hungary would have been so enormous that the Magyars would no longer have an interest in preserving the symbiosis with an Austria incapable of protecting their territorial integrity. Steed was right in his conclusion that

> the intervention of Rumania signs the death-warrant of Hungary, begins the necessary partition of Austria, and foreshadows the reconstruction of Europe on the basis of ethnically-complete states . . .[110]

5. The Czechoslovak Pivot

The Yugoslav question was closely linked with the Czechoslovak problem, but the Czechs had a great advantage over the South Slavs in that they had an outstanding representative abroad in the person of Th. G. Masaryk. The leader of the "Realist" party in Bohemia became convinced that the Entente was militarily stronger than the Central Powers when Britain entered the war. Then Masaryk received a message from Steed that the possibility of a long war was being discussed in British political and army circles; with such a prospect looming, Masaryk saw an improvement of the chances of obtaining complete independence for the Czechs and the Slovaks.

His correspondence with Steed was followed by an interview with Seton-Watson, whom he met in Rotterdam on 24/25 October 1914. The latter grossly exaggerated Masaryk's backing inside Bohemia so as to attract the attention of the government to Masaryk's ideas about "the future of Bohemia", which culminated in the quest for an independent kingdom comprising the historical Bohemia–Moravia–Silesia, to which the Slovak districts of Hungary should be added. On economic grounds Masaryk claimed the inclusion of the German parts of Northern Bohemia, but he was prepared to make concessions in the regions towards Upper Austria and in Silesia.

Seton-Watson's record of their conversation was submitted to the Foreign Office, where it did not arouse any particular interest.[111] The

---

[108] Grey to Buchanan, 28 July, *ibid.*
[109] *Ibid.*, No. 157819.
[110] Memorandum of 4 Aug. 1916, Steed papers, P.H.S.
[111] R. W. Seton-Watson, *Masaryk in England*, London 1942, pp.40–47, the memorandum is filed in *F.O.* 371/1900, No. 67456.

Czech question did not yet concern policymakers in Britain. For instance, when Ambassador Spring-Rice cabled from Washington that he had been approached by the Bohemian Committee, which had expressed its hopes for the success of the Allied forces, the answer was left to his discretion.[112]

The first prominent Bohemian politician who approached a diplomat of His Majesty's Government was František Sis, who through the mediation of *The Times*'s Balkan correspondent saw the head of the British mission in Sofia, Sir Henry Bax-Ironside, who expressed himself in favour of the preservation of Austria–Hungary and against the spread of Russian influence in the West.[113]

Although Russian interest in the Czech question was considerably greater, Masaryk, in contrast to many of his compatriots, definitely pinned his hopes on Britain and France and chose London as the centre of his campaign, because it was the centre of the Entente war effort. With the help of Seton-Watson as go-between, Masaryk established contacts with the Foreign Office and, as a result of his conversations with Clerk, he prepared his famous memorandum "Independent Bohemia",[114] in which he stated that Austria had always been an artificial state, but had now lost its *raison d'être*. He claimed that Bohemia was forced to abandon her and form an independent state. Masaryk refuted possible Allied objections by pointing out the viability of a future Czecho-Slovak state and its importance for the erection of a Slavic barrier – in conjunction with Serbia–Croatia[115] – which would be coincident with the interests of the Allies, since it was an effective means to prevent Germany from "colonising the Balkans and Asia Minor".

"The Allies have a long way to go, before the points in this memorandum come up for their practical consideration", minuted Clerk. He described Masaryk as the "recognized leader of Czech political thought", whereas for Nicolson he was a Young Czech, hardly to be considered as an exponent of the more moderate sections of the Czech party, but "still an important man".[116]

Masaryk clearly recognized that the governments in Paris and London did not desire to take much interest in the Czechoslovak exiles. (He was never received by Grey!). So he hoped to achieve his aims by appealing to public opinion, particularly in Britain.[117] Seton-Watson

---

[112] *F.O.* 371/1900, No. 60155 (6 Oct. 1914).
[113] Z. A. B. Zeman, *The Break-up of the Habsburg Monarchy*, London 1961, pp.74–5.
[114] Seton-Watson, *op. cit.*, p.116ff.
[115] "He would like to see the North Slav State connected with the South Slav State by a strip of territory running north and south along the present western border of Hungary" (!), minute by Bunsen, 10 May 1915, *F.O.* 371/1900m, No. 58359/F.53297.
[116] *Ibid.*
[117] Note in his private papers (28 Mar. 1915); L. Valiani, *op. cit.*, p.210.

had already thought of another step to propagate his cause. He wrote a letter on the significance of Hus, whose quincentenary was approaching and got 28 Oxonian dons to sign it. Beforehand the Warden of All Souls had enquired as to the view of the government on that matter, but whereas Nicolson wished to hint that it would seem advisable not to send a memorial to Prague, Grey saw no reason to discourage it and on 6 July *The Times* published it with a warm comment.[118]

To give Masaryk a permanent platform Seton-Watson urged him to accept a lectureship at King's College, where he held his inaugural lecture on "The Problem of Small Nations in the European Crisis" on 19 October.[119] Once again he tried to prove the crucial importance of the Slavonic nations for Britain as natural adversaries of Germany, which strengthened as buffer states would be the only real check upon Prussia. The important thing about this event was, however, that Asquith had agreed to take part in the ceremony, from which he was then prevented through illness! Cecil introduced him instead to the Prime Minister, who had sent a friendly but non-committal message not mentioning Bohemia.[120] This did not discourage the Czechs and when in 1916 the question of formulating the war aims became more imminent, the Czech Committee in London passed a resolution urging that they should be included in the terms of peace.[121] But in early 1916 the Foreign Office staff was not even informed whether Grey was interested in the Czech question.[122] Probably he had not yet formed an opinion on it. In a conversation on 2 May with Milyukov, then a Duma-representative, Grey made some remarks about peace terms, calling the question of the Croats and Slovenes a Russian affair, while evading the demand for a partition of the Danubian Monarchy.[123]

This problem was for the first time analysed in Whitehall, when Asquith in August invited members of the War Committee of the Cabinet to give their opinion on peace terms. The most detailed study was prepared in the Foreign Office by W. Tyrrell and Robert Paget. The latter seems to have been influenced to some degree by a conversation he had in June with Pašić, who, speaking of the creation of a South Slav state, expressed his conviction that there would be no difficulties in reaching a satisfactory understanding with Italy. With regard to the Dual Monarchy Pašić was of the opinion that:

> Austria proper will never again be able to shake herself free from Germany and it would be wise to regard her merely as a part of the

---

[118] *F.O.* 371/1900, No. 60723.
[119] Seton-Watson, *op. cit.*, p.73.
[120] *Ibid.*, pp.135ff.
[121] *F.O.* 371/2602, No. 50914.
[122] *Ibid.*, No. 86039.
[123] *Krasnij Archiv* 53/54 p.3ff.; cf. E. Hölzle, "Das Experiment des Friedens im ersten Weltkrieg", *Geschichte in Wissenschaft und Unterricht*, xxiii (1962).

German Empire; consequently she should be robbed of as much territory as possible.[124]

Pašić also favoured an independent Bohemia, which would include Moravia and be joined to the South Slav state. Although this suggestion, which was already brought forward by Masaryk, appeared to Clerk difficult to work out in practice, Pasic's ideas in general appealed to the Foreign Office, especially the conclusion that the new states with democratic ideals would be drawn towards Great Britain and France and not constitute an accession to the power of Russia. Paget and Tyrrell, in their memorandum of 7 August,[125] granted that the future of Austria–Hungary would depend very largely on the military situation at the end of the war, but if the situation should be one which enabled the Allies to dispose of its future

> there seems little doubt that in accordance with the principle of giving free play to nationalities, the Dual Monarchy, which in its present composition is a negation of that principle, should be broken up.

The Foreign Office planners were convinced that Austria would remain subservient to its ally, no matter whether the Central Powers were victorious or not in this war. The parties in Austria and Hungary which were strongly opposed to German hegemony would remain a minority and the survival of a diminished but independent Austro-Hungarian state would be no effective counterweight to Germany. However, Paget and Tyrrell found it difficult to find a solution for Bohemia. The foundation of an independent state was discarded as impractical, a link with the South Slav state as artificial. So they recommended a union with the new Polish state. To counterbalance the influence of Prussia they proposed the Anschluss of German Austria to the Reich, because despite the accession in territory and population Prussianism would be counterbalanced by the Catholic South German element.

The authors of the above scheme were, however, aware of the fact that it might have to be modified in deference to the views of Russia, geographical configuration and military considerations. Hardinge found it "an interesting report requiring a good deal of digestion" and thought it premature to express a decided opinion. Grey, who had not yet read the whole report, found it "very ably done" and ordered that it should be kept secret. His hesitant approach is demonstrated by the fact that the paper was not circulated in the Cabinet until shortly before the end of the year and then, instead of becoming a guide for British

---

[124] *F.O.* 371/2804, No. 117933.
[125] Printed slightly abbreviated in Lloyd George, *The Truth about the Peace Treaties*, i, p.31ff. The original with minutes by Hardinge and Grey in *F.O.* 371/2804, No. 180510.

foreign policy, it disappeared into oblivion until the end of the war.

The Chief of the Imperial General Staff, Sir William Robertson, submitted his memorandum on 31 August. The full extent to which the government was committed, he wrote, was not known to the General Staff, but he assumed that it was the intention to break up Austria–Hungary, obviously drawing his conclusions from the arrangements with Italy and Rumania, the latter just having signed the Treaty of Bucharest on 16 August. Robertson, however, would have preferred to keep Austria in existence in order to stave off Pan-Slavism.[126]

Balfour in his memorandum of 14 October discussed a peace settlement on the basis of the principle of nationality, but was far less rigorous than the Foreign Office planners, for he doubted the viability of the potential new Slav states. In the Czech question he said:

> Whether an independent Bohemia would be strong enough to hold her own from a military as well as from a commercial point of view against Teutonic domination – I do not know.
> If the change is possible it should be made.[127]

There was of course a great difference between a cautious consideration of possibilities for a future settlement and the official assurance for which the emigré leaders had been hoping in vain so far. The need to state publicly the war aims of the Allies came with the Austro-German peace offer in December 1916, which was immediately followed by Woodrow Wilson's appeal to the belligerents to state their terms. This duty fell on the new War Cabinet formed under Lloyd George. The discussions over the nature of the reply to the Americans were dominated by the dilemma of whether the Allied answer should be evasive – as Briand had proposed – or should clearly state the objects for which the Entente was fighting. The latter alternative was strongly favoured by Cecil who convinced his colleagues of the necessity to make a definite appeal to rouse American sympathies. He was commissioned with a draft, in which he proposed the passages:

> They (the Allies) looked for some territorial settlement that had the possibility of permanence; such a settlement must be based on principles acceptable to human feelings such as nationality and security . . .
> Above all a settlement on national lines would be essential in South Eastern Europe; the details could be a matter of discussion, but they must include the liberation of Slav peoples from German domination.[128]

---

[126] Lloyd George, *War Memoirs*, ii, pp.833–43.
[127] *Ibid.*, pp.877–79.
[128] *Cab.* 23/1, *WC* 16 (23 Dec.) and *F.O.* 371/2805, No. 260747/f.252387.

The problem was discussed at an Anglo-French conference in London on 26 December, where the French also came to the conclusion that the principle of nationality was a very important psychological weapon and it was Albert Thomas who said it was necessarý to animate the fight with great ideas.[129] As a result of this agreement on the general tone of the answer the Director in the French Foreign Ministry, Philippe Berthelot, prepared a draft which the War Cabinet considered as a basis, subject to certain amendments. This draft reply already specified the "liberation passage" naming the Slavs, Italians and Rumanians.[130]

The final wording was postponed until an Anglo-French-Italian conference which took place in Paris at the beginning of January 1917. Paris was the second stronghold of the Czech emigrés. The director of the Czechoslovak National Committee, Edvard Beneš, laboured hard to persuade the Quai d'Orsay to include the "Czechoslovaks" in the peace terms. Beneš succeeded in winning over a collaborator of Berthelot, Robert de Caix, who recommended that his superior should give the Czechs a stimulant for the Czech resistance.[131] Berthelot, who also was on friendly terms with the Slavophile Ernest Denis, acquiesced in Beneš's demand and, when it came to the actual formulation of the passage in question at the conference, managed to persuade Robert Cecil to agree. The other delegations seemed preoccupied with the planning of forthcoming military operations in Greece and the Balkans in general and their attitude towards the problem of Austria–Hungary are not recorded in connexion with the liberation-formula, but from the paper on a new strategy which Lloyd George had circulated, it is quite evident that at the turn of 1916/17 there was a strong feeling in favour of liquidating Austria:

> Germany is formidable only as long as she can command an unbroken Austria, but if Austria is beaten, Germany will be beaten, too.[132]

For these reasons, he advocated that the question of the crushing of Austria should be examined. The final obstacle was purely a linguistic one, because there was an obvious contradiction in demanding "the liberation of the Italians, Rumanians, Slavs and Czechoslovaks", but

---

[129] *Cab.* 28/2, I.C.13a (26 Dec.) and *Min. Aff. Etr.* ser. A, cert. 369.

[130] *F.O.* 371/2806, No. 264233 of 28 Dec., *Cab.* 23/1, *WC* 18 & 19 of 26 and 28 Dec. – It is interesting to note that the Italians demanded the inclusion of a phrase to affirm the principle of nationality and the liberty of the small nations in order to support their irredentist aims(!). *F.O.* 371/2806, No. 260829.

[131] E. Beneš, *Souvenirs de guerre et de révolution*, i. Paris 1928, pp. 265–66. De Caix's memo. of 2 Jan 1917 in *Min. Aff. Etr.*, *loc. cit.* Cf. also V. Kybal, *Les origines diplomatiques de l'état tchécoslovaques*, Prague 1929, p.95, n.7.

[132] *Cab.* 28/2, I.C. 13a.

the specification "Yugoslavs" would not have been accepted by the Italians.[133]

The Allied note of 10 January can be regarded as a landmark in the history of the war and it was hailed as such by the Czechs and their friends, who had profited from the new political gospel of Woodrow Wilson. However, the Allies were careful. While adopting nationality as their watchword, they safeguarded themselves against an exaggerated interpretation with implicit distinctions between "nation" and "state" and frequent references to "nationalities" and "peoples".

According to the scheme of *The New Europe*, "liberation" was only possible as the result of the dismemberment of Austria–Hungary, for its achievement involved the destruction of German hegemony. The reference to the Czechoslovaks meant that the Allies desired that Bohemia should recover her independence.[134]

But while the Allies had not, as is sometimes contended, "thus committed themselves and given hostages to the future",[135] there is no doubt as to the prominence given to the Austro-Hungarian question, which so far had been almost forgotten by the Entente. Until now the Powers had not said the last word, but in the case of an Allied victory the very existence of the Dual Monarchy would be at stake. One thing was certain: the national programme of some of the minor Allies, ratified by the others, menaced Austria with territorial diminution on the whole South-Eastern frontier. If these *"justes revendications"* were honoured, it was necessary to consider the partition of Austria–Hungary, her division into small autonomous states, or some other less radical transformation preserving the dynastic tradition.

An Austria diminished by the exclusion of all Latin and South Slav nationalities still constituted a state of about 38 million – at that time almost equal to France – and was also a geographically homogeneous entity. It is true that the probable formation of a new Polish state had to be taken into account and would have meant the loss of Galicia with another five million. But was it necessary to detach the Czechs territorially? This delicate problem remained an open though more imminent one after the Allied answer to the American President.

Until the war, few Czechs voted for a definite rupture, being aware of the difficulties involved in holding their ground amongst the great powers. Both Britain and France were against Bohemia becoming an easy prey for either Germany or Russia. They had far greater hopes in Austria, taking a new line independently from her present ally. So the

[133] J. Laroche, *Au Quai d'Orsay avec Briand et Poincaré*, Paris 1957, p.38. A. Bréal, Philippe Berthelot, Paris 1937, p.157–58, n.l. E. Beneš, *Souvenirs de guerre at de révolution*, i, pp. 262–66. pp.262–66.
[134] *The New Europe*, No. 14 (18 Jan. 1917), "The Allies' Programme".
[133] H. Hanak, *op. cit.*, p.216.

revised French war aims draft of 12 January 1917, which Paul Cambon did not communicate to Balfour before July 1917,[136] did not mention the Czechs at all and left aside the Austrian question. The sincerity of the Allied intentions also appears in a different light in the confidential note, which Balfour sent to Wilson a week after the public statement, and which merely considered the fulfilment of "the wishes . . . of the Transylvanians, of Poland and *perhaps* Bohemia".[137] At the same time the Foreign Secretary had no objections to the transfer of a substantial sum from the American Bohemians to Masaryk, whose activities were regarded with benevolence.[138] The Czech Mafia was appreciated as a useful organization and the Allies were prepared to pay a limited price to encourage it in the attempt to disintegrate the defensive force of the Habsburg army.

---

[136] G. Suarez, *Briand*, ii, p.128f. *F.O.* 371/2937, No. 133257/f.111293.
[137] *U.S. For Rel.*, 1917, pp.17–21.
[138] *F.O.* 371/2862, No. 12976 (16 Jan. 1917).

CHAPTER II

Soundings for a Separate Peace

1. The Austro-German Relationship and the Accession of the Emperor Karl

The war waged by the Habsburg Monarchy was different from that of the other powers, because for her it was no "national" war but a struggle for the preservation of her integral existence as a dynastic and economic Great Power. The Slavic population of Austria–Hungary had only reluctantly taken part in the war and the nationalities believed that they were fighting for interests other than their own.

In the first years of the war these disruptive tendencies were still weak but the looming danger was recognised by the Germans. When their ambassador in Vienna, Tschirschky, reported from Vienna that the Danube Monarchy "was on its deathbed" and would find it more and more difficult to hold out the longer the war continued, he found open ears in the Wilhelmstrasse. Tschirschky emphasized the Austrian weakness in military and economic respect and criticised incisively the pessimism and slovenliness (*Schlamperei*) in the Monarchy. He suggested that only a change of government could bring improvement. Bethmann agreed to submit the paper to the Kaiser with the introductory remark that "the picture was not painted in too dark colours", recommending extraordinary measures.[1]

The Austrian ambassador in Berlin, Prince Hohenlohe, who reported the dissatisfaction of the Germans with the state of affairs in Austria–Hungary, concluded that "relations ought to be revised fundamentally". He did not think that the association with Germany was the only blissful (*alleinseligmachende*) policy. At present, however, Austria needed German support and so there was no other way than trying to achieve Habsburg goals with a certain dependence on Ger-

---

[1] Tschirschky's report of 28 Sept. 1916 is printed in *L'Allemagne et le problème de la paix*, i, Paris 1962, No. 332. B.H.'s covering letter for W.II dated 30 Sept. was seen by the Kaiser on 1 Oct. and bears the marginal note "*welche?*" (which), reflecting the general helplessness in Berlin, concerning the Austrian problem, cf. AA. Oe. 95 secr. No. As 3465.

many.[2] Although it was clear to the Austrians as early as December 1914 that they were waging the war less to acquire territory than to assure the continued existence of the Monarchy itself, yet from the outset of the war the "chief aim" of their policy was "to get the greatest possible increase in power and security when things are rearranged".[3] After the occupation of Serbia and Montenegro, the future of these countries and the question of war aims was discussed in the Common Ministerial Council on 7 January 1916.[4] The incorporation of Serbia, the annexation of strategic strongholds on the Adriatic coast and a protectorate over Albania were considered. Besides these Balkan plans Austria wanted to annex parts of the Ukraine, Congress Poland and White Russia and in autumn 1916 the successful invasion of Rumania stimulated Austria's penchant for this *Milliardenobjekt*.

Shortly afterwards, however, the Austrian tone became somewhat milder. On 17 October 1916, at a meeting in Pless, Burián suggested to Bethmann Hollweg "that he make the attempt to bring about the end of the war without renouncing vital interests".[5] The Austrian Foreign Minister did not see how the Central Powers could gain a decisive victory in the following summer, since they were nearly exhausted. He therefore proposed to ask neutral countries for mediation by transmitting concrete conditions of peace on their behalf. This would boost home morale and win sympathies among the neutrals. Furthermore, if it were turned down by the enemy, it would probably strengthen the pacifist movements in their countries. Burián first of all wanted the territorial integrity of the Monarchy guaranteed, and to obtain this from the Germans he tried to fit in to the war aims of the Central Powers. His terms concerning the Western Allies were as follows:

1. The restoration of Belgium as a sovereign state with sufficient guarantees to ensure Germany's legitimate interests
2. Full territorial integrity of France
3. Return of German Colonies and German annexation of the Congo State
4. No indemnities for Germany except possible commercial advantages
5. Treaties to guarantee the freedom of the seas
6. Renunciation of Allied economic warfare.

Whereas this may sound rather moderate, Burián had "strategic frontier rectifications" in mind to satisfy Germany in the East, while

---

[2] Burián to Conrad 25 December 1915, H.H.St.A., P.A.I. box red. 499 No. 30 cf. F. Fischer, *Germany's Aims in the First World War*, London 1968, p.40.
[3] Cf. H. Rumpler, *Die Kriegsziele Österreich – Ungarns auf dem Balkan 1915/1916* (in Festschrift f. H. Hantsch), Graz 1965, pp.465–82.
[4] Published in Komjáthy, M. (ed.) *Protokolle des Gemeinsamen Ministerrats der österreich-ungarischen Monarchie (1914–1918)*, Budapest 1966, No. 15, p.352ff.
[5] *L'Allemagne* . . . i, No. 347.

Austria would expand in the Balkans and perhaps also to a smaller extent in Italy.[6]

Bethmann's own proposals were ready by late October and differed in several respects from Burián's. In respect to Belgium he wanted "real guarantees and securities", and from France Briey-Longwy plus indemnities for the evacuation of the other occupied territory.[7] This was hardly different from the programme of 9 September 1914 and clearly reveals the continuity of the German war aims.[8] Hindenburg's comments on Bethmann's draft went even further, as might have been expected, and on 8 November he stated that eventual peace feelers would be undertaken, but without any slackening of current operations or submarine warfare.[9] Although Bethmann tried to compromise between maximum political and minimum military aims, the basis resulting from his discussion with the O.H.L. made it apparent that the chances for a common Austro-German peace move under such presuppositions were limited.[10]

Bethmann had to defend his paper against Austrian criticism which was mainly directed against his refusal to back the claim of Habsburg integrity. But the German Chancellor on the other hand opposed the suggestions made by William II and Hindenburg for direct interference in the Monarchy's internal affairs. He argued that such an infringement of sovereignty would be politically impracticable and harmful. Germany could not afford to deal with Austria so arrogantly as to lose her ally's friendship. (An abuse of power could entail its penalty.)

> At the peace negotiations the Monarchy may be in an advantageous position, because its relations with France and England have not been seriously disturbed by the war; this, because of the illwill they bear against us, may become an important factor in the way peace will be concluded and for the future of international relations.[11]

The danger scented by Bethmann became more imminent with the accession of Karl after the death of Franz Joseph on 21 November. As long as the old Emperor was alive, his personal integrity assured Germany of Austria–Hungary's faithfulness. But his successor was of a different nature. He was brought up by the Archduchess Maria Josepha, a pious Roman Catholic and very much anti-Prussian; in 1911 Karl married Princess Zita of Parma, who did nothing to hide her

---

[6] *Ibid.*
[7] *Ibid.*, No. 361.
[8] For an interpretation of this document cf. F. Fischer, *op.cit.*, p.116ff.
[9] *L'Allemagne...* i, Nos. 365 and 369.
[10] *Ibid.*, No. 373.
[11] This passage is quoted by Z. A. B. Zeman, *The Break-up of the Habsburg Empire*, London 1961, pp.110–11; for the document in full v. A.A.Oe 95 secr.

sympathies for France and Italy and tried ambitiously to persuade her husband to abandon the fateful alliance.

As early as 25 October, Horace Rumbold, the British Minister in Berne, transmitted the information reported by a lady at court in Vienna about the "anti-Prussian sentiments of the clique around the Emperor", which were increased by the way in which the German commands on the Eastern front were redistributed to the mortification of the Austrians.[12] Rumbold thought that Austria might preserve her status as a great power, if she concluded a separate peace now. However, when he talked the matter over with Captain Briggs, the late American military attaché in Vienna, the latter pointed out the difficulty involved in a reconciliation of Italy. Moreover, the Austrians were much occupied with the idea of a separate peace before the Rumanian intervention, which initially galvanized them, but following their recent military successes a new accession of confidence severely reduced the chances for a separate peace.[13]

When Karl came to the throne, he made it quite clear that he was not inclined to fight at all costs until final victory was achieved, and the words of his inaugural proclamation "to My Peoples" reveal his intentions:

I want to do everything to put an end to the horrors and sacrifices of the war at the earliest possible moment, to restore the sadly missed blessings of peace, as soon as it is compatible with the honour of our arms, the living conditions of our States and their dearest allies, and the defiance of our enemies.[14]

The realization of his desire for peace was extremely difficult, as the Entente answer to the Central Powers showed. It did not take special notice of the Emperor thus leaving him without a starting-point for future action. As a reaction to this sharp rebuff and to stiffen the morale of his forces, Karl issued a manifesto asserting that the enemy had refused "the hand that has been held out to them without even waiting to hear our conditions".[15]

Nevertheless, Karl did not give up at the turn of the year, he telegraphed to Wilhelm asking him "to undertake another attempt", which was, however, turned down by the Hohenzollern. The Kaiser's advisers feared Karl's penchant towards peace negotiations and therefore dropped the passage in the draft answer referring to the remaining possibility "through unofficial channels" and the necessity to seize every chance for peace.[16]

---

[12] *F.O.* 371/2602, No. 218444.
[13] *Ibid.*, No. 229011 of 7 Nov.
[14] Partly quoted in May, *op.cit.*, i, p.434.
[15] *Ibid.*, p.468.
[16] A.A. Gr.Hq.23, telegram of Wilhelm to Karl of 4 Jan.; the day before Ambassador Wedel had reported from Vienna: "Emperor in a very feeble mood . . . will say that it would do good to hide longing for peace a bit." Oe 86, i, 21, AS 88.

The second major obstacle for a survival of the Empire was the internal situation. To secure the support of the Slav subject races far-reaching constitutional reforms were necessary, giving Karl's realm some sort of federalist status. Rumours reached London by the end of the year that the Emperor intended the proclamation of a Yugoslav state inside the Monarchy. "Such a move", wrote Seton-Watson in a letter to Carson,[17] "would take the wind out of the sails of the Entente far more completely than the similar move in Poland and might create a very difficult situation for our diplomacy". In fact, nothing came out of this and on the contrary Karl had himself crowned King of Hungary promptly (instead of making use of a permitted delay of six months) – a fateful decision showing the inexperience of the young ruler, whose goodwill alone was not enough to master the situation but needed the guidance of energetic professional politicians.

Karl immediately made sweeping changes in many important governmental and administrative posts, assembling around him supposedly like-minded men Polzer-Hoditz, as the new head of his civil Cabinet, and Werkmann, as head of the press office.[18] The Supreme Command of the army was taken over by himself, while the Chief of the General Staff, Conrad von Hoetzendorff, was replaced by General Arz von Straussenberg. Baden near Vienna became the new headquarters (instead of Teschen) and Karl took up residence nearby in Laxenburg. The political leadership was drastically changed too. Heinrich Clam-Martinic became Austrian Prime Minister,[19] and his Hungarian antipode Tisza was soon obliged to send in his resignation. Most important was the change at the Ballplatz, where Count Ottokar Czernin took over from Burián. When the former was still ambassador in Bucharest, he had drafted an exposé in summer 1916, the contents of which proved him to be far more moderate than Burián and thus made the Emperor believe he had chosen a Foreign Minister sharing his point of view. Czernin, in the memorandum mentioned, recommended the ending of the war "under considerable sacrifices" in a militarily favourable situation, despite which any territorial aggrandizement should be renounced.[20]

Czernin also assumed a remarkably moderate attitude in the first Crown Council held under Karl on 12 January 1917,[21] which incidentally was before the Entente note of 10 January was known in Vienna. Here Karl outlined a maximum programme, including the annexation

---

[17] Dated 21 Dec; *F.O.* 371/2805, No. 261702.
[18] cf. their biographies on Karl: Polzer-Hoditz, *Kaiser Karl*, Vienna 1928, and A. Werkmann, *Aus der Aktenmappe seines Kabinettschefs*, Vienna 1922.
[19] cf. P. Hoeglinger, *Ministerpräsident Heinrich Clam-Martinic*, Wien, 1964.
[20] This paper was also brought to the knowledge of the German Ministry, cf. *L'Allemagne. . .* No. 283, pp.401–04.
[21] *Protokolle des Gemeinsamen Ministerrats, op.cit.*, pp.440–52.

of Congress Poland, Montenegro and the Mačva, plus frontier rectifications in Transylvania, and a minimum programme restricted to the preservation of the full integrity of the territory of the Monarchy, the acquisition of the Lovčen and the change of the dynasty in Serbia. Czernin, however, was of the opinion that "much would be achieved if the territorial integrity could be secured". He did not believe in a complete defeat of the enemy and consequently a compromise peace had to be taken into consideration. To bring about peace in the near future the Minister thought it advisable "to make the Entente believe that there would be neither winners nor losers". To gain an advantageous starting-point for negotiations Czernin would have liked to see the territory of the Monarchy "cleansed", especially with regard to Italy, and he also foresaw a solution of the Polish question on the basis of negotiations with either the Entente or Russia taking part and therefore wanted to prevent a German preponderance of too great dimensions through premature arrangements.

The recent political changes in Vienna were noted by the diplomatic representatives and "observers" of the Entente in Switzerland, who reported to their chancelleries that:

> the young emperor is gradually ridding himself of officials who are bound up with the cause of Germany and substituting for them men who were in the entourage of the late Archduke Francis Ferdinand.[22]

This was seen as having the object of counteracting German and Hungarian influence. The aim to emancipate the Habsburgs from the Hohenzollern was underlined by the empress's hostility to Germany. Although these indications were not everestimated by Allied experts, who did not disregard the difficulties implied in a change of policy by Vienna, many politicians, looking desperately for every possibility to make headway in the stalemate of the war, saw new hopes with the appearance of this silver stream on the horizon. When the matter was for the first time discussed in the War Cabinet, Balfour stated on 18 January 1917:

> that there were various indications that Austria was anxious to negotiate for peace. Recent ministerial changes pointed to a desire on the part of the new emperor to emancipate himself from German control and the forthcoming changes in the Austro-Hungarian representation at the Hague and in Berne were also significant.[23]

---

[22] Notes of the French Ambassador Leon: *F.O.* 371/2862, No. 2604. This report confirmed Rombold's tel. No. 869 of 27th inst. – for Czernin's connexions with Francis Ferdinand cf. R. A. Kann, *Count Ottokar Czernin and Archduke Francis Ferdinand, J.C.E.A.* XVI (1956).

[23] *W.C.* 37a, *Cab.* 23/13. Of the announced ministerial changes (reported by R. Paget on 17 Jan., cf. *F.O.* 371/3079, No. 13580) only the one in Berne (Musulin for Gagern) was carried out, whereas L. Széchényi remained in the Hague.

After all the Emperor Karl had in his inaugural speech manifested his desire to give to the nationalities certain satisfactions. His francophile tendencies especially, which were now much greater than under the Stürgkh ministry, were reviewed favourably at Paris. The great question was:

> Could the Emperor Karl, who felt the necessity to make concessions to the nationalities to save the Monarchy, execute his project in the presence of the German tyranny?

and furthermore

> Had Austria not only the material but also the moral force required to operate certain modifications in this orientation.[24]

If this was the case there would certainly have been a readiness on the Allied side to come to terms with Austria. According to the information gathered in Switzerland the Czechs and equally the Slovaks and the Slovenes recognized the fact that they were too feeble both politically and financially to remain isolated and they needed the support of the adjacent countries. But the Czechs by no means desired an annexation of the kingdom of St. Wenceslas by Russia, because in this case they were afraid to lose the remainder of their liberty. They wanted merely a complete autonomy within a large federation under the suzerainty of the Habsburgs, no doubt a solution which, in spite of the Allied declaration of 10 January, would have been welcomed by France and Great Britain.

2. The Hopwood Mission to Scandinavia

The death of Francis Joseph was to serve as an opportunity for Austrian diplomacy to intimate to the Entente that "Austria had only entered the war to show that she could still fight as a nation, but that she was now ready for peace at any time". This message was communicated in December 1916 by the Austrian chargé d'affaires of Copenhagen legation, Baron Franz, in an interview with the King of Norway.[25] On 10 January 1917 the British Minister in Christiania, M. Findlay, was approached by a certain Axel Christensen, a Danish merchant, who handed him an account of communications between himself, his partner Knud Scavenius (cousin of the Danish Minister of Foreign Affairs), Baron Franz, and an Austrian manufacturer of dynamite and landed proprietor in Hungary, Ernest Westfried, respecting a separate peace between Austria–Hungary and the Entente.[26]

---

[24] Report by M. de Guichen to Berthelot, dated 12 Jan. 1917 (transmitted to London, Rome and Petrograd on 18th inst.), *Min. Aff. Etr.*, *Autriche-Hongrie, Mouvement National Tcheques*, vol. II.
[25] *F.O.* 371/The War 1916, No. 256037 of 17 Dec., cf. also A.A. Gr.Hq.23, No. 1500 of 2 Dec., which does not reveal to the Germans the real purpose of Franz's interview with the King!
[26] *F.O.* 371/3079, No. 7661.

This seemed a strange story to Balfour's Private Secretary, Sir Eric Drummond, who nevertheless thought it might be genuine, because there was no lack of indication that Austria was desperately anxious for peace and would break away if she could. Drummond, however, at this stage still feared that "the terms promised to the Italians seem to make it quite hopeless to attempt to detach the Austrians".[27] Robert Graham realised that concessions were necessary and referred to an obscure passage in Findlay's telegram regarding Trieste, which the Austrians "would have in six months". In Graham's opinion one should listen to what the Austrians had to say, although, "in view of our commitments nothing is likely to come of it, unless Austria is far more hardly pressed than we know". For his colleague Lancelot Oliphant it was the commitments to Rumania that precluded any possibility of such negotiations being feasible, since Rumania would not regard any terms of compensation as adequate in the place of Transylvania, whereas the latter formed, in the eyes of the Austrians, an indissoluble part of Hungary. The Assistant Under Secretary was in line with his superior who had recorded earlier that Transylvania seemed to him "as great a difficulty as *Italia Irredenta*". The Permanent Under-Secretary, Lord Hardinge, laid even more emphasis on the Rumanian problem:

> As a matter of fact it is only our engagements towards the latter country that seem to present an insurmountable difficulty. One can imagine that it might be possible to square Italy with the Trentino and the Carso up to and including Trieste.
> Servia might be given a large share of Macedonia, Bosnia–Herzegovina together with an outlet to the sea. The Yugoslav provinces of Austria could become autonomous with a personal union, but Rumania could be compensated only by Russia (Beesarabia), which is most unlikely.[28]

On January 25 Robert Paget suggested to Hardinge an offer to negotiate on the basis of the Southern Slavs (except Bosnia–Herzegovina) remaining under Austrian sovereignty. Hardinge regarded this as very workable to the Yugoslavs (he meant the Croats!) who were mostly Catholic. He felt that Italy also might perhaps be satisfied, but pointed out again the Rumanian obstacle. Paget on 8 February proposed a plebiscite as a possible solution, since here military operations hardly entitled Rumania to urge her claims in full. The above proposal would to some extent save Austria's face and Paget believed the Transylvanians would vote in favour of remaining with Austria–Hungary, but Hardinge discarded the idea, because after all pledges had been

---

[27] *Ibid.*, followed by the minutes of Graham & Balfour. Oliphant's and Graham's views were registered on 15 Jan. on No. 11312 *loc.cit.*
[28] Minute on a telegram from R. Paget to Hardinge, dated 17 Jan., No. 13580, *ibid.*

given to the Rumanians.[29] This shows that the Foreign Office in early 1917 still felt bound to honour the secret treaty obligations to some extent, but no longer in their entirety, depending on the military effort made by the minor Allies.

The impact of a separate peace with Austria on the military situation was analysed by the Chief of the General Staff on 18 January before the War Cabinet. General Robertson regarded it a decided advantage from the military point of view, because it would eliminate 47 Austro-Hungarian divisions from the Eastern front and set free 149 Russian divisions to deal with 78 German divisions. It would also remove the submarine menace from the Adriatic and this counter-balanced the possibility of Italy's withdrawal from the war. The Minister of Blockade, Lord Robert Cecil, admitted that the blockade situation would be more difficult, but that the (German) shortage of shipping would enable the British navy to prevent any substantial supplies reaching Germany through Austria. Finally the War Cabinet agreed to inform the Allied ambassadors that Britain would probe these approaches. Negotiations would not be entered without previous consultations with the Allies. As a first step the British Minister in Christiania should ask for further information.[30]

On February 19 the Foreign Office informed Findley that the War Cabinet were sceptical as to the credentials of Christensen & Co. but had decided to investigate the matter. On 23 January Balfour asked Sir Francis Hopwood, a Civil Lord of the Admiralty (later in 1917 elevated to the peerage as Lord Southborough) to go to test the *bona fides* of the proposals. He was instructed to make no advance of any kind to the other side. If he was satisfied as to the *bona fides*, he might receive an emissary from the Austrian government, but he was not supposed to take the initiative in suggesting an interview.[31]

Hopwood left London on 1 February and visited Christiania, Stockholm and Copenhagen, where Westfried explained to him his idea of how proceedings should develop. The Austrians would give notice to the Germans of their intention of abandoning the war effort. Pressure would be put on Berlin by three methods when chances of peace with the Entente became more hopeful; withdrawal from military action, fomenting of political agitation in Austria, and the threat of an independent peace. Balfour approved of these tactics but ordered that nothing should be said which might be represented as entering into negotiations. On 14 February Mensdorff was appointed by Czernin to

---

[29] *Ibid.*, No. 25651 of 25 Jan. and draft reply approval by Balfour, answered by R. Paget on 8 Feb., the latter minuted by Hardinge.
[30] *WC* 37a, *Cab* 23/13.
[31] For this and the following cf. Hopwood's report (CX547) 8 Hankey's summary: Note in Lloyd George papers (F/160) and *F.O.* 371/3133–34.

come to Copenhagen and conversations seemed to be in the offing. While this was well under way, another Danish mediator, the State Councillor Hans N. Andersen, after carrying out exploratory talks in London with numerous influential politicians and the King,[32] had gone to Berlin where he expected to be sounded out as to the chances of British willingness to consider peace overtures. Andersen in his interview with the Chancellor, the Minister of Foreign Affairs and the industrialist Albert Ballin, suggested that an emissary be sent to discuss peace with Sir Francis Hopwood, of whose activities the Germans – according to Andersen – knew a good deal. Actually it was Andersen himself who was trying to evoke the impression that it was impossible to keep the Viennese move from the knowledge of the Germans, because he obviously wanted to initiate general peace talks.[33] This fabricated allegation robbed the British of the advantage of having secret peace talks with the Austrians. Lloyd George in a private letter to his Foreign Secretary revealed his attitude on the matter:

> Has an answer been sent to Hopwood's last telegram?
> Do we want even informal conversations with Germany at this stage? Austria is quite a different matter. To open negotiations with Germany through the Danish King might destroy any chance there is of detaching Austria. What is your view?[34]

No answer by Balfour has been found, but from his instructions sent to Paget on 17 February it is clear that he too did not approve of Hopwood's readiness to see a representative of Germany in order "to break the ice" in a not unfriendly exchange of thoughts on the general situation. Hopwood's plan was foiled by this unequivocal order:

> Object of your mission was to test alleged Austrian desire for a separate peace. This object could obviously not be fulfilled under most unfavourable conditions. We have no desire to negotiate with Germany . . .[35]

In the end this Scandinavian affair had come to nothing, but it had the useful effect of crystallizing the views of the Foreign Office in regard to Austria–Hungary. Drummond summed up Whitehall's opinion in a lengthy memorandum of 21 February.[36] He believed the Paget-

---

[32] On the high esteem of Andersen held by George V and the F.O. cf. H. Nicolson, *King George V*, London 1952, p.294, n.1. His activities in the early war years are documented in *l'Allemagne. . .*, i., his journey to London in Jan. 1917 is reported by Brockdorff-Rantzau to the A.A. on 30 Feb., *ibid*. No. 477, p.687, his Berlin visit announced *ibid*., ii, No. 6, p.6 (10 Feb.). Hopwood's commission to contact the Austrian was never realised in Berlin cf. *ibid*., No. 27, pp.44–46, 22 March.
[33] *F.O.* 371/3080, No. 33142 (telegram from R. Paget of 11 Feb.) and No. 36932 (message from Hopwood of 16 Feb.).
[34] *F.O.* 800/199, dated 17 Feb., copy in Lloyd George Papers, F/3/2/13.
[35] *F.O.* 371/3080, No. 36932.
[36] G.T. 43, *Cab.* 24/16.

Tyrrell memorandum (of 7 August 1916, see above) best for the future of Europe, so long as the Allies achieved a decisive victory. But apparently hopes for a *victoire intégrale* had almost vanished. In the search for a new effective means to crush Germany, attention focussed on Austria: the latter was exhausted militarily and economically, hoped for better terms now than later, was anxious to throw off German domination and, so Drummond and most of his colleagues thought, felt that the only method to do so was by a separate peace. Drummond deemed an absolute break between Germany and Austria an advantage, even dreamed of the Southern German States (Bavaria) turning to Austria; but in his view even without them a powerful barrier against German "*Drang nach Osten*" could be erected. For this purpose the non-German nationalities inside the Habsburg Monarchy had to be strengthened by forming a separate kingdom of the Yugoslavs of equal status with Hungary and by giving similar rights to Bohemia. Drummond rightly anticipated Magyar opposition to such a federal scheme, but weighted heavier the fact that the Emperor was in favour of it. Concerning the goodwill of the nationalities themselves he had little doubts. It should be possible to persuade the Austrian Yugo-Slavs, who on religious grounds opposed the orthodox and backward Serbs. (Previously Supilo had admitted that in a plebiscite they would probably vote against a union). Besides the hopes held out to the latter the chief difficulty was the agreements with Italy and Rumania. To overcome them Drummond offered the following solutions:

To Serbia Austria would have to cede Bosnia–Herzegovina and a portion of Dalmatia (as reserved in the London Convention) to give her a "reasonable" access to the sea.

Rumania was the most difficult of the Allies, because her demands entailed not only Transylvania, "but a large strip of Hungary itself, which made it impossible for Austria to assent" (*sic*). It was therefore necessary to consider an arrangement with Rumanians who were in a precarious situation and not unwilling to stop fighting. Drummond expected Austria to be willing to agree to certain boundary-rectifications, especially in the Banat, and also to give guarantees for the just treatment of the Rumanians in Transylvania and Hungary(!) by according various local privileges *or* even local autonomy. Rumania could also be compensated with Bessarabia.

Such ideas reveal the scanty knowledge in the Foreign Office which seemed entirely uninformed about the territorial extension of the Kingdom of Hungary and its constitutional rights concerning the treatment of the minorities. It is also hard to see how, at this stage of the war, Russia could have been won over to pay the bill for the Rumanian failure on the battlefield by transferring Bessarabia to her and simultaneously seeing her influence in the Balkans diminished by a Habsburg revival.

Drummond equally misjudged the attitude of the third country, Italy, to which Austria would have only to cede the Trentino – it is not clear whether he meant the whole of South Tyrol or just the Italian-speaking Southern part of it – while Trieste could be made a free port. There was indeed a considerable peace party in Italy and Sonnino's mistrust of the Yugoslavs is well known, but neither of the two groupings could be expected to forego Istria, Poland and part of Dalmatia which Italy obtained under the London Convention. Certainly the yielding of *Italia irredenta*, if this included merely ethnologically justified claims, would not have been a basis to end the Austro-Italian enmity, just because there was a vague prospect of a common opposition to Germany. Drummond, who finally reckoned with the hostility of national and naval circles to his scheme, thought it was possible to compensate their demands in Asia Minor or by the cession of British Somaliland. But in fact the offer of overseas territories only served to increase the insatiable appetite of the Italian imperialists without reducing their claim to the areas already bequeathed by treaty.

On the whole, Drummond's memorandum bears the mark of improbability and it does not matter that a separate peace on such lines would have been welcomed by France (where similar projects were under way), and such "powerful" allies as Belgium, Portugal and Japan. All the parties involved, not least the Austrians and the Hungarians themselves, were supposed to make large and simultaneous concessions so that a swapping of territories could settle the problem. This came close to the 18th century style of bartering away of territories, modified by a cynical manipulation of the principle of nationality, and throws some light on the anachronistic thinking in the Foreign Office, but the plan hardly offered a realistic approach to a negotiated peace.

Opinion in the Foreign Office only differed as to the belief in the feasibility of a peace with Austria, whereas there was general agreement about the methods by which it should be achieved.

Hardinge, whose minutes had considerable influence on Drummond, was not too sanguine. Austria would be called upon to make considerable sacrifices and this might "prove the stumbling block in the way of peace". Austria should make some territorial concessions based upon the principle of nationalities, but the Foreign Office was not convinced of the efficacy of a rigid realization of this doctrine. Cecil preferred a personal union of four states, for the settlement sketched by the Paget-Tyrrell Committee (see above) had necessarily to end in a large increase of German influence, while a defection by Austria greatly increased the chances of victory over the former.

A review of the attitude of British policymakers in this period shows a mounting disregard for the subject nationalities of the Habsburg Monarchy. Their claims were only to be honoured in so far as it was useful to weaken Germany. The same can be said of the treaty obligations to the minor allies. As long as their entry into the war promised a quick decisive victory, London was inclined to meet many of their demands, but now that this strategy had failed, the British were ready to consider abandoning them. The question was whether all commitments which had been entered into and above all the force of nationalism could be squared with the recently renewed desire to preserve the Habsburg Empire as a power in Europe.

3. America's Attempt to Mediate

The Entente note of 10 January 1917, with its stress on liberating subject peoples from foreign domination, was interpreted in Vienna as an open threat of complete dismemberment. Czernin immediately lodged protest in Washington, denouncing the Entente governments for craving "the annihilation and spoliation of the Austro-Hungarian Monarchy" and blaming them for the continuation of the war.[37] There was similar indignation in Berlin. Bethmann Hollweg characterized the Allied answer as "criminally impudent". Like Czernin the Chancellor came to the conclusion that the Entente was resolved to continue the war to rob Germany of provinces in the West and in the East, to dismember Austria–Hungary and to destroy Turkey.[38]

From the German point of view, however, this development was not deplored. On the contrary, if the enemy wanted to convince Germany's ally that its rescue could only be achieved by a closer union under German leadership and an increased display of force, "they succeeded in it", as the new ambassador in Vienna, Count Wedel, observed, "with their answer to President Wilson".[39] Wedel reported a noticeable change of mood in Vienna, where people were surprised over the Allied decision to let a weakened Germany exist, while erasing the Danube Monarchy from the map. The belief in "Old Austrian" circles that the Habsburg Empire was represented as the victim of the alliance with Germany, a victim whom the Western Powers had every interest to protect from the covetousness of neighbours eagerly striving for territorial aggrandizement, seemed now illusory. The German ambassador stressed the fact that Austrian indignation was particularly directed against England:

> The last *beau reste* of a slumbering anglomania has been swept away,
> because England is now recognized as the true representative of the

---

[37] *U.S.For.Rel.* 1917, Supp. II, p.10 (Penfield to Lansing, 11 Jan.).
[38] A.A., Gr.Hq., 12a/2 (12 Jan., B.H. to W.II) and *German Official Docs.*, (Reichstag Inquiry Commission), ii, p.45f. (No. 57, B.H. to Bernstorff, 16 Jan.).
[39] *A.A.*, Wk. 23, secr./2, No. A 2905 of 28 Jan.

will for war and the English statesmen are made responsible for the inclusion of the unholy plan for partition.[40]

Reading this despatch the Kaiser could rejoice:

> Lloyd George and Briand have done good work for us. They have become the unifiers of *Mitteleuropa*. We might have hired them to do it.[41]

Indeed, the Allied declaration provided the German militarists with solid arguments for persuading Austria of the necessity for unrestricted submarine warfare. Both the Emperor Karl and his Foreign Minister had so far not been convinced of the efficiency of the new German submarine policy. Now they were pressed relentlessly by Admiral Holtzendorff who came to Vienna on 20 January. Czernin had to realize that the Germans were adamant, and since the Austrians, dependent as they were, were in no position to carry their point against their giant ally, he acquiesced with a heavy heart. At any rate the intransigent Allied attitude left him no choice.[42]

"We must once more do something ourselves, . . . to do nothing is always worst", Czernin told Joseph Redlich when discussing the decision.[43] This "something" was not necessarily war with America. On 22 January President Wilson had delivered his "Peace Without Victory" speech phrased in an ambiguous language, but endorsing the principle of nationality. But only Poland was mentioned by name. This left Czernin room for manoeuvre. Wilson apparently was not in agreement with the war aims of Britain and France, where his recent speech was passed over in silence. Czernin might have been informed about Wilson's terms which were also ascertained by the British ambassador in Washington from his Spanish colleague. In his view and that of other sources Wilson had declared himself somewhat vaguely in favour of free access for Russia and Austria to the Mediterranean, while the principle of nationality should be observed in regard to Italian or Balkan possessions.[44] However equivocal and imprecise such phrasings were, they nourished the rumours that the President adopted a middle course between the two camps. When the Central Powers declared unrestricted submarine warfare on 31 January, the Austrian note (although otherwise almost identical with the German one) acknowledged with approval Wilson's speech of 22 January. But the time

---

[40] *Ibid.*
[41] *Ibid.*, marginal note.
[42] See his memoirs *Im Weltkriege*, Vienna 1919 and Polzer-Hoditz, *op.cit.* p.317f.
[43] *Schicksalsjahre Oesterreichs* (Jos. Redlich's political diary), ed. F. Fellner, Vienna 1954, ii, p.185 (24 Jan.).
[44] *F.O.* 115/2263, Nos. 50 (draft of 18 Jan.) and 53 (telegram of 19 inst.) – Vienna had excellent channels of communication to Madrid, but Alfonso XIII was jealous of Wilson's role as mediator and might have prevented the transmission of his alleged terms.

for the President's former campaign for open declaration of war aims had passed. From now on, in their public statements both groups of belligerents called for a peace with victory. The public feeling aroused by the slaughter on the sea, effectively barred any public move towards peace talks, and more devious means of communication had to be found. The situation was aptly described by a French diplomat talking to an Austrian in Berne:

On va fermer avec fracas les grandes portes de la paix pour entr'ouv-rir les petites.[45]

A loophole for semi-official negotiations was left by the presence of Adam Tarnowski, ambassador designate, who had been surprised by the rupture of diplomatic relations between the U.S.A. and Germany on the day of his arrival in Washington on 3 February.[46] Following the advice given by Colonel House, the President tried "to use Austria for peace" by making peace proposals to Germany through the Habsburg channel. After Tarnowski had been received amicably by the American Secretary of State, Robert Lensing, Czernin responded instantly. He declared himself ready for peace negotiations on the basis of "peace without victory" and pointed out that Wilson should feel obliged to use his influence with the Entente to make them accept that basis too, instead of threatening to dismember Austria–Hungary.

This suggestion was taken up immediately in Washington. On 8 February instructions were sent to ambassador W. H. Page in London to the effect that the President wanted to keep the channel of official intercourse with Austria open. The chief obstacle was

the threat apparently contained in the peace terms recently stated by the Entente allies that in case they succeeded they would insist upon a virtual dismemberment of the Austro-Hungarian Empire.[47]

It was the President's view that Austria had only to be assured on that point, chiefly with regard to the older units of the Empire. Wilson regarded the large measure of autonomy "already secured there" as a sufficient guarantee for peace and stability. Page brought forward Wilson's proposal in an interview with Lloyd George on 10 February. The Prime Minister replied that he knew that Austria was eager for peace and wanted to quit the war, since, even if the Teutonic powers

[45] Quoted in F. Charles-Roux, *La paix des Empires Centraux*, Paris 1947, p.163.
[46] For the following cf. Ch. Seymour, ed., *The Intimate Papers of Colonel House*, Boston 1928, ii, pp.451–52 – the bare facts of this episode are known since the publication of the corresponding volume of the U.S. For. Rel. (1917, Suppl. I). For a first brief comment cf. E. C. Brunauer in *J.M.H.* IV (1932), p.517. V. S. Mamatey, *The United States and East Central Europe*, Princeton 1957, p.52ff, relates the American background in depth, but mistakenly sees it as an American attempt for a separate peace. A. S. Link, *Wilson*, v, Princeton 1966, pp.315–18 and 385–87, stresses Wilson's interest in using Austria for mediation between Germany and Britain.
[47] *U.S. For. Rel.* 1917, Suppl. I, pp.38–40.

were to emerge victorious, she could expect no higher role than that of a German vassal. Understandably the new Emperor wished as far as possible to save his Empire:

> We have no objection to his retaining Hungary and Bohemia. We have no policy of sheer dismemberment, but we must stand by the nationals of our Allies such as the Rumanians, the Slavs, the Serbians, and the Italians. Their just demands must be met by the principle of nationality.[48]

From this statement it would appear that the British government had modified its view as expressed on 10 January. No mention of the Czechoslovaks features any longer, but the continuance of Bohemia as an integral part of the Monarchy is explicitly approved. The Slavs are listed alongside the Serbs, which means that South Slav aspirations were to be honoured beyond the promissory *aide mémoire* to the Serbian government. Possibly Lloyd George was thinking of the assurances made to Supilo by Grey. These would be difficult if not impossible to harmonize with the agreement reached secretly with Italy. The latter's claims and that of the Rumanians are called "just", but meeting them by the principle of nationality could very well imply reductions of their ambitions. Was Lloyd George's pronouncement a marked dissociation from the Allied contractual obligation? A definite answer cannot be given, because the language used is very ambiguous, not to say Wilsonian. The tone of the conversation rather points in the opposite direction. It contains an emphasis on cutting down the size of the Habsburg Empire. The peoples enumerated above were to be "freed from Austrian control". How far this was envisaged is shown by Lloyd George's unwillingness to grant the Monarchy an access to the sea. He was not even prepared to give any assurance for the survival of a rump Empire, when specifically asked to give it.

What was the reason for the British obstinacy in face of Wilson's proposal? Lloyd George contended that present conditions made it undesirable to receive even a formal offer of peace from Austria, whose withdrawal from the war might bring disadvantages to the Entente. Not only did it entail the danger of losing Italy, but also of helping Germany, for which Austria was more of a burden than a relief. Can these arguments be taken at face value? In view of the simultaneous British attempts to establish contacts with the Austrians in Scandinavia, the explanation for these sometimes partly ridiculous excuses (Lloyd George pretended he feared the recruitment by Germany of soldiers released from the Austrian army) is quite clear: so long as the British saw a chance of inducing Austria into peace talks themselves,

---

[48] *Ibid.*, pp.41–42.

they did not need American mediation, which was altogether undesirable. Any commencement of peace conversations would have ⸱een an obstacle to American entry into the war.

The other reasons for the unexpectedly harsh terms given by Lloyd George so far as they are not merely designed for that purpose can only be conjectured: Firstly Lloyd George obviously did not want to give the impression that the "liberation note" of 10 January was not a serious programme. He only took the opportunity to extricate his country from the passage referring to the Czecho-Slovaks, which had never been a firm commitment and which could now become a liability for British diplomacy in its attempts to wean away Austria. Secondly, after the "peace without victory" speech the British government had to make it clear that they were not prepared to abandon their war aims and subordinate their idea of a settlement to Woodrow Wilson's.

Ten days later, on 20 February, Lloyd George let Page know that Britain was now prepared to receive an Austrian offer and he repeated what he had said about the willingness not to disrupt the Austrian Empire. He told Page that he had changed his mind "after discussions with his associates".[49]

There is no record of such discussions or any correspondence with other Cabinet members. Moreover, it seems unlikely that the Prime Minister would have yielded to the opinion of Balfour or Milner in such an important matter, in which he was to take a great interest throughout the war. The motives for Lloyd George's different attitude, can, however, be inferred from what happened with the Hopwood mission in the meantime. (This had been broken off abruptly, when it was drifting into soundings which were to include the Germans.)

It is therefore extremely unlikely that Lloyd George at this stage contemplated negotiations with Vienna which would subsequently be joined by Germany. Why did he consent at all to Wilson's proposal, which involved the same danger? Perhaps Lloyd George no longer believed in the possibility of a *détente* between the U.S.A. and Germany In any case, the British had a formidable trump in reserve to thwart an understanding between Washington and Berlin. On 23 February the deciphered Zimmerman telegram was communicated to the Americans and this certainly contributed to the alienation of Wilson from the Germans.

On the same day the Foreign Office was informed by Spring-Rice that "the President probably desired a separate arrangement with Austria which would be the first step towards detaching Austria from the German alliance".[50] This line of action met with full British

---

[49] *U.S. For. Rel.*, 1917, Suppl. I, p.55.
[50] *F.O.* 371/3109, No. 497554, f.27635 of 23 Feb.

approval. On the other hand, the Germans protested that Austria had no intention whatever of taking a different standpoint, while among themselves they suspected Czernin of having given instructions to Tarnowski secretly. Czernin was aware of having gone beyond the frame of the former declarations of the Central Powers by agreeing with Wilson's formula of "no victors – no vanquished". He justified his undertakings by pointing out that he wanted to bring Wilson into a contradictory position to the Entente and saw a great advantage – also for Germany – in holding up diplomatic relations.[51]

The Germans were bound to sanction Czernin's action as long as they were not at war with Italy. No doubt they had an interest in postponing the American declaration of war, but for Zimmerman

> Wilson's mediating role has been played to the end. Should the President approach us with such an offer, we would decidedly refuse it.[52]

On 14 February Wedel cabled to Berlin that Czernin "shared our view completely" and that he would not any longer mediate with the United States.[53] The ambassador's confidence that he had won over Czernin for the hard line of the Germans was justified. On the same day the Austrian Foreign Minister sent his instructions to Mensdorff, who was told to intimate the absolute impossibility of a break with Germany and particularly to stress to Great Britain

> that we and Germany form an inseparable whole and that there is the fullest harmony between Vienna and Berlin both in major and minor questions.[54]

An exact *status quo* was impossible in regard to Poland, boundary rectifications elsewhere were indispensable, but "of course by no means" at the expense of Austro-Hungarian territory.

While this intransigent attitude was never conveyed to the British, the latter's viewpoint as given to Wilson via Page was presented to Czernin by the American ambassador Penfield on 26 and 27 February, when he informed the Austrian Foreign Minister that the Entente did not desire to break up the Habsburg Monarchy and that, if the Austrian government expressed a desire for peace, the American government could secure a definite assurance against the separation of Bohemia and Hungary from Austria. This was the Wilsonian interpretation of Lloyd George's far more hesitant and non-committal statement to Page. Since the American *démarche* insisted on absolute secrecy to "any other government", Czernin understood it as a separate peace

---

[51] *A.A.* Wk. 23 secr./2, Nos. AS 551 (5 Feb.) & A 4639 (9 Feb.) & A 5199 (11 Feb.).
[52] *Ibid.*, (A 5199), Zimmermann to Wedel.
[53] *Ibid.*, (No. 76).
[54] H.H.St. A., P. A. Preussen III/175, tels. No. 77 (to Hohenlohe) and No. 40 (to D. Széchényi), cf. W. Steglich, *Die Friedenspolitik der Mittelmächte*, Wiesbaden 1964, p.20 and A. May, *op.cit.*, p.485.

offer. There was no way left for a preliminary arrangement with Austria when Czernin handed Penfield a written reply stating that Austria–Hungary could only enter into negotiations for peace *simultaneously* with her allies.[55]

Czernin had at last given in entirely to the German demands. The Americans never communicated their failure in London, where it could have had a salutary effect on exaggerated hopes concerning future feelers. Instead, in the middle of March the Americans suggested to the Austrians "that the next American ships which were en route to England might be 'overlooked' and not torpedoed".[56] When this abstruse scheme was turned down by the Germans, war between them and the Americans was only a matter of time. Finally Wilson asked Congress for its approval on 2 April and after the declaration of war rupture of diplomatic relations with Austria was unavoidable, while war with each other was postponed. The American entry entailed an enormous upsurge of confidence on the British side, which was to be reflected in the reaction to a forthcoming Austrian feeler in Switzerland.

The Austro-American episode typified Czernin's idea of a settlement. He saw himself as a mediator for a gradually extending *rapprochement*, which could be initiated by Austria, while Germany was standing by, ready to be included later at a suitable moment. In that sense Czernin had proposed in his last answer to the U.S.A. to send a confidant to a neutral country for conversations with a representative of the Entente.

There was a chance for such plans with the appearance of French agents in Berne, who promised to establish contacts between the *Ballplatz* and the *Quai d'Orsay*. Czernin obtained Berlin's consent for this in principle, but at a Vienna Conference on 16 March he failed to get any territorial concessions, which made him complain that Austria had made "the most heroic sacrifices only *ad maiorem gloriam germaniae*".[57] But the Dual Monarchy had to "grasp and spin every thread of peace" – even if it involved certain sacrifices. The renunciation of Galicia and/or South Tyrol, however, would be useless, because not Russia and Italy but the Western Powers take the important decisions.

> I am convinced the key of the situation lies in the West. If Germany hands out France and Belgium *and something more*, then peace will be there.[58]

---

[55] *U.S. For. Rel.*, 1917, Suppl. I, pp.52 and 62f. (italics mine).
[56] Memorandum of the Austro-Hungarian Embassy, Berlin, dated 14 Mar. printed in *Ger. Off. Docs.*, ii, p.1334f, quoted in A. S. Link, *op.cit*, p.387. The American version was communicated to the F.O. in May 1917, cf. *F.O.* 371/3113, No. 97230/f.28438.
[57] *L'Allemagne. . .* ii, No. 20.
[58] H.H.St.Á., P.A.I., box red 501 (italics in the original), (no date), *A.A.*, Gr. Hq., Oe.23/2, No. 336 of 2 Apr., cf. also F. Hopwood, *Interalliance Diplomacy: Count Czernin and Germany 1916–1918* (Stanford Univ. Ph.D. thesis).

In a private interview with the Chancellor Czernin elicited a vague promise for this solution and thereupon sent Mensdorff to Switzerland, where the emissary tried in vain to meet competent French envoys.[59] Already before Mensdorff arrived in Berne on 21 March, the Austrian legation there had approached a Mrs. Barton, a British agent, about the possibility of arranging a meeting between a British and an Austrian representative, at which the Austrian conditions of peace – as distinct from the German – could be made known. Now that the Austro-French *caquetages* had come to nothing, Mensdorff was waiting impatiently to communicate the Austrian terms to the British.[60] When he insisted on seeing Mrs. Barton, the British Minister in Berne, Sir Horace Rumbold, authorized such a meeting. Mensdorff made it clear from the beginning that there was no question of a separate peace. He said he could, however, state "pretty positively" that Germany would give up Belgium and Alsace–Lorraine, but France would have to give something in return. Mensdorff gave no indication as to his country's attitude towards Serbia and Rumania and made only some bitter remarks over Italy. In the Foreign Office this was considered as "not in the least hopeful as regards detaching Austria".[61] Rumbold also came to the conclusion that after the break with America

> the Austro-Hungarian government are bound hand and foot to Germany, any idea of detaching Austria by means of a separate peace is out of the question.[62]

4. The Sixtus Letter Affair

Even before Count Czernin had tried to initiate conversations with Allied or neutral negotiators, another action had been launched with utmost secrecy. This contact involved the young Emperor himself and he was assisted by his wife Zita, who may have seen the double chance of helping her husband in his desire for peace and supporting her brothers Sixtus and Xavier (who were serving in the Belgian army) in their aim to strengthen the position of the legitimist movement for a restoration of the Bourbon dynasty in France.[63]

Already in August 1914 Sixtus had submitted his plans to the imperial couple, but only now that Charles had come to the throne did the Prince find the response he had hoped for. Sixtus aptly appealed to

---

[59] *L'Allemagne*. . ., Nos. 22, 26, 46, 59, 124, 139, – cf. G. Ritter, *Staatskunst und Kriegshandwerk*, Munich 1966, vol. iii. From the German sources it is evident that B.H. had only in mind the exchange of some small strips of territory in Lorraine against compensation elsewhere, preferably Briey-Longwy!

[60] *F.O.* 371/2863, No. 64156 of 26 Mar., tel. Rumbold to Hardinge.

[61] Minute by R. Graham on Rumbold's tel. of 5 Apr., *ibid.*, No. 71717. For Mensdorff's reports of 4 and 5 Apr., H.H.St.A., Kg.25w, cf. W. Steglich, *op.cit.*

[62] *F.O.* 371/2863, No. 49863 of 16 Apr.

[63] The second point is stressed by R. Fester, *Die Politik Kaiser Karls und der Wendepunkt des Krieges*, Munich 1925, and J. Joll, "The End of Dynastic Diplomacy", in *The Listener*, 23 June 1966.

francophile feelings whilst simulatneously warning of the Prussian military power, which he described as equally threatening for Austria and France.[64] Pursuing this argumentation Sixtus awoke the idea of a political re-orientation of the Habsburg Monarchy reminiscent of the Kaunitz pattern. The meanwhile existent opposition to Russia and Italy was intentionally left aside.

The first practical steps were taken shortly after Karl's accession, when the Empress's mother came to Switzerland at the end of January 1917 and intimated the Habsburg readiness for peace negotiations. On 13 February Karl sent his messenger Count Erdödy with instructions to Neuchatel, where he received document intended as a basis for negotiations compiled by Sixtus and Jules Cambon.[65] The striking fact of this draft is the complete omission of any reference to Italy. On the other hand war aims were listed, which were not within the sphere of Habsburg interest. In so far Sixtus's paper could well have become the basis of a general peace over the head of Italy. But the Prince was clearly aiming at a different solution. He had prepared two drafts for Karl, whom he expected to sign either a *projet de proclamation* or a *projet de convention militaire préliminaire*, which was no less than an armistice declaration for the Austrian front. Confronted with such far-reaching decisions, Karl became insecure and consulted his Foreign Minister, although Czernin was only told half the truth, because the matter was presented to him as a French feeler. This seemed logical to Czernin, who saw a Cailleaux ministry "on the horizon", a feeling which was founded on the appearance of semi-official French negotiators in Switzerland.[66]

Czernin advised Karl to continue the personal contacts through Sixtus. But in an eight-point memorandum he categorically refused a break with Germany: the alliance was indissoluble and the conclusion of a separate peace permanently barred by it. It was, however, wrong to suppose that Austria–Hungary was politically subordinated to Germany although in Czernin's view this freedom of action was very limited. Austria would make no opposition in the case of Germany consenting to relinquish Alsace–Lorraine. Contemplating that this note would prevent any further discussions, the Emperor made several addenda, the first and most important one being: "We will support France and use all the means in our Power to bring pressure to bear

---

[64] The only available sources for the reconstruction of these events are all Bourbon: 1. Sixtus, *Austria's Peace Offer, 1916–17*, London 1920 (ed. G. de Manteyer); 2. Xavier: *Secrets diplomatiques 1914–18*, Brussels 1963, (J. de Launay); 3. Zita: G. Brook-Shepherd, *The Last Habsburg*, London 1969.

[65] Ph. Amiguet, *La vie du prince Sixte de Bourbon*, Paris 1934, pp.102–103, Manteyer; *op.cit.* pp.47–48.Zita recently contended that there was a simultaneous initiative by the Quai d'Orsay, cf. Brook-Shepherd, *op.cit.*, p.80.

[66] Czernin to Zita, letter dated 17 Feb. 1917, printed in K. F. Nowak, *Der Sturz der Mittelmächte*, Munich 1921, p.419.

upon Germany".[67] This point was further elaborated during conversations between Karl, Sixtus, and Xavier, which took place at Laxenburg on 23 March. As a result of them Karl drew up a letter, formally addressed to Sixtus in which he assured him that he would use all his personal influence and every other means in his power to exact from his allies a settlement of France's "just claims" in Alsace–Lorraine. Belgium was to be restored as a sovereign state and to receive reparations. Serbia had to abandon her relations with all forces demanding the disintegration of the Monarchy, but then she could be allowed an approach to the Adriatic. The Slavs in the Monarchy were promised, rather vaguely, that they should have equal rights, while there was no mention of Italy's claims.[68] The hub of the letter was Karl's support of the "reannexation" of Alsace–Lorraine. Though according to the law of nations the Monarchy was not obliged to guarantee the German frontiers, Karl's approval of the French demands was an offence against the loyalty requisite within the framework of the Central Alliance. It is true that for an international détente the transfer of Alsace–Lorraine would have been more effective than the cession of the Trentino. (In this theory the Emperor was encouraged by his Foreign Minister.) At any rate, for Karl the fulfilment of the French claim was only conceivable as a high price for a general peace. A break of the alliance with Germany would have meant a unilateral cease-fire on the Austro-Hungarian front, as it was urged by Sixtus. But the Sixtus letter does not contain a formulation in agreement with this by word. Its general tenor, however, could induce people who were not fully informed about the real state of affairs in the Dual Monarchy, to assume that at the back of the imperial letter was the writer's desire to carefully express his inclination to conclude a separate peace with the Entente.

When shown the letter by Sixtus the French President was sceptical about the Austrian "offer": "How could Austria detach herself from Germany", Poincaré asked himself, "in order to render us Alsace and Lorraine?"[69] But the prospect of drawing Austria away from Germany was promising enough to investigate the matter. If the proposals took an official form, the French government thought it necessary to inform their allies.

This was done on 11 April, when Lloyd George received M. Ribot at Folkestone. The new French Foreign Secretary, who had just succeeded M. Briand at the Quai d'Orsay, showed Lloyd George the now famous letter from the Emperor. According to Ribot the Prime Minis-

---

[67] G. Manteyer; *op.cit.*, pp.51–54.
[68] *Ibid.*, pp.83–84.
[69] R. Poincaré, *Au service de la France*, ix, p.70.

ter exclaimed: "That is peace".[70] From his perusal of the letter and the discussion with Ribot, Lloyd George gained the impression that Austria wanted a separate peace. The Allies could then prosecute War against Germany alone to complete victory.[71] For the achievement of this ultimate aim Lloyd George was eager to proceed with the negotiations. A new difficulty arose from the fact that Sixtus had insisted on a strict pledge of secrecy. Originally the possibility had been discussed with M. Martin of the French Foreign Ministry that Sixtus should visit King George V who would then bring the proposals of the Austrian Emperor before the War Cabinet or at least to the knowledge of Lloyd George, Balfour, Curzon, and Milner. Ribot did not let things go so far. He made sure that Lloyd George would say nothing to any of his colleagues in the British Government and would only mention the matter, without details, to the King.[72]

So the Prime Minister was not able to discuss the matter fully before the Cabinet. Thus both the War Cabinet and the Foreign Office were seriously hampered in their deliberations by ignorance about the extent of Karl's commitments in writing. Rumours had, however, been published in the newspapers of an offer by Austria of a separate peace with Russia and this gave the Prime Minister an opportunity to raise the matter in a general way on 17 April.[73] In the Cabinet session on this day the First Sea Lord and the Director of Military Operations agreed as to the advantage of an Austrian withdrawal from the war. On Lloyd George's request they promised to provide expert information on this problem.

Lloyd George, who from now on became obsessed with the idea of a separate peace with Austria–Hungary, wanted to be briefed for the forthcoming discussions with the Italians. The first encounter with them was scheduled for 19 April at the Savoyan episcopal see St. Jean-de-Maurienne. On his journey to this Inter-Allied conference the Prime Minister was accompanied by Major-General Macdonough (D.M.I.) and Hankey, who was the first of his countrymen to learn of the true nature of the meeting, because Lloyd George let his secretary into the secret in case of an accident.[74] Before the conference Lloyd George saw Sixtus personally on 18 April in Paris, where they had an intimate colloquy at the Hotel Crillon.[75] The Prince had heard of the Allied plan to consult the Italians, to which he objected strongly. He urged Lloyd George to withhold information about the letter. In the

---

[70] *Journal d'Alexandre Ribot*, Paris 1934, p.67.
[71] *War Memoirs*, ii, p.1184; Lloyd George Papers, F/50/1/3.
[72] Manteyer, *op.cit.*, pp.92 & 97.
[73] *WC* 121, *Cab.* 23/2.
[74] M. Hankey, *The Supreme Command*, ii, p.735; Lloyd George Papers, F/160/12.
[75] The dialogue as reported by Sixtus is reproduced in Manteyer, *op.cit.*, pp.113–117.

course of their conversation Lloyd George expounded his ideas about the key problem:

> *Lloyd George.* We had an old feeling of friendship towards Austria. We would willingly shake hands with her even today if she would leave Germany. And I dare say that in France you are in the same disposition. But Italy nourishes rather bitter feelings against Austria. Italy is our Ally. We cannot make peace without her.
> *Sixtus.* The ambitions of Italy are great. And contradict in a certain manner the principles of nationalities.

After being "informed by the Prince that Istria and Dalmatia were purely Slavonic and that there were "more Italians in Marseilles than in Trieste"(!), Lloyd George answered, according to Sixtus: "we ought to give the Italians the Trentino triangle as far, perhaps, as Bozen". While it is doubtful that the British Prime Minister was so precise in his diction, he clearly seemed in favour of a diminution in the Italian claims. Although Lloyd George has never been recorded outlining a solution in such precise geographic terms, it can be assumed that he was thinking in terms of an ethnological settlement which would give Italy no more than the Italian-speaking part of the Trentino (not German-speaking South Tyrol).

The immediate question to be solved was how to bring up the Austrian offer during the conference without revealing the parts played by Sixtus and the Emperor. Lloyd George had the idea of basing the discussion upon Mensdorff's manoeuvres in Switzerland. (The former ambassador had by then already returned to Vienna. The French reluctance to send a negotiator plenipotentiary to Berne was mainly due to their preference for the Sixtus link).

The conference of St. Jean-de-Maurienne took place in a railway carriage and at the political conversations no one was present except the three Prime Ministers (Ribot was also the *président du conseil des ministres* from 20 March to 7 September) and Sonnino.[76] The ostensible topic of the conference was Italy's aspirations in Asia Minor. Being aware of the Italian lack of interest in, if not opposition to, a separate peace with Austria–Hungary, Lloyd George thought of compensating her in Turkey. This suggestion had been made in Folkestone by Ribot, who surprisingly proposed to give Italy Cilicia (which was a French zone of influence) instead of the Trentino. Between the Folkestone and the St. Jean meeting Ribot's Roman ambassador, Camille Barrère, pointed out that

---

[76] Sonnino and his P.M. Boselli have left no record. Anglo-French sources of three kinds have been consulted: 1. inf. given by the returning P.M.s, to their respective governments; 2. personal remarks to their fellow-travellers (Hankey, Barrère); 3. description in the recollections of Lloyd George and Ribot.

(a) Karl's letter was probably known to Germany and did not mean an offer of a separate peace as assumed in Paris,
(b) Sonnino could become distrustful, thinking that Italy should bear the burden of a negotiated peace alone. If told that Italy was omitted in Karl's letter, Sonnino would refuse talks with the Austrian Emperor.[77]

Ribot was impressed by this interpretation. It came too late to postpone the conference but explains why the subject was only dealt with at random. When it was broached by Ribot, Lloyd George himself kept quiet seeing that it was useless and dangerous to insist. Sonnino had cut off all discussions by bluntly declaring that a deviation from the Treaty of London would entail his dismissal and the abdication of the King of Italy. Finally, during the Smyrna debate Lloyd George lost his temper and threatened: "If we cannot act together, we alone could come to an understanding with Austria", and to Boselli he intimated in private that his envoy (Mrs. Barton!?) had *negotiated* with Mensdorff.[78] From Lloyd George's own testimony[79] it can be inferred that he also spoke straight to Sonnino, making it clear that the British Admiralty and military authorities in general considered the elimination of Austria a very decided advantage. To press his point Lloyd painted the picture of Austria–Hungary concluding a separate peace with Russia in the event of which she was unlikely to employ her troops on the Western front but expected to concentrate them against Italy. Sonnino did not respond at all to this little piece of blackmail and he was not even tempted by the offer to obtain *desiderata* for Italy in Turkey (he managed to achieve the latter without renouncing the others). Sonnino argued that it would be difficult to induce public opinion to carry on the war if peace were once made with Austria. On the whole, the Italian Foreign Minister expressed the belief that the Austrian feelers aimed at destroying the Allied unity and he therefore thought it would be inadvisable even to listen to any suggestion for a separate peace.

Eventually the assembled statesmen reached an agreement that:

> it would not be opportune to enter into a conversation which, in present circumstances, would be particularly dangerous and would risk weakening the close unity that exists between the Allies and is more than ever necessary.[80]

The British optimism, seconded by French goodwill, had suffered a first rebuke. "We realized", stated Ribot,

---

[77] C. Barrère, "Souvenirs diplomatiques", *Revue des Deux Mondes*, 15 Apr. 1938.
[78] *Journal d'Al. Ribot*, p.70, id., *Lettres à un ami*, p.277; cf. M. Toscano, *Gli accordi di San Giovanni di Moriano*, Milan 1936, pp.273, 275, n.87.
[79] I.C.-20, S18, *Cab.* 28; *War Memoirs*, ii, p.1187.
[80] *Ibid.*, p.1188.

that the Italian Government did not concede any compromise over the territorial results, which it expected from the success of our armies.[81]

Lloyd George rightly accused Sonnino of being the stumbling block in the way of a separate peace with Austria. Sonnino was the champion of Italian nationalistic and imperialistic aims. He had helped bring his country into the war to entitle it to reclaim the *terra irredenta*. Only a complete victory could secure for Italy what had been promised in the secret treaty, namely the Trentino, Trieste, Dalmatia and the various Mediterranean islands. This was Sonnino's price for a separate peace. Not believing that, in the spring of 1917, Austria–Hungary was inclined to pay so much, he refused negotiations with her.[82] But Sonnino like his Allied colleagues expected or at least wished the Habsburg Monarchy to survive, because he feared that its dissolution would bring Germany to the Brenner. His wrong inference was that Austria–Hungary could survive even after all the Italian aspirations were fulfilled, not to mention the *desiderata* of other nations and nationalities. (Despite an amicable treaty with Rumania, Italy was never much concerned with her or other claims such as the Czech.)[83]

Be that as it may, the St. Jean-de-Maurienne conference had not borne the results, which the British and French had hoped for. Prince Sixtus was told the bitter truth by Lloyd George and Jules Cambon. There was no indication at the moment that either Austria or Italy was ready to abandon some of their war aims in order to pave the way for a compromise peace. Consequently it seemed useless to policymakers in London and Paris to continue their efforts of mediation.[84] Thus R. Graham wrote on a dispatch reporting on an American visitor's talks in Vienna that "all intention of coming to separate terms with Austria has been abandoned for the moment".[85] Yet the Ribot-formula adopted at St. Jean, though it precluded conversations, did not prevent, as R. Cecil observed, "hearing anything the Austrians have to say".[86]

For the Foreign Office, which had not been informed about the Sixtus mission, the Austrian project was shelved until a better opportunity promised success. For the Quai d'Orsay, which regarded the Alpine barrier as insurmountable, the Bourbon attempt had failed. The mercurial Welshman who determined the policy made at Whitehall was still eager to set in motion what would have been one of the greatest diplomatic feats. As the Italian point of view proved

[81] *Min.Aff.Etr.*, Conf. Int., 1917; Carton 369/3/viii.
[82] *War Memoirs*, ii, pp.1188–89; O. Malagodi, *Conversazioni della guerra*, ed. B. Vigezzi, Milan 1960, pp.122 & 252.
[83] *Ibid.*, p.373; cf. L. Valiani, *op.cit.*, p.318, n.22.
[84] *War Memoirs*, ii, p.1190; Manteyer, *op.cit.*, pp.118–126.
[85] R. Paget to Hardinge, 30 Apr. 1917, *F.O.* 371/2863, No. 88575/f.64156.
[86] *Ibid.*

insuperable, Lloyd George pinned his hopes on a softening of the Austrian attitude to overcome the deadlock:

> It is essential that Austria give up something to Italy. Italy is our Ally, and we cannot make peace without her.
> . . . .
> If she really wants Peace, she must make these concessions.
> . . . . . .
> Austria will be obliged to come to terms . . . she must sacrifice something to Italy.[87]

After the experience of the Inter-Allied Conference at St. Jean Lloyd George was willy-nilly more inclined to meet the Italian demands, which meant abandoning the previous ethnological criterion. The principle of nationality was preferred by him, and by Britain on the whole, as a means for a lasting settlement. But an exact observance of this noble principle contravened the contractual engagements between Italy and the Allies. The diplomatic ties as well as military calculations necessitated satisfying Italian covetousness to some extent. This was the only way to keep Italy as a belligerent ally before and after a separate peace with Austria–Hungary. So Lloyd George repeatedly said that Austria had to show herself willing to cede the Trentino (no doubt Lloyd George in this instance means the whole of the province of South Tyrol from the lake of Garda to the Brenner) and the Dalmatian Islands. Trieste might perhaps be left subject to discussion, though the Italians were very keen to get the town. From the dialogue as recorded by Sixtus it is impossible to ascertain the extent to which the North Dalmatian coastline proper was regarded as a *sine qua non* by Britain.[88] It is hardly conceivable that a viable Austria–Hungary could have tolerated the acquisition of maritime strongholds on her threshold by a naval rival. The emergence of an autonomous South Slav state, possibly connected with an enlarged Serbia would have increased the Slav title to this area (as it later did on the Paris Peace Conference). Again the Allies in general and Lloyd George in particular dodged such a complicated territorial issue which was considered as of secondary importance. A politician like Lloyd George who thought in great categories, overlooked the fact that the leaders of Austria and Italy staked all the national prestige in such strips of territory, which in comparison with British imperial possessions were minute. The states contiguous to the Adriatic regarded these territories as decisive for their status as a Great Power. The irony lies in the fact that the fate of the Habsburg Monarchy depended on a realistic self-assessment. Hitherto

---

[87] G. Manteyer, *loc.cit.*
[88] Sixtus noticed a partly different, but basically unclear concept of minimum terms in Paris, cf. *ibid*.

the justification of its position in South-East Central Europe was founded on an increase in its capacity to form an *Ausgleich*, in the sense that it constituted a factor of balance both between the adjacent rival powers and even more so for the rival nationalities within its own boundaries. What was needed in 1917 was a token that Austria–Hungary's rulers were prepared to return from the haphazard pseudo-power policy demonstrated in 1908 and 1914 to the true historic mission of the Habsburgs. The situation was meanwhile becoming more and more precarious for Austria–Hungary. Both the Emperor and his Foreign Secretary realized this and tried to persuade the Germans to reconsider their "all or nothing" approach to the conduct of their war diplomacy. The cause for the persistent urgency with which Vienna was pressing Berlin was the events in Russia. The first news about the spring revolution had reached Vienna in mid-March. The most shattering threat was Milyukov's speech in the Duma on 8 April. The Russian Foreign Minister was the first Allied statesman of rank who explicitly pronounced the desire to see the Habsburg Monarchy dismembered by declaring himself in favour of the independence of Poland, Czechoslovakia and Yugoslavia.[89] The nationality problem and the demand for the independence of the small nationalities were not new in 1917. But with the fall of Tsarism it was going to explode in a revolutionary manner. So it is not surprising that the fall of the Romanov dynasty caused anxiety at the Viennese court. This fear of a spread of the revolutionary spirit is best expressed in Karl's letter to Wilhelm of 14 April:

> We are fighting against a new enemy which is more dangerous than the Entente: against the international revolution, which finds its strongest ally in the general starvation.[90]

Karl implored Wilhelm to consider a prompt termination of the war – perhaps with heavy sacrifices – in order to be able to combat the movements of subversion. Czernin added that by late summer or autumn the war had to be concluded "at any price". Therefore it was important to initiate peace negotiations at a moment when the enemy was not yet fully aware of the waning force of the Central Powers.

But the O.H.L. and the Kaiser did not believe that Austria was at the end of her resources. Ludendorff argued that the Russian Revolution also strengthened the military position of the k.u.k. army, which was now able to recruit more men for the Italian front. Zimmermann confided to Grünau that under certain circumstances Germany would

---

[89] Quoted in Beneš, i, pp.329–339. On the ambiguous nationality policy of Milyukov cf. M. Ferro, "La politique des nationalités du gouvernement provisoire russe", *Cahiers du monde russe et soviétique*, 1961.
[90] *L'Allegmagne...* ii, No. 68.

continue fighting alone to avoid a premature and disagreeable peace. The Wilhelmstrasse, trying to avoid such an extreme showdown, decided to support Czernin against the Imperial family and their Kamarilla. Ambassador Wedel was instructed to point out to Czernin that he must not conclude an "anxiety peace" at Germany's expense.[91]

On the other hand the Austrian Foreign Minister was confronted with his Emperor's lack of interest in a total victory of the Central Powers. Karl bitterly complained about the exchange of German with Austro-Hungarian officers, because abroad this evoked the impression that Austria was entirely under the influence of "Prussia". "A flagrant military victory of Germany", Karl wrote on 14 April, "would be our ruin . . . A peace *à l'amiable* on the status quo would be the very best for us."[92]

As long as Austria was reluctant to contribute her share to a peace involving a loss, Germany could easily justify her own attitude and the Berlin government could count upon the support of patriotic public opinion. Moreover, it soon became apparent that the formerly expressed readiness to cede Galicia and/or the Trentino, if this was helpful, was a mere lip-service. At the end of March a mysterious Italian feeler was put out, the origins and background of which have never been cleared up satisfactorily.[93] But what matters in this context is the Austrian as well as the Allied reaction to it. The German mission in Switzerland was approached by an agent of the Italian High Command, who surprisingly offered very moderate terms for a separate Austro-Italian understanding. All of a sudden no more than the Trentino proper and the transformation of Trieste into a free port were deemed necessary to come to an arrangement with Rome. These terms, which were in contrast even to the opinion of Giolittian circles at that time, suggest that the offer was not honest, but rather an attempt to block Austrian military operations through negotiations, which would have given some breathing space to the Italian army. For Berlin the Italian approach served as a useful lever to test the reality of the Austrian readiness for a sacrifice and the warmongers of the A.A. and the O.H.L. could be pleased, when hearing from Czernin that an acceptance was out of the question.[94]

The Emperor Karl was not informed about what was going on until this negative answer had been sent. He himself was known to be most stubborn against the Italian "traitors". In spite of this Karl tried to

---

[91] *A.A.*, Gr. Hq., 23, No. 853 of 18 May.

[92] A French translation of Karl's letter to Czernin was published by Sixtus in *La Revue de Paris*, XXXIX (1932), p.5f.

[93] Cf. the article by R. Fester, "Die Sonderfriedensaktion des Prinzen Sixtus von Bourbon-Parma und die Legende des italienischen Friedens-fühlers", in *Berliner Monatshefte* XV (1937), pp.596–97.

[94] Tel. by Czernin, dated 1 Apr., No. 199, H.H.St.A., Krieg XLVII/13.

make use of the offer, which obviously boosted his confidence. When he passed on the information to Sixtus, the Bourbon must have seen a new chance to resume his role. When called by Zita, the Prince communicated the terms which Lloyd George had accepted personally on 20 April. According to Sixtus the Prime Minister would have been satisfied with the transfer of the Italian-speaking Trentino and some of the Dalmatian islands, while Lloyd George in retrospect added that he at least insisted on Trieste, too.[95]

Karl's reluctance to renounce even the southern part of the Trentino became already apparent from the evasive remarks of his messenger to Switzerland, County Erdödy. The alleged Italian offer – as well as a Russian feeler – were used by Karl to stiffen his bargaining position towards Britain and France. The idea of a plebiscite in the disputed area was turned down, not because the Emperor feared a vote for secession but because it would form a precedent for the other nationalities. Only a slight rectification of frontier might be made on the Isonzo, but Gorizia and Trieste had to remain Austrian. As for the Dalmatian islands, the anti-Italian feeling of their inhabitants was stressed.

During another visit at Laxenburg Castle Sixtus tried to convince Karl of the necessity of ceding something to Italy. With the reservation that popular feeling had to be taken into account and no arbitrary frontiers be traced upon a map, the Emperor – now under the influence of his brother-in-law – seemed to be prepared to cede the "territories Italian in speech and sentiment". But the gallantry of his troops in defending Tyrol demanded a compensation. Silesia and a German or an Italian colony were mentioned.

Left alone Karl drew up his second letter addressed to Sixtus, in which he again dodged the issue, writing that he had postponed the examination of her (Italy's) demands, until he heard from Sixtus what answer France and Britain might make to his offer of peace. The attached four addenda by Czernin emphasized that a definite reply could only be given, when the compensation for a frontier adjustment and the integrity of the Monarchy was guaranteed, since "only then can Austria–Hungary discuss the situation with her Allies". The fact that Czernin by now regarded a territorial exchange deal as "ventilatable" was a slight progress on Austria's side towards a compromise. However, firstly, it neither satisfied the Italian claims nor came up to what Britain and France wanted to secure for Italy as an acceptable minimum. Secondly, both Karl and Czernin did not commit themselves to a separate peace. So Sixtus took refuge in the "device" of a

---

[95] For this and the following compare G. Manteyer, *op.cit.*, p.129ff and Lloyd George, *War Memoirs*, ii, pp.1188–98.

very free translation and in Paris he presented a French text which made it appear as if Austria–Hungary agreed to a separate peace provided the two preconditions demanded by Czernin were fulfilled.[96]

Nevertheless the Prince found deaf ears at the Quai d'Orsay. On the other hand, Lloyd George believed in the authenticity of the Italian offer, which had emanated from the High Command, possibly inspired or backed by King Victor Emmanuel. The British Prime Minister was resolved to try to verify the latter's intention of installing a government which would conclude a negotiated peace.

Ribot was far more sceptical about the steps taken by Italy with a view to making peace. For him it was unthinkable that any request of the kind mentioned in Karl's second autograph letter had been made with the consent of Victor Emmanuel or General Cadorna. The French Foreign Minister repeated to Sixtus the impossibility of doing anything without Italy and in his correspondence with Lloyd George he added that there were undeniable pledges to Serbia and above all Rumania. The "impetuous Celt", as he was called by Poincaré, had far less scruples with these minor obstacles:

> We want, if possible, to concentrate our efforts so as to crush the military power of Germany. No other Power counts in comparison.[97]

The Prime Minister wanted to grasp the unique chance to divide the Central Powers. He considered Karl's second letter "a document of grave importance", and only the passage on Italy worried him. In the resumption of the talks between Lloyd George and Sixtus the question of a colonial compensation cropped up again. This solution which could be a means of depriving Germany of her African possessions without adding them to the British Empire, did not appeal to the Austrians, since it involved ill-feeling in their future relations with the Reich. Sixtus therefore hinted at the possibility of joining the question of the Trentino with the problem of Alsace–Lorraine. But apart from French objections this was only feasible if the reported moderate trends in Italy had any responsible support.

Observing the vagueness of the information gathered by Sixtus, Lloyd George suggested a meeting between himself, Ribot and Czernin. After realizing the inherent risks he then championed a Conference between the Kings of Italy and Great Britain and the French President, who should meet at the front. But when Sonnino was approached on the matter without being told the real purpose of the projected summit

---

[96] The passage in the German original is phrased: ". . . da Österreich-Ungarn erst dann mit seinen Verbündeten in Besprechungen treten kann". Although Sixtus's interpretation is conceivable with much imagination, the sense of the document points in the opposite direction. (cf. Manteyer, *op.cit.*).

[97] Lloyd George, *War Memoirs*, ii, pp.1198–99 (Ll.G. to Ribot, 23 May 1917).

meeting, he must have suspected its object and came forward with all sorts of excuses. Lloyd George asked his Cabinet colleagues in vain for suggestions as to how to contact the Italian King in order to clear up the incident by asking him if he had made any offer.[98] Later in June Sonnino finally agreed to attend a conference on the general European situation regarding the developments in Russia. But he declared at once, in view of current rumours, that: "If there were any question of a separate peace with Austria, he could not be expected to agree to that".[99] Also subsequently Sonnino stated that under no circumstances would he discuss a separate peace with Austria–Hungary.

The Italian attitude proved insuperable and the blame for the failure of the Sixtus mission has been laid on Sonnino by most Austrophile politicians and historians.[100] While there is no doubt about the uncompromising attitude of Italy, it should not be overlooked that the hopes for a separate peace with Austria were founded on the false assumption that the Habsburgs were prepared for a substantial sacrifice. This assumption was fostered by the attempts of a private mediator who was led by personal ambition. Sixtus deceived both sides about the degree of compromise to which the other opponent was inclined. His advantage of finding a way into the studies of all the leading policymakers concerned was more than balanced by his distortion of the information obtained.

In the end the hard facts could not be camouflaged by secret dynastic diplomacy. It was the governments which determined the war aims and peace terms of their respective countries. The widespread sympathy for the Habsburg Monarchy ended whenever the latter showed a corresponding imperialist ambition. To attempt to come to a consensus these differences were almost passed over in silence by the Bourbon mediator, who tried to create an atmosphere of mutual trust by outlining the common interests of the Allied powers and Austria–Hungary. But the realization of these lay in the distant future. What was needed in addition to the mere goodwill on the part of the Emperor, which naturally met with sympathy on the part of the British Prime Minister, was a constructive policy of accommodation by Austria's leadership in order to gain united Allied support for the rescue of the "ramshackle" Empire.

---

[98] *F.O.* 371/3082, f.106290, *WC* 150a & 151a (30 & 31 May), *Cab.* 23/2, 1.
[99] Rodd to *F.O.* (15 June), *F.O.* 371/3082, f.119193.
[100] Typical are the judgments by Lloyd George and Sixtus as well as a contemporary resumé by Hankey, which have been rather uncritically accepted by G. Brook-Shepherd, *op.cit.*

CHAPTER III

Austrophiles and Austrophobes in Britain

1. "New Imperialism" and the Habsburg Empire

The approach of the Austro-Hungarian Empire had been handled by the Prime Minister alone, who felt himself bound to his pledge of secrecy. It was only on 30 May that he introduced Prince Sixtus to several of his Cabinet Ministers, namely Bonar Law, Lord Curzon and Sir Edward Carson.[1] These three belonged to the new supreme body of power, the War Cabinet, which was formed under Lloyd George to facilitate the effective direction of the war. Most of its members were unencumbered by departmental responsibilities. They met daily to decide British policy. The leading figure in respect to co-ordination and organization was Lord Milner, who by his own personality as well as by the launching of friends into key positions, exerted a strong influence in and outside the Cabinet.

The former proconsul had assembled around himself a group of young intellectuals, the so-called "kindergarten". Some of them were now taken over into the personal Secretariat in Lloyd George's Garden Suburb. Thus the *religio Milneriana* found a direct channel to permeate the corridors of power. Among Milner's adherents were Leopold Amery, who with the rank of an Under-Secretary of State was to direct a "Far Eastern Committee", the Oxford historian Lionel Curtis, who took over the editorship of the *Round Table* from Philip Kerr.[2] The Round Tablers tried to promote their idea of a "New Imperialism". Before the war they were anything but over-occupied with the "extraordinary Austro-Hungarian Empire", which was "held together by one of the most remarkable and delicate systems of checks and balances that the world has seen".[3] It was realized that one of the main objects of

---

[1] G. Manteyer, *op.cit.*, pp.177–79. Also present were Lord Reading and Lord Stamfordham, the King's Private Secretary. Sixtus had seen George V on 23 May, cf. H. Nicolson, *op.cit.*, pp.313–14.
[2] Cf. A. Gollin, *Proconsul in Politics*, London 1964 and P. Guinn, *British Politics and Strategy in the First World War*, London 1966.
[3] *Round Table*, No. xi (June 1913), p.409.

the system was to maintain the joint supremacy of the Germans and the Hungarians over the conglomeration of miscellaneous races which composed the rest of the Empire and were to a great extent in a position of political inferiority.

For the *Round Table* this was deplorable inasmuch as it increased international tensions by giving an impetus to the Pan-Siberian movement during the Balkan Crisis of 1912/13. A conceivable line of action was to conciliate the South Slavs by a Tripartite solution by which the Empire would assume a Slavonic colour and might even aspire to a hegemony of the Balkan states. This "heroic" policy would encounter many difficulties and did not provide for the northern Slavs. Another conceivable outcome was therefore that Austria might be compelled to abandon the task of controlling her Slav population, which would then have to form a new state or "enter into some combination the vaguest outline of which cannot yet be imagined".[4] The first alternative was removed by the hand of an assassin. In 1914 Germany felt strongly the duty of "promoting Germandom – with its higher civilisation and culture – from the lesser civilisation of the Slavs".[5]

Although the Milner group could appreciate the German motivation for entering the war and perhaps even shared their racial arrogance towards the Slavs, they could not sympathise with it. After being accused of standing "for German, or rather Prussian ideas in English politics" Milner had adopted an ostentatious anti-German attitude.[6] But above all there was an urgent need to counter the *Mitteleuropa* plans, which were designed to establish a German dictatorship over Europe. They would mean, the *Round Table* commented, "the triumph of the Prussian theory of international relations against that of the Commonwealth". The essential condition of peace, therefore, was "the liberation of the non-German peoples from the political and military control of Berlin". In summer 1916 the writer saw no need to attempt to prophesy the exact territorial terms of which the details were "immensely complicated". Racial toleration, however, was necessary for a lasting peace and the races of Eastern Europe should be enabled "to settle their own future for themselves". The freeing of those peoples was regarded as a *sine qua non* of the Allied terms.[7]

Milner was a member of the British delegation to the Inter-Allied Conference, which in early 1917 adopted a declaration with a corres-

---

[4] *Ibid.*
[5] *Ibid.*, No. xvi (Sept. 1914), p.597.
[6] For reproaches of this kind by the Radicals cf. A. G. Gardiner's articles in the *Daily News* of 29 Mar. 1913 and 12 May 1917, cit. A. Gollin, *op.cit.*, pp.170–71 & 431. Milner's reference in the House of Lords to rumours of "the existence of some occult German influence in the heart of the administration" (Haldane!) was countered with the same argument by the Irish Nationalists. *Ibid.* pp.319–20.
[7] *Round Table*, No. xxiii (June 1916): "The Principle of Peace: The essential conditions of Peace."

ponding formula on the East European nationalities. This did not mean that he insisted in the pursuance of this aim. On the contrary, he advised a final withdrawal from European affairs. The essence of Milner's thinking was that a really consolidated Empire should emerge from the war. Only the failure of the "Britons" to make the Empire strong and cohesive enough to ignore the balance of power in Europe had required war against German domination on the continent. To break the German power it was considered an effective device to deprive the Reich of the 30 million non-Germans within the orbit of the Central Alliance. It was understood that Germany had to be forced by a decisive military defeat to resign her overlordship over these peoples, but the failure of some of Britain's Allies now endangered a complete success in the near future.

In January and February, 1917, during a mission to Russia, Milner experienced the war-weariness of the Tsarist colossus. He returned disillusioned by the much admired "steam-roller" and wrote to Sir Henry Wilson that he considered the defeat of the "Boches" in the field as impossible.[8] This feeling of his was greatly increased after the first Russian Revolution, the coming of which he had, despite his pessimistic impression, not expected and which was thus a tremendous shock to him. Milner came to the conclusion "that it is perfectly impossible to feel any confidence about the ultimate results", because of the world convulsion: "What will become of Russia? – of Italy? How much can the Americans really help?"[9] These questions could not be answered with precision. But whatever the weakness of the links of the Entente Powers, Milner thought the cohesion of the Central Alliance was even more threatened. His great hope remained that the growing embarrassment of Germany's allies might soon lead to a break.[10] This conviction as well as his concern for the British Empire were combined in Milner's suggestion that the Allied war aims be revised. In an interview which he granted Sidney Low on 30 March 1917[11] he explained that he was "in favour of trying to detach Germany's allies by offer, in due course, of moderate terms of peace", because it was useless to insist on the break-up of Austria–Hungary and the expulsion of the Turk from Europe. The Imperial interest in the Ottoman Empire was much greater, but the only inducement to the Sultan and his Pashas the British were ready to make was Constantinople, whereas Mesopotamia and Palestine were regarded as indispensable for "Imperial security".

---

[8] C. E. Calwell, *Field Marshal Sir Henry Wilson: His Life and His Diaries* (London 1927), vol. II, pp.322–323.
[9] Letter to M. G. Glazebrook (Toronto office of the Round Table), dated 21 April 1917, Milner papers, box 210.
[10] Letter to Lady Walburga Paget, dated 16 April 1917, British Museum, *Add.MMS.* 51239.
[11] The account of the interview is printed in D. Chapman Huston, *The Lost Historian, A Memoir of Sir Sidney Low*, London 1936, p.267.

Austria–Hungary was quite a different matter. It seemed to Milner that the representatives of the Dominions could not be expected to consider prolonging the war for the sake of the oppressed minorities in Eastern Europe. Moreover, Milner probably liked the idea of a preservation of the Habsburg Monarchy, not only for the immediate goal of a separate peace but also as a bulwark against a revival of German aggression after the war. Its recently ascended half Bourbon Imperial family had the Latin touch which the *Round Table* had already noted benevolently in Francis Ferdinand and which promised an anti-Teutonic policy for the post-war period.

Certain constitutional changes in the system of the Monarchy seemed to be on their way. For the Imperial Federationists they must have been highly desirable. Now they could argue that there was no need to fight for the freedom of the subject nationalities. If these remained inside the body politic of the Habsburg realm, they could continue to enjoy the advantages of a common market, the efficiency of which had always impressed the Round Tablers, who were faced with similar problems in their special sphere. As they had to consider the question of imperial economic co-operation and the transformation of the British Empire into some sort of federal union, they must have sympathized with a comparable undertaking in Europe, which might even have served as a model. That is to say, by taking a pro-Habsburg stand the "New Imperialists" could hope to achieve two aims: firstly, to end the war in the foreseeable future, which was regarded as necessary for the safety of the Empire and secondly, to popularize the idea of a federal commonwealth by supporting an analogous experiment on the Continent.[12]

Since Milner's ideas on peace in general and on Austria–Hungary in particular differed in several particulars from the official Allied line, no prominent British paper would have published them.[13] But after Wilson's "Peace without Victory" speech there seemed to be an outlet for planting revisionist ideas overseas. So Milner encouraged Low to publish his programme in the *Atlantic Monthly*.[14] After stating clearly that he did not believe that the Allies could inflict a defeat on the central Alliance that would enable them to impose peace, Milner specified

Regards the creation – as part of the settlement – of Czechoslovakia,

---

[12] The analogy of Habsburg and British imperial constitutional problems was also obvious in the question of Irish dissension. The Conservative M.P. James F. Hope urged Milner to "build on the basis of Federalism, not of Dualism. By dualism I mean independent or overlapping Parliaments in the same realm, and wherever this system has been tried, it has in different ways ended disastrously, e.g. Norway, Hungary, Croatia and Ireland itself". (letter of 20 March 1917, Milner papers, box 210).

[13] Cf. A. Gollin, *op.cit.*, pp.535–37. Milner's terms for Eastern Europe were incompatible with Wickham Steed's.

[14] *Atlantic Monthly*, CXX (1917), pp.47–49 (partly quoted in A. May, *op.cit.*, ii, p.542).

Jugoslavia, enlarged Rumania, as impracticable. Very doubtful if these changes are in themselves desirable; but if they are, should be left for a post-war settlement.

As an irreducible minimum he demanded the evacuation of Serbia and occupied Russian and Rumanian territory and from Austria the cession of *some* territory to Italy. But Milner laid stress on the fact that

> We did not go to war for Czechoslovakia, Jugoslavia, or Rumanians, or Poles. We ought to try to make some arrangements for their autonomy, etc., but we ought not to insist that we shall go on fighting till their aspirations are satisfied. . . .[15]

Low did not content himself with voicing Milner's ideas in America. He also published them, in a more elaborate form, in the *Nineteenth Century*,[16] presenting the case as inspired and determined by the consequences of the American entry into the war. The participation of America in the reconstruction and remodelling of Europe was recognized as desirable to gain her support for a League to Enforce Peace. To achieve this goal, Low argued, it was worthwhile to make some sacrifices with regard to the secondary or ultimate issues of the war, which the Allies expected from a victorious peace. This restriction concerned the aspirations of Serbia, Italy, Rumania, and Poland, to some of which the Allies had given their formal adhesion and added the note to Wilson. This foreshadowed the deprivation of Austria of more than half or perhaps two thirds of her inhabitants and the establishment of new states across Central and South East Europe. The question posed by Low was whether the "bold surgery" of a release of all people groaning under alien domination might lead to a permanent peace. The idea behind the intention of completing the arrested development of dissatisfied nation-states was to erect a territorial zone thwarting Germany's *Mitteleuropa* designs. But could one be sure of the efficiency of a chain of small contiguous self-governing states or were they not more likely to quarrel for generations than work together?

Low warned of the need to be careful not to commit the Allies in haste to a reconstruction scheme which would weaken Germany's allies more than herself and might in fact strengthen her commanding position in Central Europe after she had recovered from the loss.

> The break-up of Austria would make Prussianized Germany the only strong power between the Baltic and the Mediterranean. She would be free from contact with another great and partly Germanic state, which has indeed lately shown itself her subservient tool, but is nevertheless always her potential rival.

---

[15] Chapman-Houston, *loc.cit.* The full text is reproduced in *The History of The Times*, iv, p.328ff.
[16] No. 483, May 1917, p.1000ff. ("The United States and the Peace Settlement").

Besides such future considerations there were indications that Austria was weary and the time might soon come when she would be glad to be out of it "on any terms short of extinction". But if the Allies would only give her peace when she consented to her own dismemberment, she evidently refused to yield until her predominant partner was forced to do so. To achieve this end of beating Germany it suited the Allies better to let her clients lay down their arms so that they could concentrate on Germany. This should be attempted, Low advised, not by granting Austria, Turkey and Bulgaria "easy conditions but conditions that would leave them some political cohesion and might serve as a stepping-stone towards the wider reforms we contemplate". Germany would have little scope to incorporate into her *Mitteleuropa* an Austria

> which continued to exist by the mercy of the Allies; and which would be under guarantee to them of good behaviour both in their external and their domestic relations.

In such circumstances Austria–Hungary, in conjunction with Serbia and Rumania, could be built into the hedge of barrier-states which the Allies wanted to set up in opposition to the German *Drang nach Osten*. Milner and his followers preferred this projection to the alternative offered by the *New Europe*. Their "sacred lamp of nationality" was not accepted as the perfect guide to the Austrian problem, because the carving-up and pegging-down of Europe in accordance with the demands of nationality might not satiate and pacify the peoples concerned. Against the partitioning of Austria it was argued that one could not be sure of the feelings of various nationalities. It was doubtful whether the Croats and the Slovenes would prefer either Italian or Serbian rule in exchange for Magyar domination. The Slovaks were believed to have developed no national consciousness marked enough to make them desire an incorporation with their Czech kinsmen. The Czech question itself was viewed dispassionately by Low alias Milner. A proposed Czecho-Slovak state, without a maritime outlet for its industry, would not have been in an enviable position. It would be burdened with almost a third of its population consisting of a resentful German minority. Hence, genuine Home Rule and racial equality under a Viennese Central(!) government, Low suggested, might be preferred by many Czechs and Slovaks to a precarious independence. At least it was more attractive to the New Imperialists in search of a stable settlement. They did not see a promising international future as a result of an application of the doctrines of nationality and self-government. Those who demanded that wanted to stamp out the material basis of Pan-Germanism and Prussian Imperialism. The Milnerists also looked for a means to contain the German threat to Britain's role in the world. The aim of the dissolution of the Habsburg Empire was regarded as unsuitable. Firstly, it seemed to imply a prolongation of the war and secondly it did not offer a comforting post-war outlook. The ultimate result of a *finis Austriae* would be the absorption of the Austro-Germans into the German *Reich*, which would more than compensate Germany for the eventual loss of Alsace–Lorraine and a couple of millions of Poles. Europe would then be faced with a solid block of nearly eighty million German speaking people, all under Prussian control, reaching down to the Tyrol, the northern spurs of the Dolomites and the Julian Alps. This formidable colossus within easy reach of the Adriatic was a potentially bigger menace to the European equilibrium than the pre-war constellation. The territorial reorganization of Europe, Low advised, should therefore be undertaken with the utmost circumspection. If possible, a means of separating peace-making and reconstruction should be found, thus the inexorable preoccupations of the moment might be successfully hindered from taking precedence of "the wider demands of the future and the world", which in Milnerian vocabulary was congruent with the security of the British Empire from German (or any other) competition.

The argument of Milner and his group was that the settlement at the end of the war would not merely redraw the map of Europe but govern the foreign policy of the Empire for years to come. Those who had to bear the burdens of the Empire, i.e. also the Dominions' representatives, who had hitherto only vaguely and remotely discussed peace terms during the imperial conferences, were now questioning what they were actually fighting for. They were "confused" and lacked "order and harmony". The Milnerites wanted to "make them in the true sense the peace terms of the whole Empire".[17] Finally they gained a temporary forum in the Imperial War Cabinet. This institution was opened on 22 March with a wide-ranging analysis of foreign policy by the Foreign Secretary. Balfour's discourse[18] was to show that after all the ideas of Milner and his adherents were not so much different from the rest of the Government and the Foreign Office, where meanwhile similar considerations had led to similar conclusions.

Balfour saw the greatest danger as Germany's strategic position which, if she managed to preserve it, provided her with an "unbroken avenue of influence from Berlin to Baghdad", and he doubted whether the I.W.C. could be confident about shattering German ambitions in Europe. With Russia rapidly moving towards disintegration there seemed nothing to stop Germany from pressing on in the East. In Balfour's view Germany not only dominated the whole central coalition, but none of the other powers had aims which were inconsistent or

---

[17] *Round Table*, No. XXXVI (March 1917), p.248.
[18] The document is printed in full in *The Lansing Papers*, ii, p.19ff.

divergent from hers.

At least this had been so in the earlier years of the war. Now, according to rumours,[19] Austria was so exhausted that she would desire to have a separate peace. The difficulties about it were, however, great, if one considered the Allied commitments which affected Austrian territory, and Balfour rightly put the question: "What, by the terms as interpreted in our Note to President Wilson, will be left of Austria, if we do make a separate peace?" It was indeed necessary to do some detailed stocktaking of the factors involved, before one could pursue a decisive Habsburg policy. Hence the Foreign Secretary reviewed the Secret Treaties to see how far they permitted a flexible interpretation of the clauses concerning Austria–Hungary.

Italy had been promised not only the districts bordering her frontier, where the population was of Italian origin (and for Balfour *Italia Irredenta* seemed to comprise the whole of the south Tyrol province, which he did not differentiate into a northern and southern part) but also parts of Dalmatia, "which neither ethnologically nor for any other valid(!) reason can be regarded as a natural part of Italy". Except from a naval point of view Balfoour could not see that it was justifiable to hand over the Dalmatian coast, but there was the treaty to which the Allies were bound, and furthermore they had agreed not to make a separate peace.

Without attempting a solution of the Italian dilemma Balfour passed on to Serbia, which was promised Bosnia and Herzegovina. He thought that this was "a most legitimate promise". They were of the same race and not old provinces of Austria, in the event of their being lost "nobody could say that Austria was destroyed". The matter became different with the Croat and other Slav communities to the South of the Danube. Their separation from the Austrian Empire would undoubtedly mean a great break in its tradition.

At this point Lloyd George interrupted his Foreign Secretary to point out that the promise to Serbia was conditional. The transfer of Bosnia–Herzegovina depended on Serbia giving up certain positions of Macedonia to Bulgaria and only if the war was won by the Allies could she hope to be given an access to the Adriatic. The Prime Minister definitely wanted to make use of this loophole to gain more freedom of action for negotiations with the Austrians. So far as Italy and Serbia were concerned, Balfour maintained that "even if we had the sort of peace we liked, it could not be said that we had destroyed Austria, certainly not the historic Austria of the eighteenth century, in any sense of the word at all". Obviously he would have been satisfied, if a

---

[19] Balfour did not learn about the Sixtus letters before their public disclosure in April 1918. All deliberations of the Foreign Office were based on the reports from their missions in the neutral countries.

reduced but still viable Habsburg Monarchy survived. But the number of promises in which the Allies were involved, had not yet been examined *in toto*. Rumania was offered that part of Hungary, which was predominantly Rumanian in race and language and should Transylvania be handed over to Rumania that would touch, if not break up, the historic kingdom of Hungary. Balfour gave consideration to the argument saying that there were Rumanians in Hungary who did not wish to join an enlarged Rumania, but he expressed little faith in it. On the whole he seemed to believe that all people of equal nationality had an inherent desire to live in the same community. If this considera-tion was driven to its logical conclusion it meant the inclusion of the Austro-German into the Reich. But an extension of Germany's border to the South had already been discarded when the future of Germany had been surveyed. In order to keep the Austro-German interest in the Habsburg Empire alive, it had to remain attractive enough. Some of its vital components had to remain as the pillars on which the Monarchy could rest. One of them was Bohemia, which had a history and tradi-tion of its own and according to all accounts known to Balfour had developed an inextinguishable hatred of German civilisation and prop-aganda. However, he was not sure whether all those feelings could not be satisfied by giving Bohemia some sort of autonomy in the Austrian Empire.

Balfour had met the Archduke Francis Ferdinand a few months before his assassination and was then informed about the heir appar-ent's scheme of raising the South Slav element to equal status in the Monarchy. Balfour was prepared to go yet another step forward:

> It seems to me that if you made it a quadruple Empire and gave Bohemia autonomy, it would be a very curious construction, but not a more curious one than Austria has been through all these centuries, and it might really meet the views of the populations without abso-lutely destroying Austria as history knows it.

But Balfour saw no way to overcome the Rumanian obstacle, while he did not seem aware of the Slovak element in Hungary, although it can be assumed that he would have approved of its union with the Czechs in what he called "Bohemia". Last but not least there was the Polish part of Austria. Balfour thought it absurd to regard this as historically Austrian. The future of Poland, however, was for him the "greatest crux of European diplomacy".

Summarising his ideas, he then excused himself for not having been able to offer any solutions for the difficulties he had stated. If the Allies were not successful in the war, he saw no hope of solving them. If the war ended in a drawn battle, he was afraid that the British could not deal satisfactorily with them; only if they won triumphantly should they be able to influence the settlement along their lines.

Some members of the I.W.C. found Balfour's programme too vague and asked for clarifications. Smuts wanted to clear up whether Austria should be completely cut off from, or have an outlet to the sea. Lloyd George thought that she must have one and named Fiume, which implied the negation of a union of Croatia with Serbia and Dalmatia.

The Prime Minister being driven so far, Milner realised a chance to discuss "such secondary objects as the question of the enlargement of Jugoslavia and an extended Poland". Were the Central Powers to be much more disposed to peace than at that time, Milner wanted the government to be clear in its mind about the relative importance of those secondary objects. So the raising of the Habsburg question by Smuts and Milner was no less than the starting point of their attempt to induce the I.W.C. to formulate minimum terms, if not for a public announcement then at least for the case of secret negotiations which might come up, possibly via Vienna. Balfour imagined that on such an occasion a communication could be made saying that the Central Powers were prepared to permit Italy to "go round the head of the Adriatic" and cede to her the Italian-speaking places there; further that they would cede Bosnia–Herzegovina to Serbia; and most important that they would really try to make a "liberal arrangement" about Poland. It was the latter case which Balfour doubted would arise, namely that the Germans were ready for a compromise. Neither was the majority of the I.W.C., and Lloyd George himself was reluctant to be drawn into a discussion of a basis for a general peace at this stage and therefore even declined to decide the Italian aspect of it under the pretext that any offence to the Italians had to be avoided. Meeting the opposition of the Prime Minister and the Foreign Secretary, Milner and Smuts were obliged to shelve their plan not without expressing their hope to talk over these things later.[20]

However, the immediate task of the government was not to fix terms for a final settlement that would find the approval of the Central Powers as a whole. What was required was a programme that was acceptable to the Austrian government alone. In order to entice it to forsake Germany, the C.I.G.S. had forwarded on 29 March a note to the Cabinet recommending a review of the agreements with Russia, Italy and Rumania "in view of their small contribution". This paper was appreciated by Balfour's Permanent Under-Secretary, Lord Hardinge, another former proconsul who was prepared to sacrifice the interests of the smaller Allies for those of the British Empire.[21]

Hardinge stated that Italy's efforts were not commensurate with her

[20] *Cab.* 23/24.
[21] *F.O.* 371/3081, f.78326.

claims and could only be obtained at Austria's expense, and except for an unconditional surrender her claims were irreconcilable and unrealisable. From indirect yet official sources Hardinge had gathered the information that Italy would be satisfied with the Trentino, and the non-occupied territory at the Isonzo and Trieste, the latter perhaps to become a free port.

As for Rumania, if her territory was restored and commercial prosperity assured, she might realize that her ambitions were unobtainable. In Hardinge's view it was desirable to try to secure rectifications of frontiers at the Peace Treaty "so as to induce the most Rumanian part of Transylvania, and if possible, autonomy for the Rumanian part of Hungary". In the meantime there would be no advantage in entering upon negotiations with Italy and Rumania for the reduction of their claims, since to do so would reduce their effort in the war. A concrete Austrian offer had to be awaited, because it was not impossible that with the satisfactory progress of the war the attitude of the Austrians would change and they would again (!) be ready to negotiate for a separate peace. Hardinge appreciated the inherent difficulties, but did not regard them as unsurmountable. He calculated that if very moderate terms were made acceptable to Italy and Rumania and if Galicia was added to the Polish state,

> Austria might well be satisfied with a federation of the four autonomous states of Austria, Hungary, Bohemia and Yugoslavia under personal sovereignty.

So Hardinge arrived at the same conclusion as his superior with the slight variation that he was prepared to give a little more power to both the Habsburg Empire as a whole and its subdivisions in relation to the Imperial Crown. Such a solution, he concluded, might, "if a guarantee of the support of the Allies were given, create a powerful barrier against the German *Drang nach Osten*".

This was also declared to be the supreme aim of British policy by the newly established Sub-Committee of Territorial Desiderata, which held two meetings on 17 and 28 April.[22] As regards the conclusion of a separate peace with Austria–Hungary, the chairman, Lord Curzon, informed the members (R. Cecil, A. Chamberlain, Smuts, W. Long, G. Clark, *et al*). that Italy had emphatically vetoed the idea. Consequently the problem featured only at random during the discussions. Sir George Clerk outlined the Foreign Office view of a quadruple federation as depicted above. Even he, who had formerly been in close contact with the South Slav leaders and their British friends, now considered that it might be possible to reorganize Austria on national lines. This

---

[22] Minutes: *Cab.* 21/77.

might fit in with the feeling of the Serbs, who would not like to be dominated by the Croatian element. A more extreme view on the lines of Milner – who himself presided over a Sub-Committee on economic desiderata – was represented by the Committee Secretary Amery, who drafted a conclusion, which said "It might be the right policy to make peace, even if it involved leaving the Czechs, Poles, Rumanians, and possibly the Yugoslavs in the Austro-German orbit, with such measure of independence as we might be able to secure for them".[23] The final report of the Curzon Committee, probably because of a clash of opinions, did not set down detailed recommendations at all and was particularly vague on Austria–Hungary. The precise mode in which this object was to be achieved was a matter which in the main concerned Britain's Allies more than the Empire–Commonwealth. The principal British interest in the settlement was that, while it should reduce the power and resources of the Central Powers, "it should correspond as far as possible with the wishes of the populations concerned and be inherently stable and calculated to promote a lasting peace".[24] General as these terms were, they meant a dissociation from the aims as declared at the beginning of the year. The liberation of the oppressed nationalities was now only demanded for the Turkish Empire, while in conspicuous distinction to it the Habsburg Empire was implicitly granted a solution based partly on pseudo-historic, partly on modified national lines.

2. The Public Discussion on Austria–Hungary

When in 1917 the diplomatic activities in connection with the Habsburg Monarchy were reaching their peak, those in favour of its destruction and those opposed to its dismemberment waged a fierce struggle against each other to win the sympathy of public opinion, and what was more important, to convince the government and the Foreign Office of the soundness of their respective standpoints.

The pro-Habsburg elements were labelled by their political opponents as "those who advocate the detachment of the Habsburg Dominions from Germany", which meant attempting a separate peace.

J. Annan Bryce, M.P. and follower of the *New Europe*, surveyed this "strange company" in a Commons debate on 14 May.[25] He saw, first of all, a strong body of financial opposition to the dismemberment of an economic unit, in which cosmopolitan finance had invested a great deal. The severing of the links between the Habsburg provinces would have caused a weakening if not upheaval of the commercial and monetary system in that area. The *Credit–Anstalt*, the *Wiener Bank* and other

---

[23] Quoted in H. I. Nelson, *Land and Power*, London 1964, p.20.
[24] *Cab.* 21/27; the report was presented to the I.W.C. on 1 May 1917, *Cab.* 23/40.
[25] *Hansard*, 5th ser., cxiii, 1367ff.

institutions of that kind would probably collapse and bring about damage to the City. Many financiers, bankers and industrialists had not been in favour of the war from the very beginning. Now that it was going to last for several years, these businessmen congregated to warn the public of its eventual consequences. Their best-known representatives were Hugh Bell, R. Holt and D. A. Molteno. Their weekly *Common Sense*, edited by F. Hirst, voiced the fear that a continuation of the war for the sake of destroying the Austro-Hungarian Empire would unnecessarily endanger the prosperity of the British. The peace-minded tycoons, under cover of what was known as the "yellow circle", also tried to get into touch with enemy financiers. In summer 1917 the War Office became worried enough about their activities to send a Mr. Kingham to Switzerland to obtain information about the participation of British subjects.[26] This turned out not to be the case and on the whole the influence of "the economy" was not so much exerted by actions but consisted of an ever present factor, which was to be observed whenever the decision between war and peace had to be made.

The fate of Austria–Hungary also concerned a number of people in England who had even less direct power but could make themselves heard on an influential level because of their descent and social reputation. Aristocrats and old Conservatives fostered a sentimental sympathy for the "nice" Austrians and regretted the disappearance of dynasties in general. Typical amongst this class of society was Walburga Paget, the wife of the former ambassador to Vienna, Augustus B. Paget. Lady Walburga had watched with great misgivings the influences at work which strove to "prussianize" the Austrians and predicted that if Germany was victorious in the war, Austria would be absorbed by the stronger nation. This problematical outlook should make the new Emperor, whom she credited with character and courage, understand the necessity of concluding a separate peace at the cost of cessions to Italy and the Balkan states. The loss of her Italian, Slavonic, and Rumanian territories would reduce Austria's population from fifty to approximately twenty millions, the exact number depending on the fate of Hungary and Bohemia, which Lady Paget found too complicated to forecast. But even with little more than her German provinces left, Austria might be intrinsically stronger than before by becoming the centre of attraction for the South German states. Thus out of the old Austria–Hungary there might emerge a national and have caused a weakening if not upheaval of the commercial and monetary system in that area. The *Credit–Anstalt*, the *Wiener Bank* and other expected to contribute in the future by assisting the Allies to reverse the Bismarckian solution of 1871. The beginning ought to be a separate

---

[26] *F.O.* 371/3085, No. 186478/f.172966.

peace, for which the Habsburgs should be given Silesia as a first fitting restitution.[27]

The raising of such unrealistic Austrian possibilities (which were instilled to some extent into official minds[28]) can only be explained by the desire to see the British Empire freed once and for all from the menace of German rivalry. This aspect dominated the thinking of British Conservatives and Royalists just as much as that of the majority of the Liberals. But while the latter tried to appeal to British self-interest, the Austrophile aristocracy hoped to save the House of Habsburg by the methods of the Congress of Vienna. Their outdated conceptions never became a guideline for official policy, though they were in a position to instil their pro-Habsburg sentiments into high quarters on an intimate personal level. As regards their competitiveness in public opinion, they could be easily denounced as reactionaries to whom one need not listen any longer and therefore only played a modest role in the ideologically tinted discussion over the Habsburg case.

Dynastic and ecclesiastical loyalties were much more at work on the Continent. The *New Europe* brandmarked

> shortsighted ultra-montanes who in their ignorance regard the decadent and corrupt Catholicism of Austria and Hungary as a bulwark of the Universal Church. . . the black reactionaries who still linger in a few corners of Rome and Paris, dreaming of the restoration. . . of some degenerate Bourbon dynast in France or Spain.[29]

This early hint at the Carlist pretenders was of course not founded on any knowledge of the Sixtus mission, but it shows how well the anti-Habsburg group scented their potential enemies. Regarding the Roman Curia the *New Europe* contended that her view was not contradictory to the Entente aims. Benedict XV's appeal for a just and durable peace was incompatible with the German designs for *Mitteleuropa* and the latter could only be thwarted by giving freedom to the subject nationalities.[30] A. Bryce [31] went so far as to note a new attitude of the Holy See towards the Habsburg Monarchy and maintained that the Vatican had shifted to a policy of saving the nationalities instead of the Habsburg dynasty. His belief in a complete conversion of the traditional attitude of the Curia was far too optimistic, though the Papacy avoided siding openly with the Habsburgs. Benedict XV was reserved when asked to support the peace offer of the Central Powers in December 1916, and the Pope was also wrongly accused of acting as a tool of the Austrian Emperor when he launched his appeal for a general

---

[27] *Nineteenth Century*, Mar. & May 1917, pp.563–65 and 1098ff., *Spectator*, 13 Jan. 1917.
[28] For attempts to convince Balfour cf. Paget papers, *B.M. Add. MSS.* 51239.
[29] *New Europe*, ii, No. 21, 8 Mar. 1917.
[30] *Ibid.*, 22 Mar. 1917.
[31] Cf. n.1 (*Hansard loc.cit.*).

peace in August 1917. Benedict had tried in vain to persuade Karl to make concessions to Italy, but apart from this he favoured the continued existence of a Monarchy that had paid all due deference to Rome. The Papal attempt to bring about a peace on a modified *status quo ante* implied the preservation of Austria–Hungary and Allied diplomats in the Vatican were requested to follow a policy of *"ménagez l'Autriche"*.[32] Only when events proved that a peace by compromise was impossible did the Vatican intensify its relations with the subject nationalities, particularly the Croats, but even Benes had the honour to be received by the Pope. But this flexible adaptation of Curial policy, which was facilitated by its cautious public pronouncements throughout the war, can only be regarded as the recognition of a development which the influence of the Roman Catholic Church was unable to prevent.

If the intimations from the Vatican were always received with attention in London, this was in the hope of gathering information about the real state of affairs in the Central Powers. A direct papal mediation could not be considered, for Italy had become an ally on condition that the Holy See would be excluded from a peace conference. There remained the indirect influence exerted by the English Roman Catholics. Some of their distinguished writers like G. K. Chesterton and Hilaire Belloc took a surprisingly anti-Austrian stand.[33] But their opinion had a limited impact on the political scene. More attention is reserved for the Catholics in the middle and lower charges of the Foreign Office (Theo. Russel, Drummond, Gregory). H. W. Steed tried to convince them that Austria was not the great Catholic state, either in the religious or the Roman sense. He wrote to them about his discussions with Cardinal de Cabriere, the doyen of the Church in France, and also sent them a detailed analysis, presumably by Ch. Loiseau, who played an important part at the French Embassy in Rome. The conclusion of his argument was that the interest of the Roman Church was in the redemption of the peoples of Austria and that the fate of the Habsburgs was an entirely secondary consideration.[34] Apparently the Foreign Office staff was not moved very much and a year later the Austrophobes still attacked who they called the "Vaticanists" planted in various departments and the diplomatic service, and accused them of working hard to entangle Britain in private pourparlers with Vienna.[35] While the pillars of the nineteenth century establishment

---

[32] L. Valiani, *op.cit.*, p.328; for the Austrian side cf. F. Engel-Janosi, *Österreich und der Vatikan*, ii, Gr 1960, p.291ff.

[33] Cf. H. Hanak, *op.cit.*, pp.128–30; cf. also the articles by the Rev. W. Barry, entitled "Break Austria", *Nineteenth Century*, 1917, pp.441–53 and 885–902.

[34] Steed to Theo. Russel, 26 Feb. 1917, Steed papers. The enclosed anonymous article "Le Saint-Siège et l'Autriche" appeared first in *La Revue de Paris* of 15 Jan. 1917; extracts were printed in *New Europe*, 22 Mar. 1917.

[35] *National Review*, Feb. 1918.

remained largely quiet under the surface, there was one almost traditional group of the English political life which made itself heard in the most articulate way. These "trouble makers" were the Radicals, Liberals in opposition who were often too quickly denounced as "amiable pacifists". The dissenters from British Foreign policy demanded the conclusion of a negotiated peace with the Central Powers. They believed in an Austro-German readiness to agree to a restoration of the *status quo* and blamed the Allied war aims as the main obstacle to peace. Thus one of the most curious political episodes of the war came into being. The Liberal slogan was: "Hands off the Austrian Empire". Among those who styled themselves Liberals and Democrats over and above their fellows, we find the strongest desire to preserve the Austrian Empire and the most patent willingness to postpone to other considerations the aspirations of the small nationalities within the Austrian Empire. Their mouthpiece was *The Nation*, a weekly edited by H. W. Massingham. Until mid-1916 the *Nation* had been rather critical of the "Habsburg idea". Agreeing with the pre-war view of Steed and Seton-Watson, it was admitted that the Monarchy was becoming much more a unity and much less a "ramshackle" empire. But the unifying Austrian idea was not a democratic one, there was no satisfactory parliamentary system and it scarcely touched the masses of any race. Since the Habsburg idea was not consistent with democracy, Austria had made war, which in a relative sense had proved her viability. The anonymous columnist, usually Henry N. Brailsford, wrote that

> Austria has endured the strain of the war rather better than the whole generation of students would have predicted. She has suffered disaster after disaster in the field. . . But with all these handicaps and trials there has as yet been no definite collapse and no actual disruption.[36]

The Radical sympathy for Austria was awakened when it was learned that the German peace offer of December 1916 was due to her initiative. Suddenly *The Nation* saw a new role for the Habsburg Monarchy in Central Europe. When the young emperor came to the throne and dismissed "German" politicians, for whom he called upon what they regarded as "Czechs" who belonged to the group "which worked for very definite aims under Francis Ferdinand" Karl himself seemed to be of the same school and although the Radicals did not know how precisely the late Archduke meant to go and still less what his successor contemplated they were sure that he wanted the creation of a "big South Slav State" which might even have the status of a subordinate kingdom. By such a reconstruction of the Empire the Magyar ascendancy, which for the Liberal dissenters did not have the same romantic

[36] *Nation*, 28 October 1916.

feelings as for the Gladstonians, could be reduced and the Monarchy would no longer be tied necessarily to Germany in the sense of Naumann's *Mitteleuropa*. Karl's personal equation was still an unknown factor, but for *The Nation* the tidings from Vienna sounded ideal. It was said that

> Austria, in the last stages of privation and at the end of her endurance, without actually contemplating a separate peace, is trying to open separate conversations with Britain and France in order to prepare the basis for a general peace.[37]

At that time it was difficult to see how Austria could extricate herself from the "octopus embrace of her ally", as a letter to the editor depicted it.[38] But a time might well come, when the pressure of warfare would become so effective that it might even extend to the anti-Prussian South German States. It would then be the obvious duty of the Allies to facilitate such a tendency.

However, this way seemed barred by the latest declaration of war aims on 10 January 1917. Radical criticism was immediately alarmed by the liberation clause, which they regarded as an extension of the Allied programme, with the effect of threatening the Monarchy with dismemberment, thereby foregoing the possibility of coming to terms with her peacefully.

One of the first prominent comments on the liberation clause came from Noel Buxton. He had the reputation of a Balkan expert and in a book, which he published together with his brother Charles Rhoden in 1915,[39] he had advocated the liberation of the subject nationalities to the extent of giving them complete independence. Now he regarded this as an immense task for the Allies. At the bottom of his theory lay the belief that the coming of peace might be hastened if the government could show that the allied aims were moderately conceived. So he joined the bandwagon of the so-called "rational peace movement" striving for a "decisive settlement", which, in his opinion, a decision on the battlefield could not secure.[40] To prevent a solution of this kind it was necessary to prosecute the war vigorously on the diplomatic front, that is to say, changing the *status quo* by pacific means. For the Habsburg Monarchy this implied a reform of her internal structure. Dualism was dead – Federalism became the catchword of the day. Buxton acknowledged that the Czechs and other Slavs desired political emancipation. Their freedom was also useful from a British point of view, because it would curtail the military force at Germany's disposal. But this could be met by Home Rule. N. Buxton observed that the quest for

---

[37] *Nation*, 13 Jan. 1917.
[38] *Ibid.*, 20 Jan. 1917.
[39] *The War and the Balkans*, London 1915.
[40] T. P. Conwell-Evans, *Foreign Policy from a Back Bench*, London 1932, p.14.

complete independence was not universal among the nations of Austria–Hungary. The anti-Russian parties, for instance, had a certain genuine loyalty to the Habsburg union. Furthermore, a break-up of the Monarchy would destroy the balance of Europe, while the multi-national Russian Empire remained intact. Last but not least, an indefinite continuation of the war involved further losses of British soldiers and increased the military and economic risks.[41]

The radical appeal to British interests was not confined to material arguments. While not being opposed to the principle of nationality as such, they warned of its outright application. The nationalities of South East Europe had not reached the standard of culture and civilisation which entitled them to full independence. Their demands were destructive and dangerous by giving impulses to nationalistic democracy. German *Kultur* was threatened by the onslaught of semi-illiterate Slav races – even dissenting among themselves.

The difficulties of the Habsburg Monarchy were similar to those of the British Empire, "and its aims . . . consistent with our safety", as V. Arnold put it.[42] The problems of the Habsburgs were comparable to British Imperial policy. Austria had already gone too far to transform herself. Only Hungary was still a hopeless phenomenon, but the Rumanian irredentism was doubtful, too, because of the higher economic status of the Transylvanian peasants. In her dealings with the Galician Poles Austria had done well and in Bosnia, which she released from Turkish rule, "she worked the same miracle in evolving order and material prosperity that we wrought in Egypt. If the Serbs of Bosnia are as yet only partially self-governing and by no means grateful," *The Nation* asked, "do their sentiments differ very much from those of the Egyptian Nationalists?"[43] While the irredentism of the Orthodox Serbs was recognized, the Catholic Croats would perhaps prefer an autonomous "Illyria" to an independent South Slav kingdom, of which their exiles were speaking. But there were no data how far their countrymen followed them. The same applied to Professor Masaryk, who before the war stood for Home Rule and now took an uncompromising view in a letter to the *Nation*.[44] This did not discourage the Radicals

> Roger Casement did not speak for Ireland, and one must remember that every subject race evolves its Sinn Fein minority.

For the Radicals Bohemia had its parallel in Ireland and they did not think it was entirely unfavourable to Austria. Vienna at least tried to do good with the Manhood Suffrage Act of 1907 and the Czechs were then

---

[41] *Nation*, 20 Jan. 1917.
[42] *Cambridge Magazine*, 9 June 1917, cit. H. Hanak; *op.cit.*, pp.157–58.
[43] *Nation*, 27 Jan. 1917.
[44] *Ibid.*, 3 Feb. 1917.

rallying to an Austria which was becoming a better home for Slavs. The *Nation* conceded that the status of the Czechs was unenviable. They were the most advanced Slav people of the Monarchy and deserved more political freedom. But the creation of a Czechoslovak state was questioned. Firstly, there was a much bigger "Ulster" in Bohemia, which could lead to future unrest, as the Radicals feared with foreboding. Secondly, the Slovaks were a "simple and backward peasant race" with no authentic national history, submerged under Magyar misrule and not yet fit to govern themselves.

Above all, the crucial question was: Is the independence of Bohemia desirable? The Radical argument against it was that the Czechs should have no "right" to an independent army with power to attack its neighbours or be in a position to invite a rival Great Power to utilize its government.[45] In short, the aspirations of the Czechs had to be subordinated to the wish for security of the Big nations, who did not want to become involved in trouble arising from the creation of a new state.

Noel Buxton was the first who broached the topic of "the most interesting item in the Allies' programme" in the Commons.[46] He asked for clarification on two points. Firstly, whether the formulation used meant no more than Home Rule within the Austrian Empire and secondly, whether the new term Czecho-Slovacks (*sic*) was to be understood as Bohemia. Buxton was inclined to assume that the government did not consider absolute political liberation as minimum terms since the word independence did not appear in the note. The total dismemberment of Austria, he warned, could not be secured without total moral and military extermination of the enemy.

The more vociferous pacifists Outhwaite and Ponsonby had no doubt that the ominous passage meant the break-up of Austria–Hungary. They questioned the independence of the Czecho-Slovaks, a people whose existence was widely unknown in Britain.[47] Ponsonby could not help feeling "that those responsible for foreign affairs in this country are also a little doubtful as to the territory occupied by the Czecho-Slovaks" and Outhwaite referred to "rumours going about that the Prime Minister has been making inquiries as to who the Czecho-Slovaks are".

The Foreign Secretary and his deputy simply refused to make any comments on the issue, which went beyond the January statement and Sir George Cave, the Home Secretary, found it premature to discuss the question of the German minority in Bohemia.

The numerical strength of the Radical parliamentary group was

---

[45] *Ibid.*
[46] *Hansard*, 5th ser., xc, 69–70 and 1134–1178 (7, 14, 20–21 Feb. 1917); cf. A. J. P. Taylor, *The Trouble Makers*, London 1957, p.147.
[47] *Hansard*, loc.cit.

negligible, but their repeated interpellations were nevertheless embarrassing for the government. It found itself exposed in the pursuance of a very ambiguous policy towards the nationalities, which meant a loss of the intended psychological and propagandistic effect of the note to Wilson. To thwart the impression caused by Radical publicity, the circulation abroad of the *Nation* was forbidden in April. This measure did not remove the problems of British policy makers. Were they merely out for the dismemberment of enemy countries to produce a diminution of the Central Powers' military forces or had they a genuine interest in seeing the freedom of the small nations secured? If they demanded complete independence for all the various nationalities of the Austro-Hungarian Empire, what about Russia, Ireland and Finland? Although this comparison was drawn by Charles Trevelyan,[48] it was not the aim of the Radicals to drive the government towards a doctrinal nationality policy. They considered this principle as outdated and reactionary and were of the opinion that other criteria like historical tradition and geographical lines should equally determine the drawing of boundaries, which ought to be left to an international Conference. Only in some extreme cases like Italian-speaking Trentino a cession of territory was supposed to be reasonable as a means of settlement. In general the Radicals believed that one could not get a moderate Germany before a moderate Entente. For this reason they wanted both sides to agree to their liberal solution: an autonomy for the South Slavs, the Czecho-Slovaks and the Rumanians inside the Habsburg Monarchy, which would assure to them "the reality of self-government".[49]

The problem for the Entente statesmen was that they did not know whether, by the offer of moderate terms, Austria could actually be detached from her ally, an event which could then very well lead to a general *sauve qui peut* among the Central Alliance. Short of this, however, *The Nation* argued, the knowledge that Austria–Hungary could obtain moderate terms, without bringing Vienna to an open breach with her ally, might induce her to accept peace without delay on terms which would satisfy British and Allied intentions. These were still ambiguous and therefore the next step ought to be to define their real intentions, which alone might go far to disintegrate the hostile coalition.[50]

Radical appeals were suddenly seconded by the outbreak of the March revolution in Russia. The Lvoff declaration of "No annexations and no indemnities" showed that there was a considerable pacifist body in Russia. Since the new regime in Petrograd as well as the new

---

[48] *Ibid.*, 1189–91 (20 Feb. 1917).
[49] *Nation*, 3 Mar. 1917.
[50] *Ibid.*, 28 Apr. 1917.

leadership in Vienna favoured an anti-annexionist peace, it seemed not unlikely that the announcement of the Russian Socialists had more appeal to the Habsburg rulers than the "gratuitous contributions to greater Prussia"[51] of the Entente note.

The revolution also stimulated the discussion of the Habsburg problem in circles which had hitherto been indifferent to it. The Conservative and highly patriotic *Saturday Review*, for instance,[52] had formerly mistrusted all news which reported that Austria was at both her wheat's and wit's end. Now the weekly paid attention to the rumours about an Austrian move towards a separate peace and admitted that the advantages of an understanding were very great, although the main danger was not that Russia would conclude a separate peace but that her internal conflict would be intensified. The weekly's columnist found it even more interesting to consider the permanent effect of the Russian change on Austria and the future position of the Austro-Hungarian Empire in Europe. Until now the Pan-Slavist protectionist policy of the Romanoffs had forced Austria into subservience to Germany, whenever her Slav or Czech subjects showed symptoms of revolt. Now the writer in the Saturday Review saw an alternative:

> We believe that one of the possible results of the great change in Russian government is that Austria may emancipate herself from German tutelage and may thus preserve something from her ancient position in Europe.

With a decisive military victory more remote than ever, it was Radicals and Conservatives alike who asked themselves whether a dismemberment of the Habsburg Monarchy was a fixed and immutable part of Allied policy. Was such a dismemberment most likely to secure the best chances for civilisation for the "subject nationalities" and the prospect of peace for Europe at large? Austria had to be beaten in the field just as Germany to achieve a settlement worth having, but once Austria and Germany were beaten, it did not follow automatically that they would be divided up into "a host of small and jarring nationalities and principalities". If they were, Europe would only be converted into "one gigantic Balkan problem".[53] Assuming a general fear of the balkanization of Central Europe the Radical and also the Conservative press believed that, in the natural order of things, there would be an Austria after the war. The momentum of political tradition should not be underestimated, the Monarchy's remarkable achievements should not be forgotten, when an attempt was made at the settlement to re-model or supersede the structure the Habsburgs had built.[54] The Radical

[51] *Ibid.*, 19 May 1917.
[52] *Saturday Review*, 21 Apr. 1917 ("Austria and the Russian Revolution").
[53] *Ibid.*, 9 June 1917.
[54] *Nation*, 31 Mar. 1917.

Liberals recognized that in the last resort it depended on the people themselves. The Conservatives were more reluctant to grant them this freedom of deciding their own fate and doubted its political wisdom.

> As to the nationality principle, up to a certain point, we all believe in it. But beyond a point, we do not. If the whole of Europe, the whole earth, is rearranged, would the nations live happily?[55]

The answer in respect of Austria–Hungary was in the negative. This did not mean a clearcut approval of the "No annexation" formula. The various forces of irredentism could not be neutralized without any territorial changes at all. Some sacrifices had to be made, especially to Italy. She had to acquire those districts which were largely inhabited by her own race, and the problem of the Adriatic had to be settled by giving Italy a dominant role. On the whole, however, the best solution would be an "honest" federalism giving autonomy to the chief racial divisions and protection to the subject minorities. Rounding up this argument, the *Saturday Review* concluded that the intricate problem of the Austrian nationalities and its solution depended so largely on the policy ultimately adopted by the young Emperor. It might involve considerable territorial changes, but

> a great state in which the Slav races must be influential would be an invaluable counterpoise to the German Empire and would be far less likely to disturb the future Europe than a congeries of small nations.[56]

The *Saturday Review* stood by no means alone with this argument. C. P. Scott of the *Manchester Guardian* was equally doubtful about a policy of dismemberment:

> It is a large order to break up the Austrian Empire and to reconstruct its fragments. . . Would a South Slav State, I wonder, hold together? These small Slavonic nationalities seem to have a wonderful capacity for fighting each other.[57]

The *Manchester Guardian* had regarded the Allied note to Wilson as "maximum rather than minimum terms" and though the Allies probably wished to secure some greater measure of liberty for the Slav population of the Habsburg Monarchy, they were not committed to any specific means by which it was to be attained. The desire for the break-up of the Monarchy was ascribed merely to the now vanished Imperialist Russia. After the revolution the diplomatic situation called for a policy of detaching Austria from the Central Alliance by guaran-

---

[55] *Saturday Review*, 9 June 1917.
[56] *Loc.cit.*
[57] A. May, *op.cit.*, p.548. Cf. C. P. Scott papers, *B.M. Add. MSS.* 50901–09.

teeing her integrity after suitable cessions to Italy.[58] The trend in public opinion towards a pro-Habsburg attitude in spring 1917 is perhaps best illustrated by the remark in the *Westminster Gazette*: "We have always doubted the wisdom of making it appear", the liberal evening paper stated, "that an Allied victory meant the destruction of Austria–Hungary and we doubt it even more now".[59] The *Nation*, however, exaggerated when it claimed that no section of opinion in Britain either vetoed or disapproved a closer approach to Austria.[60] It is true that the idea even fascinated jingoists like Northcliffe, who after having been approached by an Austrian Pole (Retinger) about a separate peace, wrote to Steed on 18 January:

> I see no harm in pourparlers which do not pledge us to anything. I know that it will get up the back of Russia, but someone's feelings have got to be ruffled before we win, and after all, Russia is going to get her piece of cake in Constantinople.[61]

He argued that it would be fatal at this juncture to get caught in a snare of this kind. Only when Austria was ready to declare war on Germany would it be time to deal with her authorized representatives but not before.[62] From his last conversations with Drummond and Russel he had received the impression that the Foreign Office was far more lenient towards Austria and inclined to revise the official attitude as made public in January. Steed warned strongly against such a step:

> Our attitude towards the Austrian question is a most important matter. We – that is to say the government – ought not to take up any attitude whatever, nor to suggest by implication that we might eventually take up this or that attitude without the most careful consideration, especially if the attitude be in any way, directly or indirectly, a departure from the policy outlined in the reply to President Wilson.[63]

Before revising its Austrian policy the Foreign Office should clear its mind over a number of crucial points. The first question to be answered frankly was the nature of a future Austria. If the Monarchy was to survive, there was the alternative between a "Habsburg rump" shorn of regions like the Trentino, Galicia, Dalmatia and Bosnia–Herzegovina with the Dual system intact; or a new Federal State which would be "a kind of imperial Switzerland". Assuming that the Foreign Office favoured the second solution Steed questioned the practicability of

---

[58] *Cit.* H. Hanak, *op.cit.*, pp.217, 250.
[59] 21 Apr. 1917.
[60] 12 May 1917.
[61] The letter was intercepted by the War Office and sent to the F.O. Filed in *F.O.* 371/3079, f.7661 (No. 17654), minuted by Balfour!
[62] Steed to Robinson, 23 Jan. 1917, Steed papers.
[63] Steed to Theo. Russel, 26 Feb. 1917, *ibid.*

breaking the dual system against the opposition of the German and Magyar bureaucracy and the grip of the German military. He denounced the Emperor Karl as "a possibly well-meaning but degenerate young man", accusing him of becoming a habitual drunkard, on whom one could not base a policy. A reduced, federalized, independent Habsburg Monarchy could not withstand the German economic pressure without economic guarantees from the Allies. How could the Allies expect a proportion of the indemnity which they required from a country that was "utterly bankrupt, disorganized and half-starved?" Furthermore, the "Prussians" – aided by the Austro-Germans and the German Jews (!) – could organize a stampede of the Austro-German provinces into the German Empire and thus frustrate all Allied designs. It was even conceivable that the Germans were winking at the separate suggestions through Austria to weaken the cohesion of the Allies. Considering all these difficulties Steed issued the warning that

> we should not allow ourselves to be led into any imprudence of thought or speech by conceptions that may once have been sound but are no longer real.[64]

If Steed could not totally convince the Conservative elements in the Foreign Office, his argumentation, made under the pretence of expertise, could at least induce the Foreign Office staff to waver and hesitate in embarking on a pro-Austrian policy. How far they were to proceed would in any way be largely determined by the nature of an eventual Austrian offer.

At this stage Steed contented himself with appeals not to change British policy opposing his personal schemes. He did not yet dare to ask the government to come round all the way to his point of view, namely to make the destruction of Austria–Hungary and the creation of new nation states a declared war aim. The time to realize demands of this order had not yet come. Steed even failed to persuade the editor of *The Times* to give him a forum for his programme. This led him and Seton-Watson to the foundation of the *New Europe*, a weekly on foreign affairs which from December 1916 onwards became the vociferous organ of the anti-Habsburg group.[65] The *New Europe* argued that the disruption of Austria–Hungary could not be bought off by a new federalism, "as some good-natured Englishmen suppose". A new Slavonic federation might, indeed, arise from the *disjecta membra* of the Habsburg Monarchy, but it could not be founded within the Monarchy without practically restoring that very German–Magyar dominion which the Allies hoped to destroy. The emergence of three powers from victory – Jugoslavia, Bohemia, and Greater Rumania – would bring

---

[64] *Ibid*.
[65] *Through Thirty Years*, ii, pp.94–95 and 127, cf. H. Hanak, *op.cit*, p.175ff.

about the end of German domination in Central Europe.[66]

The *New Europe* also hailed the Russian Revolution, for it promised to transform Russian diplomacy from top to bottom. The formerly "theocratic" Empire had finally liberated itself and was now seen as an Eastern pendant to the British Commonwealth and therefore could claim what was beforehand reserved to the Dominions of King George, that is, to be an empire and a democracy. This was the fundamental difference between the Russian and the British Empire on the one hand and the Austrian on the other. In the latter the dominant State was itself founded upon denial of the right of small nations to live their own life and there seemed nothing but to withdraw subject peoples from its yoke. Where their right was at last partially admitted, as by Britain and of late Russia, self-government within the state might reasonably be expected to satisfy the craving of national self-expression. This applied to Ireland and Finland. Only Poland was a serious problem in the eyes of the *New Europe*. The Asian nationalities within the Russian realm were comparable to the British Crown colonies. That is to say, the right of self-determination had to comply with Allied interests. When a people's demand concerned their own territory, this nationality was supposed to enjoy "democratic liberty" within the boundaries of a more civilised empire. The same development was denied to Austria–Hungary, because indirectly it endangered the prosperity of the British Empire and its Allies by keeping up the prospect of a *Mitteleuropa* dominated by Britain's continental rival. Hence the *New Europe* argued that a democratic development in the Austro-Hungarian Empire was not possible. The Slav nationalities could only enjoy real freedom when fully independent.

Taking for granted an Allied military victory there remained one major obstacle to this: the Italian aspirations in Dalmatia. This was clearly an imperialist aim and in flagrant violation of the new Russian formula, which, together with the entry of the United States, could have a salutary effect on Italy.

With Russia renouncing her hegemonial role in the Balkans, Italy's statesmen could duly be expected to be animated by the new democratic spirit. The Foreign Office was summoned by Arthur Evans[67] to undo the secret treaties as far as possible. The "legitimate" need of Italy for protection on her eastern maritime flank was recognized by him and should certainly outweigh any "pedantic" application of the principle of nationality. No peace could be satisfactory for Italy, Evans pointed out, that did not place a series of key positions (Pola, Lussin, Lissa, Valona) as strategic strongholds into Italy's hands. But to endeavour to lay hold of Dalmatian or Croat territory *en masse*, and more especially

---

[66] *New Europe*, 26 Apr. 1917.
[67] *Ibid.* and *Saturday Review*, 9 June 1917.

any mainland tract, would antagonize the whole Slavonic world and could only be a prelude to a new War of Liberation in the near future.

So for the *New Europe* "no annexations" and *la victoire intégrale* became perfectly compatible. Masaryk enthusiastically greeted it:

> The Oriental question, which is the real issue of this war is gradually being merged in a world-question . . . The insolence, the Hybris of Pangermanism, will be finally crushed by democracy; that is the reason why the Russian revolution is so much feared by Germany and Austria–Hungary. These enemies of democracy know that the Russian Revolution is the surest pledge of the Allies' victory.[68]

Despite this displayed optimism the *New Europe* realized that the partition of Austria–Hungary might prove a stumbling block to the anti-imperialists in Russia. In fact, the Council of Labour and Soldiers' Delegates soon objected to Milyukov's policy for a decisive victory, which it wanted to be substituted by a decisive victory of democracy. Such vague statements introduced an element of doubt and uncertainty, which was not eased by the inconclusive policy pursued by the Kerensky government.

An authoritative article expressing the views of the leading Minority Socialists (Chkeidze, Skobolev, Tseretelli) appeared on 9/22 April in the *Rabochaja Gazeta*.[69] It took up the allegation that the Council of Workmen's and Soldiers' Delegates supported at any cost the inviolability of the old territorial frontiers between States. This was declared an untrue bourgeois smear. It was merely the case that they did not bring forward concrete terms because they rejected the continuation of the war as a means of deciding the questions affecting a whole number of nationalities. Moreover, the Russian branch of the International alone could not consider itself competent to work out these concrete decisions of peace on the fate of Poland, Serbia and the Austrian nationalities. Taking the question of Austria–Hungary, they acknowledged the "abnormal" position of that country and that "there is no reason to think that a number of nationalities there are striving to free themselves from the yoke of Austro-Hungarian Dualism". The Entente Imperialist, however, made capital out of these aspirations, but their support was a mere lip-service, as the promises to Italy and Rumania showed.

Allowing that the various Austrian nationalities were beginning to demand independence, the inherent difficulties to this were also pointed out. The Czechs could form themselves into a separate State, but they would be separated from the sea and their economic development would thus be shaken to its very foundations. On the other hand,

---

[68] *New Europe*, 22 Mar. 1917.
[69] *Ibid.*, 24 May 1917.

the Serbo-Croats by forming themselves into a separate State, might cause serious harm to the other nationalities by separating them from the sea. The Russian Socialists were of the opinion that such questions could only be decided at a general meeting of the International, where representatives of all the nationalities interested in the solution of this problem would be present and where representatives of the remaining branches of the International would play the part of arbiters. A platform of this sort was to be the Socialist Conference planned to take place in Stockholm, which the Soviets called for on 15 May. This request immediately sparked off a debate in the Commons the day after.[70]

There the pacifist M.P. Philip Snowden issued a similar declaration to that of the Russian government, i.e. a repudiation of all proposals for imperialist conquest and aggrandizement. The policy of the scheduled conference should be "to secure such re-adjustment of territory as will remove one cause of war", namely the resentment at being subjected to an anti-racial alien rule. But Snowden emphasized that it would not be easy "to redraw the map of Europe and to make race and governmental area co-terminous". A. F. Whyte, a close associate of Seton-Watson, replied that the possibility of a permanent settlement in the Balkans implied the "disturbance" of the present Austro-Hungarian Monarchy. This would only be a dismemberment in the eyes of the Habsburg dynasty. He was seconded by his colleague Mackinder who claimed that the "rescue" of the Serbs, Rumanians and Italians had nothing to do with "Imperialist conquest". Austria was not a nation but something quite different from the other states of Europe, a dynastic group of properties. Whyte was not prepared to believe that the Russian nationalist democracy wished to maintain the enslavement of their brother Slavs. He stated that one of the foremost of the Allied claims had to be "to secure a re-sorting of the peoples of South-Eastern Europe in such a way that it should be built of free nationalities and not a mere heap of peoples kept together by military control".[71]

Robert Cecil, who defended the government's policy in the House of Commons, was cautious in his reply. He also made qualifications for the term "annexation", which he did not want to be applied to the release of misgoverned populations under the Ottoman Empire and in the German colonies. He dwelt at large on these cases where British interest was directly concerned and a transfer of sovereignty seemed justified on moral grounds. Touching upon Central Europe Cecil singled out Poland, Alsace–Lorraine and Italia Irredenta. The restoration to Italy "of provinces populated by Italians" was a commitment which the government could not give up but in view of the "no annexation"

---

[70] *Hansard*, 5th ser., cxiii, 1625ff.
[71] *Ibid.*

demand abroad and at home Cecil found it impossible to defend the Italian claims *in toto*, though by omitting the Adriatic question he paid tribute to the demands of public opinion. Both Radicals and the *New Europe* could be pleased about this abandonment of British support for Italian Imperialism. They did, however, fail to extract any new utterances from the government on Austria–Hungary as such. Cecil merely repeated the clause in the note to Wilson and after a Radical "dismemberment" exclamation he added emphatically:

All that is said is the liberation of these races from alien domination. . .[72]

Instead of rewriting the note to President Wilson, which Snowden demanded, the British Government preferred to stick to those vague formulations and crude generalities, which were deemed sufficient as weapons of psychological warfare. More precise alterations in favour of Austria could endanger the loyalty of minor Allies and the disturbance wrought by obstructive subject nationalities. A definite pledge in favour of the latter could bar the second alternative of a diplomatic coup. No doubt the major reason for the cautious pronouncements by Cecil was the chance of making a separate peace with Austria. The parliamentary exponents of the *New Europe* tried to prove that this was undesirable and not feasible without German consent. J. Annan Bryce claimed that it would be ruinous to Britain's future in the East, if the Austro-Hungarian Empire was allowed to continue to exist. The only bulwark against Pan-German expansionism was a barrier of Poland in the north, Czecho-Slovakia in the middle, Rumanians, Transylvanians and Jugoslavs in the south and Italians in the south-west.

The scepticism of the government to such sweeping schemes was expressed by Bonar Law who replied on 14 May:

I do not think that anything would prove more fatal to Germany than if one of the other Central Powers were to separate from her.[73]

3. The Pressure Groups and the Formulation of War Aims

The influence of the organs of both Austrophiles and Austrophobes on the formation of public opinion was considerable, but it is difficult to measure it precisely. Even more difficult to assess is their impact on official quarters, although certain personal and/or administrative connections can be traced. Conversely, the high appreciation for a journal like the *New Europe* in intellectual and unofficial political (parliamentarian) circles was due to its competent and detailed information

[72] *Ibid.*, 1675–79.
[73] *Ibid.*, 1373.

derived from emigré underground movements and the War Office Daily Review of the Foreign Press.

The Intelligence Service, organized as the Intelligence Bureau of the Department of Information and headed by Lord Gleichen, was staffed with men who were sympathetic to the case of the subject nationalities of the Habsburg Monarchy, e.g. J. W. Headlam, the brothers Leeper and Lewis B. Namier. The latter, who worked for the East European Department of the Foreign Office, was especially friendly to the Czechoslovaks and in 1917 he published two pamphlets in which he drove home with utmost poignancy the argument that the Czechs had to be liberated from their position of being a tool of the German war machine. The Habsburg Empire had committed a crime in forcing the Czechs and other Slavs to fight their racial brethren in Serbia and Russia and hence deserved to be destroyed.[74] Namier, himself a descendent of Jewish landowners in Galicia, also fostered a special love for the country of his birth, the renascence of which he wanted to see as the result of the war. In the pursuit of his aims he submitted on 11 May a memorandum summarizing "the fundamental facts" about the Habsburg Monarchy. His main points were:

1. The Germans of Austria–Hungary will never admit an anti-German course; they were even prepared for incorporation into the German Empire.
2. The Magyars will never admit a merging of territory (Grossösterreich).
3. The Czecho-Slovaks will never abandon the idea of a Bohemian State with the same rights as the Hungarians.
4. The Rumanians and the Yugo-Slavs are left within the Monarchy while national states of their own exist.
5. Autonomy is impossible. The war has brought the emergence of nationalism.

Namier realized that there were people in Britain who feared the disruption of the Austrian Empire, because it was likely to lead to the integration of the Austro-Germans into the Reich and to an increasing influence of Russia on the Balkans. But he thought that these two factors would neutralise themselves. New national states would be in the interest of Great Britain and keep both Germany and Russia from the Mediterranean. Finally Namier warned of the fallacy of a separate peace. Germany could not be deprived of the Austrian auxiliary by negotiations. She could watch them or even encourage them in secret. Conversely, as long as the present system existed, the Habsburgs were in danger and needed German support.

Namier's report was received with mixed feelings in the Foreign

---

[74] Cf. his autobiography *Avenues of History*, London 1952, pp.90–91.

Office.[75] Whereas R. Graham saw "no danger" in it, Lancelot Oliphant strongly protested against the author's daringness in giving a political interpretation instead of confining himself to merely providing information. Such an outburst shows that some officials in the Foreign Office did not view the intake of so-called experts with much sympathy. They must have felt themselves overruled by the latter's superior factual knowledge and feared a waning of their own influence.

But on the highest level the erudition of the *New Europe* group was found valuable. Seton-Watson, who originally was designed for a mission to Russia (a move by his enemies to get him out of the way?) had been serving as a private in the R.A.M.C. On 16 April it was decided by the War Cabinet to attach him to the Information Department and hardly a month later he commented for the first time on a telegraphic report on the political situation in Austria–Hungary.[76] According to the *Berliner National Zeitung*, which Townley had read in the Hague,[77] Clam-Martinic had wanted autonomy or home rule by royal decree (octroi) instead of by Act of Parliament. His resignation, which he tendered after his plan had been vetoed by Czernin, was not accepted. If this was true, Seton-Watson observed, it of course

> knocks the bottom out of the theory (on which the proposal of a separate peace with Austria–Hungary rests) that the Clam-Martinic Cabinet aims at the Slavisation of Austria.

On 18 May the Viennese *Neue Freie Presse* contained an article on "English Overtures to Austria–Hungary" dealing with an article in the *Saturday Review* upon a separate peace with Austria. The Austrian paper called such designs a "bottomless baseness" and pointed out that the Central Alliance was based on the will of the people. Such news provided a welcome opportunity for the anti-Habsburg men of the Department of Information to state the validity of their arguments and this time Oliphant felt obliged to annex their memorandum and draw the attention of his superiors to it.[78]

The hopelessness of a separate peace was confirmed in a conversation between Gleichen and Crosbie, the Secretary of the American Embassy in Vienna (who had left Vienna three weeks previously[79]). Crosbie told Gleichen in the presence of Seton-Watson that the Austrian authorities had decided to maintain their alliance to Berlin. There was indeed bad feeling between German and Austrian military officers but this did not affect the political situation, since Germany had complete control of her ally. The Emperor was popular but without

---

[75] *F.O.* 371/2862, No. 97435.
[76] *WC* 119.25, *Cab.* 23/2.
[77] *F.O.* 371/2862, No. 1146, f.2604; minuted by Seton-Watson on 11 May.
[78] *F.O.* 371/3076, No. 101544/2 of 19 May.
[79] *F.O.* 371/2862, No. 103995 of 23 May.

definite political ideas and his wife not of dominating influence. Crosbie's analysis was obviously due to the circumstances which preceded
the Austrian break with the U.S.A. Then Czernin, who wanted to
prevent the break, changed his attitude after a visit to Berlin, where he
was pressured to the contrary.

The Austrian subservience to Germany was endorsed in the eyes of
the I.B.D.I. by a cordial exchange of telegrams between Czernin and
the German Chancellor. Apart from this leakage the I.B.D.I. had to
admit that the information recently received from and about Austria
was rather scanty. This lack of evidence made it difficult to draw very
definite conclusions, but for the Department of Information everything
seemed to point in the direction of a pro-German policy at Vienna.
There was no volte-face of government in sight and at best an abandonment of the extreme anti-Slav repression could be expected. Karl's
decision to reassemble the Reichsrat had caused dissatisfaction in
extreme Austro-German circles but the Czechs and the "Croato-
Slovenes" (*sic*) were not impressed by Karl's move.[80]

The idea behind this gesture was to appease the opposition by taking
the representatives of the people into the confidence of the government.
But in fact it provided the Slav leaders with a forum from which to voice
their grievances and ambitions. In the very first session on 30 May the
presidents of the Yugoslav and Czech Parliamentary Clubs, Father
Anton Korošec and František Staněk, read solemn declarations which
aimed at changing the fundamental structure of the Empire. They
demanded that the South Slavs and all Czechoslovaks be united into
independent states. Though their statements still professed loyalty to
the Habsburg dynasty, this was interpreted as a mere lip-service by
Seton-Watson, who rightly pointed out the change of tone from the
abject declarations made by the same men in January. But he also
willingly disregarded the possibility of a Habsburg (con-)federation
which would have put the South Slavs and the Czechoslovaks on an
equal footing with the Magyars. No more was asked for publicly by the
nationalities' representatives at home so far and there was no sign that
their ambitions went beyond such a solution, although Seton-Watson
could argue that they had to conceal their real objects.[81]

From the end of May 1917 Seton-Watson drew up weekly reports
on Austria–Hungary analysing the situation in the Monarchy as
reflected in Austrian newspapers, public declarations by the leading
politicians and changes in office. A major event in the latter category
was the downfall of Tisza, the Hungarian premier, whose position had
been described as "safer than ever" only a fortnight before the I.B.D.I.

---

[80] *F.O.* 371/2862, No. 97562 of 12 May.
[81] *G.T.* 917, *Cab.* 24/15 (2 June).

was faced with his resignation. They attributed this not so much to his disagreement with Karl on the Hungarian franchise but to the Austro-German Polish settlement, which involved the secession of Galicia to a new Poland under German influence and had an impact on the future food *Ausgleich* between Austria and Hungary. On the whole this agreement was seen in London as a further proof of Austria's inextricable integration in a Central European economy under German domination.[82]

If there was to be any development towards an alternative it depended largely on the attitude and determination of the Emperor Karl. In his speech from the throne he announced that he would take the oath to the Constitution at a later period. This seemed to foreshadow some radical changes in the Constitution. He proposed the "unity of the Empire" as a new basis, which meant centralization through the exclusion of the Poles and the Ukrainians and a curtailment of the Landtage. The only compromise envisaged was to grant the Czechs the division into German and Czech districts in Bohemia. But on 12 June in the Budget Debate Karl avoided committing himself to any concrete scheme and described the claims put forward "as a result of national passion" and said that such wishes "could not be realized if submitted in their existing form". He emphasized the need of a strongly consolidated state whose "fully tested foundations must not be shaken".[83]

Seton-Watson did not see the reasons for the appointment of Czernin and Clam-Martinic as a desire for Slavisation on the part of the Emperor. He concluded that Karl merely wished to be surrounded by new people of no political past, who were more pliable to his wishes. While this showed his strong sense of independence, the Emperor intended to maintain the dual form of the Austrian idea and was opposed to federalism. His international policy was not clearly defined and Karl had especially independent ambitions in this field, but their realization depended on the domestic situation.[84]

Prime Minister Clam-Martinic, who lacked real statesmanship resigned, because he could not find a way out of the dilemma of enjoying either German or Slav support. For the latter he would have needed Karl's support. The Emperor toyed with the idea of appointing a personality respected by all groups, but when the potential candidates Lammasch and Redlich declined, Karl replaced Clam by the bureaucrat Ernst von Seidler who was to serve as a stopgap for about a year. In Hungary Count Esterházy and his successor in turn Alexander

---

[82] Weekly Report on Austria–Hungary and Poland, 26 May 1917, *G.T.* 853, *Cab.* 24/14; initialled by Oliphant, Graham and Hardinge.

[83] *G.T.* 1039 and 1073, Cab. 24/16 of 14 and 16 June.

[84] Memorandum on the Emperor Charles by R. W. Seton-Watson, dated 18 June, filed in *F.O.* 371/2862, No. 129141, f.2604.

Wekerle formed cabinets comprising contradictory elements but showed no intention of modifying the existing system to the disadvantage of Hungary's ruling classes.[85]

Meanwhile the Emperor tried to propitiate his subject nationalities by announcing an amnesty for their condemned leaders. According to the Czech National Council in Switzerland this move was due to pressure by the German military chiefs. It was in Germany's interest to prevent an increasing opposition by the Slavs in the Monarchy, which could only weaken the war effort of the Central Powers as a whole. This explained why they were advocating a conciliatory Slav policy and Seton-Watson acknowledged that the Germans were less intransigent than the Austrians themselves.[86] From the British point of view the memorandum submitted by the Czech Social Democratic Party to the Socialist Conference at Stockholm was clearly an acceptable compromise. This paper asked for the right of every nation to constitute itself as "an independent whole with all the attributes of complete State independence". But where this was not feasible at present the nation should decide its own destiny "in the widest possible sense". With regard to the special situation of the Habsburg Monarchy they demanded the establishment of an independent Czech state within the limits of a United Danubian State on a Federal basis. This was to have all the attributes of a sovereign state to which a federal state could lay claim – thus excluding only foreign policy, common defence and common action to secure the economic and financial functions of the Union.[87]

While the "democratization" of the Habsburg Empire was the necessary precedent to a speedy and sincere peace for the Czech Socialists, it was of secondary importance for the British Government, which was trying to ascertain the peace conditions of Austria's rulers. According to vague allusions in the press the Viennese Foreign Office contemplated the following in mid-June 1917:[88]

1. restitution of the status quo
2. occupation of Mount Lovčen
3. freedom of the Danube (commission to be abandoned)
4. Serbia to be united with Montenegro
5. Customs union between Austria and Rumania, Serbia and Bulgaria.

However, as the I.B. pointed out, these were conditions for a general peace. The economic situation was bad but did not force the upper classes in power to make peace. A revolution was out of the question

---

[85] *G.T.* 1251 (30 June), *ibid.*
[86] *G.T.* 1323 (7 July), *Cab.* 24/19.
[87] Transmitted by E. Howard on 30 June, *F.O.* 371/3007, No. 140383.
[88] *G.T.* 1039, *Cab.* 24/16.

because of the racial diversity and the presence of the German army. Karl did not want to abandon the alliance and the utmost he could do was to put pressure on Berlin for a peace on the basis of "no annexations and no indemnities".[89]

In a memorandum on "war feelings in Austria–Hungary", which was requested by the secretary of the War Cabinet for the Prime Minister and the Foreign Secretary, Seton-Watson warned the government of the true nature of the Austrian advances, whether official or unofficial, which were taking place in Switzerland. Referring to Mensdorff's attempts to get into touch with the British legation at Berne, Seton-Watson wrote:

> His aim was not so much to extricate Austria from the war as to implicate the Entente in negotiations in which Berlin and not Vienna would have been the motive force. The primary object of Germany's and Austria's many agents in keeping the idea of a separate peace always to the front, is to create bad blood between the various members of the Entente and to exploit conflicting interests and to play upon the naiveté of well-meaning but ignorant pacifist politicians.[90]

Seton-Watson criticised the Entente for wasting time by its absurd passivity towards the irredentist nationalities. The Entente had to begin to "will its own peace", start a political offensive and define its war aims.[91]

But even if the government intended such a step, the political climate soon made it impossible. Realizing the importance of the non-annexation formula for Austria–Hungary, Czernin contacted the influential Reichstag politician Mathias Erzberger to have this principle included in the forthcoming *Reichstag* declaration.[92] Eventually this resolution of 19 July called for "peace and a mutual understanding and lasting reconciliation among the nations" and condemned forced acquisitions of territory and political, economic and financial violations.[93]

The Reichstag resolution caused a sensation and there followed a flurry of speeches by statesmen on both sides. It also led to a discussion in the House of Commons, where the Radicals questioned the government on war aims and drew particular attention to the Austro-Hungarian question and Allied commitments and declarations about the Habsburg Monarchy.

---

[89] Foreign Office survey on Austro-Hungarian war-weariness, compiled on 7 July after special request by Hankey to Balfour, *F.O.* 371/2864, f.134202.
[90] WP–37 of 9 July, *F.O.* 371/2864, No. 137019.
[91] *F.O.* 371/3081, No. 133073, f.97807 of 4 July.
[92] *G.T.* 1512 (17 July), *Cab.* 24/21.
[93] Text in Scott, *op.cit.*, p.114.

Noel Buxton opened the debate on 24 July[94] with an attack on the "apostles of the doctrine that Austria is the chief enemy". He regarded their arguments that it was an Allied duty to allot Europe to independent national status, because they were fighting for the nationalities, as sentimental and non-practical for Allied protection, because a South Slav state as a barrier against Germany was only an attractive idea without any reality. Buxton admitted that he himself had advocated a national redistribution in South East Europe, but this had depended on the belief in the ardent effects of Russia and the disaffection of the component nations in Austria and Hungary. These premises proved to be false. Buxton now realized that there was a genuine *"idée autrichienne"*, or traditional attachment to Austria, largely prevalent in the people of the Dual Empire. Furthermore, the new Russia declined to lift a finger to break Austria up and there was no evidence for America's attitude in this direction. As to the political representatives of the nationalities in the Reichsrat, Buxton could see no proof in their eloquent speeches of a conversion to independence. They rather pictured a genuine Eastern Federal State "combining nationalism with Habsburg continuity".

Buxton found "congeries of small states" like the Balkan states no attractive proposition. Such a system would have grave economic disadvantages, might even increase the opportunities of Germany and would lead to friction and greatly augment the local causes of war:

> If we rely for the making of a long period of peace on some improvement in international machinery, most of the arguments used by our fire-eating Austrophobes are knocked on the head.

Those found themselves heavily attacked by a growing Austrophile alignment, which regretted that the agitation of the emigré leaders was assisted "by a little group of professors and journalists in this country, who are 'working' the Press and public opinion". They were accused of discouraging the peace party in Austria by enabling the pro-German and the Magyar extremists to say that Britain would be content with nothing less than complete annihilation.[95]

Buxton's colleague King drew the attention of the House to their activities in connection with a Yugoslav statement addressed to the Commons, which was also signed by three War Cabinet Members, Barnes, Carson, Milner, and also by John Buchan and Seton-Watson, whom he suspected of being in a position where they had immediate and direct access to the Prime Minister without intervention of the Foreign Office. King as well as Dillon believed Buchan and Seton-Watson were members of the "Garden Party" (*sic*) in Downing Street. In

---

[94] *Hansard*, xcvi, 1173–4 (24 July).
[95] *Saturday Review*, 28 July 1917.

their opinion they had taken the opportunity of using information which they must have had through diplomatic and "special" sources.[96]

The Acting Foreign Secretary, Robert Cecil, refused to comment on Buchan and Seton-Watson but repudiated the responsibility of the named War Cabinet members for the mentioned leaflet of the Serbian Society. Referring to Noel Buxton's request to broach war aims he found himself in agreement that "Austria is not our chief enemy", which for him was no more than a mere platitude. But Cecil was not willing to discuss how far the government accepted the doctrine of the Yugoslav movement. He considered it dangerous to go further than the position occupied when the government made their reply to President Wilson, but his stress on the wording of the liberation passage was of moderate significance:

> We did not go any further than that. We did not pledge ourselves to the particular form of liberation which we should advocate at the Peace Conference.

As a second principle Cecil added that the government wanted a stable settlement, secured by a "sound and satisfactory peace resting on some natural principle *as far as may be*", which would guarantee that settlement.[97]

On 30 July A. J. Balfour was equally reluctant to go into details, thereby anticipating what he considered the work of a final Peace Congress. The government could not venture to commit itself, because it depended upon allies and did not know how the balance of forces would go. He therefore thought it was a folly for a Foreign Minister to be definite in dealing with events still distant, as for instance the problem of joining Serbia with Croatia or separating parts of Bohemia and parts of the Slovak country from Hungary. How one was going to deal with "such a great and ancient monarchy as Austria, how Austria and Germany are going to deal with their internal problems *which they must settle*", nobdy could discuss in the Commons and Balfour was only prepared to hint that the peace he desired would involve a certain rearrangement, "such a modification of the political forces in Europe that there will not be a balance of power in precisely the old eighteenth century sense of the word".

> What we desire, I believe, on every side of the House is that the nationalities composing that heterogeneous state should be allowed to develop on their own lines to carry out their civilization and determine the course of which their development should take place.[98]

---

[96] *Hansard, loc.cit.*, 1181 and 1189.
[97] *Ibid.*, 1898–99.
[98] *Ibid.*, 1847–51.

This was a broad principle and left plenty of room for manoeuvre. Not surprisingly both Cecil's and Balfour's speeches were received favourably by the Austrian press, where they evoked a considerable echo. Semi-official papers like the *Neue Freie Presse* and the *Pester Lloyd* pointed out the eventual *arrière pensée* to drive a wedge between Germany and Austria. But if Cecil wanted to hint in a delicate, diplomatic manner that the road to an understanding with Germany led through Austria–Hungary, then it could be safely confirmed that Austria–Hungary would "not adopt an attitude of hostility towards such an intention, but would consider in accord with Germany the advisability of stepping on the bridge which England might erect for the purpose of a possible peace by agreement".[99]

The *Reichspost* treated Balfour's speech as deliberately vague and as proving his desire to say neither too much nor too little. It praised his remarks on Austria–Hungary as containing nothing insulting, "nothing even which we ourselves do not want".[100]

On the other hand the Czech press showed itself alarmed and the Croat *Radic* explicitly protested against Noel Buxton's statement in the Commons. On the other hand, Buxton noted with satisfaction that the utterances of Balfour and Cecil had an extremely conciliatory effect in Austria. Quoting a favourable comment from the *Fremdenblatt* he presumed that the government desired to produce just this spirit. He therefore urged the government to refuse to take up the support of those who suggested policies of an extreme character and had "not proved good guides". Their advice had been in favour of policies "which have led to disaster".[101]

Balfour, however, declined to be made a party to these "friendly controversies" between Buxton and Seton-Watson and their respective followers. He expressed his appreciation for the expert knowledge of either side, but like other experts they differed profoundly among themselves and were looking for aid for pressing their views. Balfour then denied that his July speech was intended as a declaration of policy regarding Austria, but he had only intended to be evasive. He wanted to be judged by what he had said, and not by what the Austrian press interpreted. He regarded the newspaper reports about a development in the direction of autonomy as a hopeful sign and welcomed everything increasing local autonomy and "sound" liberty. But for Balfour it was perfect insanity to discuss openly what the government would do, if these changes really took place. He did not know whether these forecasts were true. They could be an expedient of enemy politicians in difficulties.

---

[99] *F.O.* 371/2863, No. 154252 of 31 July (press review of Seton-Watson).
[100] *Ibid.*, 11 Aug. and *G.T.* 1768 (18 Aug.), *Cab.* 24/23.
[101] *Hansard*, 20 Oct., 1389–1398.

Moreover, Serbia, Greece and Rumania were Britain's allies, who were undergoing great sacrifices and to whom the government was bound "by every tie of loyalty".[102] Under these circumstances any idea of an "open" diplomacy was impossible for the British government. However pressed by pro- and anti-Habsburg circles, its attitude remained to avoid public commitments on the future of the Habsburg Monarchy, which was regarded as the best way of keeping open the door for either development.

The pleadings of the pressure groups could be dealt with more frankly in secrecy inside Whitehall. Here Noel Buxton's pamphlet "The Entente and the Allies of Germany" was most carefully considered and L. S. Amery made it the starting-point of his analysis of the chances for a separate peace.[103] Amery was extremely sceptical because of the practical and political difficulties involved. He took into account many factors which the *New Europe* used in its campaign against the Austrophiles. Amery saw the main problem in the inextricably intermingled armies of Germany and Austria and was deeply impressed by the cohesive block of the Central Powers:

> A provincial government in Birmingham would find it almost as easy a task to disentangle the Midlands from the war, as Austria would find it to carry a separate peace into effect.

Apart from the purely military aspect there were permanent motives of racial sympathy and political interest. Amery was convinced that the Austro-Germans would refuse to follow a government that had concluded a separate peace and would initiate a civil war. The Hungarians, too, were expected to refuse to give up their domination until Allied forces reached Budapest. For these governing races the maintenance of the Central Alliance was more promising in many respects, especially from an economic point. But even if they showed a willingness to come to terms with the Allies, Amery was not sure whether a satisfactory settlement could be achieved. He did not discard the demands of the nationalities as easily as his mentor Milner and did not trust the prospect of a federal Austria as sketched out by Buxton, for the internal reconstruction could always be promised and not carried out afterwards. The terms on which Austria could be detached would not satisfy the minor Allies either. The Allies would lose the service of the Serbian, Rumanian and the Italian armies, who would regard themselves as betrayed. On the other hand there was no reason to believe that the Austrians would adopt towards their old Allies an attitude of

---

[102] *Ibid.*, 1399–1904.
[103] *F.O.* 371/3083, No. 138699/f.147980. Buxton's peace terms were forwarded on 12 July 1917 (published in the *Contemporary Review*, Jan. 1918), Amery's paper (*G.T.* 1482) is dated 27 July.

neutrality less favourable than that of the United States at the beginning of the war.

Amery was almost at one with Steed when he stated that the idea of securing a separate peace was "inherently absurd", because it ignored "the essential interest and principles which have led to two Alliances". But for Amery this did not mean that a separate peace was absolutely impossible. It might be attained by a concentration of military force. For Amery, and here he was to agree with Lloyd George, the question of a separate or general peace was "at bottom one of strategy". Hitherto all Allied endeavours were directed against Germany in the hope that her collapse would involve the collapse of her allies. But if the Entente failed at the Western front, the Western Allies could not hope to get more out of a general peace than Germany was forced to concede as a result of exhaustion. If they did not find this prospect encouraging enough, they had to modify their strategy at the risk of leaving Central Europe intact. The war situation had to be changed to the disadvantage of Austria in order to compel her to agree to a settlement which was not only acceptable to Britain but also the Entente as a whole. Amery came to realize this in his conclusion:

> To imagine that we can buy off Germany's allies without beating them on terms which would break our own alliance is a dangerous illusion.

It remained another question whether the political and military leadership of the Entente was both materially equipped and mentally disposed to adjust the strategy of the Allies in a way that could bear results which were needed to facilitate a *rapprochement* with Austria.

CHAPTER IV

Strategy and Diplomacy

1. The Debate for a South Eastern Offensive

The new Lloyd George government was faced with the duty of reviewing the military position: The situation at the turn of 1916/17 was not very bright after the Allied forces had suffered a series of set-backs. The most depressing debacle for them was the Rumanian reverse, which had entirely altered the Balkan position. Instead of contributing to a decisive Allied breakthrough, Rumania's entry into the war had ended in a complete defeat of her army with the ensuing occupation of the major part of the country. Thus the Central Powers had strengthened their position, while Russia suddenly found herself isolated and exposed to a now much extended line of front.

Rumania was no longer a menace to an Austrian flank needing cover and protection and as a result the prospect of effectively attacking the Central Powers from the South East seemed ruined. If there had been a well-prepared action with the Allies attacking simultaneously at several fronts, it would have endangered seriously the situation for the Habsburg Monarchy. Austria, menaced on three flanks, could have collapsed or at least the Germans would have been forced to support a crumbling Austria by withdrawing troops from the Western front. Now the vulnerability of Austria–Hungary was much reduced. With Russia's power continuously fading, she was only left with one serious enemy: Italy. But the repeated Italian offensives on the Isonzo river had been without any penetrating success. Militarily neither Italy nor Rumania had lived up to Allied expectations. The diplomatic ring closed around the Dual Monarchy by Entente diplomacy had been broken on the battlefield.

To examine the grave problems arising from the Rumanian collapse an inter-Allied conference was summoned at the wish of the British government. It took place in Rome from 5 to 7 January. At this conference Lloyd George had a memorandum circulated, in which he raised issues of strategy and made proposals as to how to deal with them.[1]

The Prime Minister aimed at a fundamental reconstruction of Allied strategy. His most striking idea was that of a combined attack on the Italian front. Lloyd George assumed that the enemy would concentrate his manoeuvre forces against this front, and, as a first alternative, asked the Allies to make the necessary arrangements. He proposed to move heavy artillery to Italy so that the Austro-German forces would find themselves confronted with a vastly superior armament of Italian guns reinforced by British and hopefully also French artillery. By adopting this plan Lloyd George hoped to convert a repulse into a rout of the Central Powers. However, Lloyd George did not want to see the provisions limited to a defensive scheme. He wanted to ask the generals whether they could not devise plans for a surprise offensive on the Isonzo front, so as to "shatter the enemy's forces, to inflict a decisive defeat on him, and to press forward to Trieste and get astride the Istrian Peninsula".[2]

There was no doubt of the advantage of such an action, if carried out successfully. But the big question was: Could the Central Powers be routed by the Allies on the Italian front? Lloyd George was convinced of the unexploited potential in the Italian army. He believed that, with so far unused resources of infantry, the Italians could launch an offensive on a great scale and achieve a complete victory, provided that they were given heavy artillery and ammunition. But above all, on the Italian front the Allies had to deal with an enemy who was weaker than elsewhere on the Western front. The Austrians did not have the same cohesion as the Germans and were less redoubtable as a fighting unit. "Germany", he pointed out, "is formidable so long as she can command an unbroken Austria, but if Austria is beaten, Germany will be beaten too". For these reasons he strongly advocated that the question of crushing Austria should be examined.[3] Since the Austrians were the weakest among the enemies, Lloyd George suggested striking at the Italian front, which might "enable the Allies to capture Trieste, which would bring important political advantages".[4]

Such an advantageous political outcome could have been a separate peace with Austria–Hungary. In fact Lloyd George had been forwarded information from secret agents in Spain reporting that "the Austrians themselves are full of astonishment at the Allies not undertaking a proper offensive against them, as Austria's collapse would then be inevitable", and the same source of the British Intelligence Bureau

---

[1] Lloyd George, *War Memoirs*, ii, p.838ff.
[2] *Ibid.*, p.24.
[3] I.C. 15b, *Cab.* 28/2.
[4] Pt. 3 in the resolution of Lloyd George's memorandum, *loc.cit.*

learnt that there was in Austria "great depression and eagerness for peace, even in the highest military circles".[5]

This information was nevertheless vague and outdated. There is no evidence that Lloyd George took a particular interest in the Habsburg Monarchy before or at the Rome Conference. His knowledge of the Dual Empire was superficial, although he had a rough idea of its racial composition. He claims to have heard of the desertion of "unreliables" during the Brussilov offensive in 1916, which had shown the war-weariness of the subject nationalities, when some divisions surrendered without fighting:

> The heart of the Slavs and Roumans who constituted the majority of the Austrian conscripts was not in the struggle. . . . would the unwilling soldiers of the "ramshackle empire" follow the example of the Germans, French and British on the Western Front and lie for hours and days in muddy shell holes to defend their battered defences? I felt confident they would not. Their devotion to the Austrian Empire was not equal to that display of sustained heroism.[6]

Lloyd George conceded that the Slavonic regiments preferred fighting Italians to Russians, but he thought they were not concerned in the quarrel with either. However, Allied diplomacy had given them reason for concern. The Austrian authorities could exploit their inborn hatred of the Italians by referring to the Italian aspirations along the Adriatic coast. Most Croats, Serbs, and Slovenes preferred living within the Monarchy to being occupied by the Italians. As long as the Allies had no better alternative to offer, the South Slavs were likely to continue their stubborn resistance already demonstrated in the previous battles. Indeed, the frequent desertions of the Czechs on the Eastern front were never matched by the South Slavs. This did not mean that they were satisfied with the existing conditions. They were eager to free themselves from Magyar domination, but so far their dissatisfaction had not come out openly. It existed under the surface and could well turn into a revolutionary demand for peace and freedom.

So far Lloyd George had neither considered the demands of the nationalities' movements, nor had he heard of the desire for peace of the new Emperor. These factors can be assumed to have preoccupied his mind in a very general way – and later in 1917 they were to increase his obsession with the above scheme – but it must be stated very clearly that the original idea of an offensive on the Italian front was unrelated to the hope for an immediate separate peace with Austria–Hungary as well as afterthoughts of a decomposition of the Habsburg Empire in the

---

[5] Reports by Lord Derby of 21 Dec. 1914 and Murray of Elibank of 7 Jan. 1915, copies in Lloyd George paper, C/25/8/1 + 2.

[6] *War Memoirs*, i, pp.826 and 828.

event of a complete crushing of its army. In the main, Lloyd George's scheme was a military and not a political one. He was occupied with finding a way to defeat Germany. Since it seemed unlikely to him that the Allies could make a quick progress at the Western front, he was looking for another way.

His attention was drawn to the Italian front by the British liaison officer Delmé-Radcliffe, who was also in close contact with leading Italian politicians. One of them was Leonida Bissolati, a Socialist member of the Italian government, who on his own initiative said that he felt strongly that the Entente ought to make a great combined effort from the Italian front against Austria.[7]

Bissolati had discussed an eventual Allied action with General Cadorna, the Italian chief of staff, whom he had found entirely in favour of the idea and who wanted to convince Sonnino.[8] Under such auspices the chances for the Lloyd George scheme seemed promising. But at the Rome Conference the British Prime Minister stood almost alone. He had expected Briand and Thomas to be advocates of the "way round", but the French ministers showed themselves disinclined to believe in the success of the proposed operation and did not want to upset the plans worked out by the British and French general staffs for a Western spring offensive. On the other hand Sonnino was inclined to examine the problem on the basis that the Italian forces were supported with weapons and troops. Being no expert on military affairs the Italian Foreign Minister called on Cadorna to express his view. Surprisingly Cadorna displayed a lack of enthusiasm for the project, which baffled even Sonnino. Cadorna doubted that he would be left in possession of the promised material long enough to carry out a sustained offensive. He had gained this impression from conversations with Robertson and his French pendant Lyautey and therefore showed no desire to make himself the spokesman of an Allied change of strategy. He merely stated that he would consider the question. So the Lloyd George scheme was quietly buried and point seven of the conference minutes recorded that it was referred "to the military advisers of the various Governments".[9]

The failure of Lloyd George's idea is understandable. The Prime Minister had come to Rome with a plan that had not been examined in detail and was therefore regarded by the others as a hazardous enterprise. The political background also seemed far from explored. The information about the Dual Monarchy was still scanty and Austria was just beginning to play a prominent part in the deliberations of the

---

[7] Delmé-Radcliffe to Lloyd George, 15 Dec. 1916, Lloyd George papers F/56/1/1.
[8] *Ibid.*, F/56/1/3 of 25 Dec. 1916. Cadorna's talk with Sonnino, whose interest in the partition of Asia Minor is already reported, was postponed.
[9] *War Memoirs*, i, pp.851–57, *Lord Riddell's War Diary*, p.267; Hankey, M., *The Supreme Command*, ii, p.607f.

Allies. This is best shown by the handling of the relevant passage in the answer to President Wilson, which was formulated in its final version at the same conference. But this political move against the Habsburg Monarchy was not correlated to any strategic discussions or vice versa. Lloyd George therefore should not have expected to make a deep impression on the Allied politicians without being able to outline the eventual political consequences in detail. As long as there was no substantial evidence on the diplomatic front,[10] his scheme was easily turned down. If the Prime Minister had intended to overrule his own generals by an inter-Allied political directive, he had failed to convince the other Allies. In January 1917 his scheme was presented precipitately and had no more effect that raising the idea of an alternative to Allied strategy.

But soon after the Rome Conference the impact on the Italians proved greater than expected. General Cadorna, who had been asked by Lloyd George to examine the possibility of an offensive on the Carso front, drafted a memorandum which was circulated in Whitehall on 30 January.[11] He suddenly recommended an offensive beginning on 15 March, the object being to obtain possession of the Italian Alps and thrust towards Austria. This would involve the British helping materially with artillery.

Behind this change of mind was the anxiety to see the Italian war aims secured. This was also expressed by the Italian King, who favoured an offensive, because then the whole edifice of the central empire would be undermined.[12] In conversations with the Italian ambassador Imperiali Lloyd George repeatedly attached a special importance to the operations on the Italian front, observing that

> if Austria, in a given moment, accidentally sees herself forced to make peace, it is evident that she is far more easily inclined to cede territories already taken by us, while she would be very much against abandoning the territories permanently in her hands.[13]

Meanwhile the assumption that a diplomatic deal with the Austrians was in the offing had been confirmed by the first Austrian feeler, the Mensdorff-journey to Scandinavia (discussed in a former chapter). Some general information about this incident was also given to the Italians.[14] But in Rome the idea of a separate peace was anything but favoured, because it would have involved a compromise, for which Italy had not entered the war and which nobody dared to conclude. The Italian politicians who supported an offensive on the Carso river

---

[10] The French delegates at Rome had no knowledge of the Sixtus call.
[11] *Cab*. 23/1 and 24/.
[12] Letter from R. Rodd to Lloyd George, 12 Jan., Lloyd George papers, F/56/117.
[13] Report by Imperiali of 22 Jan., cit. in L. Valiani, p.267.
[14] *F.O.* 371/3086.

were not pro-Austrian. When Bissolati came to England and participated in a War Cabinet meeting on 1 March[15] he had not only urged an Allied offensive but also spoke of the necessity of resurrecting the Slav nationalities of the Habsburg Monarchy. Bissolati, who had been told about Austrophile tendencies in Great Britain by Wickham Steed, was assured by Lloyd George that there did not exist a favourable stream of opinion for the preservation of Austria.[16]

In reality this opinion was just winning over the Cabinet and even Robertson admitted the advantage of a separate peace if it came off.[17] But in view of the Nivelle scheme and French feelings in general, he regarded it as impossible to aid Cadorna. However, the C.I.G.S., when previewing the development of 1917, thought that it was probable that (if Allied operations on the Western front were only moderately successful) the remainder of the German troops would be thrown against Italy in order to achieve a spectacular coup.[18] This danger was already imminent in 1916, but then Falkenhayn did not consent to Conrad's plans.[19] Now that the Central Powers had opened up new resources in the South East and Russia was on the brink of collapse, they might try to deal the next blow to Italy.

By mid-March the Italians were getting nervous about a possible Austro-German attack. Cadorna appealed to the British and French to allocate 20 divisions to help him if necessary, because he feared that the Germans might soon be in a position to set free troops from the East. If a combined force of 90 German and Austrian divisions was concentrated on the Italian front, Cadorna doubted whether the Anglo-French offensive in the West would be a sufficient relief. The Cabinet agreed with the Allied staffs in principle that a contingent should be provided for, but was reluctant to approve of the dispatch of such a numerous force. As a result Lloyd George received a pressing letter from Ambassador Rodd[20] describing Sonnino's regrets that Lloyd George's proposals at the Rome Conference had not been carried out. The War Cabinet shared the Italian fears and let its apprehensions be known to Robertson, who was already on his way to Italy to enquire into the matter. When he returned from the Italian headquarters, the C.I.G.S. presented a report to the Cabinet[21] stating that the Italians were in a fearful funk of a German invasion and were concentrating

[15] *Cab.* 23/2.
[16] Recorded in O. Malagodi, *Conversazioni della guerra, 1914–1919*, ed. B. Vigezzi, Milan 1960, i, pp.111 and 142 (cit. in Valiani, p.266).
[17] Memorandum on "Germany's Intentions", 24 Feb., Cab. 24/6.
[18] *WC* 37a, Cab. 23/13.
[19] G. Craig, "The World War I Alliance of the Central Powers in Retrospect", *Journal of Central European Affairs*, xxxvii (1965).
[20] *WC* 98–102, Mar. 16–22, *Cab.* 23/2. Rodd's letter of 18 Mar. read out in *WC* 102. Cf. also *War Memoirs*, ii, pp.1373–75.
[21] Circulated on 28 Mar.

entirely on the defensive. Robertson thought that their Army Commanders were "too old and inactive" to carry out a successful offensive. He was of the opinion that the Italians had all the infantry they needed and since the French military authorities were even more opposed to sending troops to Italy, the request was turned down. (The British merely sent ten batteries of howitzers and personnel.) In April it was too late to reverse the decision for a Western offensive. Moreover, a sudden change of strategy would have hit the pride of the French and British generals, who preferred to operate in the "main theatre", which was under their personal control.

The Italians had their revenge at the conference of St. Jean-de-Maurienne (19 April), where they turned down any consideration of a separate peace with Austria–Hungary. It is true that they were basically against this device, because they were afraid to be at the losing end. But if the ground had been prepared by an overwhelming military success, their response might have been different, because then they could have counted on getting the most important of their *desiderata* implemented. That even the official Italian circles did not altogether exclude such a solution can be seen from a letter by Bissolati, who in late May regretted that Trieste had not been threatened at an earlier stage of the war.

> In face of this menace the Hungarian crisis would have been hastened and a separate peace with Austria (which today is only a manoeuvre on the part of Germany to divert the Allies) would have been on the road of realization.[22]

Lloyd George was further encouraged by his personal interview with Prince Sixtus and the receipt of the second letter of the Austrian Emperor. After the failure of the Nivelle offensive and the possible defection ahead, the Prime Minister feared that Germany would become superior to the Allies in guns and men, "especially when Austria remained her ally". On 9 May, when the War Cabinet had a discussion of the possible consequences of Russia leaving the war, Lloyd George offered his panacea:

> In such circumstances the best chance for the Allies would appear to lie in a separate peace with Austria, in which Italy might have to be compelled to acquiesce. If we failed to induce Austria to make a separate peace, he could see no hope of the sort of victory in the war that we desired.[23]

At the meeting it was generally agreed that Allied diplomacy be used to assist, if possible, the military situation and that if Russia should leave

---

[22] Bissolati to Lloyd George, 28 May, Lloyd George papers, F/55/4/2.
[23] *WC* 135a, *Cab.* 23/13.

the war, every possible effort should be made to secure compensations by a separate peace with Austria. It was pointed out, however, that the Central Powers considered that the withdrawal of Russia rendered victory to them probable and it would be difficult to secure a separate peace, unless their exhaustion and general desire for peace outweighed their hopes for victory. Among the Cabinet members who were far more pessimistic than Lloyd George was Lord Curzon. He could not discover any sufficient reason why Austria–Hungary, or Turkey or Bulgaria, should sever themselves

> from an Alliance which has already proved to be successful in so far as its main objects in Eastern and Central Europe are concerned, and from which they are more likely to derive advantage in the future, even at the expense of German domination than from anything which we are at present in a position to offer.[24]

The danger that Austria and Italy could come to an understanding over the heads of their respective allies was judged unlikely by Curzon. Italy could not make peace without substantial concessions from Austria. Austria (all the more if she be freed from anxieties for her Eastern frontiers by the inaction or withdrawal of Russia) was in a position to refuse, and would not be allowed by Germany, to make them. Curzon admitted that Italy might not be "a very comfortable or helpful bedfellow in the Entente" but she might also be a rather disagreeable and dangerous factor if she went out. Anyhow, for the present it seemed to be necessary for Italy to continue fighting, unless coal difficulty or internal troubles brought her to a standstill. In the meantime her strategic value for the Entente could not be denied. She held 750,000 Austrian troops, a certain proportion of whom would be otherwise on the Western front.

In view of the Russian developments Curzon regarded Germany's allies as a *quantité négligeable*. Since they were near the brink of exhaustion, Germany would only get moderate support from them, as soon as Russia disappeared. In this point Curzon followed the interpretation of the C.I.G.S., who believed that Austria might regard the elimination of her principal enemy (Russia)

> as a means of securing relief from the necessity of further efforts and sacrifices rather than affording an opportunity to concentrate her forces for an attack on Italy – the success of which would be doubtful.[25]

The seriousness of the Russian situation also occupied Lord Milner and his friend L. S. Amery. Milner had firmly supported Lloyd George at

---

[24] Memorandum of 14 May, *G.T.* 703, discussed *WC* 137, *Cab*. 23/2.
[25] *Ibid.*

the Rome Conference. He was then of the opinion that it was the Allies' turn to disturb the enemy by taking the initiative. They should try to surprise him by undertaking a great and successful operation.[26]

At about the same time Amery analysed possible operations for 1917.[27] He thought that an offensive on the Western front was not likely "to have any decisive effect on the political situation with a view to the terms of peace", because the success would be different in nature from the German one in Rumania (where a large territory with foodstuff supply had been captured). While the Western front should continue to occupy the main effort of the Allies, Amery thought that they could now afford to consider the employment of troops in other operations, which might promise "decisive strategical results of a qualitative character", i.e. the collapse of one of Germany's allies, or the occupation of territory, valuable from strategic, economic or political point of view. With regard to the Italian front Amery saw the difficulty of working on a restricted area and the nature of the ground. But an advance which would secure Trieste and Pola (with its effect on the naval situation in the Adriatic) seemed very useful to him. But in the main his advice was to regard the Italian offensive as a "holding attack", for he expected better results from a campaign against Turkey. In a letter to Milner, Amery suggested the constitution of a small body directly responsible for correlating and crossexamining the material provided by experts. This should lead to the production of effective plans to be presented to the War Cabinet.[28] Milner took up the idea in his memorandum of 7 June which urged the need of a "fresh stocktaking" of the whole war situation. Among other things he proposed that four or five people should concentrate their minds upon the military and political situation in the "Balkans as a whole".[29]

Milner's memorandum was discussed at a Cabinet meeting on 8 June.[30] When the meeting began, General Henry Wilson was asked to provide information on the French army. He had grave doubts as to whether it would be possible to hold the French army together for another winter without some real success, "whether military or diplomatic". Lloyd George, however, believed in both a military and a diplomatic success. He thought that a peace with Bulgaria was not difficult, if only the Serbs would carry out their threat "to walk into the Austrian camp". Personally he would not regard this as a misfortune if it resulted in Austria's dependence on Slav races, instead of on Germans, but he believed he stood alone in this view. So the Prime Minister adverted to the question of a separate peace with Austria which he had

[26] *War Memoirs*, i, p.855.
[27] Notes dated Jan. 1917, *Cab.* 21/88.
[28] Amery to Milner, 1 June, *ibid.*
[29] *WC* 159a, *Cab.* 23/16.
[30] *Ibid.* and app. to *WC* 159a.

no doubt of securing on terms sought by the Entente pow ~rs. The difficulty was that Sonnino had baulked at discussing the possibility of a separate peace, owing to the fact that he was himself, for political reasons, not in a position to make peace on the Austrian terms. The latter included (according to the information which Prince Sixtus had passed on to Lloyd George and which the Prime Minister took for granted as being official): the secession of the Trentino (but not of Trieste, nor Gorizia, nor Dalmatia) in return for the cession by Italy or the Allies of Erythrea or some colony, and the independence of Serbia was also provided for.

Under the impression that a compromise between Italy and Austria could be reached it was generally agreed that the Austrian approach ought to be pursued. The opportunity ought not to be let slip, although great caution was thought necessary. The British were wary of being drawn into "a trap designed to secure the release of two million Austrian prisoners with a view to a subsequent resumption of hostilities". The Cabinet was also mindful of the risk

> that the conclusion of a separate peace with Austria might produce an atmosphere in which the crushing of Germany might become difficult . . . (but) was of the opinion that, if properly handled, these negotiations might result in the isolation of Germany and a general peace on the terms sought by the Entente Powers.

Because of the absence of the C.I.G.S. the military aspect of the problem was not discussed at this Cabinet meeting. It was, however, decided to set up a Cabinet Committee on War Policy with Lloyd George, Curzon, Milner, and Smuts as members. Their discussions mainly concerned the important question whether the forthcoming offensive should be conducted in Flanders or in Italy with a view to striking a blow against Austria, designed to compel that country to make a separate peace, because it was now believed more than ever before that some of the Italian *desiderata* should be achieved by military efforts, before the diplomatic channel could be re-opened successfully.

Lloyd George's ideas on the subject had gradually matured since the Rome Conference and he had now worked out the project in some detail. In his memorandum of 16 June[31] the Prime Minister bitterly complained that the fundamental error of Allied strategy had been the refusal to recognize the European battlefield as one unit. A corollary to this allegedly mistaken attitude had been the repeated attempt of the Allies to overcome the enemy by attacking him with the strongest armies on the strongest front. This had led to the neglect of the Balkan area, which was lost to the Central Powers in 1916. But Lloyd George

---

[31] Printed in *War Memoirs*, ii, pp.1283–87 ("Alternatives"). (The date of the document can be ascertained from a copy in the Milner papers, box 125.)

saw a second opportunity for the Allies to be successful in a secondary "theatre" of the war, and he warned of letting it slip away again. Austria and Turkey, namely, were still the weakest fronts and "if either Turkey or Austria were overthrown it could be the beginning of the disintegration and consequent destruction of the Central Powers. If Austria were defeated it would lead to a separate peace with that Empire". In the wake of an Austrian collapse Turkey and Bulgaria, then isolated from Germany, would probably crumble too. So the Allies could concentrate on Germany and the breaking of her power would only be a matter of a few months. Lloyd George saw this aim facilitated by assuming that, after a separate peace with Austria, Germany had to station a portion of her troops on the Austro-German border. That is to say he expected the Germans to respect the sovereignty of Austria–Hungary instead of forcing her to remain in the Central Alliance by leaving or increasing the German troops in Austria, which in the extreme case could result in a German occupation of Austria.

Disregarding such an eventuality Lloyd George examined the crucial military question more hopefully. Was it feasible to bring about the defeat of the Austrian army during the coming autumn? He firmly believed that it was within the compass of Allied resources to inflict a heavy and possibly even decisive blow upon Austria in 1917, because her position was an exceptionally weak one. The Austrians suffered from desertions of their Slav soldiers and their economic and financial situation was an extremely grave one. As to man-power the reports indicated that there were no reserves behind the Austrian lines. The Italian army at this stage of the war still had ample men and reserves; its combatant strength was estimated at about 1,770,000 men against Austria's 571,000 on that front.[32] Italy was also supposed to have a higher number of reserves, especially if one considered that the Austrians had to supply drafts for an army of nearly half a million on the Russian front. The morale of the Italian soldiers was reported to be good. All accounts seemed to agree that their failure to achieve greater successes was due to the lack of sufficient heavy artillery and ammunition. In these circumstances it seemed reasonable to Lloyd George and those of his colleagues who supported the plan to advance sufficiently to secure the capture of Trieste. Provided British (and French) artillery – which also were believed to be superior to the Italian and Austrian weapons – was made available to the Italians, an advance on Trieste, which was only eight miles from their lines, could bring great results. There was, however, the possibility of the Germans coming to the support of the Austrians. Lloyd George therefore proposed to send

---

[32] These figures and the following evidence on the military potential are derived from M. Hankey, *The Supreme Command*, ii, pp.675–76.

supplies to Italy in clever secret ways, so that it would take the Germans a few weeks to bring troops to the Isonzo. Moreover, if the Germans moved away troops from the Western front, that would provide a good opportunity to attack their lines in France. But the greater share of the heavy fighting would be left to the Italians on their front. Thereby one could also hope to overcome the exhaustion of the French army. A successful Italian operation carried out with British material help would be enthusiastically welcomed by the Italian public and Lloyd George rated it so high that he painted the picture of an eternal alliance of the two Mediterranean powers as the result of their military co-operation against Italy's arch-fiend. While this was no more than a dream of the future, a substantial and hardly less spectacular gain could become a reality. Lloyd George was convinced that in the event of a great military defeat Austria would make a separate peace:

> The repeated and urgent advances made by Austria during the present year, many of them emanating directly from authoritative quarters, prove that those who have the direction of affairs in Austria are nervous and alarmed as to the prospect. All the information received points in one direction – that Austria is on the point of collapse, and that it needs but powerful and vigorous pressure to precipitate her downfall.[33]

From an allied point of view a military success was necessary as a preliminary for peace negotiations because "no peace could be possible without satisfying the legitimate claims of Italy", for no Italian statesmen dared to make peace without securing both the Trentino and Trieste. But once Italian pride was assuaged by the success of their armies and Austrian morale correspondingly shaken, peace negotiations might be undertaken with greater chances of success. Lloyd George, encouraged by his interview with Prince Sixtus, continued to understand that Austria would now be prepared to surrender the Trentino and the Prime Minister believed that only Trieste stood in the way of a compromise. This commercial town was linked up with so much tradition and prestige that the Austrians were not expected to give it up, unless it was actually conquered.

Lloyd George summoned his leading generals to consider his alternative to the Flanders offensive as planned by them. Robertson appears to have been briefly attracted by the scheme. On 9 June he pointed out to Haig what difficulties could arise for Britain, if the costly attacks had to be undertaken without the full co-operation of the French.

On the other hand it was possible that Austria would make peace if harrassed enough. Would it not be a good plan, therefore, to support Italy with guns?[34]

Haig did not agree. In a memorandum reviewing the strategic situation "with special reference to the comparable advantages of an offensive in Northern Belgium as against an offensive from Italy against Austria",[35] he manifestly expressed his belief in destroying the enemy's strongest forces first. Only the next best course was to hold his main forces and attack his weaker ones. Haig found the arguments against the Italian scheme "overwhelmingly stronger than those in favour of it". The Field Marshal was not certain that, after large detachments to Italy, the Allies could still hold the Germans on the Western front. But above all, it was "at best very uncertain" that the Allies could defeat Austria, as it was in Germany's interest to uphold Austria just as it was in the interests of the Allies' to overcome her. To him the geographical advantages seemed very much in favour of Austria. Finally, the main part of the forces employed in an Allied attack would be Italian, and Haig had little confidence in their fighting strength. By 20 June Robertson had come round to Haig's point of view. He was now personally sceptical of Austria making a separate peace, "as her whole future depends upon her relations with Germany to whose wheels she is tied in a variety of ways".[36] Assuming nevertheless that she would make a separate peace, if fairly heavily punished, Robertson shared Haig's doubts about the outcome of an offensive from a strategical point of view. He also thought that Germany could always beat the Allies in concentrating superior forces in Italy, especially because after the March revolution in Russia the number of divisions at her disposal had increased.

Faced with the determined opposition of Haig and Robertson to his plan, Lloyd George considered it too great a responsibility for the War Policy Committee to take the strategy out of the hands of the military advisers, but he asked them again on 21 June to consider his misgivings.[37] His alternative, which was in the first place military, and in the second diplomatic, would cut "the umbilical cord of the Central Alliance" and set free whole forces for the Western front. Moreover, Italy would then be bound to support the Allies, for he did not contemplate cooperation with Italy without a bargain that, if Austria was reduced to terms, Italy would support them in their attacks against Germany. It was his belief that Trieste was the only thing that stood between Italy and a separate peace with Austria. If Trieste was cap-

---

[34] *Private Papers of Douglas Haig*, ed. R. Blake, London 1952, p.236.
[35] *War Memoirs*, ii, pp.1464–66.
[36] *Ibid.*, p.1461.
[37] Minutes of the 16th meeting of the War Policy Committee G179, Par. 86–87; *Cab.* 27/7.
[38] *Cab.* 21/88.

tured, Austria would have to appeal to a population that was "half Slav" to recapture it and they would refuse to do it. In view of the negative development in Russia Lloyd George thought it absolutely vital to force out Austria, which for him was "the vital necessity of the hour . . . in order to give Sir Douglas Haig a chance of victory *next year*".

But in his reconsiderations of 23 June the C.I.G.S. did not follow the Prime Minister's inference that a successful attack on Trieste would assure an Allied victory in this war.[38] Robertson regarded it as "a matter of opinion" whether it was a reasonable certainty that Austria would make peace after the fall of Trieste. From a purely military point of view the Allied troops had to go "half way up to Vienna" to constitute a serious military threat. But assuming that Austria made peace he ventured to doubt whether Italy would come to France to help in fighting the Germans, notwithstanding given promises. Once she got Trieste, Robertson argued, Italy was likely to make peace herself, because she came into the war to fight Austria, not Germany. In pursuit of this argument Robertson asked whether the Allies could rely upon defeating Austria and getting her out of the war, while keeping an *active* Italy. He questioned whether it was justifiable to transfer a large number of forces to Italy and place the decision of the war "in the hands of a foreign general". The dispatch of artillery alone could not be expected to accomplish the overthrow of Austria, for which troops were needed. Robertson thus suggested that the War Cabinet kept in their minds a clear distinction between sending artillery in order to help Italy "to get better results", and aiming at the complete defeat of Austria. This modified viewpoint of Robertson's was apparently the result of consultations he had with General Foch. The latter was also against sending infantry to Italy and merely approved of helping her with artillery in an attack. In Foch's opinion the idea of "squashing" Austria was an excellent one on principle, but a difficult matter to carry out.[39]

Having before them the pros and cons of either a Western or a Southern offensive in the form of an interim report of the Cabinet Committee on War Policy, the War Cabinet discussed the instructions to be followed by the British representatives at the forthcoming inter-Allied conference in Paris.[40] At this Cabinet meeting on 20 July Haig was authorized to carry out his prepared plans for the E.E.F. If it appeared probable in the execution of these plans that the results were not commensurate with the effort made, the whole question should be re-examined in the War Cabinet with a view to the cessation of this offensive and the adoption of an alternative plan, which was a great

[39] *Ibid.*
[40] *WC* 191a, *Cab*. 23/13.

offensive against Austria, supported by British and, if the French were prepared to co-operate, by French artillery. Although preparations for such an eventuality should be made, the Lloyd George scheme was thus more or less put aside. It was left to Robertson to discuss the Austrian alternative with Cadorna and Foch "in his own way" at Paris. Robertson had obviously succeeded in convincing the Cabinet of the unreliability of the Italians and it was agreed that it was undesirable to make definite arrangements with General Cadorna at once on this question, which might induce him to postpone or at any rate diminish the offensive operations he was planning on his own. For the same reason it was agreed that the moment had not yet come to make any bargain with the Italian government as to their continued co-operation in the war in the event of such a blow being struck as would induce Austria to make a separate peace.

The long-deferred inter-Allied conference took place on 25 and 26 July and despite the decision of the War Cabinet, which had practically referred the matter to the generals, Lloyd George again tried to make his point during conversations with French ministers and Sonnino. He pointed out that if the Russians collapsed, Rumania's collapse was also inevitable and that in such circumstances it would be very difficult to exact the claims of the Eastern Allies of the Entente against Austria. This rendered it more desirable to concentrate on the claims of Italy, who was co-operating to her full extent. Lloyd George remarked that if the whole of the Russian, Rumanian, and Serbian claims against Austria were realized in their entirety, the break-up of the Austro-Hungarian Empire would be involved, but that the Italian claims could be agreed to without such a break-up. If the Allies continued in the expectation of winning Galicia, the Bukovina, the Banat, Temeshvar, Transylvania, and all the Serbian claims, they "really were failing to face the facts".[41] Concerning the Italian *desiderata*, Lloyd George was still seeking to enable the Italians to achieve them by military means on the assumption that they would thereafter continue the war. Sonnino consented and supported him in the main, but French military opinion was dead against the proposal. Foch insisted that a decisive result could only be achieved by a double attack on the one side by the Russo-Rumanian armies and on the other by Italy. The utmost that could be hoped from Lloyd George's proposal in his opinion was good moral and tactical efforts, but not a decision which changed the war situation rigorously in favour of the Allies. Thus no immediate result, as far as any operation connected with a separate peace with Austria was concerned, followed the conference.

The deadlock on the Austrian question was also felt at a Cabinet

[41] *I.C.* 24a.

meeting at the end of the month, when the War Cabinet had another important discussion on future policy in regard to Russia and was reminded of certain overtures from "a very high Austrian quarter".[42] No answer had been sent, because in Paris the British and the French had felt that the Italians were more concerned. The latter always pretended to favour a military action to "bring Austria in a frame of mind" to agree to terms, but the Italians themselves had given no indication of being prepared to discuss terms which Austria could accept.

The same divergence between strategy and diplomacy characterized the London conference on 7 and 8 August, where the matter was discussed at length by most of the War Cabinet members, Balfour, Ribot, Painlevé, Thierry, Thomas, and Sonnino, who in turn consulted the three heads of the general staff. Encouraged by Sonnino, who strongly urged support for the Italian front, Lloyd George observed that he had always thought the best policy was to try to crush Austria. The Prime Minister deplored the fact that for three years Allied diplomacy and military plans were kept apart from and independent of each other. He appealed to the Allies to consider their political action and to attach their military action to it, that is to say he wanted the strategy co-ordinated if not sub-ordinated to the diplomatic conditions. Once a policy to detach an enemy power was decided upon, the soldiers had to adapt their strategy to it.[43]

Ribot and Painlevé did not oppose him on principle but considered it impossible to change the plans for 1917. Foch was more inclined to consider a combined military and political action. From this he did not expect a complete defeat of Austria but on the other hand a partial defeat might convince her of the necessity to enter into negotiations, although this was by no means certain.

The Italians had formerly accused the French of being jealous of any military success that Italy might achieve. Such sentiments certainly contributed to the hesitant attitude of the French, but besides these emotional misgivings French caution was based on the suspicion that Cadorna could find an excuse for not launching a full scale attack, even after he had been given much artillery. How important it was to take the Italians at their word was finally demonstrated, when Cadorna's representative Albricci (who had permanently professed to welcome any support the Allies could accord) was asked at which date Italy could start an offensive. Albricci's answer that the latest season was the end of August foiled the project at least for 1917.[14]

So the diplomatic attempts to make a separate peace with Austria

---

[42] *WC* 200a, *Cab.* 23/13, 31 July 1917.
[43] *I.C.* 25, a–d.
[44] *Ibid.*

could not be assisted by a military blow. Whether such an action would have been successful is as difficult to say in retrospect as it was for the policymakers to decide at the time. But while it proved impossible for them to clear away the political difficulties on the Italian front, the simulatneous stalemate in the West kept the way open for a resumption of diplomatic contacts, if only under the previous presuppositions. This meant that instead of strategic boldness political inventiveness was needed on the part of the British Government and Foreign Office, if they wanted to influence the future development of Austria–Hungary by using her desire for peace in order to achieve the ultimate aim of an Allied victory in the West (over Germany).

2. The Aftermath of Dynastic Diplomacy

Austria's military and political situation in the middle of July 1917 was described as being most critical by various sources reaching the Foreign Office. From a neutral diplomat (probably the papal nuncio) the British legation at Berne heard on 11 July about the deep Austrian pessimism as to the Russian front and desperate efforts to secure an early peace, because Austria–Hungary had no longer any reserves. Thereupon Hindenberg had sent reserve divisions to the aid of Germany's partner and assured Arz of a forthcoming victory in the West through the submarines, and a separate peace with Russia due to her internal conditions.

These arguments, however, had not convinced the Austrians. The Viennese government was endeavouring to induce the German government to give up all idea of annexation and indemnities and to propose a general peace before September on the following terms:

1. The restoration of Belgium and Northern France, Belgium to be compensated half by the Central Powers and half by the Entente.
2. Evacuation of Rumania and Serbia.
3. Independence of Poland.

The other questions (Alsace–Lorraine, the colonies, and the Italian-speaking provinces of Austria) should be reserved for discussion.[45]

Such terms were still too vague to evoke a response from Britain, whose leaders listened with more attention when their Acting Consul General in Zürich transmitted an account of Professor Foerster's interview with the Emperor Charles, who was said to have "always felt drawn to England and believed in her mission in the world".[46]

Apart from such polite compliments to British imperial pride the Emperor had for the first time admitted the need of a complete renovation of the Habsburg Monarchy. Karl now seemed to acknowledge that

---

[45] Rumbold to *F.O.* 371/3079, N.138769, f.2075.
[46] Vice Consul Beak to Sir W. Langley, *F.O.* 271/2864, N.155578, f.149040 (13 July).

it could only be saved by radical measures along the line of democracy and federation. The ideal solution was seen in a great confederation which would serve as a counterpoise to Germany. That confederation would be constructed on the principle of the right of the peoples to decide their own fate. Historic boundaries had to fall, the South Slavs were to be united in a kingdom of their own. A similar status was in view for Rumania.

> But there were tremendous impediments and it was probably true that, failing an impulse from without, the regeneration could not be effected. Perhaps violations inflicted upon the country by the Entente might in the end be a blessing in disguise.

This sounded like an open invitation to a peace of renunciation from the side of Austria, who seemed to wait for the Allies to dictate to her a new future. In the chanceries of Paris and London the report was read with due credit for the Emperor's good intentions, but one could still not believe that he was seriously offering anything approaching the above.[47] Indeed it is very difficult to ascertain how far the report reflected the ideas of the Emperor and to what extent the pacifist Munich professor had exaggerated the imperial identification with what was surely a sweeping scheme born in his own mind. There were some hints that Karl was sympathetic to suggestions for a federal solution, but whether he was prepared to make constitutional changes against the opposition of the privileged Germans and Magyars was another matter. Karl remained an unknown factor for the British observers of the diplomatic scene, but an attractive one, since he had shown "marked inclinations towards favouring the Slavs and especially the Czechs".[48]

Behind all the positive interpretations of an eventual Austrian transformation of their Empire stood the belief that, mainly because of the economic strain, the Austrian government would be obliged to make peace at any price very soon, as a bad harvest was likely and would entail risings in the country. An Austrian desire to initiate conversations was already reported a week after this forecast, by the D.M.I., whose agents were contacted by the Austrian councillor Skrynski, who expressed Austria's anxiety to negotiate with Britain, for which purpose Mensdorff would be sent to Switzerland.[49] This sudden interest in Britain was explained by a deadlock in France, where feelers had been put out on three separate occasions at which the French had agreed in principle but no further proceedings had followed. But before any offer was seriously considered by the Foreign Office, the French 2[e]

---

[47] Minute by G. C. Clerk, *ibid.*
[48] Rumbold's telegram of 14 July, *F.O.* 371/2862, No. 146500.
[49] *F.O.* 371/2864, 17 July (No. 143081).

Bureau had established a new contact in Switzerland. It remains a mystery who took the initiative; probably it was a French noblewoman with multiple ties to Catholic royalty and aristocracy in Europe. Her son-in-law was Count Revertera, a retired Austrian diplomat, who was introduced to the French Intelligence Officer Abel Armand at Fribourg.[50]

His superior, the Minister of War Paul Painlevé, was spoken of as the most convinced supporter in the government of Austrophile policy.[51] Painlevé, after having found the feeler promising, decided not to act alone but to inform the British. He must have expected a positive reception on their part owing to the constant pressure put by Lloyd George for a military operation on the Austrian front. Painlevé himself had earlier in the year (in April) communicated the preference for such a strategic alternative by certain French generals. Then he was in no position to support them: now he came to London as a responsible Cabinet minister to take part in a conference on the same matter. For security reasons the diplomatic aspect was discussed very privately at Lindfield near Brighton on 6 August, when Lloyd George was apprised of the situation. The topic was then discussed at a dinner the following day between the Prime Minister, Balfour, Curzon, Painlevé, Albert Thomas, and Ribot.[52]

The Intelligence Section of the French General Staff had prepared a paper as a basis of a peace proposal to Austria. This argued that it would be worth paying a high price for the gains which would accrue from an Austrian withdrawal, e.g. the maintenance of her integrity or an actual increase of her power. This could be achieved by creating a federation of the states in which the Slavs formed a majority under the Habsburg dynasty. To this the non-Prussian part of the German people would be added and thus a hostile barrier erected against Prussia. For this aim the French were prepared to sacrifice most of the extravagant Italian aspirations, of which merely the Trentino ought to be recovered, whereas Trieste could become a free port. Since the draft was produced by the French negotiators three days later, it can be assumed that the British found it suitable for an offer. The British point of view on eventual negotiations with Austria had been summarized by Gregory, a Senior Clerk in the Foreign Office, on 3 August. He had analysed the situation in view of a continuation of the Sixtus mission, of which the present affair was practically an aftermath.[53]

Gregory started with a very favourable appreciation of the Austrian

---

[50] Mamatey, *op.cit.*, p.142.
[51] Memorandum by R. W. Seton-Watson, *F.O.* 371/3081, No. 133073, f.97807 (4 July).
[52] Ribot, who had previously been little inclined to the idea, was said to have fallen under the influence of banking and financial circles interested in Austrian industrial and shipping concerns.
[53] Enclosed in *F.O.* 371/3134, No. 88265, f.13977.

Emperor. He credited Karl and his wife with being entirely pro-French and pro-British and consequently strongly anti-German. Karl was supposed to be full of character and autocracy. This view seemed indicated by the recent changes which he had made alone and Gregory thought that Czernin and Berchtold were without real influence, while Karl followed the advice of the Empress to a certain extent.

To break the power of Berlin and Budapest, Karl was believed to be "politically determined on *Trialismus*" on the lines of his murdered uncle. Moreover, the Emperor "was naturally anxious in principle to make a separate peace with England and France". But at this moment there were two self-evident obstacles: Firstly the Russian Revolution had changed the Austrian outlook. They now thought the Central Powers would be victorious and supposed even Italy to be on the verge of revolution. Secondly, Austria would be expected to make a separate peace "on the basis of her own liquidation as decreed by England and France in the Italian and Rumanian agreements and the note to President Wilson". Gregory regarded the treaties as still valid and put the "liberation" note on an equal footing with them. But that did not mean that he wanted them honoured, because unless they were revised the Emperor had no incentive to make any advance to England or France or to accept theirs.

Gregory felt that the nationality question "generally might be capable of readjustment but that Trieste is vital". In other words Britain should be lenient towards the Habsburgs and not insist on a radical implementation of the aspirations of the subject nationalities. If one proceeded in this way, only Italy stood in the way of peace. She was a belligerent of some rank and her claims could not be swept aside easily. But Gregory did not rule out a drastic recasting of the situation resulting in an Italian republican revolution which could eliminate the anxiety of the Emperor and prompt him to make overtures to the Allies.

Once the political gap was bridged there remained the problem of the practical realization. Gregory held the withdrawal of German units from Austria as an essential prerequisite. This could only take place when German reserves were exhausted. The task for Germany to hold up the South Eastern flank would be increased by the quitting of Bulgaria. A separate peace with Austria's neighbour would also be an incentive to herself to follow suit. Such a snowball reaction could have confronted the Germans with a rapid crumbling of the whole Balkan theatre, making it impossible for them to control both the military and the diplomatic action of her allies.

Another incentive to Austria to combine particularly with Britain was the danger of a Socialist peace. At least in London, where the idea of a Socialist Conference met with the sternest opposition, one thought in terms of a sort of common ideological basis. Conversely, Britain was not regarded by Austria as the adversary most likely to be inclined towards peace. Vienna hoped to find more sympathy among French traditionalists than in "democratic" Britain, where progressive ideas about self-determination had found their way into statements on war and peace. The Habsburg mistrust of Britain went so far that the Emperor and his messenger Revertera toyed with the idea of a continental block against "the perfidious Albion".[54]

On 1 August the Viennese impression of an intransigent Britain was changed by what was mistaken for a British separate peace offer dating back to April, when it was forwarded to the Spanish Queen Mother. It had not been transmitted to Vienna immediately by the Spanish royal family, because they believed that Karl would not be interested before the German desire for peace was proved. For King Alfonso and his mother assumed that Britain was "in any case precisely informed that the Monarchy could not, for moral and material reasons, conclude a peace without her allies". Consequently Britain must have used the offer of a separate peace as a pretext to come into indirect contact with Germany by means of Austria–Hungary.[55] But this interpretation of the so-called British offer reflected at that time more the intentions of the Spanish Court than those of the British government. This was also recognized by Czernin, who in spite of this tried to win Berlin's support for the newly opened channel. Czernin largely shared the Spanish point of view and obviously counted on a changing British attitude during the course of eventual negotiations, but what he could not see was that he had not received a proposal by the British government. It was not revealed before 26 August that none other than Lady Walburga Paget stood behind this offer. She had tried to convince Balfour of the necessity of a separate peace with Austria, but there is no sign that she acted in accordance with the Foreign Office.[56]

Meanwhile the belief in a British desire for negotiations was soon increased by another report from a neutral country. On 9 August the Habsburg minister in the Hague cabled that his British colleague, Sir Walter Townley, had offered him an accidental meeting. Upon this news Karl promptly remarked: "One can see that England wants to talk after all. At any rate the matter ought to be protracted without being broken off until Revertera has been here".[57]

Again there was no official British intiative. The mediator was a certain Leipnik, a journalist of Hungarian origin who had offered to

---

[54] F. Engel-Janosi, *Die Friedensgespräche Gf. Nik. Reverteras mit Comte Abel Armand, 1917/1918*, Graz 1965, p.374.
[55] Tel. Fürstenberg from Madrid, 30 July 1917, H.H.St.A., Vienna, Krieg geh. XLVII/13.
[56] *Ibid.*
[57] Tel. L. Széchényi, transmitted to Czernin on 10 Aug., *ibid.*, Krieg 25/2. The addendum by Karl on the same day, *ibid.*, Cabinet of the Min.IIn.

work in the Hague for the Allies,[58] but apparently he had not given up his Habsburg loyalty. When Leipnik was told by Townley that the War Cabinet was divided over the matter, this must have instigated him to offer the wavering British more conciliatory terms. Leipnik was assisted by the Austrian minister L. Széchényi, who wanted to sound out whether peace proposals from Vienna would receive a polite hearing. He said that Czernin had complained that his previous overtures had met with so much rudeness that he was not prepared for further rebuff.[59]

Czernin himself had gone to Berlin to present the Austrian terms there personally. The same suggestions, which were said to follow instructions given by Karl, were put forward in the Hague, although somewhat "inspired" by Leipnik:

1. Complete and unconditional evacuation of Belgium and Serbia.
2. Compensation for the devastation in the occupied countries.
3 *Some* concession in Alsace–Lorraine.
4. A League of Nations to guarantee peace after the war.

The Austrian minister objected to the idea of compensation, unless the principle was accepted as a general one and also applied to Galicia and East Prussia. He also thought that Serbia had to be the Serbia before the Balkan Wars. A League of Nations was not deemed practical.[60]

These terms showed a certain concession by the Austrians but were not far-reaching enough to be taken up, as had been done with the feeler to the French General Staff. These undertakings had made more practical progress and what was decisive for Lloyd George was indicated in a telgram from Paris which briefed the British leader on the Swiss proceedings. The Prime Minister was pleased to hear that Austria was now not only anxious for peace but also willing "to pay the price of a break with Germany".[61]

Balfour, too, now believed that a great advance had been made and that Austria was "prepared to quarrel with Germany". Thereupon the Prime Minister observed that Austria wanted to come out of the war as the dominating factor instead of Germany, which the Austrians wanted "to put in fee" particularly in reference to the Poles. It was much easier for the Allies to agree to any such ambitions than to solve the conflict between Austria and their own minor allies. But Balfour was now more inclined than ever to scratch the secret treaties. It sounded to him that Italy would be content if Trieste was made a free port. As to Rumania she had proved "incompetent to the verge of a crime". Smuts had the

[58] *F.O.* 3/i/3076, No. 97879 (Townley's telegram of 14 May).
[59] *F.O.* 371/2864, No. 157121, f.134262 of 10 Aug.
[60] *Ibid.*, No. 157704 of 11 Aug.
[61] Draft minutes of a Cabinet meeting of 14 Aug. 1917, enclosed in *Cab.* 23/16 (fol. 25–6).

idea of bribing her with Bessarabia and new markets. But if Austria refused to cede Transylvania the Foreign Secretary feared that the secrecy of the talks could not be kept, because then the Rumanians would go to Germany. Asked what his policy was, the Prime Minister, who had pressed his colleagues to move swiftly, at first expressed himself in favour of getting the best terms one could for Rumania. But after Smuts had advised proceeding with the negotiations as far as possible without bringing in Rumania, Lloyd George took up immediately this tactical proposal and instructed Balfour to begin with Italy, then Serbia and if an agreement was reached, the fight on behalf of Rumania should be put up; but if it came to the point he would have no hesitation in sacrificing Rumania, who found herself at the bottom of the list of Allied obligations which the British were prepared to implement. Curzon agreed with Lloyd George that Rumania could not expect to get much. If she got back where she was and something on the Russian side she would not fare so badly in British eyes.[62]

Reverting to Austria's future Lloyd George emphasized that the Habsburgs wanted economic support. He concluded that they were hopelessly bankrupt, for they did not reveal the figures of their budget. Economically the Austrians were getting more and more in the grip of Germany, but they would rather owe money to the British.

The last doubts were ventured by Milner, who in this critical stage surprisingly did not believe that Austria was prepared to break with Germany. He was countered by Lloyd George who reproached him for underrating the extent to which the Austrians were disgusted with Germany. After all, the Prime Minister concluded, it was not the first time that Austria had betrayed her allies and finally one ought not to ignore religious considerations and their sympathy for Bavaria.

The great expectations expressed at the Cabinet meeting had been aroused by a cipher telegram from Lloyd George's special envoy Sir Henry Norman, who had had two interviews with Painlevé, of which he sent a detailed report the day after.[63] Norman stressed that the outstanding fact emerging from the conversations between Revertera and Armand was "the profound desire of the Emperor to have peace at the earliest possible moment". Karl was credited with being extremely tenacious in his views and acts and willing to act independently of Czernin. The Emperor only needed some "plausible ground" for breaking away from his ally. This was an indispensable condition to safeguard his own personal honour. He would not "betray" Germany,

---

[62] Austrian diplomacy was well aware of the Allied disinterest in the Rumanian aspirations. Skrzyński said, to the Germans at Berne, that they should not trouble their heads about Rumania, for nobody within the Entente had a real interest in her fate. (Transmitted by Romberg to Berlin on 18 Aug., Wk.2 geh/48, AS 3204).

[63] Dated 15 August 1917. Lloyd George papers, F/60/1/13.

138

but if an acute difference of opinion should arise on the conditions of peace, Karl would "assert his own right to decide independently what the interest of Austria demanded of him". The method to realize such an "honourable" independent action was visualized by the Austrian representative on the following day: Britain and France were to communicate to the Emperor the terms of peace they would be prepared to recommend to their allies, i.e. Italy and Rumania. These terms might be very hard but not "absurd" in the sense that the restitution of Alsace–Lorraine would be hard but not absurd as the secession of territory up to the left bank of the Rhine.

If the Emperor received a communication of terms of peace which he found useful – and that meant they were also such as Austria could possibly accept – he would then forward them to the German Emperor urging him to accept them as a basis for peace. Should the Kaiser refuse to consider them (and this was expected to be the case),

> a situation would have arisen in which the Emperor of Austria would without any sacrifice of his personal honour declare to his ally that he considered them acceptable terms and that in the interests of Austria he felt it his duty to take independent action to this effect.

Concerning the terms for Austria Revertera intimated that Karl was prepared to go a very long way and in a democratic direction to secure peace *and* the future of Austria. He agreed willingly to the principles of a federalized Austria, the restitution of Serbia (with a sea-port) and Rumania. The different races of Austria were to receive autonomous government in an Austrian confederation to which Poland would be associated as an independent kingdom with an Austrian prince on the throne. An economic link in the form of a *Zollverein* with Bavaria was also suggested in the conversations.

Norman learned from his informants that Karl had considered Britain his enemy and that his representative was amazed to hear that the Allies might be expected to regard a solution such as the foregoing and that "they certainly were willing under such conditions to see a strong Austria as the result of the war". This meant a definite turning point in Allied policy. So far they had been prepared to accept a diminished but viable Austria–Hungary. Now they not only removed the threat of dismemberment by telling the Austrians that they did not want to break up their Empire, but they also paid tribute to the new military situation and offered her an increase of power with a dazzling outlook on her future role in Central Europe.

In turn the Emperor seemed to meet the Allied request for the liberation of the nationalities by regarding "the United States of the Danube" as an acceptable solution of the difficulties *after* the war.

This federal scheme could in Painlevé's view provide the way out of the commitments with Rumania and Italy. In the former case it needed only a sincere desire on both sides. The second, Italy, was the "black point". Here Karl was extremely reluctant to satisfy the Italians "without hopelessly antagonizing his own peoples". Too much Austrian blood had been shed for the defence of the lands demanded by Italy. Not only the sentiment of the Emperor but public opinion in the Monarchy was hostile to the Italian demands on the Adriatic coast, which were so excessive as almost to preclude any arrangements. Trieste could not be ceded as well, but the question of making it a free port would be considered. Altogether the Austrian unwillingness to give in to Italy could not be overlooked. Painlevé therefore thought of letting loose her ambition against Germany. However, the French Minister of War warned the British to avoid attaching an exaggerated importance to these conversations which were nevertheless possibly not without distinct elements of promise. He believed the matter well worth pursuing as in any event affording a line of counter-assurance against German aims.

The first meeting between Armand and Revertera clearly aimed at finding a way for a separate peace, which the Emperor – according to his representatives – was willing to conclude under certain circumstances. But the Imperial Chamberlain, if not misunderstood or carried away by his own eagerness to come to results, had gone further than the Emperor was prepared to go. Karl, opposed to increasing the territorial possession of the Monarchy at the expense of his ally, gave the order to refuse a separate peace *a limine* and to find another basis, which would be acceptable for *both* Austria and her major ally.[64]

A telegram from Rumbold on 12 August had pointed in the same direction. Skrynski had told him that there was no question of a separate peace. Austria hated Germany but would remain loyal. The only way was to "work on Germany" to make her conciliatory.[65] G. C. Clerk commented that a separate peace was welcomed but only possible after a blow to both Germany and her ally. Meanwhile Britain should be ready to listen, for which Lord Newton's forthcoming visit to Switzerland was an opportunity. But Balfour disapproved a mix-up between negotiations for prisoners and negotiations for peace.[66] On the other side Czernin was once again ready to send Mensdorff. The Austrian aims were achieved – but there was no question of a separate peace. Being explicitly told this Clerk no longer found the feeler promising, because "the Austrian mentality did not grasp the present situation". Moreover, he feared that talks with a British personage could not

---

[64] H.H.St.A., XLVII/13.
[65] *F.O.* 371/2864, No. 157767.
[66] *Ibid.*; cf. also Clerk's and Cecil's minutes on No. 166490 of 15 Aug.

be kept secret.[67]

Czernin also complained about the ambiguous British reaction. He had noticed a "lack of unity" in the recent speeches by Balfour, Cecil and Lloyd George. In spite of this he gave this serious step a chance of success. Formal overtures being rejected he asked for the guarantee of a satisfactory "form", e.g. a meeting between the two ministers in the Hague.[68]

The British inclination towards a direct meeting with the Austrians was definitely discouraged by a cable from Washington according to which there was indeed a strong feeling for peace in Austria and every possible pressure was being brought to bear on Germany, but there was no chance of a separate peace. This estimation by a reliable source[69] made it extremely questionable for the Foreign Office whether it should embark on negotiations with the Austrians. The pros and cons of such an undertaking were weighed thoughtfully by H. Nicolson on 22 August,[70] who started off with the assumption that the Austrian proposals were *bona fide*, i.e. with the full knowledge of the Austrian government and also known and possibly approved by Berlin. He therefore submitted that:

> We should consider the possibility of entertaining negotiations with these Austrian representatives from the point of view, *not* of detaching Austria from the alliance (which is impossible) but of placing the German government in a position which it would be difficult for them to justify either to their own people or to their allies.

Nicolson admitted that any such negotiations were "a double-edged tool". He wanted to confine the negotiations to Austrian problems and thereby come to a preliminary arrangement with Austria on such "middle" questions as compensations (for Belgium, Serbia and Galicia!) and the future of Poland. This would not be so difficult as a settlement with Germany, but any arrangement with Austria–Hungary would "immeasurably strengthen us for an eventual settlement with the Central Powers as a whole".

If the negotiations for peace came to nothing, because the Central Powers were not in a fit state to discuss it satisfactorily with the British, they could at least be used as a means of propaganda by being brought into the open. This could lead to a loosening of the fatal solidarity between the enemy powers. If their alliance did not disintegrate, at least a weakening of the moral forces by which that Alliance had been

---

[67] *Ibid.*, No. 162604, Rumbold to F.O., 20 Aug.
[68] *Ibid.*, No. 164751/f.134202, Townley to *F.O.*, 21 Aug., transmitting a report by an agent (Leipnik) on Czernin and the Pope's letter.
[69] *F.O.* 371/2863, No. 163289/f.49863, Spring-Rice to F.O., 20/21 Aug.
[70] Minute to No. 164751 (cf. note 1).

so firmly cemented might well be secured.

However, the enthusiasm of H. Nicolson's superiors was shattered by two factors: firstly that Austria would not conclude a separate peace and secondly – and this was a new observation – that she would collapse very soon at any rate. The foundation for the latter argument was the revelation of the gloomy April memorandum by Czernin. Its text had leaked out through the indiscretion of the German parliamentarian Erzberger and was known in Entente circles in the second half of August, and passed on by Leipnik in the following formulation:

> I believe the Austro-Hungarian desire for peace to be perfectly sincere. Austria cannot undertake to enter a new winter campaign. This undeniable fact ought to be the basis of all considerations.[71]

The effect of this advice which must have reached the French equally swiftly is already noticeable in the proposals which Armand made to Revertera at their second meeting on 22 August. The Austrian desire of playing a mediating role was forestalled by the harshness of the terms suggested by France for a general peace. These included the secession of Alsace–Lorraine up to the frontier of 1814, reparations for France, military neutralization of the left bank of the Rhine, secession of Heligoland; only a vague willingness to help Germany recover or obtain colonies by restitution or exchange sounded promising.

On the whole this document can only have been intended to test whether Austria–Hungary would break with Germany or not. Simultaneously a definite offer was held out for this purpose. But Austria was also asked a higher price by that time, namely the cession of Trieste with merely some economic precautions.

In the case of an independent Habsburg Confederation being established, the prospect of an alliance with both France and Britain was held out. But Revertera retorted that an alliance with Britain was not popular. The campaign in the British press for the dismemberment and destruction of Austria had brought Austria to the highest pitch of exasperation with Britain. When arranging the further procedure Revertera tried to keep out the British from the negotiations. He argued that if a British as well as a French representative was sent, Austria would be obliged to insist on the presence of a German one, too. Following instructions by Karl he therefore proposed a meeting / between Painlevé and Czernin only.

British hopes in the affair were further diminished by a Hague telegram saying that Czernin at the present time could not lend his name to the evacuation of Belgium and Northern France but might do so later, in the event of a complete change in the views of the Allies on

---

[71] *Ibid.* (Leipnik report).

the German colonies. In London the proposal was not thought to be good enough. The terms were not sufficiently comprehensive to be worth anything, and Cecil thought this would come to nothing, although a formal offer should be awaited if it came.[72] But the Austrians were far from committing themselves. On 13 September Townley cabled that he had information that Austria's forthcoming reply to the Pope's peace proposal would not reveal her real views, because it would afford no opening for peace negotiations with the Allies. According to his Austrian colleague in the Hague "Italy might be detached from the Allies by an offer of the Austrian territory she covets".[73] Since France would leave the war after Italy's departure and as Russia could be neglected in any case, only Britain and U.S.A. would remain of the Allied coalition. The motive behind such wishful thinking, passed on from Vienna to London, was to give the impression that Austria was in a powerful position. Thus it was implied that it was advisable for Britain to bargain with Austria, before she was deserted by her allies.

But the effect of the Austrian intimations was the reverse. Cecil suspected that the intention was to entice Britain into secret negotiations with Vienna which were to help the Austrians to persuade the Italians to make peace with the Habsburgs instead of continuing the fight on the side of the Entente.[74]

Cecil's suspicion was hardened by reports from Rome and Berne which appeared to prove the unreliability of the Austrian advances. Rodd wired that there had been a moment when the Italian conditions had been on the point of being accepted by Austria–Hungary. The main difficulty was the immediate execution of a transfer of territory, which in fact the Italians had insisted upon in full anticipation of its constituting an unsurmountable obstacle.[75] This description of the talks seemed to fit the Austrian attempts to keep Italy neutral before she entered the war and the information was therefore taken seriously in London although there is no evidence that any Austro-Italian negotiations took place in 1917, and although the source of Rodd's report was obscure (the late Greek minister in Vienna). The same can be said of Rumbold's telegram about a South Slav intrigue afoot to split Britain and France against Italy. The British minister warned that all dispositions discernable at Vienna for the conclusion of a separate peace would be passed on to Berlin. Germany possibly winked at these efforts to leave the door open for a peace without victory for which the Austrians could be blamed, if it was ever necessary to agree to it.[76]

[72] *Ibid.*, Townley to F.O., 23 Aug., No. 165510.
[73] *Cab.* 23/4, *WC* 233 of 14 Sept. 1917.
[74] *Ibid.*
[75] *F.O.* 371/2864, No. 182467 of 14 Sept.
[76] *Ibid.*, No. 182437 of 5 Sept.

Again there is no evidence that the Germans encouraged the Austrian undertakings to this effect. The Germans on the whole were rather embarrassed by the diplomatic activity of their ally and suspicious of becoming involved in negotiations on terms to which they did not subscribe. But the mere possibility of Germany being behind the Austrian offers stiffened the attitude of the Foreign Office against what was now regarded as "Austrian peace manoeuvres" as part of Germany's game. This view was shared by the leaders of Britain and France and at a meeting in Downing Street on 15 September they agreed that for the time being nothing could be done in the matter of a separate peace with Austria.[77]

Some positive change was needed in the situation of the war to re-enliven the project of coming to terms with Austria. Lloyd George had always believed that this could be achieved after scoring a remarkable success on the battlefield and had laboured in vain throughout the summer of 1917 to win over his generals for the idea. Suddenly there was a revival of activity on the Italian front in late August. Cadorna's operations showed more promise than usual and Delmé-Radcliffe implored the British government to send arms to help the Italians to exploit their initial advance to the full. Unless this report was over-sanguine the events taking place in Italy seemed to offer overwhelming possibilities and Lloyd George pointed out his renewed optimism to Robertson.[78] The Commander-in-Chief was, as usual, opposed to the Prime Minister's view and tried to counter the now favourable reaction of the French General Staff. Robertson admitted that diplomatic considerations could not entirely be ignored, but he was unwilling to release more than fifty guns from the British front in Flanders. Finally Haig agreed to free a hundred and Lloyd George was confident of achieving much with them. His view was that a comparatively small success on the Isonzo front might lead to great results and have a decisive effect on the war whereas a considerable success in the West might have small results, because the Germans were much more stubborn and tenacious than the Austrians.[79] But once the guns had arrived in Italy, Cadorna modified his plans and decided not to attack. Rodd could not explain this strange and sudden change of policy within a few days, but the result of it was that the artillery was withdrawn again from Italy.[80] This meant a definite end to the policy of striking a blow at Austria as a preliminary to a separate peace.

---

[77] The participants of this meeting were Lloyd George, Milner, Curzon, Balfour, Painlevé, Thomas, and Ribot. Cf. *Journal d'Alexandre Ribot, op.cit.*, p.174.
[78] *War Memoirs*, ii, pp.1385–86.
[79] *Cab*. 23/13, *WC* 227c of 4 Sept.
[80] *Cab*. 23/4, *WC* 237 of 21 Sept.

CHAPTER V

The Climax of Secret Diplomacy

1. The Crisis of the Allies

From the Foreign Office point of view the most critical and difficult stages of the war were reached in autumn 1917, when despite the severence of diplomatic relations, the possibility of peace negotiations was in the air. The Foreign Secretary explained to the Cabinet that the "middle stage" of diplomacy had been reached, when the natural channels of diplomacy were still choked, but when some of the belligerents were "endeavouring to start informal conversations about the terms of peace".[1] Balfour (before concentrating on the German peace feeler via Madrid[1a]) reviewed the advances made so far from Germany's allies Austria, Bulgaria, and Turkey. In the case of the latter two the advances had come from opposition circles or "would-be rebels" who were apt to take too rosy a view of their powers and prospects. In the case of Austria the advances had come from "the highest quarters in the established Government", which induced the Foreign Office to take the Austrian proposals more seriously than the others. But, on the other hand, Balfour concluded,

> all the indications appear to show that Austria is so tightly bound to Germany, that, *as things are at present*, she could do no more for the cause of peace than press moderation upon her arrogant partner. Whatever change in her attitude the coming winter and spring may produce, it seems more than doubtful whether *at the present moment* anything will induce Austria to break away from Germany.[2]

The situation was this: Austria, or at least the Austrian court, desired peace, but would not act without Germany, which had just expressed a desire for a non-committal talk about terms of peace. Balfour preferred the German offer to the Austrian feelers, because it had come through

---

[1] Balfour's memorandum on "Peace Negotiations", dated 20 Sept., is printed in full in *War Memoirs*, ii, pp.1237–40.

[1a] Cf. Fest, W. B., "British War Aims and German Peace Feelers during the First World War (December 1916-November 1918)", *Historical Jornal*, xv, 1972.

[2] Italics in the original.

an orthodox diplomatic channel. In the Cabinet, however, hopes for a separate understanding with the Austrians were still alive. Bonar Law, when faced with the same alternative, advised his Prime Minister not to act before knowing what had happened to the French negotiations with Austria.[3]

The reason for the preference for negotiations with Austria is obvious. As long as there was a chance that they would lead to the actual defection of the Habsburg Empire from the Central Alliance, this would have made superfluous any consideration of a compromise with Germany, which was basically undesirable for the British and only envisaged by some Cabinet members as an ultimate emergency solution.[4] But after the Germans had decided to make an advance themselves, the Austrian diplomatic position had lost in value. Those who were sceptical about her desire to conclude a separate peace, like Balfour, lost interest in the matter as well as those who were inclined towards a general peace, like Milner, because her role as a mediator or informant was less necessary at the moment. Only if Austria exerted a much stronger pressure on Germany could this lead to results which the British government would regard as positive. An Austrian threat to act independently and even the prospect of the virtual execution of such a step therefore aroused high expectations in London.

On 29 September W. Townley reported from the Hague that Czernin was "determined to make a last effort to get Berlin to agree to peace proposals". If the Austrian Minister for Foreign Affairs failed, he would propose to his Emperor "to take such steps as may be necessary to obtain peace on other lines, presumably a separate peace". On this point the Austrian minister in the Hague would not commit himself, but his declaration that Czernin would resign, if Karl did not entertain his proposal, was received with great attention.[5] However, this dramatic announcement was not followed by any substantial action. The basis for negotiations which was communicated a few days later was disappointing from a British point of view. Only the evacuation of Belgium and Northern France and the restoration of Serbia were granted *a priori*. The questions of Alsace–Lorraine, Italy, and Russia were to be left for discussion. For Townley it was not apparent how far Germany approved of the new move, but it all pointed to a rupture between Austria and Germany, he wrote, if the Austrian views were found acceptable.[6] Yet the new proposal made hardly any concessions: all the disputed problems were singled out: and the emphasis was on German and not on Austro-Hungarian territorial questions. The whole

---

[3] Bonar Law to Lloyd George, 21 Sept., *ibid.*, p.1240.
[4] For the minutes of the discussion on the German offer cf. *Cab.* 23/16.
[5] *F.O.* 371/2864, No. 188934/f.134202; Milner diary, entry for 1 Oct.
[6] *F.O.* 371/2864, No. 162950 of 6 Oct.

tenor was in the direction of a general peace on the basis of the status quo with some modifications. Under these circumstances the Foreign Office was not interested in responding to the offer of meeting a special negotiator from Vienna. Townley was instructed by Balfour and Hardinge:

> The Austrian terms are quite inadmissable, but if we tell them so, they will immediately communicate the fact to the Germans. I am not sure that this is desirable.[7]

The Foreign Office did not want to produce the ill effect of strengthening the German extremists, who might gain preponderance, after the explicit refusal of an Austrian offer. The best course therefore seemed to be to do nothing, since the Austrians, though anxious for peace, showed no signs of desiring a separate peace. The Cabinet did not doubt that Austria was clamouring for peace – all government information pointed in that direction. It was uncertain, however, whether they were prepared to pay the price for it. "But for Germany", Balfour commented, "they would be willing".[8] His verdict shows the dilemma of British diplomacy. Nothing could be done from London to clear up the crucial questions without committing Britain to negotiations, if only on an unofficial level. Balfour showed no inclination to initiate such conversations. Nor could he offer to the government any alternative means of promoting the matter. His attitude was marked by indecision. It was left to Vienna, whether "the flirt over the fronts" was renewed and perhaps intensified. The Foreign Office remained in a state of alert – ready to react but unwilling to act.

Although Austrian diplomacy had so far been successful in its attempts to arrange informal conversations between representatives of the two countries, Czernin expressed himself confident about the prospect of making peace, when pressed for it by the Czech Socialist leaders Tuzar and Staněk.[9] The Foreign Minister explained to them that the main problem was to bring the other side to the conference table, because "once Austria was at it, she would not leave". Accordingly it was his object to entangle the Entente in negotiations from which there was no return. Concerning the interior reform of the Empire Czernin asked the Czechs "to keep order a few months longer" and in all his conversations with the Slavs he could refute the alleged support of the Allies for the small nationalities by referring to the recent speeches of Lloyd George and Asquith which kept silent in respect of Austria–Hungary and its nationalities.[10] For Czernin this was a proof

---

[7] *Ibid.*, 8 Oct.
[8] *Cab.* 23/13, WC 247b of 11 Oct.
[9] *F.O.* 371/2864, No. 200207 of 17 Oct.; despite the indirect evidence (from Czech circles in Switzerland) the report is illuminating and deserves attention, which it also found at the time!
[10] E.g. Czernin laid great stress on Asquith's speech on 26 Sept.; held in Leeds, printed in Scott, *Official Statements* . . ., p.162–67.

that the Entente no longer thought of the dissolution of Austria–Hungary and that "England in particular has completely abandoned the idea". Thus the demonstratively friendly British attitude together with an ostensible Austrian peace campaign served as a means of keeping the interior peace of the Monarchy. In this connection Prince L. Lubomirski, a cousin of a member of the Polish Regency, approached Sir Esme Howard in Stockholm and suggested an Allied statement that the dismemberment of the Habsburg Empire was not aimed at.[11] But the Foreign Office could not carry out such a move without consulting the Allies and Balfour was sure that under existing circumstances "no such declaration would ever be assented to by our friends". Moreover, the Foreign Secretary doubted the wisdom of expressively saying anything which suggested the view that England alone was ready to make it. Evidently he wanted to avoid two things: firstly, to give the impression that the Entente was split over war aims and secondly, to give the Austrians assurances in advance. It was much better tactics to leave them in suspense about Allied intentions about the Habsburg Empire. A British assurance in favour of the preservation of the Monarchy would have fortified the position of the authorities in Vienna and Budapest and thereby relieved the pressure of coming to an early peace with the Allies at all costs in order to anticipate a revolution of the subject nationalities. So Balfour allowed the proposal to slide for the moment and tried to test the actual state of desperation in Vienna. "If Austria is really *in extremis*", he minuted, "she must come to us again".[12]

But it was the position of Britain's Allies rather than that of Austria which deteriorated. On 24 October combined Austro-German divisions attacked the Italians, who suffered a crushing defeat and lost heavily in men and material. As a result of the rout of Caporetto they were driven back to the Tagliamento and Piave, and the road to Venice or even Rome seemed open to the Central Powers. The consequences that threatened were great. The cracks in the Austro-Hungarian conglomerate would be cemented and furthermore Austria would be free to assist Germany on the Western Front. On 7 November Hankey noted in his diary that "the Italian position proves to be critical in the extreme".[13] The Vatican and to a lesser degree the Socialists were regarded as responsible for an active peace propaganda. Lloyd George feared that the peace party in Italy might succeed in persuading the victorious enemy to grant moderate terms of peace and if this was accepted by the Italian people, another member of the Entente would

---

[11] *F.O.* 371/2864, No. 201856 of 19 Oct.
[12] *Ibid.*
[13] M. Hankey, *op.cit.*, ii, p.720.

drop out.[14] Then the contrary effect of a separate peace by Austria–Hungary would be achieved. The British (and the French) had been thinking in terms of cessation of hostilities on the part of Austria while Italy would continue on the Allied side. The military situation, however, rather suggested the reverse. After Caporetto Lloyd George's idea of an offensive against Austria had to be abandoned once and for all. It made no difference that the Italian King now regretted that this advice had not been followed.[15] The only positive outcome was the establishment of a unified Allied command. At the opening proceedings of the new Supreme War Council the question of whether the Allied attitude in Italy was to be purely defensive or whether an offensive should still be considered was raised by Clemenceau, who had come to power three weeks after the Italian disaster. His proposal was received lukewarmly by the Italians, and the British and French had to be content that their new premier Orlando at least expressed the resolution to carry on fighting, for which he was given the necessary support to stabilize the Italian front.[16]

As a matter of fact, Caporetto diminished the possibility of an Austro-Italian understanding by a territorial compromise. The prospect of the Italians satisfying their ambition by helping themselves to some Habsburg territory was now far removed. Conversely, the prestige of a resounding victory had made the Austrians less inclined towards any concessions. The Emperor Karl, shortly after the victorious battle, alluded to the "handsome compensations" offered several times by French and British statesmen to Austria if she made a separate peace. He admitted that these efforts had undoubtedly had a considerable effect among certain nationalities and parties in Austria–Hungary and he deplored the fact that in certain circles (Poles, Magyars) victory over the Italians was not properly appreciated. Karl now publicly repudiated a peace policy of renunciation. The Habsburgs and the Hohenzollerns were more closely united than ever and the Venetian offensive "offered a good lesson" as to what the peace policy should be.[17]

The lesson that Caporetto was a turning-point found its way also into the Foreign Office, where the conspicuous analysis of a businessman whose letter was transmitted from Berne by Rumbold,[18] was studied with interest. The writer argued that Caporetto was a serious blow to the Italians, but the fact that the Austrians had only been able to obtain

---

[14] *War Memoirs*, ii, p.1390.
[15] *Ibid.*, p.1401.
[16] *Ibid.*, p.1618–19.
[17] Reported by Townly on 11 November after it was reproduced in the *Kölnische Volkszeitung*; *F.O.* 371/3081, No. 215380/f.97807.
[18] *Ibid.*, No. 235883 of 13 Dec., minuted by Balfour and Cecil ("interesting"!).

such tremendous success with the help of the Germans put Austria into a still more dependent position upon Germany and still further removed "the already distant possibility of Austria being able to go her own way and making a separate peace".

The Italian set-back was not only one for the Allied war effort. On the day when the Western statesmen had agreed upon assistance for Italy events came to a head in Russia. While Lloyd George, accompanied by Smuts and Henry Wilson, conferred at Peschiera, Milner, who had stayed behind in London, noted in his diary on 8 November that there was "very bad news from both Italy and Russia" which put "a new and worse complexion on the war".[19] Similarly Balfour was disturbed by the two events and although he hoped for better things he concluded that "we must consider all eventualities". If Russia made a separate peace, he rated the effect far greater than the American entry.[20] On 19 November, the C.I.G.S. addressed a grave warning to the War Cabinet that after a separate peace with Russia the greater part of the enemy forces could be moved to the Western front, which might prevent the Allies from obtaining decisive results in the coming year. If victory was not possible in 1918, Robertson implied, the Allies – particularly the Italians and the French – might be too war-weary to make a great offensive in 1919, despite the addition of the American forces to the Allied arms.[21] There could hardly be better evidence for the prevalence of this estimation than the fact that in the other camp Czernin counted on internal disorder in Italy and France and a separate peace with Russia.[22]

When part of the hopes fostered by Czernin had materialized, the Foreign Minister informed his representatives in the Hague and in Switzerland that he was much interested in establishing contact with Britain and instructed them to let Britain know *officieusement* that if she was prepared to have an *officieuse* conversation on the subject of peace, the Austrian government would pledge its honour to keep the matter secret. Czernin emphasized that the defeat of the Italians would not alter in any way the peace proposals already submitted and that he was "clearly fishing for an answer".[23] The previous offer had found no response because it aimed at a general peace. Now, because of the favourable turn of events on the Italian front, he had nothing to offer but "a declaration guaranteeing the integrity of Italian territory as it existed before the war". In view of the renewed Austrian self-

---

[19] Milner papers, box 280.

[20] *F.O.* 371/3086, f.218315: "The Position on 8 November, 1917".

[21] Copy of the memorandum in the Milner papers; partly quoted in R. H. Ullman, *Intervention and the War*, Princeton 1961, i, p.40.

[22] *F.O.* 371/2864, No. 200207 of 17 Oct.

[23] *F.O.* 371/2864, No. 208754 of 31 Oct. and No. 209341 of 1 Nov. For the Austrian side cf. H.H.St.A., Krieg 25/27, on the basis of which Steglich wrongly assumes that the initiative came from London (cf. *op.cit.*, p.224).

confidence the Foreign Office instructed its go-between to reply that in Britain the moment was not regarded as favourable to fall in with the Austrian suggestions.[24]

When the British minister in the Hague learned that the Austrian proposals held good only until 20 November, the British government, in the belief that this would appear to indicate "something more than a feeler", instructed its minister to convey the same answer that had been given to the German advances through Madrid:

> that if the Austro-Hungarian government wishes to make any communication to the British government as regards peace, the latter will be prepared to receive it and to discuss it with their allies.[25]

After their successful military co-operation with Germany the Austrians were placed on the same footing as their bigger ally as far as the diplomatic treatment by the Foreign Office was concerned. At the moment London did not dare to agree to a discussion with an enemy power, be it for a general or a separate peace. The danger of giving ground to the pacifist movements in Allied countries, which would have exploited any facts or rumours that could have leaked out from talks, however secret, must have held back the British from contacting Austria. Moreover, the strong language used in the instructions for Townley which were communicated to all Allied embassies – even to Petrograd after some hesitation – was apt to evoke the impression that the morale of Britain was unbroken and could thus add to the strengthening of the resistance of the other Allies.

Clemenceau, obviously for the same motive, would have preferred Austria–Hungary being told to put proposals officially for the consideration of the Entente.[26] This had "probably put an end to any overtures", as Clerk minuted, but it was only a personal interview, which the Foreign Office did not authorize, disregarding Townley's conviction that the only way to get a written communication was a preliminary conversation with the Austrian minister.[27]

When Czernin learned the conditions from London, which put Vienna in an inferior position for negotiations, he refused to be tied to a programme of renunciation. He ordered his minister in the Hague, L. Szechenyi, "not to contribute *anything* to the arrangement of a meeting with an Englishman."[28] Now the informants of both chanceries had the order to behave purely passively and the soundings had come to a

---

[24] *F.O.* 371/2864, 3 Nov. (No. 209391).

[25] *Ibid.*, 16 Nov. (f.134202); the quoted text with explanation was communicated printed (with wrong date!) U.S. For. Rel. 1916, Sp. p.65.

[26] *F.O.* 371/2864, No. 220252 of 18 Nov. (Bertie to F.O.). Balfour in his minute explained the unreasonable request with Clemenceau's ignorance of the nicety of the German –Spanish proposals and not with a rigorous opposition to any peace diplomacy!

[27] *Ibid.*, Townley's tel. of 17 Nov. and F.O. answer of 19 inst.

[28] Underline in the original, H.H.St.A., *loc.cit.*, quoted in Steglich, *op.cit.* pp.50304, n.638.

complete deadlock and only a modification of the instructions on the British side promised the chance of a new *rapprochement*. An eventual change of mind in London depended on how valuable the political leaders considered a direct communication with the Austrian government and whether they could get the necessary consent of their Allies, who had meanwhile been advised of developments.

Despite the temporary deadlock of the Austro-British soundings the go-betweens in Switzerland continued their efforts. The confidant of the British legation was the Egyptian Prince Djemil Toussun, who conferred with Baron Aleksander Skrzyński, a councillor to the Austro-Hungarian legation. On 22 November the latter communicated that Czernin was "ready to send to Switzerland a person in the confidence of the Austro-Hungarian government".[29] In the event of Britain authorizing a representative for the prospective *entrevue* Czernin was disposed to send either Mensdorff or Mérey, an official in the Ministry of Foreign Affairs, holding the rank of an ambassador. The Austro-Hungarian government, which pledged its honour for absolute secrecy, felt obliged to ask for an assurance because of the failure with the French in the past. This was the main reason for Czernin to turn towards Britain, although Skrzynski tried to fabricate a special Austrian preference for the British:

> The Austro-Hungarian government has no sort of animosity towards England and does not in the least share the sentiments of Germany in that respect. The Austrian nation is very favourably disposed towards the English nation.[30]

On the surface these compliments were only the expression of an Anglophile Austro-Polish nobleman to give proof of his country's anxiety to create an atmosphere of conciliation by the greatest courtesy towards the opponent. Besides, the formulation "Austrian and English nation" was apt to indicate the common problem of the nationalities in the two Empires. From an Austrian standpoint such a comparison associated the belief that Great Britain with her Empire–Commonwealth would show more understanding and respect for Austria's interior situation. These allusions to mutual interests could create a congenial climate for negotiations but they were not enough to bring about a meeting. That required a serious desire on the part of the British to sound out what Vienna had to offer. It was Lloyd George himself who thought the matter worth while pursuing and overruled the cautious and unyielding Foreign Office. The Prime Minister could count upon the support of the War Cabinet (where incidentally the whole affair was never formally discussed before January 1918), in

[29] *F.O.* 371/2864.
[30] *Ibid*.

particular of Milner, who thought that British diplomacy heretofore had been too timid to listen to any of the peace proposals, but that under the new circumstances the Allies "ought to listen to every peace whisper".[31]

The greater problem was to persuade the other Allies. At the inter-Allied conference which was convened in Paris on 29 November they were confronted with Skrzynski's telegram.[32] Balfour, who read it out, informed his audience (Lloyd George, Addison, House, Clemenceau, Pichon, de Margerie, Orlando, Sonnino) that previously he had instructed his ministers to insist on a written communication and he asked whether now he should go so far as to allow them to "listen without comment". Lloyd George wanted to go further: he claimed that "we are free to try to render account of what Austria, Bulgaria, and Turkey had in their breast". Lloyd George did not fail to give reason for his anxiety to negotiate with the Austrians. He showed himself very alarmed at the growing liquidation of Russia. This meant that 100 to 120 divisions would be freed for the Italian and French fronts, whereas the American assistance could not be obtained in full before late 1918.

> Well, then; we will be one ally less without one enemy less. Can't we diminish them? Until now we have not sounded them out. Here is Austria. She is very tired. We have very official proposals. The Austrian question is neither a French nor an English question. Austria is an Italian question. It is Italy that has to decide.[33]

Lloyd George emphasized that he did not want to demand from Italy that she drop her war aims, but asked why the Austrian terms should not be investigated. How could such an investigation lead to positive results without sacrificing at least part of the Italian claims? The subtle difference in Lloyd George's calculations was that he did not intend to force Italy to any renunciation until it was proved that this would be honoured by the Austrian side. For the moment Lloyd George contented himself with appealing to the Italian delegates to reconsider their demands in view of the general situation of the Allies, which was no more than a request for a voluntary moderation of the Italian demands.

In his efforts Lloyd George was backed by President Wilson's personal representative Colonel House. The *éminence grise* of the White House was the first American delegate at an inter-Allied conference, where he attempted to exert a moderating influence on Allied war aims. The Americans could make use of the fact that they were no party to the secret treaties. Lloyd George, obviously realizing the chance of pressurizing the Italians indirectly, had won Colonel House for his

---

[31] Quoted in A. Mayer, *Wilson vs. Lenin. The Political Origins of the New Diplomacy 1917–1918*. Cleveland 1964 (2), p.282.

[32] Minutes taken by de Margerie, *Min.Aff.Etr., Confer.Int.*, Ser. A, Carton 269, doss 1 sd/10.

[33] *Ibid*. (retranslation from the French).

cause before the conference started. Now Wilson's adviser ruthlessly exposed the weakness of the Italian position. He pointed out that with a population almost equal to that of France she had not done enough and left her the alternative between an equal military effort or an "honourable" peace with Austria.

From this moment Sonnino was on the defensive and did not object that one could listen to the Austrians. Nevertheless he warned the others of the risks involved in premature negotiations, which could dissociate the Allies, who might lose their moral resistance once the affair was made public by Germany. This was the point at which he found the support of Clemenceau, who did not tolerate any intrigue for a separate peace that included Germany. His determination to fight the enemy to the very end was unbroken and he waited with confidence for the arrival of the Americans. But the "tiger" had also to face the military crisis after the Russian "treason". Besides he was far from being Austrophobe. He had family connections with Austria through his brother Paul, who was married to the sister of the director of the *Fremdenblatt*, Julius Szeps, and these contacts were used from both sides during the war. It is most probable that Clemenceau would have continued the policy of his predecessors and spared the Habsburg Monarchy, if he had believed that it was still possible to detach her from Germany. He rather objected to the timing of the proposed *prise de contact* than its aim, with which he can be assumed to have sympathized.[34] Certainly his basic approval of a separate peace with Austria also determined his answer in the negative, when asked by Lloyd George, whether he was opposed to listening to the Austrian proposals in order to elucidate them. Balfour hastened to add that he would turn to the Allies if one made "approaches", and after two and a half hours the British had succeeded. Britain was authorized to ascertain what terms Austria had to offer for a separate peace.[35]

Lloyd George, who was "full of the separate peace with Austria",[36] could regard the outcome of the conference as a great success for himself and Great Britain. The extent of the British contribution to the cause of the Allies had given British diplomacy the lead in the determination of the foreign policy of the Entente.[37] But Britain's new role had to remain subject to the limitation that pressure must not be exerted to a point which might alienate the Allies. In this respect House criticized

---

[34] For Clemenceau's pre-war links with Austria cf. R. Pinon, "Clemenceau et L'Autriche", *Revue polit. et parl.*, 1948, p.154f – Reports about the Austrophile circle around Clemenceau's sister-in-law were regularly sent to the A.A.; cf. *L'Allemagne* . . . . . ., ii, Nos. 172 & 180.

[35] Ch. Seymour, *The Intimate Papers of Colonel House*, Boston 1938, iii, p.276 (House to Wilson, 30 Nov. 1917).

[36] *Ibid.*, entry for 1 Dec.

[37] On 12 Feb. 1916 the C.I.G.S. had already expressed the view that G.B. should attempt to control the diplomatic policy of the Allies. The War Committee accepted his suggestion on 22 Feb. 1916, cf. the minutes of the War Committee. *Cab.* 42/22.

Lloyd George for acting too precipitately instead of consulting Clemenceau first before talking to Sonnino.[38] Such a gradual persuasion of the other Allies would have smoothed the discussion at the conference and prevented the falling out between the advocates and the opponents of entering into conversations.

It is, however, possible to imagine that Lloyd George deliberately aspired to expose the isolated position of Sonnino, whom he might have expected to be the only one to be unmoved by his plan. The Italian Foreign Minister was indeed a stubborn opponent of any deal with Austria–Hungary. His obstinate and inflexible attitude found expression in the Sonnino project, which he forwarded the day after the discussions on Austria, when the draft of the answer to the Bolsheviks was debated and Sonnino simply circulated a draft advising that nothing be done.[39] He did not want to recognize that the conditions had changed since the beginning of the conflict through the collapse of the Russian front and the disaster of Caporetto. Notwithstanding those setbacks he kept insisting that the Italian aims had to be maintained *integralmente*, as they were sanctioned by the treaties.[40] He was not moved by the argument of the Swiss minister in Rome, who suggested that there were political and economic solutions to which Austria could assent without losing face, both with respect to her Italian crown lands and to the Adriatic.

Rightly so, Sonnino thought this was quite improbable. Moreover, the situation did not look so bad as to consider what he regarded as a peace of renunciation. Since the American factor could be expected to count in three or four months, he saw no reason "to throw in the sponge" for a mess of pottage that might be offered.[41]

Sonnino had only consented to the British initiative on the condition that the big Allies, i.e., Italy included, were informed. After the conference had dispersed he continued to warn against too much complaisance in receiving the Austrian proposals, for he had noted "an English tendency to make more of them than was suitable".[42] His Prime Minister, Signor Orlando, was also apprehensive of Lloyd George's attitude towards Austria and his *idée fixe* of concluding a separate peace. For both Italian statesmen the British move was a cause of uneasiness and unrest, and was resented vividly. It was regarded as a dangerous adventure adding to the existing difficulties of the internal Italian situation, which could really become serious if the neutralists, Giolittists, Socialists, and clericals were strengthened by reports of pacifist

---

[38] Ch. Seymour, *loc.cit.*

[39] *Min.Aff.Etr.*, *loc.cit.*, text printed in A. Pingaud, *Histoire diplomatique pendant la Grande Guerre*, ii, p.?.

[40] O. Malagodi, *op.cit.*, p.260–62.

[41] This interview was reported to Berlin: A.A., Wk 2 geh., 54, AS 5853 of 21 Dec. 1917.

[42] Barrere to Pichon, 7 Dec., *Min.Aff.Etr.*, *loc.cit.*

conversations with Austria.[43]

But the Italian anxiety was relieved by the cautious attitude of Clemenceau and Pichon,[44] who were emphatically asked to beware of delicate soundings by their ambassador in Rome, Camille Barrère. The critical analysis of this conspicuous observer of the goings-on reveals the weakness of Lloyd George's argument:

> It is not now, when the Austrian armies are on the Piave, that the court of Vienna would consent to concessions acceptable to Italy. If Lloyd George thought of compensating Austria at the expense of Germany for what she would cede to Italy, it seems to me audacious to believe that one could not only detach Austria from Germany but even turn her against the latter. This would be, at the point where we are now, a pure chimera.[45]

2. The Polish Problem in its bearing upon Austria

The extent to which Lloyd George desired to do nothing that could render an understanding with Austria more difficult was demonstrated by his attitude at the Paris conference during the discussions relative to a declaration on Poland.[46] The Polish question had been internationalized by the Central Powers, who in November 1916 promised to establish an allegedly independent Polish state. The Entente, in its answer to Wilson in January 1917, did not go beyond a vague reference to the future status of the Poles, subject to Russian objections.[47]

The leaders of the various streams in Polish politics stated their views to the British delegation at the Petrograd conference in February 1917, where G. C. Clerk made a note of all shades of opinion for Milner.[48] Count Wielopolski of the Central Polish Committee, in Clerk's eyes the one with the most authority and the most practical view, contended that the majority of the Polish nation was for a victory of the Entente, because a German victory would imply the loss of the districts inhabitated by Poles both under German domination as well as the Polish parts of Austria–Hungary. The Monarchy, Wielopolski argued, did not count "since the day when she became a plaything in German hands". Now the European equilibrium demanded the resurrection of a Polish state.

Among the Poles the belief in the incorporation of Galicia in a new Poland was stronger than the hope for the German lands. On the other hand the Galician Poles, with their happier experiences of Habsburg

---

[43] *Ibid.*
[44] The British misinterpreted Pichon's silence during the discussion as a tacit approval; cf. P. Cambon, *Correspondance*, Paris 146, ii, p.214.
[45] *Min.Aff.Etr.*, *loc.cit.*, 8 Dec. 1917.
[46] *Min.Aff.Etr.*, *loc.cit.*
[47] *Cab.* 28/2, I.C. 16 (g).
[48] *F.O.* 371/2806, f.2.

rule, were not yet whole-heartedly at one with their countrymen in Russia and Germany.

Clerk concluded his survey with the remark that any advance towards Polish unity at that time had to recognize the first essential for Polish independence, namely that it depended on Russia's initiative.

Russia's exclusive interest in that matter was always respected by the Entente. But when the new Provisional Russian government showed itself also against real Polish independence, the Foreign Office was disturbed, since the attitude of Milyukov facilitated the German attempts for a Polish army. Balfour suggested that the Russian government be urged to go as far as possible on the lines of independence "to prevent Poland being drawn in the future within the German orbit".[49]

Apart from such negative aims British policymakers were not yet decided as to how the Polish problem could be solved best in their interest. The only fact that Balfour took more or less for granted was that Galicia ought to go to Poland, for "it would become absurd to call it a part of historic Austria", which was what the Foreign Secretary wanted to see preserved after the war according to his personal "historical" interpretation.[50]

In May 1917 the Poles at the Vienna *Reichsrat* and the Galician diet voted unanimously for a "free Poland with access to the sea". Roman Dmovski, soon to become the leader of the Polish National Committee in Paris, went further in his demands. In July 1917 he published a pamphlet in English to attract the attention of British statesmen. Dmovski proceeded from the presupposition that a complete reconstruction of Central and Eastern Europe was necessary. Otherwise a beaten Germany would quickly regain her prewar preponderance. Therefore Dmovski demanded with particular pungency the disappearance of the Habsburg Empire and the dissolution of what he called a "Medieval relic" on the principle of nationality.[51]

But Dmovski's strong anti-Habsburg sentiments were not shared by a large number of his compatriots. In Stockholm E. Howard gathered that "all the Poles desired complete independence but if they could not obtain this the next best thing would be autonomy under Austria which would unite them with Galicia".[52]

This solution was regarded as a *pis aller* among radical Polish leaders. They foresaw the danger of an inclination in certain quarters to look to Austria for the realization of Polish reunion, for since the collapse of the

---

[49] *F.O.* 371/3000, f.7684.
[50] Balfour's review of foreign policy of 22 Mar. 1917 is printed in *The Lansing Papers*, ii, p.19ff, –. (cf. above ch. III, 1).
[51] Cf. T. Komarnicki, *Rebirth of the Polish Republic*, London 1958, pp.177–78.
[52] *F.O.* 371/3001, No. 179918/f.7684 of 15 Sept. & No. 184057 of 20th inst.; for the following *ibid.*

Russian army it was feared that the latter could not be counted on to effect it. So the efforts of the Conservatives of Cracov, who were closely tied to the Habsburg dynasty, tended towards reviving an Austrian policy in Galicia.

The Habsburgs had never entirely abandoned the idea of a Polish Kingdom attached to Austria–Hungary by the links of a personal union, though the Austro-German agreement of 18 March 1917 had allotted Poland to the German sphere of influence. In the meantime the Germans had doubts as to whether the convention of Kreuznach was advantageous to them. They realized that the Poles were extremely hostile to Germany and that their separation from a Galicia remaining Austrian would be the cause of constant unrest. Moreover, the Germans started to look with rising interest at the economically richer Rumania, which was to fall under Austrian domination as a compensation for renouncing Poland. Besides these inherent difficulties there was a more general source for German uneasiness. German observers in Vienna had noticed a growing hostility against Germany that threatened the alliance. The Ententist inclinations of the court did not remain unknown to Berlin. Its confidants came to the conclusion that "those detrimental trends and leanings could be eliminated if a certain event forced the Emperor (Karl) to side openly and honestly with us. The solution of the Polish question (in favour of the Austrians) ought to be that event".[53] The matter was settled in that spirit on 22 October when Austria and Germany signed an agreement that regulated the economic and military co-operation between the two countries to the advantage of Germany and also conceded trade rights for Rumania to her. In turn she consented to a personal union between Poland and the House of Habsburg. In public the Central Powers tried to produce the impression that nothing was to be decided before the conclusion of peace, but if the Poles should voluntarily choose to associate themselves as a third state in the Austro-Hungarian Monarchy, no difficulties would be created.[54]

Rumours about the assumption behind the agreement soon spread. Both in Vienna and London it was speculated that Germany's reason for accepting Karl as King of Poland was a similar hold over Lithuania and Courland.[55] Basing his argument on this assumption a Socialist deputy (speaking during a *Reichsrat* debate on 9 November) treated the intention of uniting Austria and Poland as "bound to antagonize the Entente", because its realization "involved the overthrow of the rival coalition", and hence a great prolongation of the war for purely dynas-

---

[53] A.A., Wk 20 c geh. ad No. As 3778 of 1 Oct. 1917; cf. also Z. A. B. Zeman, *op.cit.*, pp.160–62.
[54] *Ibid.*, p.162; text in *L'Allemagne* . . . . ., ii, No. 299, pp.521–22 – the public impression was reported by E. Howard on 30 Nov.; F.O. 371/3002, No. 235106/f.7684.
[55] *New Europe*, v, No. 59 of 29 Nov.

tic reasons.[56] This precipitate judgment did not take into account the real effect of the Bolshevik revolution. A month later the impact of the Russian collapse on the fate of the Poles was seen quite differently by Czernin:

> No discerning critic can expect that the West–Entente will have the forces to bring about a solution of the Polish question against Austria–Hungary *and* Germany.[57]

Indeed, the exit of Russia from the front against the Central Powers was not anticipated when the Allies were ready to support a proclamation on Poland. Then the unification of the Poles by force of arms might have been possible. Now the British were not willing to prolong the war by committing themselves in a way that excluded a negotiated peace.[58]

However, it was essential to express sympathy for the Poles fighting on the side of the Allies. Dmovski used the Bolshevik revolution to press the Foreign Office through his London representative Sobanski, who submitted a memorandum which asked to pay attention to the Polish question in view of Russia's defection and again demanded the dissolution of the Habsburg Empire.[59]

The Allies were obliged to deal with this complicated question at the inter-Allied conference at the beginning of December. Balfour, together with Pichon, had prepared a formula saying that "the creation of a Poland, politically, militarily, and economically independent and indivisible" constituted one of the pre-conditions of a solid and just peace.[60] Hereupon Lloyd George observed that "any statement about Poland might be very dangerous, as it would have an adverse effect upon any discussion with Austria". Lloyd George asked his colleague to consider the Italian position:

> If Austria would give all that Italy wanted, it would, nevertheless, be impossible to make peace unless Austria was willing to hand over Cracov and Lemberg, districts which had always been perfectly well governed and had been better treated by the Austrians than by the Russians under their domination.[61]

Above all Lloyd George found the present moment unpropitious to express more than sympathy for the Poles. The above formula suggested setting up a Polish state by military means at a time when the strength of the Entente was very debatable and the Western Allies had almost broken with Russia. If they included Polish independence in their war aims, the Yugoslavs and the "Tzeks" (*sic*) would immediately

[56] Quoted *Ibid.*
[57] H.H.St.A., Krieg XLVII geh., note of 16 Dec.
[58] Minute by Gregory; *F.O.* 371/3001, No. 189230/f.7684 of 29 Sept.
[59] *F.O.* 371/3002, No. 218943 of 16 Nov.
[60] Minutes of the inter-Allied conference, 3 Dec. 1917, *Cab.* 28/3, *I.C.* 35 a & b.
[61] *Ibid.*

ask for the same and thus embarrass the Allies, who had at least "some hopes from Austria".

In this situation Lloyd George and some of his closest political friends (certainly Milner and Smuts) envisaged with much sympathy the eventuality of Austria–Hungary and Poland forming in Central Europe a political system capable of resisting Russia and Germany at a time. This was the Austro-Polish version of the now slightly modified theory to build up Vienna as a counterpoise to Berlin. This new combination counted on the collaboration of the Poles, for which the British had encouraging evidence, as well as the Magyars, who in this context were never even thought of in London. The whole calculation had a tinge of phantasy and was undoubtedly very difficult to put into practice. At the time it seemed the only viable alternative to *Mitteleuropa* on the one hand and the formation of new national states on the other. The British government, in the most critical phase of the war, made it the long-range aim of their diplomatic actions. On the eve of a direct Austro-British diplomatic contact the Austro-Polish solution had become the mainstay of the British conception for a reconstruction of the Habsburg Empire and the whole of East Central Europe.

3. The Smuts–Mensdorff Meeting

It followed from the promotion of the Austro-Polish solution to a *desideratum* of British foreign policy that the opinion of those Austro-Poles who looked with sympathy at the tentative feelers between London and Vienna, found increasing attention among the British politicians who were responsible for the decisions to be made. It was in fact a memorandum compiled by two prominent Polish leaders, both said to be pro-Allied, that formulated the vision of an Austrian settlement as it was desired by the most decisive personalities residing in Whitehall.

The authors of the paper in question were Professor Pininski, the late governor of Galicia and a member of the Upper House, and Perlovski, a leading Polish exile in Switzerland, who gave the final touch to the former's draft and partly modified it.[62] Both pleaded for peace and a strong Austria, but they gave a more differentiated answer as to how to achieve it than many previously consulted so-called experts. As long as the war went on, they argued, it would be impossible for the Monarchy to break the bonds that united her to the German Empire. Pininski explained:

Those who suppose that she will conclude a separate peace commit an error and I daresay an injustice. She will stay at this to the end of

<hr/>

[62] Rumbold's tel. No. 871 of 5 Dec. 1917, filed in *F.O.* 371/3002, No. 238348/f.7684; minuted by Gregory, Clerk, Graham, Hardinge, Cecil; seen by Smuts and Milner, copy sent to the P.M. (Lloyd George papers F/59/9/9).

the war. But I feel equally entitled to express my deep conviction that she will rejoice in her complete independence after the war.

Then a renovated Danubian Monarchy would be in a position to defend her independence and she would also secure to every one of her nationalities the freedom "Germanism" rendered impossible for so long.

> She will brilliantly succeed, if the Allies do not oppose her effort. Will they commit such an error? It can hardly be supposed. Every political man perceives that after Russia's breakdown, the destruction of Austria means a general break-up and that it would be equivalent to the removal of the last barrier, opposed in the East and the South to unrestrained Germanism. . . . The world needs a great and prosperous Austria and knows that the greater she is, the more will she be freed from any German influence.

These "interesting and attractive" reflections found a wide readership in the Foreign Office and the War Cabinet. The Foreign Office staff was sceptical as to the practicability of some points. Gregory saw an irreconcilable contradiction between the assumed unwillingness of Austria's part to make a separate peace and the aspired re-unification of Poland with Austrian help, which in the opinion of the Assistant Clerk could only be achieved with military means, "as no diplomatic combinations at (the) peace settlement will ever force Posen out of Germany". But Gregory's superiors were not disturbed by such objections.

Three leading figures in the War Cabinet, Lloyd George, Milner and Smuts, increasingly thought in terms of a diplomatic settlement of the war, which was also to include Germany but in such a way that Britain was left as the political winner. Such a situation presupposed that Germany did not achieve an equal position to that of the British Empire after the settlement. In some respects this attitude is a reflection of the attitude of the "New Imperialists", the little but influential group around Milner and Amery that had put before the Cabinet the proposal that Europe should be left "to stew in its own juice" and that Britain and her Dominions should "ride off with the German colonies and Mesopotamia".[63] The contemplation of such a "bad peace" had formerly been rejected. Now the unfortunate military situation revived this plan in a subtle variation, in which the Habsburg Empire was supposed to play a leading part.

A compromise in Europe was barred by the many disputed problems between Austria and Britain's Allies. In order to withdraw unscathed from the scene the latter's claims had to be sacrificed by Britain. In the

---

[63] Hobhouse to C. P. Scott, Scott papers, *B.M. Add. MSS.* 50903, 26 Sept. – on the movement as a whole cf. above, ch. III, 1.

case of Russia and Germany the problem seemed to be solved by events and in the minds of hopeful Britons could also help to bridge the Franco-German gap. Austria's "grave-diggers" were shaken, too. Italy had almost suffered the same fate as Russia. Officially she remained as bellicose as ever, but under the surface a surprisingly pacifist mood could be perceived inside the Italian government. The new minister of the Treasury, Signor Nitti, when pinned down by Lloyd George on Italy's minimum aims, expressed himself extremely moderately. Nitti named the Trentino and Trieste, but, if Italy was compelled to negotiate for peace now,[64]

> it would be necessary that the interest of Italian subjects residing in these districts should be properly protected. This should satisfy the Italian people now that we have been beaten hard.

Smuts did infer from "this most important answer" that Italy, as a result of her humiliation at Caporetto, was prepared to renounce even the Trentino, provided cultural autonomy was conceded. But it seems that Nitti's stand was somewhat ambiguous, for Lloyd George also remembered that he said something about improving Italy's military frontier, which the Prime Minister "understood to mean the Trentino".[65] Never did it occur to the British to scrutinize how far the strategic border of the watershed and the ethnographical divisions between the German-speaking and the Italian population differed from each other. Nor did the British dare to ask the Italians officially about the true nature of their minimum demands. They were satisfied with a remark from a rival politician that Sonnino did not count. From this contention Foreign Office scheming immediately derived that Sonnino's influence was waning against that of Nitti and Giolitti. Being afraid to talk face to face with their Allies about the revision of war aims the British leaders hoped that a sensible attitude on the part of Italy would prevail once they could be confronted with a concrete offer.

The British tactics favoured clearing the ground with the Austrians first. After the Paris conference the position of the Habsburg Empire was analysed under various aspects of H. G. Nicolson. Distinct from most of his senior colleagues, he had a sound knowledge of Austro-Hungarian affairs. Nicolson was neither captured by the Austromania within the Cabinet nor did he sympathize with the extreme demands of the exiles. From his detached personal angle he was able to give an impartial appreciation. Its tone was basically pessimistic. He did not see a way out of Austria's "eternal dilemma between vassalage or disruption". The fruits of victory could mean complete subservience of

---

[64] The interview between Lloyd George and Nitti took place on 1 Dec. in Paris; it was reported by Reading (*F.O.* 371/3086, f.231940) and the P.M. himself (*Cab.* 23/13, *WC* 290a, 4 Dec.).
[65] Marginal note on Smuts's memorandum of 27 Dec., *Cab.* 1/25/27.

the Habsburgs to Berlin, the corollary to defeat being at best a "crowned federation". The chances for a reconstruction on a loose federal basis with a Slav orientation were regarded with reservation:

> It may be doubted whether even if the Emperor Karl were forced towards that ("sense of reality") he would find it possible to re-establish the former equilibrium of discontent which has been the sole cohesive force in the Empire by an adoption of that Slav policy to which he is stated to show so strong an inclination.[66]

Nicolson did not overlook the exhaustion of the Monarchy through the blockade, the lack of organization and sectional distribution. He rated the longing for peace in Austria stronger than in any other country and likely to increase after the collapse of Russia and Italy, because then the menace that had justified patriotism was removed. In spite of this almost universal feeling in Austria, namely that a continuation of the war led to ruin for the sake of Germany, Nicolson felt obliged to emphasize very clearly that there had been "no indication that the Austrian government or people were desirous of concluding a separate peace". Nicolson based his judgment on the records available to him in the Foreign Office. That means that he did not know of the offers of the personal envoys of the Austrian Emperor. But this did not matter for the recent intimations, which were acts of official Austrian diplomacy. They could, therefore, enable the British before long to ascertain

> how far the Austrian government are sincere in their proposals and to what extent they are prepared to induce the German government to a reasonable basis for discussion.

Nicolson's conclusions are symptomatic of the growing disillusionment in the Foreign Office about the possible results of an Austro-British contact. The belief in a separate peace had almost vanished. It would have been the ideal solution from the British point of view, but since there were no indications that it could be achieved, the strained military situation forced politicians and diplomats to think of an alternative which might have similar effects. The method for solving the problem which came more and more under serious consideration in Britain was a sort of diplomatic capitulation of Germany due to Austrian pressure.

This way to end the war by diplomatic negotiations had also advocates on the Austro-Hungarian side. One of them was Count Michael Károlyi, who was free to travel frequently to Switzerland to instil the idea of a peaceful settlement into the minds of both the benevolent enemy and her bigger ally. Károlyi deplored the Kühlmann declaration on Alsace–Lorraine made in October and proposed to transform

---

[66] Memorandum by H. G. Nicolson of 8 Dec. 1917; *F.O.* 371/3986, f.230895.

this land into a federal state, for which Germany should be compensated in Courland. But if Germany remained obdurate, Austria could not continue to fight and had to consider the eventuality of dissociating herself from Germany, "since at present national interest had precedence over a sentimental policy".[67] While this warning was addressed to the Germans, Károlyi already told British agents in Switzerland[68] that he wanted an Austro-Hungarian peace in agreement with the Entente. He captured his listeners by sketching out a startling scheme for a renovated Habsburg Empire, which was to be subdivided into five independent states under the old dynasty: Austria (without the Trentino), Bohemia, Poland (Austrian and Russian parts only), Hungary (including Transylvania), and Yugoslavia (consisting of Croatia, Dalmatia, Serbia and Montenegro).

Károlyi's stress on confederation rather than federation was in accordance with the policy of the independence-party in Hungary. The proposed reorganization of the Dual system into a pentagonal one was unpopular among the Magyar magnates who determined politics in the transleithan part of the Empire. They never ceased to insist on the territorial integrity of the kingdom of Hungary and argued that a federation of five states within the borders of the Monarchy would leave them powerless against Rumania and the Balkan *irredenta*.[69] Károlyi tried to circumvent the latter threat by uniting all South Slavs inside an enlarged Habsburg Empire. Supposing that his proposition was meant seriously, Károlyi had modified his pre-war plans of a Greater Hungary (where the subject nationalities were to be "equal" under Hungarian leadership.[70] Now he offered a conciliatory and broad-minded scheme of full equality to all major nationalities. Only the Rumanians were exempted. Probably Károlyi was aware that a Hungarian state reduced to its purely Magyar population was not attractive enough to the ruling classes in Hungary. After the collapse of Rumania the position of the Transylvanians lacked material support, though there were still sporadic voices of an *irredenta* towards the Monarchy, which were perceived as far as in London.[71]

The Foreign Office reaction to Károlyi's *ballon d'essai* was mixed.

[67] *A.A.*, Wk 2 geh., 53, No. A.40315 of 29 Nov. (report by Romberg).
[68] *F.O.* 371/2864, No. 230982/f.134202; telegram by Rumbold of 3 Dec.
[69] On 9 Oct. Rumbold had reported the supposed attitude of Wekerle, the Hungarian premier, to such proposals. *F.O.* 371/2864, No. 194970/f.2604.
[70] A. J. P. Taylor, *The Habsburg Monarchy*, Peregrine Ed., p.244; Károlyi had already discussed the possibilities of a Danube Federation with a new orientation with Poincaré and Clemenceau during his visit to Paris in 1913. He met with no response, because the French thought that Austria–Hungary was already too much involved in the opposite direction. Cf. *Fighting the World* (M. Károlyi), New York, 1925, pp.78–80.
[71] A notorious spokesman of a Greater Rumania in personal union with the Habsburgs was the conservative Reichsrat deputy from the Bukovina, Ritter v. Onciul, whose speeches were briefed by Seton-Watson; cf. Weekly Report on Austria–Hungary, v. 16 June, *Cab.* 24/16 (G.T. 1073) and New Europe, v. No. 59 of 29 Nov. 1917.

Graham understood that the proposals pre-supposed an Allied victory before negotiations could be commenced, and Hardinge found Károlyi "not strong-eyed" and not deserving serious attention.[72] This verdict being seconded by Balfour the matter could be left aside, had not Drummond made Károlyi's suggestions the starting-point for a detailed memorandum, in which he tried to bring the Foreign Office *desiderata* in proportion to reality. Since his previous account, given in February, decisive changes had taken place which affected the question of a (for Drummond still "separate") peace with Austria–Hungary.[73] The main factor was the collapse of Russia. Up to the present she had been looked upon as the great barrier to German expansion towards the East and the South East. Now it seemed unlikely that Russia would recapture her old strength and coherence for many years to come and be capable of stemming the tide of German influence.

> The smaller Slav states cannot in the near future look to her (Russia) as the protector against Teutonism. Is it not, therefore, advisable to turn elsewhere to find a bar against German expansion? It may be a reconstituted and liberalized Austrian Empire that the Allies desire.

If such a solution was really in the minds of the Austrian and Hungarian statesmen, as Drummond assumed from the Károlyi interview, a strong and efficient barrier against German predominance in *Mitteleuropa* could be constructed – at least in the workshop of the Foreign Office. For Drummond the difficulties involved did not seem insuperable. He was only troubled by the Serbian question. His answer to this hardest obstacle was a fusion of Serbia, Montenegro, Bosnia, Herzegovina, Dalmatia, and Croatia under the Habsburg crown, which "would have probably come to pass if the Archduke Francis Ferdinand had come to the throne". Drummond was convinced that the Serbians of Serbia were attracted by this solution. He made the future dynastic loyalty a matter of education. The Serbians of the Monarchy were, "on the whole, of a higher class and on a higher intellectual level" than their independent brethren. Consequently it was "in the interest of everybody that the future Yugoslav state should ... have complete autonomy under the nominal rule of the Habsburgs", while the Serbian dynasty should remain "like the kings of Bavaria and Saxony". Even if the Károlyi scheme proved unacceptable – as it did to Hardinge – a solution of the Serbian question should be possible. A strong Austrian *bloc* was not regarded as necessarily antagonistic to a Balkan *bloc*, which might constitute still another barrier against German expansion eastwards".[74] Obviously the shock of Germany's recent military successes

---

[72] Minutes on No. 230982; cf. n.2, p.275.
[73] G.T. 2976 of 10 Dec. 1917, *Cab.* 24/35, copies in Balfour papers (*F.O.* 800/200) and Milner papers, box 125.
[74] Minute by Hardinge, *ibid.*

had frightened the Foreign Office so much that they wanted to build up a whole series of compact geographical entities with an anti-German orientation as an assurance against a repetition of the German *Weltpolitik*. But the mobilization of potential candidates became problematic when Germany had a direct hold over the people that should be organized against her. This applied to a section of the Poles. If the Allies were sufficiently successful to impose their own terms on Germany, German Poland "could well be added to Austrian and Russian Poland". The question of German Poland, Drummond advised, should be reserved till the end of the war in view of Austria making peace independently of Germany.

The proviso of the Polish resolution at the Paris conference was a first attempt to create a basis, on which Austria could be induced to liberate herself, a desire she showed increasingly, both as regards the present and the future. The prospects for negotiations were judged to be positive by Drummond, in spite of the military situation, which could in fact prove an advantage for diplomacy in closing the gap between the territorial promises of the secret treaties and the demands that could actually be exacted from Austria.

In the wake of the crumbling Russian colossus the Rumanians could not resist the Central Powers. From recent telegrams it appeared that under the new conditions the Rumanian king and government would be content if they could secure the territory formerly belonging to them.[75] The claim for Transylvania had been dropped: the legal title to it was invalidated by the military realities. Italy was spared a similar fate to the Rumanians, but she had suffered a grievous defeat and might be induced "to be content with much less than they are strictly entitled to by the treaty made at the time of entry". The Trentino plus the transformation of Trieste into a free port might after all satisfy "the larger part of the Italian nation". Britain was always prepared to defend this minimum on moral grounds. The legal claim to Adriatic and other districts which were unjustifiable on the principle of nationality were, in British eyes, forfeited on the battlefield. If the Italians could not obtain them with their own men, the British did not stand up for these aspirations. They sent troops to prevent the catastrophe of a collapse of yet another ally, which was useful to bind part of the enemy forces. They refused to support Italy's hankering after imperialist dreams, which they saw now as a threat to their own Empire, because she would necessitate continuing the war at a stage when it seemed no longer desirable from a British imperial point of view.

Bearing this aspect in mind it is perhaps not too surprising that the

---

[75] They also showed themselves willing to cede part of the Dobrudja to Bulgaria, if compensated in the Bukovina and Bessarabia.

negotiator nominated by the British side was someone whose political thinking was dominated by his concern for the future of the Empire–Commonwealth: General Smuts. He had naturally only a limited knowledge of the intricate structure of the Habsburg Empire and its border disputes. But this did not deter the War Cabinet from commissioning him. Habsburg experts like Seton-Watson and Steed were not considered as attendants because of their bias. For the purpose of the mission they were not necessary, either. The idea of the government was to prepare the ground for an understanding on broad lines, for which the negotiator need not know geographical *minutiae*. Vociferous criticism against the selection of Smuts on these grounds is unjustified. On the other hand the choice of an Englishman who had personal links with Austria looked more promising at first sight to produce a good climate for the meeting. Lord Derby, for instance, called himself a personal friend of Mensdorff and thought he could find out what his real opinions were.[76] But the journey of a well-known personality like him to Switzerland was bound to be detected and would have aroused suspicion. The Cabinet thought that a "colonial" might be let off more lightly than an Englishman, when the expedition came to be revealed. Moreover, within the War Cabinet Smuts's authority was highly appreciated and his views on war aims and peace were particularly valued by Lloyd George and Milner, whose opinions on the prospect of the war converged after the Bolshevik revolution.

Smuts had already approached Milner's position in Spring 1917, when he set down as one of the four major war aims of the British Empire, "A settlement of Europe which will limit or destroy the military predominance of the Germanic powers, though the actual details of such a settlement may be left open for the peace conference".[77] Smuts believed that the time factor was in Britain's favour "only up to a point". The foundations of Europe were loosened in the convulsion of the war and Russia and America might "well prove a diplomatic embarrassment at the end".[78] Smuts therefore became an advocate of defining the essential objects and the best means to realize them in the shortest time, because this was perhaps the "road to an early victorious peace".

Smuts was guided by the presupposition that the Allies could not overcome Germany by defeating her completely in the near future. In his opinion only a limited military victory was obtainable. Germany had to be convinced by a certain measure of military success and the assurance that the destruction of her national existence (for which

---

[76] Letter by Derby to Lloyd George, 1 Sept. 1917, Lloyd George papers, F/14/4/65.
[77] Memorandum of 29 Apr. 1917, printed in *War Memoirs*, i, p.909ff.
[78] This and the following quotations are from Smuts's notes for a speech during Mar./May 1917, printed in *Selections from the Smuts Papers*, iii, No. 748.

Smuts assumed she was fighting!) was not the aim of the Allies, or at least the British, whose policy was traditionally based on the balance of power in Europe, and Smuts feared that the destruction of Germany might create a vacuum into which "seven worse devils may enter". This applied *mutatis mutandis* to the Habsburg Empire. Smuts stood up for the restoration of Serbia and Rumania and the cession of *Italia irredenta* to Italy but demanded a clear seaway for Austria. The matters of Poland, Bohemia, Transylvania, Bosnia, Macedonia, and Dalmatia should be settled at the peace conference. That is to say a change of the internal structure of the monarchy should not be enforced during the war. Speaking at Sheffield on 24 October[79] Smuts spelled out his ideas in public:

> We do not want to break up Germany or Austria, we do not wish to break up anybody or anything. But lines must be laid down by which the small nations can come into their own. If they cannot be independent, let them be autonomous and not tyrannized over by imperious Empires. I do not think the world will split up into small states. The tendency will rather be the other way. But it will be along national lines.

All this implied that pledges to the minor Allies could not be implemented. Smuts largely agreed with his regular correspondent Lord Loreburn, who drew gloomy consequences from a continuation of the war on behalf of the other European Allies:

> If we are to carry out the claims of Sonnino, Ribot, Pashich (*sic*) and others, the war cannot possibly be ended till famine and epidemics and anarchy have destroyed civilization.

The Liberal peer (later to become a member of the Lansdowne Committee) was disturbed by the disintegration in Russia and the mutinies in France. He offered the suggestion to Smuts that he and another (Bryce) should "meet face to face someone on the enemy side . . . to learn if there is a way which may open the prospect of peace". With the concurrence of her Allies Britain could then find out what the Central Powers were ready to do, either by direct informal communication or preferably through the U.S.A. and Austria.[80]

Although the idea appealed to Smuts, he was at the same time "profoundly impressed with the enormous difficulties and perplexities surrounding the whole object of peace". He suspected Germany of manoeuvering for a conference, at which she could hope to win more than in the field. Knowing that informal feelers had been put out between France and Austria he doubted whether anything could be usefully done before the fighting season closed in winter.

---

[79] *The Times* of 25 Oct. 1917.

[80] *Selections from the Smuts Papers*, iii, No. 777, letter from Loreburn of 9 Sept., answered by Smuts on 12 inst., *ibid.*, No. 780.

By that time the fall of Russia and the defeat of Italy had changed the situation to being "far from favourable but equally far from despair". Smuts warned against exaggerating the bearing of the events in Italy and Russia. If the Bolsheviks made a separate peace with a great surrender of territory that might produce a new situation politically:

> Germany might say: Russia was the real enemy, now she is destroyed. England is not a military nation, France is done for all time. We can afford to make great concessions in the West – restore Belgium, give the Trentino to Italy, compromise on Alsace–Lorraine. As to our colonies we can let them go. It should be difficult to resist such a proposal. If the war is won without a direct military victory, it will I am sure be a greater triumph, because it will be the conquest of the instruments of war by the instruments of peace and will demonstrate that peace hereafter can be maintained.[81]

This was a clear-cut option for a general peace on a compromise basis. But could one expect Germany to react in the way Smuts had optimistically sketched out? They were conditions which the British would like her to accept. Balfour, who was asked by Smuts to comment on a paper of his which elaborated the above proposals in detail,[82] expected America and also France to be content with them, but he did not see the slightest chance of Germany admitting defeat diplomatically. Therefore it was questionable to Balfour whether one would gain from proposing these terms at all. Negotiations could only bear success, if the British made tentative qualifications in the extreme demands of their minor Allies. If the negotiations broke down nevertheless – as Balfour thought they would – the enemy had a powerful instrument for a peace propaganda that could split up the Entente, though this danger was partly obviated by the fact that every proposal had to be *ad referendum*. In any case, Balfour disliked the idea of a settlement at which all the compromises were at the expense of Serbia, Rumania, Poland(!), and Italy (and perhaps France), none at the expense of Great Britain or America. Differing from Smuts and the leading Cabinet members, the Foreign Secretary stuck to a solution which satisfied the small nations and perhaps also the subject nationalities. Balfour cannot be called a champion of the principle of nationality and he did not follow the extreme aspirations of the exile politicians. But he sensed that there could not be a political system of Europe that ignored their demands entirely. Britain's entry into the war had been motivated on high moral principles. Now she seemed to embark on a policy that abandoned them almost completely, if only the continued prosperity of the Empire was saved.

---

[81] C. P. Scott papers, *B.M. Add. MSS*. 50904, 12/12 Nov. 1917.

[82] The Smuts paper has not been found, but it can be reconstructed from Balfour's answer of 15 Dec., Balfour papers, 49697, *B.M. Add. MSS*.

The catchword to overcome such scruples was "federalism". If the general policy of building up a new Austria on federal lines was accepted, Balfour saw several stumbling blocks in its way if one did not want to alienate the opinion of the peoples concerned. This applied to the Austro-Polish solution as well as to the Serbian question. Here Balfour did not like the latter at all to come out of the war smaller, that is without the "uncontested zone" and merely gaining Herzegovina. The Czech and Yugoslav problems were "very hard to judge" for him. When he was pressed by Horodyski (an agent of Polish origin working in the interest of the Allies) to make a further announcement in favour of an independent Poland and an independent Bohemia, he did not conceal from the Cabinet the fact that his personal sympathies were with the "Bohemians", who he thought deserved the greatest consideration, because they had made great sacrifices for the Allies, but he feared that "owing to their geographical position the ideal of independence appeared chimerical, the utmost that they could hope for being home-rule within the Austro-Hungarian Empire".[83] When Smuts suggested that it might be impossible to do anything for Bohemia or the Yugoslavs, Balfour concurred, but "if so it is greatly to be deplored".[84] Balfour's cool comments upon General Smuts's efforts to find a *modus vivendi* reduced all deliberations to the simple question: should the British, for the sake of a mere chance of an anti-German course by Vienna at some uncertain time, sacrifice the lot of the subject peoples of the Habsburgs?

British voices that left the internal structure to the discretion of Vienna and Budapest and did not question the Berlin–Vienna axis did not represent the official policy in London. This was recognized realistically at the Ballplatz and the exaggerated attention devoted by the Austrian press to singular pacifist utterances had only propaganda value.[85] When these forces were gaining ground in Britain after the Bolshevik revolution, Vienna tried to use the new climate created by the conciliatory mood for negotiations that took into account this increasing pacifism. The *Neue Freie Presse* considered it "almost a duty that a word should be addressed from Austria to the British nation as to whether a conversation would be possible."[86]

Count Czernin himself stated the view of his government publicly in a speech held in front of the "delegations" (the two parliamentary committees by which alone the Foreign Minister could be called to

---

[83] *WC* 279 of 21 Nov. 1917, *Cab*. 23/4.17.

[84] Cf. p.284, n.1.

[85] This counter-propaganda particularly annoyed Seton-Watson, who accused the Austrian press of "telling tales about England". Cf. Weekly report on A.-H. xv, G.T. 1999 of 8 Sept. 1917, *Cab*. 24/25.

[86] Articles of 30 Nov. and 4 Dec. 1917.

account for his policy), which met on 4 December.[87] On this occasion Czernin justified the reorganisation of the Monarchy on a Dualist basis fifty years ago. He bitterly attacked the "brutal formula" of the Entente that asked for self-determination for the single nationalities without respecting the sovereignty of the Austro-Hungarian state and its right to control its territorial existence. For him the Allied demand for self-determination was no more than a mantle to cover forcible detachments of Habsburg territory on behalf of her minor Allies, whereas the Entente had never run short of pretexts for not allowing the right of self-determination to be applied to herself. The accusation of pursuing selfish annexationist aims did not of course work out with the Czechs. For Czernin, however, "the question of nationalities inside the various states regulating their relation to one another and to the State, this is not an international but an internal question." With the same determination he rejected all idea of a separate peace, which culminated in the phrase "I know no difference between Strassburg and Trieste". For the ears of those Britons who still fostered hopes Czernin had only a sarcastic retort:

> If, then, there are still people in the Entente who live in the illusion that they might succeed in separating us from our ally, then I can only say they are bad psychologists and childish minds.

Under these circumstances Balfour felt bound to warn Lloyd George:

> Personally, I have always feared that success is not likely at the present stage; but is it not rather rash to make what is in any case difficult almost impossible?[88]

Balfour's main concern about sending Smuts, who, incidentally he regarded as "a most admirable choice", was that it was almost certain to be detected. Balfour was led to believe by the Austrian insistence on incognito that they manoeuvered independently from Germany. Lloyd George seemed to think that secrecy was unimportant, because the Austrians acted with German consent.

In actual fact, Berlin's ambassador was briefly informed immediately after Mensdorff's departure. Czernin told him that he had accepted the British proposal of a meeting with Smuts "according to a previous agreement between Vienna and Berlin".[89] It had been communicated to the British government that Mensdorff would be merely commissioned "to listen to what Smuts had to say". Mensdorff had

---

[87] All essential parts quoted hereafter are printed in *New Europe*, v, No. 64, 3 Jan. 1918.
[88] *F.O.* 800/199, letter by Balfour to Lloyd George of 10 Dec. 1917.
[89] *A.A.*, Wk 2 geh., 54, No. AS5025 of 17 Dec. – the agreement to which Czernin referred must be Kühlmann's consent to a continuance of the feeler to Painlevé. The Austro-British approach was not prepared in accordance with Berlin!

corresponding instructions and should remark that a separation between Germany and Austria–Hungary was out of the question. Britain
should finally give up her illusions and face facts. As a matter of fact, the
British did so to a certain extent, as the instructions for General Smuts
show. He was given clear and definite limits for his mission to Switzerland and was not entitled to discuss a general peace, but conversely his
trip did not merely aim at sounding out the Austrians directly whether
they finally accepted a separate peace offer or would even make one
themselves. This question played only a secondary role in the considerations of the British side. Smuts personally described his principal
object: "to instil into the minds of the Austrians that in case they freed
themselves from German domination and made a fresh start in sympathy with the British Empire they would have our full sympathy and
support".[90] This could be done in three stages:[91]

1) discussion of the possibility of a separate peace,
2) demonstration that the destruction of Austria was not included in
   British (and Allied) war aims,
3) general attempts to pave the way towards an understanding with
   Austria.

British confidence in the feasibility of the first stage (although first in
terms of desirability) had been disheartened by previous events and
notions. So Smuts did not even dare to raise this first point. It was his
interlocutor who took the initiative and made it clear from the beginning that a separate peace "was entirely out of the question" that
Austria would follow the example of Italy by doing "anything so
treacherous and dishonourable". Mensdorff explained that Austria
was prepared to do anything to secure "an honourable peace short of
deserting her ally during the war".

Smuts, who was evidently prepared for a declaration of this kind,
thereupon commenced to expound a conglomeration of ideas on the
Habsburg Monarchy according to the line he had discussed before his
departure with Lloyd George, Balfour, and Milner.[92] Smuts did not
conceal their anxiety about the future of Europe because of the downfall
of Russia, which had taken a form that made it not only a disaster for
her allies in the war but a factor of uncertainty and concern for the more
distant future. Smuts and his colleagues did not foresee the later impact
of Bolshevism. The fear of them and "many influential quarters" was
rather based on the precarious situation which would be intolerable in
their eyes: a Europe without a counterweight to Germany.

---

[90] Smuts's account of the conversations is contained in Lloyd George, *War Memoirs*, ii, p.1478ff.
Unless otherwise indicated the following quotations are from this source.
[91] Acc. to Smuts's statement in the War Cabinet on 18 Jan. 1918, WC 235a, Cab. 23/16.
[92] For the latter cf. Milner-diary, entries of 10 and 11 Dec. 1917.

From this point of view it was a matter of grave concern that Austria should no longer continue her role of subordination to Germany, that she should be emancipated from German domination, and should, with the assistance of the Entente, and especially the British Empire, make a fresh start of complete independence *vis-à-vis* the German Empire. If Austria was prepared to play that role and break with Germany she would have not only our active support, and we would do everything in our power to uphold and strengthen her and to assist her economic reconstruction.

To prove the Allied and particularly the British benevolence Smuts categorically denied that it was their intention to break-up and partition Austria–Hungary as the Austrians thought was foreshadowed in the Allied statement of January 1917. Then and still more at present, Smuts assured Mensdorff, it was their object to assist Austria to give the greatest freedom and autonomy to her subject nationalities. The liberalisation of the Austro-Hungarian "local institutions" was the best way to convince the British of the value of friendly mutual relations. Smuts left open the form which the liberalization was expected to take. He stressed that the Allies did not want to interfere in Austria's internal affairs. What they were interested in was that the subject nationalities were "satisfied and content" like the peoples of the British Empire, which he held out as an example worthy of emulation. Austria should become a League of Nations comparable to the Empire–Commonwealth.

Together with this internal emancipation there should be a marked dissociation from Germany, which seemed absolutely necessary to "thoughtful people in England" to secure the full sympathy and co-operation of the Entente, especially of Britain and the U.S.A. Such a new orientation would give Austria a justification for her existence in the future. To sum up, the Habsburg mission after the war was to keep a peaceful stalemate of the balance of power on the continent against the expected renewed attempt of a not completely beaten German militarism.

The territorial details affecting Austria–Hungary were to be solved by the establishment of a South East European confederation. This was most obvious in the case of Poland, which would get Galicia for accepting an Austrian ruler on its throne. For the other states to which the Allies made pledges during the war "means should be found to satisfy the reasonable claims". The procedure would be similar to the one sketched out for Poland. Their irredentas should be acquiesced in order to create the climate for togetherness under the Habsburg patronage. Austria–Hungary was summoned by Smuts to "approach these questions in a broad spirit, sacrifice a little to gain indirectly a great deal more".[93] Evidently she was invited to profit politically and economically from all the advantages inherent in a great economic unit, which was to comprise Poland, an enlarged Serbia, and possibly Rumania.

Smuts's sound territorial arrangement would have given Serbia Bosnia–Herzegovina and brought her to the Dalmatian coast (which left the margin of interpretation between a free port and the actual acquisition of a strip of coastline). Mensdorff appeared to be not unfavourable to this solution of the South Slav question. He was on the other hand vehemently opposed to making concessions to a beaten Rumania and Smuts had to withdraw his advance for Transylvania. He tried to secure at least part of the Bukovina, which Mensdorff admitted to be on a different footing. But the Austrian envoy expressed the hope that eventually no proposals would be made by the Allies which went in the direction of a "partition" of the Hungarian kingdom as this would be most fiercely resisted by the Hungarians.

The German Austrians were, however, not going to set them an example of conciliation in their dispute with Italy. Mensdorff denied all Italian claims, because they were not in accordance with the principle of nationality! He categorically refused any compromise and said that Austria would never cede Trieste and its hinterland.[94] Smuts insisted on the cession of at least the Trentino (Trient, Trento) and felt that Austria would be prepared for a deal, although Mensdorff did not expressly say so. Actually Mensdorff wrote in his report that he had declared that Austria would never cede "a foot of ground" to Italy. He added with reference to the Trentino that one had to be prepared for British support of the Italian point of view.[95]

The whole conversation between Smuts and Mensdorff was conducted on an "academic" level. Smuts purposely abstained from going into details of territorial questions at this stage;

> for he "intended merely to have a preliminary canter over the ground in order to satisfy (himself) in (his) capacity as a scout of the general attitude of the Austrians on the question of territorial concessions.

The impression he formed was that Austria was in an accommodating mood, which is a surprising conclusion because Mensdorff did not make a single suggestion that Austria would compromise on any issue concerning her pre-war territorial possessions. Mensdorff's main

---

[93] Quoted (in English!) in Mensdorff's report for Czernin, which was published (as a reaction to Smuts's version in Lloyd George's Memoirs) in *Berliner Monatshefte*, xv, 1938, pp.401–419.

[94] When Buxton asked Smuts on 17 March 1918 whether the Mensdorff interview did not imply leaving Austria intact and in possession of Trieste, Smuts answered: "Not intact, but it would be mad to cut off Austria from the sea, when we are claiming a port for Poland." Cit. T. P. Conwell-Evans, *op. cit.*, p.150.

[95] Cf. footnote 93 above.

interest, which he repeatedly tried to manifest, was to offer Au
help in mediating between Germany and Britain through prelim
conversations between London and Vienna. Smuts refused to disc\
general peace or any terms concerning Germany. But in fact his l\ -g
range aim and that of his British mandatories was exactly that, as long
as they could be sure that the Austrians would help them to force
Germany to accept terms which the Allies, due to the most unfavourable circumstances of the war situation, considered by now unavoidable
to agree to. In Smuts's opinion the chances for Austria thus acting in
the interest of Britain were increased by his talk with Mensdorff:

> From the very depth of her abasement and despair, Austria has been
> made to see daylight, and I expect that she will strain every nerve to
> induce Germany to accept moderate terms, and that she will there-
> after strive, with our assistance, to recover and assert her political
> independence of Germany.

Smuts had finally come to a conclusion which had been more or less
preconceived by the British leaders, before they sent him to Geneva,
namely that a separate peace with Austria–Hungary was not feasible.
On the other hand peacemaking with Germany would have been the
acknowledgment of defeat at that stage. But the continuation of the war
seemed to overcharge the forces of the British Empire and its partners.
So the British were tentatively thinking of a third way to peace. Their
ideas, which were still in a very indefinite form as regards the actual
peacemaking, were led by the desire to find a way of defeating Germany
with diplomatic means.[96] Smuts outlined the direction in which the
efforts of British diplomacy should go; every opportunity should be
taken to drive a wedge between Germany and Austria, should be made
so that Austria would "look to us rather than to Germany for her future
after the war".[97] Smuts, who was convinced more than any other
British statesman that a conference including Germany was unavoidable finally, laboured to "prepare a general peace" that satisfied both
the Central Powers and the Allies. For this goal a constellation had to
be brought about to convince the enemy that it was not worth continuing the fighting and that it would be better "to concede to us most of our
legitimate war aims". So far a conference for a general peace could not
be entered into by the Allies, because they would have been in a
position inferior to Germany. If she turned out the unscrupulous
negotiator she was expected to be, she could play off the Allies against
each òther because there was no unity on the other side.

The first step to be taken, Smuts proposed, was to destroy this

---

[96] The suggestion that the Smuts mission aimed at a political solution including Germany was
made by W. Steglich, *op.cit.*, pp.259–62 & 311, although he overrated the British willingness to
negotiate with Germany.

[97] Memorandum on "Peace Preparations" by Smuts, 27 Dec. 1918, *Cab*. 1/25, No. 27.

advantage by seizing every opportunity to drive a wedge between Germany and Austria. Secondly, Smuts advised them to continue to hold out a helping hand and an open ear to Austria, on the assumption that she was talking behind the back of her ally. Britain as the trustee of the Entente should exploit the Austrian mood to talk and use her privileged position gained at the Paris conference to "clear the ground at least as far as Austria was concerned". Smuts hoped to reach "rough provisional conclusions" by this informal "spade work", to use his term.

If the Austrian issues, which formed most of the intricate topics that stood in the way of a satisfactory peace, could be settled in advance, Smuts argued, there would be ultimately, when one came to settle accounts with Germany, only two questions left: Alsace–Lorraine and the colonies (assuming that Germany was prepared to evacuate Belgium and Northern France). There were of course also the more general questions of trade, disarmament, and a League of Nations, but they were considered to be of secondary importance in reaching a settlement, which Smuts believed would have been immensely facilitated if the "numerous and dangerous pitfalls" of the territorial problems had been removed from the slate beforehand.

The weak points of Smuts's proposals are quite obvious. Firstly, he could not offer a practical procedure as to how to get guarantees for Austria's behaviour at a peace conference and still less as to the nature of her post-war policy. Secondly, despite her leading position in the Entente, Britain had not yet succeeded in clarifying what exactly were the minimum aims of her allies, not to mention the difficulty of persuading combatants to reduce their claims. Thirdly, it would have been extremely difficult to establish a Habsburg confederation by secret diplomacy and practically over the heads of the peoples concerned.

Were the hopes fostered by Smuts, Lloyd George and Milner, to name only those who were most influential and could determine the further development, more than odd, visionary dreams? Smuts came away optimistically from the Geneva meeting. He had

> the impression that, if we had to deal with Austria alone, there were no insuperable difficulties in the way of a satisfactory arrangement, though these difficulties were increased by the resentment felt at the conduct of Italy and Roumania.[98]

Since France had also not responded very enthusiastically to the British proposals, although they were presented at Paris as if they aimed exclusively at a separate peace with Austria, the only potential ally for Britain on the Austrian question was America. Balfour, who personally

---

[98] *F.O.* 371/3133, No. 3465/f.2002 of 29 Dec. 1917 (copy in *B.M. Add. MSS.* 49738).

was quite indifferent to the whole matter, undertook to draft a telegram to President Wilson to inform him about what had happened in Switzerland. Robert Cecil, who was consulted on its wording, strongly objected to the inclusion of the above passage, because thereby Wilson would be given the qualified approval of the British of a settlement that was "not an easy one to carry through".[99] For Cecil it clearly involved a German Courland and Lithuania and therefore German predominance in Finland and Sweden, for which the Allies would get the evacuation of Belgium and perhaps part of Alsace. "As far as Europe was concerned", he concluded,

> this cannot be regarded as a brilliant result of the war, though it may turn out to be the best we can do. It is all that is likely to come out of the Geneva negotiations.

Cecil's scepticism in a settlement through Austria was confirmed by his doubts about the prospect of reconstructing the Habsburg Empire. He attached very little importance to the Emperor Karl's alleged liberal leanings, but even if they were sincere and enduring,

> Autocrats and Ministers have very little power. The policy of Austria–Hungary will always be the policy of its German and Magyar populations.

4. The Revision of British War Aims

One practical suggestion by Mensdorff fell upon fruitful ground. He had urged the British to state their peace terms clearly and definitely so that there could be no misunderstanding as to their aims. If the Central Powers felt that they were reasonable, Mensdorff declared, they would be accepted. If they did not form "a basis for discussion", they would be rejected, but then at least the ground had been cleared.[100]

The campaign for a broad revision of Allied war aims had been persistently pursued by the Petrograd Soviet and after some hesitation this demand became the official policy of the Provisional Government. When the Western Entente partly gave in to this pressure, it was already too late, and the scheduled inter-Allied conference to revise the Allied war aims never took place. The procrastinating attitude of the Western Powers towards the Russian demand for a "democratic" programme became partially responsible for Kerensky's fall. The Russian call for peace, however, could not be stopped. After the Bolshevik uprising their decree proposed the immediate opening of negotiations.[101] This was the beginning of an independent Russian peace

[99] *Ibid.*; this telegram was shown to the Prime Minister and Gen. Smuts who concurred!
[100] *War Memoirs*, ii, p.1489.
[101] A. J. Mayer, *op.cit.*, p.261–62.

policy aiming at an armistice. Militarily it meant the collapse of Russia as a fighting ally, while at the same time another (Italy) was apparently following suit.

Disquietened by this outlook Lord Lansdowne made his second attempt during the war to convince the government of the advisability of a negotiated peace.[102] He did not believe that the Central Powers, and especially Germany, could be brought to their knees. As long as they were unbeaten, Lansdowne argued, they could not be expected to accept all of the conditions specified in the Allied note of 10 January. Some of the proposals in this enumeration remained essential, such as the restoration of Belgium, Alsace–Lorraine (to a degrée that France considered indispensable), Serbia, and Rumania. On the other hand, the Russian claims could no longer be regarded in the light of 1914. The pretentions of Italy were "always exorbitant" and Lansdowne believed that the Italian government would welcome a peace under which she might only obtain a part of the concessions upon which she insisted as the price of their adhesion to the Allied cause. Lansdowne distinguished between aims which were regarded as not open to discussion and those which required "further examination, probably by the light of the wishes, not yet clearly ascertained, of the populations immediately concerned". The latter qualification was to be applied to the demand for the "liberation of the Slavs, Rumanes, and Czecho-Slovaks from foreign domination." Besides the obvious threat to the Habsburg Empire Lansdowne was concerned that Allied policy might aim at the economic annihilation of Germany and therefore wanted the government to declare that it did not seek to bring about the destruction or dismemberment of either of the Central Powers.

Faced with these reproaches the Foreign Secretary assured Lansdowne that he did not desire the destruction or dismemberment of Germany, if this did not exclude the transference of certain territorial fringes (Poles, Alsace–Lorraine) and what was true of Germany might "surely be applied, *mutatis mutandis*, to Austria also".[103]

Encouraged by the attitude of the Foreign Office Lansdowne had his appeal for a "co-ordination of the Allies' War Aims" published in *The Daily Telegraph* of 29 November. The crucial part of the letter dealt with the note of 10 January; which the author asked to re-examine:

Some of original desiderata have probably become unattainable. Others would probably be given a less permanent place than when they were first put forward . . . when it comes to the wholesale rearrangement of the map of South-Eastern Europe we may well ask

---

[102] The relevant documents for the Lansdowne move are published in *Nineteenth Century*, Mar. 1934, pp.370–84.
[103] *Ibid.*, p.378, Balfour to Lansdowne, 22 Nov. 1917.

for a suspension of judgment and for the elucidation which a frank exchange of views between the Allied Powers can alone afford.

Lansdowne practically invited the Government to repudiate all interest in Eastern Europe and return to that attitude of detached *désintéressement*, which had marked British Balkan policy before the war. The reaction to his letter was divided. It was polemically attacked by the Northcliffe press and severely criticized by the *New Europe*.[104] The Government spokesmen publicly condemned it, although they had privately arrived at very similar conclusions. Lloyd George was annoyed, because the letter had been published at a very inconvenient moment, namely when he himself was intending to persuade the other Allies to a more moderate course at the Paris conference. Now it looked as if his careful move and the publication of the letter were a concerted action and the government could be suspected of pacifist tendencies.[105] The Radical peace propaganda had indeed found a powerful ally, as the *New Europe* realised with horror:

> In revolutionary times extremes meet, and it need not surprise us to note the gradual formation of a new coalition between reactionaries like Lord Lansdowne and Radical doctrinaires like *The Nation* . . . It is not yet sufficiently realized that there is a small but active school of individuals who would have us "scrap" as Utopian many of the war aims of our Allies – especially, of course, those of our small Allies – and concentrate upon our own selfish aims.

The support for the Lansdowne letter was actually more widespread than the *New Europe* was prepared to admit. The *Manchester Guardian* welcomed the letter as an attack on "profitable patriotism" and the *Westminster Gazette* commented that it expressed a great body of public opinion which so far had been inarticulate in order not to embarrass the government.[106]

The emergence of a new section of moderates among industrialists, merchants, and bankers was observed with interest by the Americans. Colonel House hardly disagreed with Lansdowne and thought on similar lines as his associate Loreburn, with whom he conferred on the eve of the Paris Conference, when he informed himself about the war aims movement in Britain, where he also spoke to Hirst, Brailsford, Massingham, Lansbury, Spender, C. P. Scott, and Asquith.[107]

After the American attempt for a common war aims declaration had failed, Wilson made his own statement on 4 December. On that day he

---

[104] No. 61 of 13 Dec. 1917.
[105] *WC* 290a of 4 Dec., *Cab.* 23/13; *Min. Aff.Etr., loc.cit.*, note by J. Cambon of 2 Dec.
[106] 30 Nov. 1917.
[107] Seymour, *op.cit.*, iii, p.232–33; regular reports on Radical opinion were sent to the House by W. H. Buckler, a special agent attached to the American Embassy in London. Cf. L. W. Martin, *Peace without Victory*, Newhaven 1958, p.115.

announced the declaration of war by America on Germany's allies including Austria–Hungary. He had been driven to this decision by the military events on the Italian front. Paradoxically this was not an American move towards an anti-Habsburg policy. Wilson reassured the Austrian statesmen and their Allied sympathisers that the Americans did "not wish in any way to impair or to re-arrange the Austro-Hungarian Empire". Wilson disclaimed all desire of dictating to them how to handle their economic or political affairs. All he asked for was that Austria–Hungary should be freed from Prussian influence, and while declaring war on that power, he apparently offered peace with her on almost any terms provided that she would break with "Prussia".[108]

In substance there was no difference between Lansdowne and Wilson who both wanted to remove the impression that the Allies desired the annihilation of any of their enemies. But Lansdowne had to restrict himself to the argument that some of the Allies' war aims had become obsolete and should be restated. The hint of a possible understanding with Austria, as it was implied by Wilson, would have been impeached by the patriotic press, which tended to denounce the idea of a separate peace as indicative of a compromise policy towards Germany.[109]

Wilson's declaration was immediately taken up by the Radical opposition in the Commons, where Philip Snowdon asked whether, in view of the President's statement, the British government and its Allies now intended to revise their war aims. Balfour refused to attempt an interpretation of Wilson's speech, but in the long run he could not avoid a discussion on the subject which now concerned more than just a handful of Radicals.

Their stalwart, Noel Buxton, realized the importance of increasing support at home and abroad in order to make an impact on the British government. The President's influence was the foremost factor, the second being Asquith's attitude.[110] Buxton and Wedgwood were puzzled by Asquith's recent utterances, which reiterated the demand for the dismemberment of the Habsburg Monarchy.[111] Such pronouncements presumably were designed in order to represent any terms made by Lloyd George as a bad peace. Now Buxton and his parliamentary friends tried to bring Asquith on a more conciliatory line with an appeal which was circulated to all Liberal M.P.s. The passage condemning "extravagant aims such as the destruction of Austria" found the qualified approval of men who had hitherto loyally supported the

---

[108] For a corresponding comparison cf. Cecil's letter to Lloyd George; Lloyd George papers, F/6/5/10, 5 Dec. 1917.

[109] Cf. *Spectator* of 3 Nov. 1917 & *National Review* of Feb. 1918.

[110] Letter by Noel Buxton to House of 12 Nov. 1917; L. W. Martin, *op.cit.*, p.151.

[111] E.g. his speech at Birmingham on 11 Dec., which was disapproved of by Lloyd George for the same reason (C. P. Scott papers, *B.M. Add. MSS.* 50904).

government. George Greenwood demanded "a just and much needed rectification of the Italian frontier", but beyond this he agreed that the dismemberment of Austria–Hungary was no part of the Allied terms. He thought, however, that "the deliverance of the misgoverned Slavs under Austrian rule" would immensely benefit humanity. A. F. Whyte, meanwhile the editor of the *New Europe*, also did not cherish the explicit call for dismemberment, but he thought

> it wrong to suggest as is often done now that we have no quarrel with the Habsburg Monarchy. Doubtless the extent and depth of the quarrel depends on the relations of Vienna with Berlin, but as long as they are now and as long as the whole system of Government is unchanged in Austria – and especially in Hungary – the Monarchy will be a menace to European peace.[112]

These answers to Buxton are typical of the anti-Habsburg spokesmen in Britain. They did not demand the destruction of the Monarchy *per se*. What they insisted on was the liberation of its Slav subjects. This involved a drastic curb of Germany's reserves, both economically and militarily, for once the Slavs could determine their own fate, they could not any longer be used as pawns in the calculations of Berlin. So the primary source of the anti-Austrian argument was in fact anti-Germanism. The eventual form of Slavization in the Danube basin was of secondary importance and depended on circumstances. Theoretically it could happen within the Monarchy or by the establishment of new independent states. The latter solution was the declared aim of the Slav leaders in exile who therefore regarded *Austria delenda est* as a presupposition for their success. Their British supporters (Steed, Seton-Watson, Whyte) were inclined to agree with them in this conclusion but the erection of an anti-German barrier was the supreme motive and goal. Only when this could not be achieved within the existing political entities did the dissolution of the Habsburg Empire become a necessity.

Notwithstanding their different conceptions of a future settlement all major political circles in Britain agreed upon the need to reformulate the war aims. The final incentive was the publication of the secret treaties by the Bolsheviks.[113] In an extended debate in the Commons[114] Balfour attempted in vain to defend them and gave a rather irritated and muddled reply to the protest of the Radicals. But this time the Liberal opposition was numerous and could not be silenced easily. Wedgwood branded Balfour's view as outdated and J. W. Wilson

---

[112] The above correspondence from the Buxton papers is quoted by H. N. Fieldhouse, "Noel Buxton and A. J. P. Taylor's Trouble Makers", *A Century of Conflict*, ed. M. Gilbert, London 1966, pp.189–91.
[113] The *Manchester Guardian* started to print them on 12 Dec.
[114] For the following cf. *Hansard*, 5th Ser., c, 1917, 2011–2084 (19 Dec.).

thought that the developments in Russia had freed the British government from any hesitation in regard to restating their "original" war
aims. Many M.P.s held the view that the obligations owing to the
participation of Russia, Rumania, and Italy in the strife were to a large
extent cancelled by the present situation. A. Rendall felt that the
Russian defection had made all speeches by Asquith out of date.
Knowing that there was a strong feeling in Austria about the pronouncements of the ex-Prime Minister, he could not see any harm in
putting these things out of the Allied programme, whereby "the friction
and the unnecessary sense of grievance and doubt on the part of the
Austrian people, might as well be got rid of".

A more prominent speaker calling for moderation was the former
President of the Board of Trade, Runciman, who showed some understanding for the Foreign Office being cautious in its pronouncements in
regard to Serbia, or Rumania or Dalmatia, for there was an Allied
audience. But Runciman warned against giving Italy the impression
that Britain was prepared "to act in the Italian ambition by pressing for
the break-up of the Austrian Empire". Having been a member of the
government at the time of the making of the secret treaties, he now
agitated against their implementation. His attitude is a striking example of the fact that British public opinion was not likely to support a
government which would go on prosecuting the war – after having
solved the dispute with Germany over Belgium and France – purely
with the object of attaining the extreme demands of the minor Allies,
notably Italy.

The dissenters concentrated their attacks on Italian aims, because
they were more than any other in flagrant violation of the high principles for which the Allies were declared to be fighting. Now their real
ambitions were exposed by the Soviets and the Liberals turned towards
the only moral figure who presented an acceptable alternative to them:
Woodrow Wilson. They preferred the terms adumbrated by the President to any speaker in Britain and tried to create the impression that
the country was not able to resist the strong American views on Allied
aims. If the latter really implied, as many of them believed or
insinuated, the dismemberment of the Habsburg Empire, they could be
assured of Wilson's opposition to such designs.

To meet the Wilsonian wave Lloyd George undertook a first step on
20 December at Gray's Inn. Steering a middle course he announced his
general agreement with Wilson's policy but attacked the suggestion of a
"half-way course between victory and defeat" as it was demanded by
Lansdowne.[115]

Eloquent Liberals and Conservatives had created the intellectual

---

[115] Scott, *op.cit.*, pp.210–14.

basis for an alternative foreign policy, but they were no threatening factor as long as they lacked the support of the masses. The great majority of the Labour movement had so far loyally supported the government. At an inter-Allied Socialist conference that took place in London in 1915 the British section including the I.L.P. expressed their support for the Allied cause, asserting that the victory of the Allied powers "must be a victory for the popular liberty, for unity, independence and autonomy of the nations in the peaceful Federation of the United States of Europe and the World".[116]

Labour's entry into the new Coalition formed under Lloyd George cemented working class support for a prosecution of the war until final victory. This decision was defended before the Annual Conference[117] as giving the party a voice in the question of the terms of peace. The plea for an international Socialist conference to discuss war aims, which was put forward by the I.L.P., was turned down (as well as the appeal by the International Socialist Bureau) in favour of an inter-Allied conference. Only the call of the Russian revolutionaries changed the mind of the Labour Executive, which now regarded a British participation as inevitable. In preparation of the proposed Stockholm conference the Labour leaders tried to bring about an agreement between the Allied Socialists on the conditions of peace. A special sub-committee was appointed to formulate a statement on war aims. The wording of the draft was largely determined by Sidney Webb, who produced an amended version of the "Report on Peace Terms", which the Fabian Society had issued in 1916. Therein territorial changes were recommended as opposed to a return to the *status quo ante*, since the forcible denial of nationalist aspirations had formed a perpetual danger to world tranquillity and a settlement redressing nationalist grievances was indispensable to an enduring peace in Central and South Eastern Europe. The Fabian report generally approved of the principle of nationality, save in the instances where "geographical and strategic requirements of other States needed to take precedence of nationalist aspirations".[118] This applied to an outlet to the sea. In such a case transfers of populations might be carried out. Plebiscites were regarded as useless and dangerous as a means of settlement.

Fabian thinking was always attracted by the advantages of comprehensive political entities which by necessity ruled the world while the small states had to be confined or extinguished. Upon the outbreak of war Ensor, addressing an audience at Essex Hall, saw the hope of peace in a world concert of "satisfied" Great Powers, whose presumable reduction in number he regretted as one of the calamities of war.[119]

---

[116] Quoted in A. Henderson, *The Aims of Labour*, London 1918; p.83.
[117] *Report of the 16th Annual Conference of the Labour Party, 1917*.
[118] Quoted in A. M. McBriar, *Fabian Socialism and English Politics*, Cambridge 1962, pp.140–41.
[119] A. M. McBriar, *loc.cit.*

Among the potential "candidates for decay" he must have thought of the Habsburg Empire, which in many respects did not at all comply with the utilitarian approach of the Fabians to a "clean" settlement. In May 1915 Ensor eventually went so far as to express his conviction of the "imperative need" of dismembering both the German and the Austrian Empire and suggested "setting up Hungary and the Slav provinces of Austria as independent states, while adding South Germany to a Germanized Austria".[120] His attitude was regarded as "complacent" by Beatrice Webb and obviously not shared generally in Fabian circles. For instance, the League of Nations envisaged by Leonard Woolf[121] would include Austria among the eight great powers.

The vagueness on Austria–Hungary in the Fabian statements is also present in the August draft of the Labour Party. Whilst there is no explicit passage on the Monarchy, it contains a section on the Balkans, for which a special conference of the representatives of the peoples concerned is suggested. This or an authoritative International Commission would deal with the reorganization of the Balkan peninsula on the basis of "the complete freedom of these people to settle their own destinies, irrespective of Austrian, Turkish or other Foreign domination".[122] The exaction of this recommendation could well lead to the formation of a South Slav state cutting off Austria from the Adriatic. A Customs Union embracing the whole of the Balkan states, which was also suggested, could have fulfilled the economic needs of a diminished Austria, provided she had trade privileges in it. The reduction of the Monarchy at another point was unequivocally demanded. The British Labour movement declared "its warmest sympathy with the people of Italian blood and speech who have been left outside the inconvenient and indefensible boundaries . . . and supports their claim to be united with those of their race and tongue".[123]

The inter-Allied conference was unable to accept the British or any other draft compromise and suggested the postponement of the Stockholm conference. During the next few months the Labour programme was redrafted for adoption by the special Joint Conference of the T.U.C. and the Labour Party held in London in late December. The influence of the left-wing movements in Britain and in Allied countries during the previous months clearly accounts for the endorsements in the December draft. The I.L.P. and B.S.P. and vigorously opposed some provisions, which in their view should have been a rigid alternative to the Allies' note to Wilson, the anti-Habsburg implications of

[120] *Beatrice Webb's Diaries*, i, 1912–1924, ed. M. I. Cole, London 1952, p.33.
[121] *International Government*, London 1916.
[122] *The Labour Party Memorandum on the Issues of War*, London 1917.
[123] *Ibid*.

which the B.S.P. organ *The Call* brandmarked on 15 March:

> We submit that the dismemberment of Austria, the cession of Constantinople and the Straits to Russia, the satisfaction of the European demands of the Italian imperialists, the absorption of all Poland by Russia, the enlargement of Roumania are proposals that override the concept of nationality.

The organization which agitated most vociferously against the provisions of secret diplomacy was the Union of Democratic Control, which was primarily an offspring of Liberal dissent but included also many prominent left-wing Labour leaders, MacDonald and Jowett being among its founders in 1914. Through them the I.L.P. adopted the U.D.C. programme more or less unaltered.[124]

The suggestions for a peace settlement made by the U.D.C. ruled out all claims based on conquest or imperialist ambition. Where a change of the pre-war frontiers appeared justified on national grounds, no transference of provinces should be carried out without the consent of the populations concerned. For the U.D.C. the best process to decide the future of Alsace–Lorraine and the Trentino was by plebiscite or possibly a policy of autonomy or partition. Austria–Hungary was treated as a national state like Germany and the existence of the Habsburg Empire never questioned.

The increasing influence of the U.D.C. spirit is indicated by the changes in Labour's December statement, which asked for an Alsatian plebiscite and modified the endorsement formerly given to the Italian claims. It continued to realize that "arrangements may be necessary for securing the legitimate interests of the people of Italy in the adjacent seas" but had "no sympathy with the far-reaching aims of Italian Imperialism".[125] The official statement of the Labour movement was supplemented by a brochure which Henderson compiled at the end of 1917.[126] He believed that questions like Serbia, Poland and the extension of Italy and Rumania to their "natural boundaries" were all capable of being settled on the principle of the right of self-determination. But its rigorous application would have clashed with the desire not to bar the way for a negotiated settlement with Germany and her allies. The idea of self-determination and the desire for an early peace proved incompatible, especially in the case of the Habsburg Monarchy. The result of Labour's endeavours to conciliate the two principles was a manifestation of aims which left a wide margin of interpretation, and avoided an explicit statement on the future of

---

[124] H. M. Swanwick, *Builders of Peace*, London 1924; A. J. P. Taylor, *The Trouble Makers*, repr. London 1969, ch.v. The identity of the U.D.C. terms with the Labour programme on the whole is exaggerated by H. Hanak, *op.cit.*, p.237.
[125] *The War Aims of the British People. Statement of the War Aims of the Labour Party*, London 1918.
[126] A. Henderson, *The Aims of Labour*, London 1918 (foreword, 22 Dec. 1917), especially p.43.

Austria–Hungary.

Their own vagueness did not prevent the Labour leaders asking the government for a public declaration in very definite terms. However, their request for a clarification of the official policy concentrated on the areas disputed between Germany and Turkey and the Allies. These were the cases which in Labour's view demanded a revision, though the secret treaties with the minor Allies were not forgotten. Examining the facts for and against the continuance of the war, G. N. Barnes, Henderson's replacement in the War Cabinet, listed as the supreme advantage that Austria was "on her last legs", but on the other hand the same applied to Italy and Rumania and Barnes observed with distinct disapproval that Britain's burden was increased by being "entangled with Rumania and Italy by arrangements made".[127]

When Cecil suggested not to mention these difficult questions in a statement of war aims, Barnes asked the Cabinet "to recognize existing facts in Italy and Rumania".[128] Actually this demand met the majority inside the War Cabinet, which felt that any declaration omitting such important items as Alsace–Lorraine or the Trentino would be too vague. There was practically no difference of opinion between Lloyd George and Labour on any essential territorial war aims.[129] In fact the Prime Minister might have been thankful to have found an ostentatious excuse for the revision of his position against the expected opposition of the extreme patriots on the right and Allied criticism abroad.

Labour's interest in foreign policy was no danger for Britain's rulers. The Labour Party basically agreed with the Allied interpretation of the fundamental principles of reconstruction. A reason for more concern was the Bolsheviks. In their negotiations with the Central Powers they had pushed the principle of the right of self-determination to the forefront. But they had shown a reluctance to insist upon the same rights for the Slavonic peoples in Eastern Europe. The Allies tried to persuade the Bolsheviks not to be satisfied with "empty phrases" from the Germans. Milner and Cecil, in a memorandum for submission to the French,[130] advised them to induce the Bolsheviks to ask the Germans for "specific undertakings from them as to such questions as Poland, Bohemia, the Roumanian parts of Transylvania, not to speak of Alsace–Lorraine and the Trentino".

Balfour noticed a certain inconsistency in the pursuit of British policy. On the one hand General Smuts had been sent to Geneva in order to explain that the destruction of the Austrian Empire was no part of Britain's war aims, though it was desired to see autonomy

---

[127] Notes on the War, 30 Dec. 1917, *Cab*. 1/25, No. 28.
[128] *WC* 308a of 31 Dec., *Cab*. 23/13.
[129] *WC* 308, *Cab*. 23/4 & *Report of the 17th Annual Conference of the Labour Party, 1918*, p.12.
[130] The document, dated 21 Dec., is printed in *War Memoirs*, ii, pp.1550–51.

introduced in its various portions. On the other hand the Bolsheviks were assured that Bohemia, Moravia, Croatia, etc., were to determine each for itself what their future status was to be.[131] On 22 December Trotsky had put forward terms which demanded the right of the nationalities which had hitherto not enjoyed independence to decide their own future by plebiscite.[132] The British could not swallow the Bolshevik programme *in toto*, but Balfour found the general spirit in which it desired to rearrange the map of Europe "in harmony with our sentiments".[133] The Bolshevik overtures were answered on behalf of the Central Powers by Czernin, who on 25 December accepted the Bolshevik formula provided it was agreed to by all Russia's allies.[134] Lloyd George was much impressed by this declaration and thought it deserved a serious reply. He was "in a very pacifist temper"[135] and wondered whether there was still anything to gain from continuing the war. In a Cabinet meeting on 28 December all members were surprisingly moderate. Faced with Smuts's report that Austria would not discuss a separate peace, the possibility of a general peace was seriously considered.[136] Milner proposed a three-stage proceeding: first the Cabinet had to agree on a minimum programme; secondly, the attitude of the enemy had to be ascertained and thirdly, the other Allies had to be consulted. There followed a clash of opinion over the practicability of fixing an irreducible minimum, to which Balfour was opposed. His and others' attempts failed to carry much conviction without a knowledge of what Britain's partners really wanted.

A more immediate task was the restatement of war aims in public, which Lloyd George advocated on a "less requisitive basis than the reply to Wilson a year ago".[137] After the Cabinet discussion Hankey was the first to draft what the reaction to the Central Powers' statement should be.[138] He observed that certain positions of the enemy were in accord with the Allied view, for instance the assurance that there should be no forcible acquisitions of territory. But all depended on the interpretation of such phrases and the ambiguity of the original Russian proposals had been increased by the enemy's reply. The most difficult article was the one demanding a referendum for national groups, to which the Central Powers had observed that every state must deal with its people "independently in a constitutional manner". The Allies were not in entire agreement with either the Bolshevik or the

[131] Private letter to Cecil, 26 Dec., Balfour papers, *B.M. Add. MSS*, 49738.
[132] Pt. 3 of the Bolshevik programme. Cf. *War Memoirs*, ii, p.1549.
[133] Balfour papers, *loc.cit.*
[134] Scott, *op.cit.*, p.221.
[135] Remark to C. P. Scott, quoted by Hammond, *C. P. Scott of the Manchester Guardian*, *op.cit.*, pp.221–23; cf. also Thornton diary (Milner papers, box 301), p.272.
[136] *WC* 307a, *Cab.* 23/13, 1 (draft minutes).
[137] *Ibid.*
[138] Dated 29 Dec., Lloyd George papers, F/23/1/38.

German point of view. Despite a general agreement with the sovereignty of every state over its subjects, Hankey remarked that there were exceptional cases "of people who are linked by ties of race, history, or language, more closely to other nations than to those under whose temporary allegiance they have fallen". The reunion of such "historic" *irredentas* was regarded by Hankey as an inescapable condition for a just and durable peace. The cession of the Trentino (and perhaps of such islands in the Adriatic as had a predominantly Italian population) came under this category. In this case opinion in all British quarters agreed and a referendum was deemed superfluous.

The settlement of the racial problems in South Eastern Europe was more complicated. Philip Kerr, who was the next to consider counter-proposals, saw the essential basis of a lasting peace in the grouping of the various nationalities, as far as possible, in "autonomous units".[139] As to the relations between these national units, the Allies had "no fixed idea, provided that they were not brought under the political and military domination of Berlin". This aspect determined the British Habsburg policy. If the Empire was to continue to exist, "the granting of equal rights to the subject nationalities (namely the Poles, Czechs, Slovaks, and South Slavs) with the Hungarians and the Germans in the *direction* of Austro-Hungarian policy" was a guaranty for the "democratization", which Britain and her Allies desire to achieve in Central Europe. Kerr did not consider this transformation of the Monarchy to form a direct war aim of the Allies, but it entered largely into their dispositions. If these became true, Kerr concluded, they should be prepared to defend the settlement by some kind of supra-national organization. In view of this

> it would be one of the finest objects of Allied statesmanship to draw a liberalized Austria–Hungary into union with this concert of democratic powers.

When the nature of the British declaration of war aims came up for discussion in the War Cabinet early in 1918, it was agreed that the statement should show the audience at home, in the Allied countries and the "peoples" of the enemy powers that it was not the object of British policy to destroy the enemy nations. In regard to Austria the following guideline was set out:

1. The Italian claims for the union with their countrymen under Austrian rule should be supported in general terms with no specific reference to all the Italian war aims.
2. Some reference ought to be made to such races who sought "some form of autonomy" (Italians (!), Croats, Slovaks, Czechs, etc.)[140]

---

[139] Dated 30 Dec., *ibid.*, F/89/1/12.
[140] *WC* 312 of 3 Jan. 1918, *Cab*. 23/5.

A discussion of the terms with the Allies was ruled out as well as sending a direct answer to Czernin, because this would n.ean an opening of negotiations. Though the Cabinet and especially Lloyd George were mindful that the statement was formulated in a way that left open the possibility for a diplomatic understanding, this was not to be its primary purpose. For Lloyd George it was "essential that the statement should be a war move rather than a peace move".[141] The Prime Minister imagined that it was possible to paralyse the Austrian war activities comparably to Russia's in the past 18 months. A clear indication that the British did not want to destroy her should "make her people lukewarm in the war", thus deterring her from using her full strength actively against the Entente (Lloyd George calculated that Austria might send up to 300,000 men to the Western Front). Despite this tactical motivation Lloyd George met objections from Cecil, who warned against abandoning the obligations to Rumania and Italy, for which there were also strong military grounds. If either of these two was discouraged by the other Allies, the peace parties in their countries had a forceful argument in hand. But at this moment it was very important to uphold the resistance of the two partners of the secret treaties. Rumania could become an important link to the anti-Bolshevik forces in Southern Russia and hopes for a South Eastern barrier including her had not yet been given up. Italy for her part also had a more immediate effect on the military movements of the Central Powers than any psychological warfare could produce. The Italians had thrown back the Austrians from their advanced position and would engage large forces for another year.[142] Cecil had prepared a draft, in which a qualified assurance to the Habsburg Empire was given. After demanding an independent Poland it continued:

> Similarly, though we agree with President Wilson that the break-up of Austria–Hungary is no part of our war aims, we feel that, unless genuine self-government on true democratic principles is granted to those Austro-Hungarian nationalities who have long deserved it, it is impossible to hope for the removal of those causes of unrest in that part of Europe which have so long threatened its general peace.[143]

The immediately following reference to the "legitimate" claims of the Italians and the Rumanians made it obvious that some cession of territory in these two cases would be supported by the British, though only as far as they were justified on ethnological grounds, a proviso which was underlined by the promise to discuss the secret treaties with the Allies.

---

[141] *WC* 313 of 3 Jan. 1918, *Cab*. 23/5.
[142] Cf. the report of the D.M.O. on the Italian front given in *WC* 311 of 2 Jan., *ibid*.
[143] *War Memoirs*, ii, p.1514.

But through Mensdorff it was known that the Austrians were reluctant to consider any territorial satisfaction of their Latin neighbours. The only feasible way to ease the renunciation seemed by territorial compensation and the prospect of a comprehensive Balkan settlement.[144] This was regarded by Lloyd George and his closest advisers as a means of leaving the Habsburg Empire in a position to exercise a powerful influence in South Eastern Europe. The idea had already been sketched out to the Austrians during the intimations in Switzerland. Now the Prime Minister insisted on a similar public assurance by the inclusion of a corresponding phrase into the original draft:[145]

> If these conditions (Italy, Rumania) are fulfilled, Austria–Hungary would become a Power whose strength would conduce to the permanent peace and freedom of Europe, instead of merely being an instrument for the pernicious military autocracy of Prussia that uses the resources of its allies for the furtherance of its own sinister purposes.

Lloyd George was fully aware of his leniency towards Vienna and apologetically admitted to Steed that he had "not been able to go as far as you would like about Austria".[146] In fact he had moved in the opposite direction, which the *New Europe* was pointing out. British interest in the integrity of the Habsburg Empire had become apparent and the implied conditions were made transparent to shrewd examiners of the speech. Gustave Hervé of *La Victoire*[147] depicted the peace which was in Lloyd George's mind. The writer recognized the intention of building a "golden bridge for the Habsburgs" by offering them Allied support for a reconstructed Empire consisting of five autonomous nations extending from Fiume to Danzig and which including Poland would comprise sixty million inhabitants of whom forty million would be Slavs. The crucial point was that these Slavs of the "new Monarchy" should not be manoeuvered and that the Habsburg state continued to be a Prussian vassal state. The only pledge that Vienna could give was to turn against Germany in the present war, but how could she?

British diplomacy was as distant as ever from any concrete results in the Austrian question. Lloyd George's speech to the Trade Union Congress was a bold move as it declared openly the designs of the British government. Whether it was daring enough to evoke a positive

---

[144] This was proposed by Smuts in his draft (*G.T.* 3180). For the Cecil draft cf. *G.T.* 3181, both of 3 Jan., in *Cab.* 24/37/1.

[145] *WC* 314 of 4 Jan., *Cab.* 23/5.

[146] *Through Thirty Years*, ii, p.180.

[147] 7 Jan. 1918. Reported on the same day by Bertie (*F.O.* 371/No. 5124/f.4070), minuted by Cecil, who claimed that Hervé had "read a good deal into the P.M.'s declaration that was not there".

response depended finally on the frame of mind of policymakers in Vienna.

5. The End of an Illusion

When the War Cabinet had discussed the Smuts mission and the Czernin speech following the Geneva meeting, it was virtually agreed that Smuts should travel again to Switzerland, this time to have an interview with Czernin himself as Mensdorff had proposed. Balfour showed himself "a little alarmed at the almost inevitable publicity", but Smuts and the Cabinet as a whole were of the opinion that the advantage of dealing directly with the man in authority outweighed the danger of detection.[148] The second objection brought forward by Balfour was his permanent concern not to act without being certain of Allied approval. If a member of the Cabinet was "to confabulate with an Austrian Prime Minister" (*sic*), this could be regarded as going beyond the mandate the British received at Paris, which was to carry on informal conversations. The agreement of the French was, however, obtained in Paris by Bonar Law after seeing Clemenceau. Disregarding the fact that the possibility of a leakage had increased (due to Rumbold's indiscreet mentioning of Smuts's name) the War Cabinet on 2 January agreed that Smuts might with advantage resume his contacts with the Austrians. The British were not even held back in their intention by the conjecture of a likely German complicity.[149] But when a week later Lloyd George wondered whether the time had not come to put the Cabinet decision into practice, it was Smuts himself who was not too eager to go. He managed to persuade his colleagues that it would be a mistake to appear too anxious. It was therefore decided to wait for the reaction to Lloyd George's speech of 5 January.[150]

On the Austrian side the guesswork about the true intentions of the adversary and the most advisable steps to take at this moment was leading up to the same questions. Mensdorff had returned to Vienna with the impression that the talks with Smuts had not been unsatisfactory. They had not borne immediate success, but it was a beginning, "*le premier jalon*", and Mensdorff hoped that others would follow. His optimism was based on his experience of British policy when he was an ambassador in London, from which he drew conclusions which were aimed at convincing his superiors at the Ballplatz:

> I can only repeat again and again that the English are past masters in the art of dropping something which has proved impracticable, but

---

[148] Balfour to Cecil, 29 Dec. 1917, Balfour papers, *B.M. Add. MSS.*, 49738.
[149] *WC* 311a of 2 Jan., *Cab.* 23/16.
[150] *WC* 318a of 8 Jan., *ibid.*

that they will never condescend to explicitly giving up a declaration which they have made once.[151]

But Mensdorff had to take note of a certain mistrust against Britain on the part of both Mérey, to whom he spoke first in the Foreign Ministry, and also Czernin, who showed himself particularly perturbed over an agent's report from the Hague, which resumed the old demand for a written assurance as a condition for an Anglo-Austrian approach. This information was evidently superceded by events, since meanwhile a direct contact had taken place without any such preliminary concession by the Austrians. Despite this Czernin was led to believe that "this infamous action by England" was a further proof how necessary it was to be cautious. His accusation that the British move merely aimed at pumping out information about the Austrian fighting strength was unjust. The question is whether the Minister for Foreign Affairs was really misguided in his interpretation, or whether he intentionally insinuated a false play on the part of Britain. He might have found it necessary to counteract the Anglophile leanings of his envoy and the favourable reception which his report could be expected to get from the Emperor Charles.[152]

Czernin was meanwhile over-occupied with the peace negotiations at Brest–Litovsk, from which he had only returned for a brief spell during the first pause of the proceedings. A quick and efficient exploitation of the Russian defeat could give Austria the much needed relief and perhaps enough breathing space to continue the struggle on Germany's side, if the planned spring offensive in the West led to a final victory. But to be capable of holding out at least a couple of months longer the Monarchy desperately needed victuals from the occupied territories in the East. This could only be done after the signing of a corresponding peace treaty, which was delayed by the Bolsheviks who hoped to gain time for their revolutionary propaganda by which they hoped to create the atmosphere for a general peace. The German delegation remained unimpressed with this tactic and Vienna had to wait until their expansionist aims were met. In this precarious situation Charles authorized Czernin to conclude a separate peace with Russia,[153] but beforehand Czernin tried to moderate the German demands. Here the Anglo-Austrian entrevue could serve as a lever in two directions. Firstly, the threat of a separate peace forced Germany to consider the wishes of her ally. Secondly, the prospect of a general peace through the channel London–Vienna made it advisable for the German politicians, if not for

---

[151] Mensdorff diary, H.H.St.A.; Mensdorff papers, pt. 4, entry of 29 Dec.; Mensdorff papers, pt. 2, undated note (spring 1918).
[152] Mensdorff diary, 31 Dec. & H.H.St.A., Krieg 25/27, Czernin tel. to Demblin for Charles, rec. 23 Dec. 1917. Cf. W. Steglich, *op.cit.*, p.262–63.
[153] *Protokolle des Gemeinsamen Ministerrates . . ., op.cit.*, p.627ff.

the military, not to bar the way completely for a final understanding with Britain by creating an irreversible situation in the East. So Mensdorff was taken to Brest–Litovsk, where he gave Kühlmann a detailed account of his recent journey, although he did not tell him everything in order to make sure that the German Secretary of State took the "right" view of the affair.[154]

Though there is no record of what Mensdorff told Kühlmann at Brest, one can imagine that he tried to play down the anti-German point in the Smuts offer, as he did when explaining the British ideas to Baernreither.[155] According to the latter's notes Mensdorff depicted the British scheme for a reconstruction of Central Europe, in which Germany's power should be balanced by a system of combinations of states, which should prevent a preponderance of Germany but form a certain equilibrium *with* Germany; in other words that the federative complex under Austria's leadership was to be connected with Germany, but in a way that the latter would not predominate.

Similar inferences were drawn by Aleksander Skrzyński, whose analysis of the Geneva meeting was circulated in the Austrian Foreign Office.[156] His assumptions of the "general line" which the British had in mind were also determined by the desire to find a solution that could be arrived at with the Entente without offending Germany. So Skrzyński argued on the basis of his observations in Switzerland that Britain was finally seeking an agreement that included Germany and would even secure "good terms" for the latter, though it would compromise German militarism. To achieve a conciliatory settlement everything was to be discussed step by step with Austria: firstly, the aims of the Monarchy and Austria, next those of Bulgaria, Italy, and France, and then Germany. The British, so Skrzyński calculated, would understand the Austrian endeavours to get just terms especially for her larger ally. When an agreement was eventually reached between Vienna and London, Britain together with her Allies and with Austria and Bulgaria would be in a position to confront Germany with a *fait accompli* and thus be able to achieve peace. This would take time:

> The English must proceed slowly and cautiously, since they have to consider our, partly justified, *idée fixe* that one merely wanted a separate peace with us.
> They only wanted to continue these conversations, if they were convinced that they could be – for the time being – kept secret and conducted without commitment, thus not affecting the combativeness of the Entente peoples.

---

[154] Mensdorff diary, 4 Jan. 1918.
[155] Baernreither diary, 28 Mar. 1918, H.H.St.A., (pt. vii, vol. xix).
[156] Memorandum of 20 Dec. 1917, H.H.St.A., Krieg 25/27.

Skrzyński's elaboration was a mixture of right anticipation and wishful thinking. While there had been definite signs of a British willingness to come to terms also with Germany, this did not mean that a common ground between the two main enemies had been found. The British government was far from accepting a draw as a result of the war. But Lloyd George realized that Germany could not be expected to surrender her colonies and compromise in Alsace–Lorraine without getting any compensation. He was therefore seriously thinking "of paying the Germans in the East in order to square them in the West".[157] If the Germans were to agree to such a bargain, it was not very meaningful for the British to continue the war. A complete victory seemed more than doubtful and at that moment the enemy was already driven out of all overseas positions. They had been the only target of a direct British interest, whereas the ambitions of their Allies lay mostly on the continent. If there occurred a peace by negotiations along such lines, French and Italian aims could not have been satisfied to the same extent. Aware of their accusations of British selfishness and also in view of the "new diplomacy" of ideas led by Wilson and Lenin, the Cabinet considered camouflaging the acquisition of the colonies and Mesopotamia and Palestine by introducing a mandatory status. This could have possibly helped to assuage the French and Italians when requested by the British to give up a remarkable amount of their aspirations.

At the moment they should only assent to private conversations with the Austrians, because a direct approach to Berlin was ruled out in London as a diplomatic capitulation. The matter was different with Czernin, who had nevertheless been in touch with the Germans and consequently, so Lloyd George pondered, must know what they were up to. As the Prime Minister explained to C. P. Scott, he had intentionally avoided "playing up to Czernin" in his speech to the Trade Unions, because then the Germans "would at once have been suspicious of a secret understanding and called the Austrians to order".[158]

Meanwhile the negotiations at Brest were progressing and the likelihood of a separate peace between the Central Powers and Russia became more imminent every day. To guard against the <i>Diktat</i> of the Germans in the East, which would have put an end to all his considerations, Lloyd George insisted on the resumption of the contacts in Switzerland. While he was still restrained in his eagerness by the scepticism of some of his colleagues, the decisive move came from the other side.

Skrzyński approached the Anglo-Egyptian Parodi, whose report of

---

[157] Scott papers, <i>B.M. Add. MSS</i>, 50904, 7/8 Jan. 1918.
[158] <i>Ibid.</i>

the interview was uncritically passed on to London by Rumbold.[159] It was stated therein that the Austro-Hungarian government was in agreement with a number of points in the recent addresses by Lloyd George and Wilson. Contrary comments in the Vienna press upon the views of Lloyd George should not be taken as representative for Czernin, who was in any event willing to meet Lloyd George.

The reaction in the leading Viennese newspapers had in fact been sarcastic if not completely unfriendly in tone. The semi-official *Fremdenblatt* (the mouthpiece of Czernin!) thanked Lloyd George for "so graciously" promising not to destroy Austria–Hungary, but merely wishing to cut off enormous tracts of territory. It criticized the fact that the catchword "self-determination" was only to be applied for others as the "latest invention of British cant". The *Neue Freie Presse* also repudiated the attempt to internationalize the internal problem of the Monarchy and commented that only a conqueror could speak as the British Prime Minister had done, whose public programme was denounced as a peace of annihilation.[160]

Skrzyński had tried to assuage the British disappointment over these utterances by claiming that these voices were not representative, since part of the Austrian press was in the hands of munition manufacturers. This argument was challenged by Cecil who mistrusted the communication on the whole. The Acting Foreign Secretary was particularly suspicious of the excuses given for the dispatch of two or three Austro-Hungarian regiments to the Western front. He wrongly interpreted this as a feint for the preparation of another attack on the Italian front. Cecil also held the view that the Central Powers wanted to make Italy believe that the British "were ready to sell her to Austria".[161] Sonnino's extreme suspiciousness had already been aroused by Lloyd George, who did not conceal his opinion about the unreasonableness of Italian claims. A meeting between him and Czernin might be used with telling effect in this direction. But on the other hand Cecil had to concede that it might also be desirable to hear what Czernin had to say. To reconcile these two divergent factors he recommended that, firstly, nothing should be done without previous consultations with the Italians and, secondly, that the proposal should not be rejected but that the intentions of Czernin should be ascertained in more detail, especially as to the subjects he desired to discuss with the British. Winding up his argument Cecil set forth the whole double-edged problem of making peace by negotiations:

If the move is a genuine one, it must mean that there is really great

---

[159] This telegram (No. 39 of 11 Jan. 1918, *F.O.* 371/3133, No. 7760/f.2002) is printed in *War Memoirs*, ii, pp.1498–99.
[160] Cf. the articles in both papers on 7 and 8 Jan.
[161] Cecil's minutes on Skrzyński's telegram of 11 Jan.

pressure for peace and that the Centrals are for some reason or other in a very bad way. If it were not for the very lurid accounts that are being sent to us from Berne, I should believe this more easily. But if it be true we should increase and not diminish the pressure by holding off.

Cecil was right in doubting the genuineness of the advance. A retrospective examination of the Austrian documents proves that Skrzyński was not authorized by Czernin but had tried on his own initiative to bring about a further encounter between Britain and Austria on the very highest level.[162] However, at the time when the offer was made, Lloyd George was blinded by the apparent favourableness of the situation and was under the illusion that it had undergone a change within the last week or so. The enemy seemed perturbed by his war aims speech and Skrzyński's dramatic account of Count Czernin's "Titanic" struggle at Berlin in order to maintain the "no annexations" formula must have strengthened Lloyd George's belief as well as an article in the *Frendenblatt* which attacked Bülow as a supporter of Hindenburg. All this seemed to indicate that Czernin and Kühlmann were acting in concert against Hindenburg and Ludendorff. This split between the civil and the military authorities, Lloyd George diagnosed, gave an opportunity for a diplomatic offensive. Smuts might be able to drive a wedge which separated the civil and military authorities. On this occasion Smuts would also have the opportunity to talk quite frankly about the war aims as publicly announced. Conversely such a display of candour would enable the British negotiator to ask for an equally frank statement of the enemy's. In support of the Prime Minister's argument it was pointed out in the Cabinet that the enemy governments could well be supposed to consider coming to terms with the Allies before committing themselves to the hazardous and risky offensive in the Western theatre. There was general agreement that it was almost certain that Kühlmann was privy to this proposal, which made it advisable to be doubly cautious, because the offer might be a trap to draw the Allies into a peace conference, before their terms were accepted. Despite this danger the Cabinet thought that conversations could not be put off for ever and Smuts might "obtain very valuable information, not only about the enemy's war aims but about their general disposition towards the question of peace and war". So the War Cabinet decided that he should go in place of Lloyd George, because otherwise contemporary history would condemn them for discarding such an important overture.[163]

The War Cabinet's inclination to attempt a compromise with the

---

[162] H.H.St.A., Krieg 25/27.
[163] *WC* 325a of 18 Jan. 1918, *Cab.* 23/16.

moderate representatives of the Central Powers was suddenly also shared by Haig, who had hitherto been one of those optimistic military leaders who believed in a complete victory over the enemy. Now he doubted whether much more could be gained for the British Empire by continuing the war for another twelve months. By then Britain would be much more exhausted and face the problem of an industrial and financial recovery to an even greater extent. America, which Haig did not expect to be a serious factor in the war in 1919, would "get a great pull" over Britain. Considering that so far the British Empire had secured more than Germany out of the war Haig thought

> our best policy was to strengthen Austria as against Germany, and the latter in the direction of Russia for the future. Thus she would be taken off the path of the British Empire and would in future bump up against the greatest military obstacles.[164]

Thus the most prominent political and military leaders in Britain were in favour of an early peace if it could be achieved on those lines and in view of the recent Austrian offer there seemed to be some prospect of realization. But by request of the Foreign Secretary immediate action was, however, again postponed. Balfour had asked to wait until Orlando's visit to London, where the Italian Premier arrived at the beginning of the last week in January. He had come to express *viva voce* the Italian objections to the T.U.C. speech. Lloyd George justified it as a war stratagem without pledging himself to truncate it. To tranquilize Orlando and his Minister for Food Supplies, Crespi, who accompanied him, Lloyd George gave ample assurances of aid to the Italians in their emergency.[165] As to his policy towards Vienna, Orlando showed himself reassured after the talks, too. Lloyd George neither concealed from him the Smuts–Mensdorff negotiations, which he explained as a move to reinforce the pacifist tendencies in the enemy camp; nor their negative outcome insofar as Vienna, for the moment, was not inclined to make territorial concessions. Conversely, Orlando did not exclude *a priori* the possibility that Italy could also agree to a compromise peace in case her Allies deemed it indispensable, but he found it useless to reduce the Italian rights now for a mere eventuality. When the two leaders parted, each of them could be satisfied that the other had not dared to express his true opinion. Lloyd George is reported to have said that "England does not repudiate treaties",[166] and Orlando agreed to the continuation of the Swiss conversations which he cannot be expected to have favoured.

By now the Central Powers had decided on a public answer to the

---

[164] Reported in a letter by Smuts to Lloyd George, 21 Jan. 1918; Lloyd George papers, F/45/9/9.

[165] L. Valiani, *op.cit.*, p.383; O. Malagodi, *op.cit.*, ii, p.271ff.

[166] Page to Lansing, 31 Jan., *For. Rel.*, Supp. I, i, p.60.

announcements of Lloyd George and President Wilson. The latter's "Fourteen Points", which had followed three days after the T.U.C. speech, had exceeded the British statement in publicity. What mattered mostly was that the American President was not tied by the secret agreements of the Entente. So it was to his points that Hertling and Czernin referred in their speeches on 24 January.[167] Hertling emphasized that the questions of the Italian frontiers, the nationality problem of the Habsburg Empire, and the future of the Balkan states mainly concerned the "political interests" of Austria–Hungary and left a reply to them "in the first instance" to the Austrian Minister of Foreign Affairs. Where German interests were at stake, they would be looked after by the Berlin government, for which the alliance with Vienna was the "essential point" of its present and future policy. His reference to the problems concerning Germany and his polite but determined repudiation of Lloyd George's proposals made it evident that the Germans were in no mood to discuss a peace that was tolerable for the Allies.

Czernin's answer was exclusively reserved for the American President, whose plea for autonomy of the nationalities he rejected as an interference in Austrian affairs. He refused to make any concessions to Italy, which could not any longer expect the same generosity on Austria's part as at the time when Vienna was prepared to pay a price for her neutrality. He also refused to make any concessions to Rumania, Serbia, and Montenegro. His intransigence did not prevent Czernin from offering the mediation of a general peace by a concerted action of Washington and Vienna.[168]

Both these declarations were reviewed by the Supreme War Council at Versailles on 2 February.[169] Lloyd George pointed out that both Hertling and Czernin had shown no intention of relaxing their claims, whereupon Sonnino tried to use the situation to get some public assurance that the Allies, by whom Italy had been "placed in the shade" recently, recognized the necessity for territorial adjustments for Italian security beyond the offer made by the Austrians in 1915. But Lloyd George was aiming in a different direction. He wanted "to make it quite clear to Germany and Austria that the real barrier to peace was the aggressive and unrepentant military caste. Peace could never be made until that class was overthrown.

The declaration eventually adopted by the S.W.C. seemed to relegate to the background any possibility of political or diplomatic

---

[167] Scott, *op.cit.*, p.246ff.
[168] *Ibid.*, p.255ff.
[169] *I.C.* 44, *Cab.* 28/3.

action.[170] But Lloyd George had by no means given up his hope at least in regard to Austria alone. In a Commons debate he admitted that there was at least a difference in tone between Hertling and Czernin and wished that he "could believe that there was a difference in substance". In his speech he claimed that there was "not a single definite question dealt with on which Count Czernin did not present any terms that might be regarded as possible terms of peace."[171]

Under the surface it all looked different. Townley thought that Czernin's insistence upon territorial integrity would remain firm as long as the present military situation lasted, but should that change Austria would certainly yield and grant the nationalities administrative if not political autonomy. It was, however, doubtful to the minister in the Hague, "if this could be achieved were Austria dealing with America alone".[172] This raised the question whether the moment was favourable for the British to approach the Austrian government or whether it was more suitable to leave it to the Americans, after Skrzyński had dwelt on the expediency of America acting as an intermediary between Austria and the Entente.[173] There were two major reasons which Lloyd George outlined to his colleagues in favour of Austro-American conversations: firstly, it was easier for Austria to make peace with the U.S.A. "owing to the number of Austrian subjects in that country", and secondly, easier for the Italians to yield to American pressure.[174] Balfour was therefore requested to draft a telegram to Wilson intimating the possibility of gain from the Austrian conversations. Skrzyński had for the first time alluded to the possibility of a separate peace. This could have its reason in the fact that the negotiations with Russia were making no satisfactory progress. (On 10 February there was a break in the Brest negotiations. Trotsky declared the "state of war" at an end but refused to sign a peace.)

But even if all the insinuations made by the Austrian spokesmen did not lead up to a separate peace, in which the British had by now almost lost hope, Lloyd George thought that the question might be discussed with advantage for the Allies. This could prevent the employment of Austrian troops on the Western front and delay hostilities until the revolution broke out in Austria. The Prime Minister now became more and more convinced that Austria was on the brink of a revolution, thus agreeing in some respects with the view of the Allied agent Horodyski

---

[170] Mensdorff (diary entry of 5 Feb. 1918) assumed that the brusque declaration was the result of the strike at Cattaro. He was disappointed because the Allies now appeared to count on a revolution in Austria.

[171] *Hansard*, 5th ser. 1918, ciii, 22, 12 Feb.

[172] *F.O.* 371/3133, No. 16949 of 27 Jan. 1918.

[173] *Ibid.*, No. 21231 of 4 Feb.

[174] *WC* 338a of 4 Feb., *Cab.* 23/16.

as expressed in Versailles.[175] He gave increasing attention to the reports of reliable intelligence agents and their observations of seditious tendencies in the Habsburg Empire.[176]

In the meantime the Emperor Charles had sent a message to Wilson which was believed to have been prepared by Czernin. Its content practically amounted to *status quo ante* terms. This did not match with the accounts of conversations between Wilson's unofficial confidant Professor Herron and the Austrian Professor Lammasch, who claimed to have been sent by the Emperor to get a message through to the President. The British were well informed about these proceedings. One of their intelligence officers was present at the Herron–Lammasch talks and the Imperial telegram was deciphered by Room 40, before it reached Washington via Madrid.

The Americans were perturbed over the discordant voices emanating from Vienna. So Wilson and House agreed to ask the British for advice. On 27 February the Foreign Secretary replied:[177] He pointed out the differences between the Emperor's message and his intimations through Lammasch, which, Balfour thought, represented the opinions of the Emperor "in his then mood", i.e. unaffected by German influences. While the official proposal seemed hardly reconcilable with Wilson's public declarations on the subject of peace terms, the Lammasch scheme, as far as it went, was "in harmony with the principles laid down by the President and might therefore form a starting point for discussion". But it was open to two serious objections. In the first place it ignored Italy and secondly it might alienate the subject nationalities of Austria, whose various peoples had "so often been fooled by the phrase 'self-government' ". Balfour warned:

> The future of the war largely depends on supporting Italian enthusiasm and on maintaining the anti-German zeal of the Slav population in Austria.

Balfour feared that the Austrian statesmen could exploit the "tenderness of the President for the Austrian Empire" as a means of convincing the Slavs that they had nothing to hope for from the Allies, but he admitted that some risks had to be run and thought that it might be worthwhile to take some steps to ascertain whether the Lammasch conversations really represented the mind of the Emperor. As to how far the other Entente governments should be apprised of the character of the messages from Austria, Balfour left it to Wilson's discretion to inform the Allies of any progress of the informal conversations carried

---

[175] *Ibid.*
[176] *WC* 357a of 1 Mar., *Cab.* 23/16.
[177] Seymour, *op.cit.*, pp.385–88; cf. also Mamatey, *op.cit.*, pp.220–229.

out by Herron. Only the pourparlers with Czernin necessitated a prior consultation.

It was the Austrian move through Madrid which disquietened the British Foreign Secretary. He regarded this official approach as another attempt by Germany to create a dissension among the Allies, for he strongly suspected that it was made with at least some understanding with the German authorities. After having drawn the Americans into negotiations, the Germans could, so Balfour calculated, inform the Italians that the terms of the Entente treaty could not be squared with the President's conditions of a peace settlement. Balfour himself regretted "this unfortunate treaty" but he wanted to avoid any premature discussion of it, which would only weaken the morale of Britain's European allies.

Balfour's anxiety over a leakage of a diplomatic contact with Austria was justified by the publicity given to Smuts's errand soon after his return from Switzerland. Details were revealed in the French journal *Justice* and thereafter discussed in the Commons to the great embarrassment of both Mensdorff and Smuts.[178] The British government was attacked by A. F. Whyte for foolishly conceiving a separate peace with Vienna. He accused the government of pursuing

> the secret forms of the old diplomacy by bartering a slice of German territory in exchange for the defection of Austria from the Alliance of the Central Powers.[179]

Whyte completely misinterpreted the policy of the government at the time, as Balfour rightly pointed out in his reply. The Foreign Secretary also refused to subscribe to the doctrine of the *New Europe* that there was no ultimate gain from detaching Austria from Germany. Whyte had gone so far as to suggest that approaches to Vienna should be made with such good faith as would permit the Austrian government to pass them on to Berlin. But such an offer would have to contain all the obligations entered into by Britain and would thus be necessarily stillborn. The position of President Wilson was different. He could well present a list of terms which were of interest for Germany as well. But a Wilsonian peace would fall short of fulfilling the British *desiderata in toto*. Balfour had consciously designed his communication for Lansing but the Foreign Secretary's convictions and feelings were clear to ambassador W. H. Page, who cabled to the State Department:

---

[178] Mensdorff diary, 3 Mar., *Selections from the Smuts Papers*, iii, No. 829, p.651 (speech in Glasgow on 17 May 1918): "I deeply regret these disclosures, because it seems to me that if the war is to come to an end ultimately, it will be necessary from time to time for the combatants to try informally to get into touch with each other. It seems to me essential to do that."

[179] *Hansard*, 5th Ser., cf, 165 (13 Feb. 1918).

It is certain that he (Balfour) hopes that the President will decline to discuss a general peace with Austria alone.[180]

What Balfour did not tell the Americans was that the British Cabinet was just then discussing official advances from Austria, or at least what were believed to be official communications. According to them, Czernin would be ready to give a formal declaration that "Austria would only discuss her own affairs" in any conversations with Britain, America and the Allies.[181] Differing from Balfour, the Prime Minister was not in favour of leaving the case to America, because Wilson might agree to conditions which were unacceptable to Britain and if Colonel House came to Europe as a negotiator this would be tantamount to a conference. Therefore one should rather probe Skrzyński's proposals. Lloyd George was supported by Smuts who pointed out "the risks for the British Empire at stake" in those transactions and warned against entrusting British interest to the United States, particularly as the British had obtained from their continental allies authority to act in this matter, which was "equivalent to the diplomatic predominance in the alliance".[182]

In view of such "forceful" arguments rather than on a realistic analysis of the Austrian problem the War Cabinet decided against the strong opposition of the Foreign Office to send Philip Kerr to Switzerland to investigate the matter.[183] The decision amounted to a victory of the Cabinet over the Foreign Office on an important question of secret diplomacy. It also led up to the clarification of the real intentions of the Austro-Hungarian government, which was necessary, if British foreign policy was to be based on facts instead of expectations and illusions.

The British desire not to slam the door to further communication with Austria was guided by the development of the peace negotiations between the Central Powers and Russia. Germany seemed to be determined to confront the Entente with accomplished facts by establishing an economic hold over all detached countries from Russia. At the time of the Brest–Litovsk negotiations it looked as if any such arrangement could not be reversed by the conclusion of a general peace and the prospect of a Germany disposing of ore from the Urals was a frightening image in Whitehall.[184] Lacking the resources for adequate military reprisals the British only had the chance of playing the card of an understanding with Austria–Hungary to stop Germany from establish-

---

[180] Page to Lansing, 27 Feb., *For. Rel.*, 1918, Suppl. I, i, pp.140–44. For the attempts of William Wiseman (chief of British intelligence in the United States) to prevent the Austro-American contacts from drifting into a general peace conference cf. his tels. of 4 and 26 Feb., Balfour papers, B.M. Add. MSS, 49741. See also Lord Reading's warning of 27 Feb., *F.O.* 800/200.
[181] *F.O.* 371/3133, No. 35034 of 23 Feb.
[182] *WC* 357a of 1 Mar. 1918, *Cab.* 23/16.
[183] *WC* 359a and 360a of 5/6 Mar., *ibid.*
[184] Hardinge minute on a Berne telegram of 3 Mar., *F.O.* 371/3133, No. 40495.

ing a coherent continental block under her domination. As this looming danger had not yet become a reality the feeling prevailed in London that the Austrian approaches should not be left without a reply.

The most daring statesman in his outlook was General Smuts, who more than anybody else thought that the British had "very great cards to play" if they had "the nerve to do so".[185] After the great and surprising developments at the turn of 1917/18 Smuts visualized a very different Europe at the end of the war. He was so much impressed by Germany's victory over Russia that he believed that her *Mitteleuropa* scheme was "no longer an ideal but reality". The danger for the British Empire lay in the fact that the routes to Asia, which the British had so far successfully barred from Germany by means of the alliance with Russia, would now lie open to German expansionism. Smuts urged that this new situation had to be met by a readjustment of Allied policy. Diplomacy had to re-inforce strategy:

> If we cannot defeat Central Europe we must break it by far-sighted and daring diplomacy. The break-up of Russia has given us diplomatically a free hand in many important respects . . .
> The principal feature of my idea is still, as foreshadowed by Mensdorff, to detach Austria from Germany either before or after the peace, by holding out to her the prospect of a large increase in territory and position.

In Smuts's opinion Austria should finally have a larger territory than Germany, including not only Austria, Hungary and Poland but now also the Ukraine. One concession demanded of her was that she agree to cede Bosnia and Herzegovina and part of the Dalmatian coast to Greater Serbia and that she cede the Trentino and some minor territories to Italy and recognize Italy's claim to Valona and a protectorate over Albania.

In contrast to their proposed deal with Austria the British were not in a position to offer generous terms to Turkey, because here their own interests and ambitions were directly at stake. The Germans therefore had more to offer to Turkey with Armenia and Caucasia. Smuts proposed to counter this advantage by buying off Bulgaria with Constantinople. With this feat Smuts hoped to "fetch fox Ferdinand" and finish Turkey and the war. His plan was to break the chain of Central Europe at three points: Austria, Greater Serbia, and Greater Bulgaria. Smuts was convinced that by solving the Balkan tangle on "more or less national and satisfactory lines" and by the desertion of Austria and Bulgaria from Germany, her former allies would "become independent of and antagonistic to her, and give a quite new orientation to the diplomacy of Europe". Such an arrangement, Smuts hoped, would

---

[185] Letter to Lloyd George, 14 Mar. 1918; Lloyd George papers, F/45/9/10.

compel Germany to come to reasonable terms with the Entente and so a "favourable and durable peace could be concluded".

Through the publicity given to his mission to Switzerland Smuts's attitude had become apparent, but because of his high personal standing and reputation in Britain the Austrophobes and "Never-Endians" did not attack him directly. Knowing that he did not stand alone with his preference for imperial security they credited Smuts with being entrapped to carry out "the tortuous diplomacy of Lord Milner". The latter's policy was heavily criticized in the Commons by A. A. Lynch:

> Lord Milner's dream of diplomacy is to detach Austria from her alliance and thus rebuff or disappoint or produce lack of faith in all those who seek emancipation from Austrian rule, and who, if the occasion offered, would become the allies of the Entente Powers.[186]

For this and other indicated reasons the government was in fact at that stage already more sceptical than some of its individual members. When Milner's intimate Philip Kerr was selected to go to Switzerland on 7 March, his mission was limited to a purely informative character and he was not given any authority to commit the government to any particular policy. But the Cabinet wanted "a personal report from someone who had full knowledge of their general policy and of the present situation",[187] before taking a decision.

Balfour still believed that it would probably end in nothing, but his scepticism did not prevent him from depicting the task as "an admirable opportunity to elicit the exact meaning and scope of the recent telegrams".[188] Kerr was supposed to find out

1) whether the present proposals proceeded from the Emperor or Czernin or both,
2) whether they were made with or without German cognizance,
3) whether Austria was prepared to discuss a separate peace, and
4) if so, the general lines of the Austrian programme.

On arriving in Berne Kerr failed to see Skrzyński immediately, because the latter did not dare to engage himself more deeply without instructions from his Foreign Minister. Despite this "slight hitch" as he called it, Kerr was sanguine and from conversations with Rumbold and Parodi he gained the impression that Czernin was definitely behind the offer and was anxious for a meeting with a member of the War Cabinet. Kerr and his interlocutors at the British legation conjectured that the Austrians, and this time Karl and Czernin, were not just acting as brokers for a general peace, since they realized that they could not succeed in bringing the war to an end like that. The motives behind the

---

[186] *Hansard*, 5th ser., cv., 2219 (7 Mar.).
[187] *F.O.* 371/3133, No. 41211 of 6 Mar.
[188] *Ibid.*

new Austrian determination to get out of the war alone were believed to be their fear of the growing power of Germany as was made evident during the negotiations with Russia, and the threat of an internal revolution or national revolt, the danger of which had also been increased through the events in Russia, after many indoctrinated prisoners had returned from there. In view of the mounting revolutionary tide the long-fostered hope for a separate peace whereby Austria–Hungary

> definitely left the Prussian orbit and remodelled its institutions on federal lines and came under Entente influence[189]

could be the ideal result for Britain. But what Kerr found more likely to come out of the negotiations with Austria was

> an internal row, which would intensely preoccupy and so weaken the Central Powers, might end in a break-up and would certainly terrify Turkey and Bulgaria if it happened before Germany got an alternative route to Turkey.

Finally all the three southern allies of Germany might come out together. The adverse effect could, however, be achieved, if the terms offered to Austria were unreasonable, because then Czernin could use them as a means to re-unite the home front by pointing out that the excessive demands of the Entente made any compromise impossible. It therefore seemed essential to Kerr that Britain should discuss the basis of a separate Austro-Hungarian peace with her Allies (including Serbia!) as soon as possible (an inter-Allied conference had been proposed for 14 March) to be "in a position to reach a preliminary understanding on the spot". In the Foreign Office Graham agreed that as a basis for discussions the British ought to have "a clear idea of what we consider reasonable terms for Austria–Hungary".[190]

Lloyd George was, however, so much encouraged by Kerr's account that he decided to push ahead without clearing up inter-Allied controversies. He authorized his private secretary to arrange for a renewal of General Smuts's conversation, making it very clear that there was no question of discussing terms with Germany.[191]

Besides the attempt at peace-making the Prime Minister tried to gain as much out of the enterprise as possible, which would justify the enterprise if it failed in its main effort so that Lloyd George could not be accused later on for having engaged in a completely futile and risky action leading up to nothing. So he reminded his messenger not to neglect any opportunity of ascertaining whether any considerable

---

[189] *Ibid.*, No. 45538 of 11 Mar. 1918.
[190] Minute on Kerr's telegram, *loc.cit.*
[191] Lloyd George to Kerr, 12 Mar., *ibid.*

Austrian forces had been sent to the Western front.[192]

The meeting between Kerr and Skrzyński took place on 14 March after there had been some delay, since the Austrian had not been authorized by Czernin to engage in any contact. Eventually Skrzyński was permitted to listen to what Kerr had to say without showing any *empressement*.[193] Kerr immediately noticed his change of attitude as compared with his former communications. But he did not give up from the start and pointed out that

> the British government was not seeking to manoeuvre Austria–Hungary out of the war on any sort of terms simply as a move in the war against Germany, but that their desire was to see if a real and lasting settlement of all outstanding questions could not be made as between Austria–Hungary and the Entente as the beginning of that larger settlement which would give real and lasting peace to the whole world.[194]

But for the British the time had come to translate theory into practice. The speeches of Czernin and Wilson had shown so many similarities that one hoped to come to an agreement on a number of points with Austria as a first step towards a general peace. There could be a meeting if there was sufficient *communauté d'idées*, "the principle of settlement being not the bargaining for territory, but that justice must be done to all peoples". For instance, concessions based on the principle of nationality had to be made to Italy.

The term "separate peace" was carefully avoided during the meeting just as between Smuts and Mensdorff. But this time the British demands were greater than in December. Skrzyński would have liked Kerr to say that the British government "while not raising the question of a separate peace, thought that a discussion of the questions outstanding between Austria–Hungary and the Entente would be useful". Kerr refused this, since he understood his instructions as limiting him to agree to negotiate a separate peace and he did not consider it "politic" to pretend that the British were not out for this in the end. The interview showed that there was no basis for this aim, although Kerr did not rule out the possibility that by making "patent as many people in Austria–Hungary as possible a settlement with the Entente is the only one which will give them real and lasting peace". This method, in his opinion, could lead to a separate peace or the break-up of the Empire, about which he was not really concerned. His only ambition

---

[192] Supplementary telegram, *ibid.* In his Memoirs, ii, p.1500, Lloyd George tries to give the impression that only Kerr was so optimistic. Kerr wrote to Czernin's son on 24 Feb. 1940: "I don't think anybody expected that there would be any results from it. But I went" (Lothian papers).

[193] On 4 Mar. Czernin had warned Skrzyński that he suspected the Allies of playing a false game. Ten days later he gave his limited assent without informing Karl, H.H.St.A., Krieg 25/27.

[194] Kerr's report on the interview, *Cab.* 25/1; copies in Lloyd George papers, F/89/1/12 & Milner papers, box 108.

was to assist in finding a measure to facilitate winning the war for Britain. For this purpose he suggested preparing a more elaborate basis for the discussion of boundaries, internal reform, demobilization in the event of a separate peace, Austria's obligations after its conclusion and also raised the problem of the economic terms. A clear programme on all these issues would indeed have been necessary, if quick results should ensue from any diplomatic pourparlers. But after the last talk with Skrzyński such deliberations were not necessary. Czernin confirmed the negative response of the Austrian side unmistakably in his order to Skrzyński saying that the British move seemed to him to lack in seriousness. He rejected Kerr's criticism of the harsh treaty with Rumania and demanded that France and Italy renounce all territorial demands on Austria and Germany. As long as Britain supported their stipulations, the Central Powers could not believe that she really wanted peace. On 27 March a memorandum in French was communicated to the British to leave no doubt about the Austrian attitude.[195]

Kerr's alternative interpretations of the rebuff were that either Skrzyński, owing to his not being in close touch with Czernin, had been exaggerating or that Czernin was an opportunist awaiting the German offensive in the West. In fact both were true. In the Foreign Office there was now "little doubt as to Count Czernin being unreliable".[196] The hope of coming to terms with Austria had been severely shattered. Under the present circumstances nothing could be done and further considerations had to be postponed until the result of the German offensive was clear.

The idea of the unofficial intermediaries had been to keep the door open for later. If it was found that at that time it was impossible to achieve a *rapprochement*, this might become more feasible after the operation "Michael", but the optimistic rumours spread by them had an adverse effect on future developments. London was now disillusioned and discouraged from taking any further initiative. Since the end of the war could not be forecast the idea of a separate peace with Austria was not yet abandoned completely but it was at least put aside after the recent disappointment. Now at the moment of military crisis Britain and her Allies had to strain every nerve to hold out against the German onslaught with which the Austrians ostentatiously linked their fate. In keeping with this commitment British Habsburg policy had to become subsidiary to the demands of the military challenge. Since the Austrians had rejected all ideas of a separate diplomatic understanding

[195] *F.O.* 371/3133, Nos. 55733 & 62171 of 25 and 27 Mar., H.H.St.A., Krieg 25/27, Czernin to Musulin, 18 Mar., the communicated memorandum was passed on to the Americans and is printed in Ch. Seymour, *op.cit.*, iii, pp.390–93.
[196] Minute by Hardinge on No. 62171. – On 2 Apr. L. B. Naimier submitted a memorandum on Skrzyński which painted a very unfavourable picture of the Austrian diplomat's character. Thereupon Hardinge and Balfour thought that he might have been the liar. Cf. *F.O.* 371/4358.

207

and by their behaviour had also destroyed the British confidence in resuming the contacts at a later stage, they practically invited their desperate opponents to embark on another policy, which they found necessary to achieve victory.

CHAPTER VI

The Decision for a Policy of Disruption

1. The Demand for a Propaganda Campaign

Since the Central Powers had opened the discussion on peace, the Allied governments were in an unfavourable position with regard to the Austrian problem. On the one hand they propagated the liberation of peoples on the principle of nationality while on the other hand they had violated this principle themselves in the Treaty of London with Italy. Though the London Convention was officially secret and not published before the coming to power of the Bolsheviks, its content was generally known and made the statements of the Entente appear untrustworthy. Instead of giving the Monarchy the death blow, the entry of Italy into the war galvanized Austria into new life, and the Italians particularly estranged the previously unenthusiastic Southern Slavs with their claims to Dalmatia and by insisting that Croatia should not be united to the other regions peopled by South Slav kinsmen. Moreover, under Italian rule the Dalmatians had to fear being "Italianized", a prospect to which they preferred remaining under Austrian rule. The resuscitation of traditional anti-Italian sentiments among the South Slavs was readily exploited by the Habsburg authorities and had its effect on the battlefield, where the Croatian regiments stubbornly resisted the Italian troops. These consequences of the British and Allied policy towards Italy were noted with resentment by Wickham Steed. But he did not lose hope, having information that the Habsburg South Slavs "might even now be induced to lay down their arms if they felt that Italy had no designs upon their country".[1] Thus an Italo-Yugoslav reconciliation became the presupposition for a successful instigation of the South Slav subjects against their Habsburg masters.

The basis for a united federal Yugoslav state had been provided on 20 July 1917, when Pašić and Trumbić signed the "Declaration of

---

[1] Letter by Steed to his Correspondent in Rome, McClure, of 20 June 1916; Steed papers (*The Times* archives).

Corfu". This agreement between Serbia and the representative of the South Slavs in exile[2] demanded the inclusion of "all territory compactly inhabited" by South Slavs into the new kingdom and declared that the Adriatic must be a "free and open sea".[3] Such demands implied both the necessity of dismembering the Habsburg Empire and the nullification of the Treaty of London. But neither of these two conditions was seriously considered by the Allied governments whose representatives assembled for a conference shortly after the Corfu declaration and issued a statement assuring the Slavs that they were

> more closely united than ever for the defence of the peoples' rights, particularly in the Balkan peninsula, (and were) resolved not to lay down arms until they . . . (had) rendered impossible a return of the criminal aggression such as that for which the Central Empires bear the responsibility.[4]

In the interpretation of Steed and Seton-Watson such a phrase would have meant *Austria delenda est*. But the official plans at the time were contrary to the hopes of the anti-Habsburg group. Despite the flowery speech made on the occasion of Pašić's visit to London on 8 August,[5] Lloyd George in private showed an increasing tendency to abandon even part of Serbia's formerly recognized claims, not to speak of the aspirations for a Yugoslav kingdom. The French, who consulted the Prime Minister before the Armand-Revertera soundings, were also far from promoting a Serbo-Croat union. Nor did the Italians swallow the Corfu declaration and Sonnino made it clear to Pašić that Italy was determined to control the Adriatic and not prepared to renounce any of her claims.[6]

For Steed this obstructive attitude was incomprehensible. Without a clear conscience the Allies could hardly reply to the German peace propaganda by stating their positive peace aims and defending them by intelligent propaganda. Italy had to understand

> that the hardest blow she could hit Austria would be to be able to announce an agreement with the South Slavs as the basis for her whole programme of liberating the Habsburg people.[7]

He also believed that the British government "would be delighted to see Italy enter on this path".[8] This was only true insofar as the British would have welcomed any voluntary renunciation on the part of Italy,

---

[2] Trumbić had succeeded Supilo, who was already seriously ill and died in London in September, 1917.

[3] Quoted in W. H. Steed, *Through Thirty Years*, ii, p.166. For the full text cf. P. D. Ostović, *op.cit.*, p.275f.

[4] Scott, *op.cit.*, p.120.

[5] *The Times* of 9 Aug. 1917.

[6] Mamatey, *op.cit.*, p.166.

[7] Steed to McClure, 26 June 1917, Steed papers.

[8] *Ibid.*

which could, however, also be used to accommodate the Austrians. It was just this which Steed wanted to make impossible. If Italy's war aims had the support of Serbia and the South Slavs, this would strengthen the Italian position in the eyes of the British public and give Steed and his followers a forceful weapon against those who laboured for some kind of a settlement with Austria. Some of the Italians with whom Steed communicated in London were beginning to see "that there is no middle course between the salvation of Austria and a thorough agreement with Serbia and the South Slavs".[9] Soon afterwards he gained the impression that the apparent change of Italian attitude was rather one of tactics and he publicly warned that if Italy did not help to create Yugoslavia, it would be created without her, "either by the Austrians or by a future Balkan Confederation".[10] The event that turned the scales in favour of Steed's scheme was Caporetto. For a moment it seemed as if Italy might be defeated. Then any idea of a liberation of the Habsburg nationalities had to be given up and the German hold over Austria would become firmer. Steed understood that Germany intended to take Tyrol from Austria together with a strip of territory from the Isonzo to Trieste, so that there should be a common Italo-German frontier in the future and Germany would then obtain absolute command through Italy of the Mediterranean and the route to the East.[11] Whether Steed really believed that the situation was so desperate is difficult to assess. Colonel Repington, *The Times*'s military correspondent in France, accused him of losing his head.[12] Steed's concern in pressing the War Office to send troops to Italy immediately is understandable. For, if it was not the whole of the war that was at stake in Italy, a let-down of the Italians would have made impossible all plans for a successful operation against the Central Powers by launching an anti-Austrian propaganda campaign from Italy.

In Italy itself Caporetto served as a catalyst for a number of leading personalities who were now prepared to take a clearer position against the Habsburg Empire's internal structure and started to view more positively the aspirations of the subject nationalities. The readiness to come to terms with the Yugoslavs had so far been confined to Liberal and Socialist quarters (Bissolati, Lazzarini). Now it was also perceptible in Italian diplomatic and military circles in London. This development was helped by the Austrophile attitude shown by Lloyd George and his colleagues which embittered many Italians, and Steed's suggestion that only Italy could counter such tendencies fell upon fruitful ground. The Italians had to find a means to cope with the political and

---

[9] Steed to McClure, 14 Aug. 1917, *ibid.*
[10] *Edinburgh Review*, Oct. 1917.
[11] Steed to Northcliffe, 19 Nov. 1917, Steed papers.
[12] *Through Thirty Years*, ii, p.149.

military situation created at the end of 1917. By adopting the proposal for psychological warfare the Italians could hope to regain sympathy for their cause in Britain. They always felt that Steed and his British friends were inspired by official tendencies. As a result of collaboration with him they could expect a wholesome effect on the attitude of the government in London. Setting themselves at the head of the new movement the Italians would prove their importance for a successful pursuit of the war effort and they could no longer be compelled to renounce their claims on the ground that their contribution to the war was not in compliance with their demands. Should the propaganda have a striking success, there was even the hope that the objects of Italian policy could be achieved by first undermining and then driving back the Austrian front. Or at least the belligerent force of the enemy could be weakened to such an extent as to prevent another offensive from the North.

These aspects must have appealed especially to the Italian General Staff. Its representative in London, General Mola, was among the group of Italian, South Slav and British personalities who adumbrated the lines of a possible settlement at Steed's house in the middle of December, 1917.[13] Mola agreed that the situation in the Adriatic had changed with the elimination of the Russian factor and Italy might be able to look at the problem from a new standpoint. He also admitted the impact of the Wilsonian pronouncements. But he rejected the "everything or nothing" attitude of the South Slav representatives and insisted on Italy's strategic requirements including the "grey zones" between the distinctly Italian and South Slav regions. While he was inclined to reconsider the claim to the hinterland of Dalmatia, he vehemently opposed the South Slav maximum aims of Trieste, Pola and Istria, which were spelled out by Trumbić. Steed and the other present supporters of the Yugoslav cause were of course not concerned to secure an agreement completely on national lines. They were quite prepared to make concessions to the demands for Italian security, as long as they could win over Rome for the supreme goal of a Yugoslav state and the dissolution of the Habsburg Monarchy in general.

The formation of a "united front" comprising all anti-Habsburg forces was the whole point of Steed's scheme of undertaking a political offensive against Austria for the liberation of the subject peoples. He was still concerned that most Italians did not understand that there was no need for a detailed agreement between Italy and the Czecho-slovaks and the Yugoslavs. All that was required was Italy's general support for the idea, by which she could "at one stroke gain *il primato morale* of the Allies in Europe". Steed was certain that thereafter no

---

[13] *Ibid.*, pp.173–79.

Austrophile intrigue would be able to affect her position, because she would have British public opinion wholeheartedly on her side.[14]

The advantages that could be gained from such a policy were finally realized at the top of the Italian government. Orlando seemed determined to accept the policy scheduled in Printing House Square. During his sojourn in London at the end of January he received Steed and was persuaded to meet Trumbić on 26 January, when the two had an "interesting and cordial conversation". Steed used the occasion of the first signs of an official Italo-Yugoslav *rapprochement* to press the Italian Premier for a public commitment in favour of the principle of nationality and a compromise in the Adriatic question. "Such a speech", he cabled to Orlando, "would find the sympathetic approval of the responsible factors in England".[15] Orlando was duly impressed and complied with Steed's request in his chamber speech the next day, when he associated himself with the aspirations of the subject nationalities against the yoke of racial domination.[16] This speech was received favourably in the Foreign Office,[17] where its contrast to the stubborn attitude of Sonnino was realized as much as by Steed himself, who had been encouraged by Orlando to appeal to the Italian Foreign Minister too. Thus Steed tried to convince Sonnino of the expediency "to follow a frank policy of liberation and liberal encouragement and protection" towards the Austro-Hungarian subject peoples, pointing out that Italy could not maintain her position in the Western alliance on the basis of the Treaty of London.[18]

While Sonnino's attitude was not changed by such arguments, the "forces of movement" took shape on an international level. Representatives of the Italian Social Democratic Irredentists associated themselves in Paris with Socialists and Syndicalists of Serb, Polish, and Rumanian origin and jointly declared that the existence of the Habsburg Empire was incompatible with the right of self-determination.[19] The next step was an inter-Allied Socialist conference held in London from 20 to 24 February. Its section on territorial questions was chaired by Sidney Webb and Albert Thomas who issued a memorandum that did "not propose as a war aim the dismemberment of Austria–Hungary or its deprivation of economic access to the sea". But the Allied Socialists were much more explicit on the fate of the subject nationalities than the British Labour memorandum of last December. The claims of the Czechoslovaks and the Yugoslavs were recognized as

---

[14] Steed to McClure, 8 Feb. 1918, Steed papers.
[15] Cit. Valiani, *op.cit.*, p.387. The Italians gathered that Steed's tel. had been read by Lloyd George and Balfour before it was sent to Rome. See *ibid.*, p.436, n.159.
[16] *Ibid.*, p.387.
[17] *F.O.* 371/3228, No. 27697/f.708 (tel. by Rodd of 12 Feb., minuted by Hardinge).
[18] *Through Thirty Years*, ii, p.183.
[19] Valiani, *op.cit.*, p.389.

an international issue to be governed according to the rules of a future
League of Nations. This understood that national independence should
be granted to

> such peoples as demand it and these communities ought to have the
> opportunity of determining their own groupings and federations
> according to their affinities and interests. If they think fit they are free
> to substitute a free federation of Danubian states for the Austro-
> Hungarian Empire.[20]

The Socialists were still concerned about the economic viability of the
new political system which was to emerge in South East Central
Europe, but their British, French, and Italian spokesmen now accepted
the idea that the economic needs of the new independent states could be
secured in a (con-)federation. This had always been regarded as desirable by the *New Europe*, though with the difference that Steed and
Seton-Watson were prepared to leave a collective reorganization to the
initiative of the former subject peoples, whereas the Allied Socialists, on
the other hand, demanded the federation of the new nations as a
guarantee for their security and welfare, before they were granted
independence. As to the territorial details of the post-war settlement,
the Socialist conference went a long way to meet Italian aspirations in
the Adriatic, acknowledging that arrangements might be necessary
"for securing the interests of the people of Italy in the adjacent seas".
This problem should be settled on the principles of equity and reconciliation between the Italians and the Yugoslavs.

The Times and the *New Europe* welcomed the declaration which
created a good climate for the forthcoming Italo-Yugoslav talks. In late
February an Italian "Parliamentary Committee for the Union of All
Subject Races of Austria–Hungary" was founded. As its delegate,
Andrea Torre came to London, not with an official mandate but with
the cognizance of Orlando, to negotiate with the members of the South
Slav Committee. The outcome of their informal conference was the
so-called "Pact of Rome" signed on 7 March. It was witnessed by Steed
and Seton-Watson who sent a translation to Drummond with extra
copies for Balfour and Cecil.[21] The agreement recognized the "impre-
scriptible right to full political and economic independence" for each
people aspiring to it and condemned the Habsburg Monarchy as the
fundamental obstacle to such a development. The signatories acknowledged the vital mutual interest in the unity of the South Slav nation
and both sides pledged to settle the various territorial controversies
amicably on the basis of nationality, leaving a precise definition for the
time after the war.[22]

[20] *The Times* of 25 Feb.; cf. also *New Europe* of 28 Feb.
[21] Steed to Drummond, 7 Mar. 1918, Steed papers.
[22] For the text cf. *Through Thirty Years*, ii, pp.184–85.

Notwithstanding its generalities the agreement was sufficient for its immediate purpose, viz. to create a congenial atmosphere for the launching of a propaganda campaign. But the success of such an undertaking did not only depend on the *rapprochement* of the Italians and the South Slavs in exile. It remained to be seen how far the population within the Monarchy and more particularly the Habsburg armed forces composed of South Slavs, Czechs and Slovaks, and Transylvanian Rumanians were affected by a war of words. After the declaration of Corfu there was allegedly a serious movement of discontent in the Austrian army and Steed believed the tidings (evidently provided by his Slav collaborators) that certain Czech and South Slav regiments had been within measurable distance of defection, before the position was stabilized by the Germans on the eve of Caporetto.[23] The advocates of a policy of disruption received new encouragement from the events at the beginning of 1918. The social and political unrest culminated in the mass strikes in January. The menace of disruptive nationalism, which was again underlined by the "Epiphany declaration" of the Czech parliamentary deputies, was now complemented by serious Socialist demonstrations. The Austrian authorities were at pains to intimate via Switzerland that the strikes had been inspired by the government itself and the British minister in Berne found it plausible that Vienna used the strikes to influence the military party in Berlin.[24] In view of the strikes another British diplomatic representative, on neutral ground, E. Howard in Stockholm, suggested encouraging the Austrian peace movement by holding out to the Austrians a personal union with Poland. The Austro-Polish solution might be advantageous in stopping the Bolshevik movement from gaining ground in Poland and prevent Germany from obtaining a preponderant influence due to the Russian chaos.[25] This proposal, which did not yet comprehend the full ideological impact of Bolshevism, was strongly disapproved of by Clerk, to whom it seemed "completely opposed . . . to our real interests", whereas Hardinge thought that there was "a good deal to say for it".[25]

The idea of supporting a strong Austria against Germany was still fostered within the Foreign Office and the diplomatic service. If there were no active steps taken to bring about a split of the enemy coalition under these auspices, the adverse course of embarking on a wholehearted support of the nationalities was not followed up either. The pros and cons of a policy of revolution were weighed by the Foreign

---

[23] Steed to McClure, 25 Jan. 1918, Steed papers.
[24] Tels. by Rumbold of 24 Jan. and 5 Feb., *F.O.* 371/3133, Nos. 16375 and 27028/f.1. *The Times* of 23 Jan. 1918 drew the same conclusion from the "remarkable freedom of action left to the leaders of the Austro-German Socialists".
[25] *Ibid.*, No. 14351 of 22 Jan.
[26] Minute *ibid.*

Office, when Count Sobanski forwarded a memorandum of the Polish National Committee in Paris, which urged a political offensive against Germany by stirring up the Habsburg subjects. Gregory's extensive minute[27] reveals that the Foreign Office was anything but convinced of the success of a disruptive policy. To Gregory the present seemed hardly propitious for putting it into effect. He argued that the information about the internal conditions in the Monarchy were too scanty and mistrusted the "professional agitators", doubting whether they really represented the majority in those countries of the Monarchy for which they took the liberty to speak. Gregory believed that the Habsburg link was a very definite one, even in the Trentino and Trieste. The only exception he made was for Poland, but Bohemia could not claim the same historical tradition for leaving no alternative to political independence. He assessed the Transylvanians as "largely Hapsburgian" and dismissed the Yugoslav aspirations on the ground that the Croats did not want to be ruled from Belgrade. Then he came to this overall judgment:

> We may in fact have legitimate doubts as to how far all the peoples of the Dual Monarchy are thirsting for emancipation from the Hapsburg yoke. Privilege and autonomy were evidently all desire; but whether other than the Poles and perhaps the Czechs the majority are anxious for complete independence has still to be proved.

Under these assumed circumstances the practical effect of propaganda on the internal situation seemed doubtful and if the agitation fell on fruitful ground there was always the German army to suppress any uprising or mutiny. Yet, Gregory saw no harm in trying it, since it could hardly be less successful than the attempts for a separate peace with Austria.

Clerk was more strongly in favour of the proposal and advised that they should "do all to encourage disruption tendencies". However, Hardinge's conclusive synthesis foreshadowed the line taken by the Foreign Office in early 1918. If a disruptive policy was to be pursued, he recorded, one might "just as well advocate *autonomy* for Transylvania, Yugoslavia and Bohemia".[28]

At the bottom of this double-edged tactic was the desire to exploit the advantages of an ideological warfare as far as possible without entering into commitments from which there was no return. Thus the official Allied spokesman never promised more than an "autonomous development" and "self-determination".

The lobby in favour of a "New Europe" was alarmed by the appearance of such phrases in the speeches made by Lloyd George and Wilson

---

[27] *F.O.* 371/3002, No. 218943 of 16 Nov. 1917.
[28] *Ibid.*

at the beginning of 1918. In public, Steed felt obliged to respect Lloyd George's viewpoint as a theoretical alternative to his concept of independence and complete freedom from Habsburg rule for the subject peoples. Steed and Lloyd George concurred insofar as it was plain to both of them that no peace settlement could be acceptable to the Allies, if it left the lot of the nationalities of Austria–Hungary unchanged. But *The Times* questioned whether "genuine self-government" as demanded by Lloyd George could be introduced by the Habsburgs themselves against the opposition of the two ruling races:

> Indeed, the real test of any scheme of democratic self-government for the peoples of the Austrian Monarchy . . . will be the attitude of the Germans and of the Magyars towards it, for it is their artificial hegemony, built up in the interest of Prussian domination, that any honest scheme of self-determination for the Habsburg peoples would threaten.[29]

Steed was convinced that the dual system could not be broken within the Habsburg framework and therefore he regarded moderate pronouncements as harmful and only apt to disconcert "some tried friends of the Allies".[30] Realizing that the government was drifting into the opposite direction he wanted it to take, Steed was greatly disturbed by the possible consequences of further war aims declarations sparing Austria–Hungary. He therefore tried to persuade the British leaders to commit themselves to the loyal application of the principle of self-determination, which in his opinion should also be fully applied to the various nationalities in Austria–Hungary. In his analysis of "The Austrian Problem", which he sent to the Foreign Office for consideration,[31] Steed pointed out that vague promises had no meaning for the Czechs and the South Slavs. He warned of Austrian attempts to secure from the Allies friendly declarations that could be turned to the advantage of Austria:

> They could be used on the one hand, as a means to put pressure on Berlin, and on the other, as a means of discouraging the pro-Ally Austro-Hungarian races . . .

It was the possibility of an inconclusive peace preserving not only the Habsburg Empire but also Germany's continental position that made Steed alert against any peace rumours and soundings about which he was amazingly well informed. Steed contested the news that the Habsburgs had the will and the power to detach themselves from Germany. Nor did he consider a federalization of the Empire to be possible any

---

[29] *The Times* of 7 Jan. 1918.
[30] *Ibid.*
[31] *F.O.* 371/3134, No. 13649 of 4 Feb. 1918. Another memorandum was sent to the Prime Minister on 25 Jan. by the Serbian Society. Cf. H. Hanak, *op.cit.*, p.200.

longer. The Allied aim to establish a lasting peace "upon the democratic freedom of the peoples", as it was euphemistically phrased, implied that Germany was beaten and her power on the continent was drastically reduced. Success or failure to achieve this, Steed was convinced, depended upon the way in which the Austrian problem was solved.

To combat the struggle to save Austria it was important to get to work without delay. Steed had a powerful sponsor for his scheme in Lord Northcliffe, who on 7 February was appointed Director of Propaganda in enemy countries. This post was independent of the Ministry of Information and, indeed, from the ministerial structure and thus gave Northcliffe and his protégé a large measure of autonomy. For the powerful paper jingoist it was sufficient to be assured by Steed:

> The struggle to 'save Austria' is at the bottom of the whole pacifist and defeatist campaign in Allied countries.[32]

Once convinced of the *delenda Austria* cause Northcliffe completely relied on Steed to formulate the policy he was going to propose to Balfour. Steed drew up a memorandum[33] that proceeded from the assumption that a separate peace with the Monarchy was impossible and that therefore the only conceivable policy remaining was

> To try to break the power of Austria–Hungary, as the weakest link in the chain of enemy states, by supporting and encouraging all anti-German and pro-Ally peoples and tendencies.

To forestall any objections from the Foreign Office Steed went so far as to make the point that this policy was not necessarily anti-Habsburgian nor opposed to the interest of the Catholic religion but in harmony with the declared aims of the Allies.

Balfour in his answer of 26 February did not find the two alternative policies set forth by Northcliffe (Steed) to be mutually exclusive, for everything which encouraged the anti-German elements in the Habsburg Empire could either induce the Austrian Emperor to a separate peace and a modification of the constitution, or, if he refused to carry out such a policy, the non-German elements might bring about the change they desired. Therefore a propaganda for the subject nationalities was right no matter "whether the complete break-up of the Austrian Empire or its de-Germanization under Hapsburg rule be the final goal of our efforts".[34]

Steed was not satisfied with this answer. He wanted to extract a decision from the War Cabinet that the disruptive policy was at least to be preferred to attempts for a separate peace. But the cabinet, which

---

[32] Steed to Northcliffe, 5 Mar. 1918, Steed papers.
[33] The following correspondence is printed in *Through Thirty Years*, ii, pp.187–91. For the final drafts by Northcliffe cf. *Cab.* 24/43, G.T. 3762.
[34] *Ibid.*

was just engaged in the discussion to resume the Anglo-Austrian talks in Switzerland, took rather the opposite view. It agreed that Northcliffe should carry on his operations on the lines indicated, but subject to the ruling that:

> No promise should be made to the subject races in Austria which we could not redeem; for instance we must not promise them complete independence if the best we could get was autonomy.[35]

For the time being Northcliffe and Steed accepted this restriction. After arriving at the Italian front Steed saw himself confronted with Austro-Hungarian troops containing large percentages of Transylvanian Rumanians, Carniolian Slovenes and a purely Croat division, all of whom he hoped to seduce with "skilful" propaganda. According to Steed's report the Italian intelligence officers, supported by the French and Delmé-Radcliffe, strongly urged that the National Committees of the subject nationalities should be allowed to proclaim the independence of their respective territories on the understanding that the Allied governments would recognize such proclamations of independence though they would not pledge themselves to secure it.[36]

When Steed's pressing appeal reached London, the first German drive on the Western front, the Somme offensive, was on the wane. But the threat of the final effort of the Central Powers was by no means over and Austria contributed to it with the dispatch of several units to the French battlefield. The Habsburgs had definitely decided to stake their fate on Germany's military power and thereby challenged the Allies to employ counter-measures against Austria too. In this precarious situation the British War Cabinet was entirely in favour of Steed's propaganda project and authorized him to go ahead on the suggested lines. They were prepared to recognize proclamations of independence made by the subject nationalities of Austria–Hungary themselves, which allowed Steed the immediate use of the term 'independence' as 'explosive' propaganda in the rear of the Austrian army. However, this did not pledge the British government to anything if the undertaking failed, because they had not entered into any commitment to fight for the independence of these nationalities.

Official British policy still resembled a two-edged sword which could cut both ways, the eventual direction depending on the course of events. As long as the outcome was undecided, the political implications of anti-Austrian propaganda were not irreversibly endorsed by the political leadership in London. On the other hand, Steed and his

---

[35] *Cab.* 23/5, *WC* 359 of 5 Mar. 1918.
[36] *F.O.* 371/3134, No. 5942 of 3 Apr. Cf. *Through Thirty Years*, ii, p.205. Zeman, *op.cit.*, pp.190–91, suspects that the request was made on the initiative of Steed himself, which is very likely considering the attitude of the Italian government, which must have made it difficult for the Italian officers to demand such an outspoken policy in favour of the subject races.

collaborators always regarded their task as more than a ploy to solve an imminent war emergency. For them enemy propaganda was a direct means of achieving far-reaching political aims like the recognition of the independence of the subject peoples. In this aim they were ahead of the official administration which had adopted the view that a policy of disruption would be useful but need not necessarily lead to a policy of dismemberment.

2. The Triumph of Crewe House

Enemy propaganda had thus become a great potential in the hands of the anti-Habsburg forces. Provided that it was carried out ingeniously and met an appropriate response Crewe House could bring about a situation in which the government would be obliged to acknowledge their success by subscribing to the *desideratum* of a "New Europe". For that matter Allied propaganda had to try to obtain quick results among the Habsburg subject races. Their aspirations had to be encouraged by denouncing the deficiencies of the Dual system and the practices of the ruling classes; by pointing out the futility of expecting constitutional reform; and by holding out the prospect of real self-determination and social change as a result of the solution of the nationality questions on the basis of complete independence. These points were to be brought across to the Habsburg subjects in a rather simplified form, as Seton-Watson conceived.[37]

The ideological background and the practical demands for enemy propaganda were first co-ordinated at an inter-Allied propaganda conference in London at the end of February.[38] The next step was to incorporate the representatives of the peoples concerned. For this purpose, and also as a political prelude to the actual launching of the propaganda distribution, the Congress of Oppressed Nationalities was convened in Rome from 8 to 11 April. On this occasion the emigre groups agreed upon three major resolutions. They proclaimed the right of each of them "to attain full political and economic independence"; they exposed the Austro-Hungarian Monarchy as "the instrument of German domination" and they pledged to co-operate against the common Habsburg foe.[39] In this context the Italo-Yugoslav convention of 7 March was warmly confirmed.

The demonstration of harmony among all enemies of Austria was the main purpose of the Rome Congress, which aimed at strengthening their determination to break up the monarchy. The subject races, it was hoped, would regain confidence after the disappointment felt by them by the war aims speeches of Wilson and Lloyd George at the beginning

---

[37] For excerpts from Seton-Watson's memoranda on propaganda cf. May, *op.cit.*, pp.606–07.
[38] *Through Thirty Years*, ii, pp.191–96.
[39] *New Europe*, 2 May, 1918.

of the year. In particular it was hoped that the Yugoslavs would be reconciled by the creation of a sympathetic atmosphere in relation to the South Slavs in Italy. But the Italian government refused to take notice of the congress officially, though messages of sympathy were sent by Bissolati and Comandini, the Italian Minister of War Propaganda, and several members of former administrations were present at Rome which "gave the congress an almost semi-official character", as Ambassador Rodd emphasized in this report to London.[40]

Britain was represented by Steed and Seton-Watson, the latter having arrived there with some delay after Steed and Northcliffe had intervened successfully in his behalf at the Foreign Office, which at first had complied with the Italian ambassador's request to prevent him from going to Rome, where Seton-Watson was a *persona non grata* on account of his publicly displayed hostility to the Treaty of London.[41]

After this obstacle had been overcome and when all the principal participants were received by Orlando, Steed was satisfied and rightly called the congress "a remarkable success'. He already anticipated that it would alarm the Austrian authorities, because now a vigorous propaganda could be started thanks to the adhesion of the Allied governments.[42] Steed deliberately exaggerated the association of the Italian Premier and especially of his Foreign Minister with the affair. But publicity was secured and even the sceptical British Foreign Secretary was duly impressed and minuted: "The Congress seems to have been a great success. We have yet to see its effects."[43]

The spectacular appearance of Steed and Seton-Watson in Rome caused consternation among their political adversaries at home. The Radical M.P., J. King, asked whether the British delegates were in the service of the government and whether they had attended the conference as representatives of the government.[44] In fact, the Foreign Office, which King suspected of being in favour of the organisation of the congress, was not certain itself about the mandate of Steed and Seton-Watson. So Rodd had to make enquiries of Steed, who was at pains to explain that he had not in any way damaged the interest of the British government and her Allies. His caution had gone so far that – after consultation with Sonnino – part of Steed's speech had not been published in the press. It was true that he had accepted an honorary vice-presidency at the congress, but there he had explicitly pointed out to his audience:

I do not represent England. I am here only as an Englishman who

---

[40] *F.O.* 371/3135, No. 66462, f.64427 of 10 Apr.
[41] *Through Thirty Years*, ii, pp.197–98.
[42] Steed's report for Northcliffe was transmitted by Rodd on 13 Apr., *F.O.* 371/3135, No. 66616.
[43] On No. 66462.
[44] *Hansard*, 5th ser., cv, 117 (16 Apr.).

knows something about Austria and the Austrian subject races, but I represent nobody but myself.[45]

Thereupon Cecil laid all the responsibility upon Northcliffe, only to provoke a further parliamentary question whether the Allied governments had adopted the agreement reached at Rome. Balfour first ascertained that the French had taken no official notice,[46] and then dissociated the Allied governments from the resolutions passed in Rome.[47]

Despite the guarded attitude of the government the *New Europe* had good reason for hoping that the Rome Congress marked "the beginning of a new era in the policy of the Entente".[48] This expected change in British policy did not occur as a direct result of the Congress but nearly coincided with it, which was not just accidental.

The activities of the leaders of the rebellious nationalities at home and in exile were observed with increasing apprehension by the Vienna government. Czernin publicly brandmarked "the wretched Masaryk" and his sympathizers inside the Monarchy and acknowledged that their number was significant.[49] He had gained the impression that a change of attitude had taken place on the Allied side as a result of the social and political strife in the Austrian Empire. In a message to his Emperor Czernin expressed the belief that the predominating Entente opinion was now that the Monarchy was on the brink of collapse and that it was therefore useless to negotiate with her.[50] What Czernin did not mention in his explanation of the enemy's reaction was the effect of the annexionist peace treaties with Russia and the Ukraine and the preliminary peace arrangement with Rumania, which disillusioned the Allies in their hopes for an understanding with Austria. Only the possibility that the more compromising and reformist ideas of the Emperor himself might finally determine Vienna's official policy kept up some vague hopes in London, Paris, and Washington.

Czernin was determined to cut off "all poisoned connections"[51] of this kind. Apart from his negative response to the British and American feelers he had also given a rigorously negative reply to the French after

---

[45] *F.O.* 371/3135, No. 75021 of 19 Apr.

[46] On the closing day of the congress Pichon tel. to Barrere that he had learned that Balfour approved of the anti-Austrian resolutions formulated in Rome and that it was therefore necessary for the French to associate themselves with the British point of view. (*Min.Aff.Etr., Autriche-Hongrie, Les Yougoslaves*, Carton 313); this actually concerned Steed's formula for propaganda to be organized among the Slav elements of the Austro-Hungarian troops on the Italian front, which was not identical with the resolution of the Rome Congress. Cf. *F.O.* 371/3135, No. 64640 of 11 Apr.

[47] *Hansard, vol.cit.*, 1270 (29 Apr.).

[48] *New Europe*, 2 May 1918.

[49] Scott, *op.cit.*, p.298ff.

[50] I. Meckling, *Die Aussenpolitik des Grafen Czernin*, Munich 1969, p.343n.

[51] Baernreither diary, xix, entry of 12 Apr., cf. R. A. Kann, *Die Sixtus Affaire*, Munich 1966, pp.21–22.

a reopening of the Armand-Revertera contacts in early February.[52] Moreover, he deliberately disclosed these goings-on in his speech of 2 April, when he mentioned that Clemenceau had sought for peace negotiations.[53] His remarks had the effect of a boomerang. Clemenceau immediately countered by stating that the initiative had come from Vienna and when Czernin in turn tried to blame the French Premier for the breakdown of the talks due to the French demands, the "Tiger" struck back by revealing the secret of the Imperial letter of March 1917.[54]

The consequences of the Czernin–Clemenceau controversy were drawn unequivocally by Balfour:[55]

The French have now destroyed any chance of allied negotiations with the Austrian Emperor.

It did not matter whether Balfour disapproved that "Clemenceau had listened to his pugnacious instincts" or whether Lord Esher complained to Lloyd George that the French treatment of the Imperial letter was "disgraceful to our diplomacy".[56] Clemenceau's reaction forced the British decisively to abandon a policy which had hitherto been regarded as of paramount importance, namely to avoid everything that could forestall the possibility of detaching Austria from Germany. If the prospect for such a solution had become negligible recently, it had now vanished for ever. It was now obvious that the Allies could no longer expect to be saved by the appearance of the *deus ex machina* in the shape of a separate peace with Austria–Hungary.

The revelation of the imperial letter was also regretted by the Holy See, which had only recently informed the Allies that a separate peace between them and Austria was not possible, because all Austrian efforts were directed towards a general peace. Nevertheless Cardinal Gasparri expressed the doubts of the Holy See as to the usefulness of a union of small states in place of the Habsburg Empire . . . He rather wanted to see Austria as a strong counterweight to Germany, if perhaps only after the conclusion of a general peace.[57] His reasoning very much reflected the British point of view at the turn of 1917/18. But meanwhile London's precautions were much greater and Hardinge thought that a strong anti-German Austria was "only feasible as a federalist empire in which the Slav states enjoy complete autonomy".[58]

In other words, the British were now almost prepared to leave it to

[52] Manteyer, *op.cit.*, p.263ff.
[53] Scott, *loc.cit.*
[54] Manteyer, *op.cit.*, p.275ff.
[55] *F.O.* 371/3134, No. 65250 of 12 Apr.
[56] *Ibid.*, No. 68456 and Ll.G. papers, F/16/1/24.
[57] *Ibid.*, Nos. 55295, 55722 and 68566.
[58] Minute on No. 68566.

the nationalities themselves whether they wanted to remain united in some form or other under the Habsburg Crown. They had given up all idea of negotiating with Vienna about an arrangement that would have led to a settlement over the heads of the subject races, whose status would have depended on the willingness of the Austrian government to compromise with the wishes of the Allies. The impracticability of such an Anglo-Austrian understanding was acknowledged by Balfour in the Commons, where he declared in mid-May that the Emperor's letter offered "no firm basis for an honourable settlement".[59]

Clemenceau's action and the avalanche in its wake up to Czernin's resignation and the Emperor's humiliation in the German headquarters at Spa were welcomed with a tone of self-justification by those quarters which had preached the fallacy of any peace negotiations with Austria. They could now concentrate on their work for the dissolution of the Habsburg Empire without having to fear the counter-currents of Austrophile diplomacy. Furthermore, the task of the *New Europe* group was facilitated by an important administrative change. Balfour's appreciation for the work of the Information Bureau of the War Office had been expressed in February 1918, when he asked the Cabinet to have the staff transferred to the Foreign Office. Balfour encountered the strong objections of Beaverbrook who wanted these men for his new Ministry of Information and the Cabinet decision was reversed in his favour. The expert advisers expressed their preference for the Foreign Office by resigning in a body and finally succeeded in being employed in the Foreign Office as the Political Intelligence Department (P.I.D.);[60] which was then directed by William Tyrrell, who was assisted by J. W. Headlam-Morley. Members of the Department were L. B. Namier, A. J. Toynbee, J. Bailey, G. Saunders, E. Bevin, J. W. Simpson, J. G. Powell, and the brothers Leeper. This new organization greatly increased the influence of the anti-Habsburg forces in Britain. After the government had decided on the destruction of the Austrian Empire, they were prepared to follow the advice of those people who had advocated this policy all along. They were the only ones who had firm ideas and a detailed knowledge to offer for its execution. From now on all relevant papers on Austria–Hungary went through their hands and they were the first to comment on diplomatic dispatches, which gave them an opportunity to prejudge most of the decisions in their favour. In crucial and controversial cases they were at least asked for their opinion by the Foreign Office leadership and often could present their point *in persona*. Though it was not usual for the P.I.D. to deal with current executive work, they were also occasionally asked to prepare a

---

[59] *Hansard*, 5th ser., cvi, 569–87 (16 May). Cf. *WC* 411 & 412, *Cab.* 23/6.
[60] *WC* 349 (19 Feb.) & 367 (19 Mar.), *Cab.* 23/5; *G.T.* 3788, 3939, 3942 and 3964, *Cab.* 24/43–45.

memorandum on further action over an immediate issue, like negotiations with the representatives of the Czechoslovaks.[61]

The P.I.D. also continued the duty of the I.B.D.I. of providing the Foreign Office with regular memoranda on current events in enemy countries. But as "insiders" they could write with more authority and count on a more favourable response to their interpretations. Concerning "The Habsburg Policy" the P.I.D. could now make its point in the light of the recent events.[62] In a review of the latter incident the P.I.D. argued that Karl could never have detached his Empire from Germany, because he could not have secured "even a decent measure of self-determination" for the Slav nationalities. It was beyond his power to change the constitution and this was the crux of the matter. The Czech and the South Slav aspirations were "not incompatible with the interest of the Habsburg dynasty but (were) incompatible with the national programme of the Germans and the Magyars". The Habsburgs could only obtain the support of one group and had decided for the two ruling peoples for three major reasons:

1. The Germans and the Magyars were interested in defending the irredentist fringe of the Empire (Trentino, Transylvania).
2. Their supremacy secured the interest of Germany to safeguard the Empire from breaking up.
3. The ruling upper class was socially linked with the dynasty.

No personal sympathies of the Emperor, the P.I.D. concluded, could overcome these basic interests of the peoples.

Under these circumstances the only promising policy was a downright support of the subject nationalities and even negotiations with the Hungarian Independists (Károlyi) were regarded as being harmful, because there was

> a grave danger . . . of our alienating the only straightforward enemies of Germany within the Monarchy[63] . . . What they desire is the certainty that no illusions are entertained by Entente statesmen concerning the possibility of detaching Austria from Germany and making her into a 'balance' against her.[64]

If there remained any obscurity over a problem concerning the policy of and towards the nationalities, the P.I.D. staff took the liberty of consulting Steed and Seton-Watson.[65] The latter had not been included in the P.I.D., because as a CI man in the R.A.M.C. he had to

---

[61] L. B. Namier, *Vanished Supremacies*, Peregrine reprint, Harmondsworth 1962, p.138.
[62] *G.T.* 4629 of 6 May, 1918, *Cab.* 24/52.
[63] Minute by A. W. A. Leeper on Rumbold's tel. No. 104197 of 3 June 1918, *F.O.* 371/3135.
[64] Minute by L. B. Namier of 26 June on Reading's telegram of 3 June, *ibid.*, No. 111985.
[65] For example, over the attitude of the Polish delegation at the Rome congress. Cf. *F.O.* 371/3135, No. 75153.

await military orders. Steed took the opportunity of suggesting to Northcliffe[66] that Seton-Watson be commandeered to his purposes "as the best official expert on Austria–Hungary and a thoroughly reliable man". At Crewe House he was then able to give information and advice directly and worked at the head of the Austrian section of the propaganda department. Steed's reputation was so enhanced by his dealings in Italy that a paper on his negotiations with the Serbian government was considered as "official" by the Foreign Office staff. By autumn 1918 Crewe House, assisted by the P.I.D., was in charge of British policy towards Austria–Hungary. When Steed and Seton-Watson were absent in Paris and Alex Leeper was ill, all further action in regard to the Yugoslavs was postponed.[67] The advisers had become recognized experts, to whom the execution of the dismemberment of the Habsburg Empire was entrusted.

Northcliffe himself was not really satisfied with his position of indirectly supporting the government. After the Cabinet change which brought in Chamberlain instead of Milner, Northcliffe's mistrust of Lloyd George became so great that he was afraid of being faced similarly by "an intrigue with the Germans or the Austrians"[68] and rather wanted to resign from his post. Lloyd George expressed himself strongly against Northcliffe abandoning his duties as the chief propagandist and sent him a report on Austria which was highly favourable in its assessment of the propaganda conducted in Italy and let the Prime Minister assume that "Austria might fall to pieces after the failure of the Western offensive".[69] Information to this effect had been forwarded by Colonel Stanhope of the S.W.C., who outlined that no Austrian offensive could be undertaken, if a vigorous propaganda campaign, for which all preparations had been made, were pursued. He then expected the greater part of the Austro-Hungarian army to become unreliable and possibly unfit to even hold the line.[70] Similar assumptions were also communicated by the Allied representatives at Jassy, who agreed that it would be fruitful to exploit the increasing animosity between the different nationalities of which they had learned by suitable propaganda for there was

> reason to believe agents belonging to these different nationalities would succeed in disorganizing units recruited therefrom.[71]

Steed, who was impressed at the manner in which "the movement

---

[66] Letter of 2 Mar., Steed papers.
[67] *F.O.* 371/3137, No. 75153.
[68] Northcliffe to the liaison officer at the Foreign Office, C. J. Philips. Cf. also his letter to Milner on 22 Apr., both cit. R. Pound and G. Harmsworth, *Northcliffe*, London 1959, pp.631–33.
[69] Lloyd George to Northcliffe, 22 Apr., Lloyd George papers, F/41/87.
[70] *G.T.* 4414c of 22 Apr., *Cab.* 24/50.
[71] Bertie's telegram of 19 Apr., *F.O.* 371/3135, No. 69479.

inside the Monarchy was keeping pace with the movement outside",[72] tried to capitalize on this development. Presumably at his request Northcliffe wrote to Lloyd George that he regarded himself entitled to be informed and consulted, before a change of the present policy was undertaken; maintaining that a very definite policy had already been initiated by him with the consent of the Cabinet and the Foreign Office:

> Though no binding assurance have been given or engagement entered into, a very precise impression has been conveyed, under my responsibility, that this country at least favours a policy of liberation of the Habsburg subject races with a view to their constitution, in the event of Allied victory into a non-German polity, or Danubian confederation.[73]

This was, as Northcliffe pointed out, "a question of consistency of method". The ambiguity of British policy in this matter became more and more apparent. In late May Delmé-Radcliffe had an interview with Clemenceau and urged upon him the importance of an Allied declaration in order to convince the nationalities "that the Entente governments really meant to assist them to obtain their freedom if possible".[74] The argument in favour of such a step was evident. Only if the Allies committed themselves formally and publicly to what they promised in their propaganda, could they fully convince the Habsburg subjects, particularly the Slav politicians inside the Monarchy. If such a declaration was made, it excluded a return to the policy of coming to terms with the Habsburgs and would demonstrably manifest the will to disintegrate the Austrian Empire. Lord Derby, who had meanwhile succeeded Bertie at the embassy in Paris, confronted the Foreign Office with the necessity of clearing up the British position in the Austrian question. There were "two horses to ride", as Derby observed.

> One is Yugo-Slavia, the other is Austria maintained and strengthened. I am doubtful which horse the government mean to ride, but as they are going in opposite directions they have got to make up their mind which it is to be, as to attempt to ride both is impossible.[75]

Delmé-Radcliffe's action had been unauthorized by the London government, whose view was still that communicated to Steed on 4 April, namely that the government could not pledge itself to secure the independence for the subject peoples. The question of a public statement was still regarded as premature in Whitehall, but the direction in which British policy was going to move was now clearly indicated. The

---

[72] Steed to McClure, 9 May, Steed papers.
[73] Northcliffe to Lloyd George, 28 Apr., Lloyd George papers, F/41/8/8.
[74] *F.O.* 371/3135, No. 89828 of 20 May.
[75] Lloyd George papers F/52/1/34.

Spa meeting of the two Emperors of the Central Powers showed that the outcome of the Clemenceau revelations was an even closer union between Austria and Germany, in which the Monarchy was to take the role of a second to the German *Mitteleuropa* realization. The prospective alliance for twenty-five years removed all idea of a Slavization of the Habsburg Empire as a counterbalance to German expansionism in Central Europe. According to information gathered by a well informed agent,

> Germany (had) undertaken to assist Austria in quelling apprehended risings in Bohemia and amongst the Southern Slavs on the strict understanding of an equivocally German policy in Austria . . .[76]

In view of this development it was felt in London that the policy of detaching Austria from Germany had to be abandoned "as both inopportune and impracticable" and "that the best plan (was) to give all possible support to oppressed nationalities in Austria in their struggle against German–Magyar domination".[77]

Already the day after Cecil had sent this confidential information to Paris he confirmed the new attitude on behalf of the British government in public. Speaking at the Mansion House on the occasion of the third anniversary of Italy's entry into the war (22 May) he greeted the Adriatic reconciliation achieved at the Rome Congress and also praised "those gallant Czecho-Slovaks" and the other subject races. Cecil took the wind out of Austrophile criticism by linking the aspirations of the nationalities with the high moral principles for which the Allies pretended to fight:

> People talk sometimes about the dismemberment of Austria. I have no weakness for Austria; but I venture to think that is the wrong point of view. The true way to regard this problem is not the dismemberment of Austria, but the liberation of the populations subject to her rule. We are anxious to see all these peoples in the enjoyment of full liberty and independence;[78]

This argument sounded more credible after the Italo-Yugoslav *rapprochement*, which now proved a great asset for propaganda.

So did the speech made by Cecil, and the *New Europe* did not fail to thank him for providing "the best piece of propaganda for Austria–Hungary that has yet come from the British Government".[79] Cecil had used the sort of formulation which the propagandists had been longing to hear. After all a British statesman of rank had spoken of

[76] *F.O.* 371/3136, No. 87568 of 16 May.
[77] Cecil to Derby, 21 May, *F.O.* 371/3135, No. 89828.
[78] *The Times* of 23 May.
[79] *New Europe* of 30 May.

'independence' for the subject peoples, a phrase that was so essential
for their purpose. It might in fact not have been included by Cecil, had
not a member of the Austrian section of Lord Northcliffe's Department
"conferred with him and concerted with him those features of his
declaration that affected anti-Austrian propaganda".[80]

Crewe House was further encouraged by a personal letter of thanks
by the Prime Minister to Northcliffe, which praised him for the organization of the "admirable work" in his Austrian propaganda.[81] Steed
tried to make political capital out of the appreciation of this campaign
by pleading for more definite Allied concessions to the aspirations of the
nationalities. He urged the government to issue an official declaration
for the Czechoslovaks and the Yugoslavs arguing that the latter's
conduct in the forthcoming offensive might be determined by the
attitude displayed by the Allied governments.[82] The British already
considered a separate declaration to the Czechoslovaks[83] at that time.
The matter of a collective Allied declaration was then discussed between the British and the French. The French Foreign Minister held
the moment appropriate for the recognition of the independence of the
Czechs and the Poles and suggested that their National Councils
should be asked to draft a formula. Pichon founded his willingness to
comply with their wishes on the fact that

> all thought of a separate peace with Austria was over. We need
> trouble no more to 'ménager' the Austrians. Therefore the Allies
> should use every means to make difficulties for the Austrian front.
> They should support the Slav and non-Magyar elements in the
> Empire.[84]

While this view had also become the maxim of British policy, its
representatives were hesitant to carry out the logical conclusions from
their recent perceptions. Cecil pointed out the difference between the
Czechs and the Poles and together with his Prime Minister was
extremely reluctant to add to the war aims new pledges "that they
could not realize". Due to the precarious military situation at the end of
May Lloyd George doubted that the Allies might ever have the means
to influence the development in South East Europe in the desired way
and feared that to raise unfulfilled hopes among those small nations
would be detrimental to Britain's relations with them in future.

It was finally agreed to draft a formula for the Versailles meeting at
the beginning of June. It was also until then that all discussion over the

[80] Minutes of the second meeting of the Committee for Propaganda in Enemy Countries held at
Crewe House on 27 May, *F.O.* 371/3474, No. 99386; draft by Steed in the Steed papers.
[81] *Cit. ibid.*
[82] Letters by Steed to Davies & Lloyd George, both of 30 May, Ll.G. papers F/41/8/15.
[83] Cf. ch.VI, 3.
[84] *I.C.* 63, *Cab.* 28/3 (28 May).

Yugoslavs was postponed, because the British and the French felt obliged to act in unison with Italy. Sonnino, however, thwarted the Anglo-French intentions with his veto of any formal recognition of Yugoslav aspirations.[85] The way out of this deadlock was provided by an American declaration issued on 29 May, which announced the "great interest" of the United States government in the proceedings of the Rome Congress and expressed its "earnest sympathies" with the aspirations of the Czecho-Slovaks and the Yugoslavs.[86] Simultaneously the British were confidentially informed that Wilson had also lost all hope of making a separate peace with Austria and had decided to support the nationalities.[87] So the Allied Prime Ministers, after declaring the formation of an independent Polish state a condition for peace, associated themselves almost verbatim with the American declaration.[88]

Steed and his Slav friends were disappointed over the weakness of the Versailles declaration. For the moment it was little consolation that Northcliffe promised to use all his influence in favour of the issue of more satisfactory pronouncements at least in Britain.[89] The official Allied death sentence over the fate of the Habsburg Empire had again been postponed. But the events in Austria and especially at the Italo-Austrian front promised that the dissolution of the Monarchy would soon become inevitable. It was comforting for Crewe House to learn that mass desertions at the Piave front had forced the Austrian High Command to order machine-gun sections "to undertake 'special duties' " with divisions containing troops of the subject races. According to reliable information the morale of a large proportion of the Austro-Hungarian forces had been undermined by the propaganda actions and forced the Austrian military authorities to place their 'shock troops' in the front line.[90]

There were, however, still some organizational obstacles and the D.M.I. had to report to the Cabinet on 4 June that no report of the Rome Congress had yet reached the Yugoslavs in Austria, so that its effect would not be felt on the next offensive.[91] The government decided to await the outcome of the offensive, before any far-reaching schemes for the instigation of a revolt in Austria were considered. Lloyd George was of the opinion that a premature rising would be futile and harmful to the spirit of Czechoslovaks. Balfour pointed out that the British

---

[85] *I.C.* 66, *Cab.* 2814.
[86] *For.Rel.*, 1918, Suppl. I, i, p.808, cit. Mamatey, *op.cit.*, p.261.
[87] Wiseman interview with Wilson on 29 May, *Lansing Papers*, ii, pp.130–39, reported to Drummond on 30 May, *F.O.* 371/3443, No. 101715 (*cit.* in Mamatey, *op.cit.*, p.257 after A. Willert, *The Road to Safety*, London 1952, p.158.
[88] *The Times* of 4 June.
[89] Dispatch to Delmé-Radcliffe of 8 June, *F.O.* 371/3747,
[90] Pound & Harmsworth, *op.cit.*, p.638 and Crewe House minutes of 27 May (*loc.cit.*).
[91] *WC* 425, *Cab.* 23/6.

could not render any direct assistance in Bohemia or Galicia and Curzon doubted whether a revolt by the nationalities "would ever become a sufficient menace to Austria". Lloyd George and his other colleagues seemed more convinced that the situation in Austria was developing in favour of the Allies, but the Prime Minister was wary that "a great opportunity would be thrown away", if too much was attempted too early.[92]

The Piave battle, which was waged from 15 to 24 June, ended with a great military success for the Italians who recaptured much of their territory. It also provided fresh evidence of the extent to which disaffection was rampant in the Austro-Hungarian army. Large numbers of deserters with propaganda material in their pockets crossed the lines.[93] Those nationalities who were reported to have fought well had no knowledge of the Allied propaganda and recent declarations in their favour.[94] Admittedly many of them surrendered out of sheer war-weariness, but their decision was certainly promoted by the psychological warfare initiated by the British propagandists.

Significant evidence for the impact of the propaganda is provided on the Austrian side. Czernin's successor Burián complained[95] about its effects on the South Slav politicians in a Crown Council and after the Piave disaster the government published a *communiqué* which brand-marked individual cases of treason.[96] In retrospect the official Austrian war history stated that

> an extraordinarily dangerous weapon, perfectly employed, diminished the spirit of the Austro-Hungarian army at the front from the days of the Rome Congress.[97]

Thus the military collapse of the Empire was considerably eased by the propaganda work against it. But what was even more important was its immediate repercussions on the attitude of the leading British statesmen, who were impressed by its efficiency and became more and more convinced of the inevitability of breaking up the Habsburg monarchy. For men like Northcliffe and Lloyd George the propaganda enterprise also offered a success which they could offer to the public to improve their own image as competent war-leaders. The Prime Minister took the opportunity of the Austrian defeat on the Piave of referring in the Commons to the "very serious discontent in Austria", where he believed three-fifths of the population were in sympathy with the aims of the Allies.[98] Altogether the Austrian situation had developed com-

---

[92] *WC* 429a of 11 June, *Cab.* 23/14.
[93] Valiani, *op.cit.*, p.401.
[94] This applied to the Poles. Cf. the report of the D.M.I. of 26 June, *WC* 436, *Cab.* 23/6.
[95] *Protokolle des Gemeinsamen Ministerrats, op.cit.*, pp.662–64 (30 May).
[96] Published in the Vienna press on 27 July 1918, quoted in *New Europe* (15 Aug.).
[97] *Österreich-Ungarns letzter Krieg*, 1914–1918, vii, Vienna 1938, p.19.
[98] *Hansard*, 5th ser., cvii, 785–86 (24 June).

pletely contrary to Lloyd George's intentions a few weeks previously. But again Austria seemed the key to victory over Germany in the war and therefore the news about sedition and revolt was apt to fill the British government and public with new hope.

3. The Recognition of the Czechoslovaks

In his appraisal of the revolutionary forces in Austria–Hungary Lloyd George spoke with special admiration of the Austrian prisoners coming over to fight on the Allied side in Siberia.[99] This referred to the Czech legion which had been formed in Russia as a result of the initiative of the Czech exile politicians. The Czechs had decided to help themselves by helping the Allies in bringing about the downfall of the Central Powers. If the Czechs could provide an efficient combatant force, this would be the best means to invalidate a pro-Habsburg policy of the Allies and the fundamental basis for the claim of Czechoslovak independence.

The value of a Czech military corps was first appreciated in France, where the Czechs were permitted to establish their own army. Its autonomy under the Czechoslovak National Council was recognized in principle by the French government in August 1917.[100] While being engaged in protracted negotiations for a Czech army in Italy, Beneš also came into contact with British officials in Rome. Sir Samuel Hoare, the head of the British Military Mission in Rome knew Masaryk from the time when he held a similar position in Russia. He undertook to act as a go-between in Beneš's attempt to secure also the British consent for the military enterprise of the Czechs. Hoare prepared the ground in London by sending the information and memoranda compiled by Beneš to the Foreign Office. Beneš's dossier on the Czechoslovak question outspokenly rejected a federalization of the Austrian Empire and demanded an independent Czechoslovak state. Since it was impossible to federalize the Empire, Beneš argued, the plan to detach Austria was "based on an absolutely erroneous supposition".[101]

Urged by Seton-Watson and Steed, Beneš came to London on 20 October 1917 and talked to several Foreign Office officials. In a conversation with Clerk,[102] he explained that every utterance of a British statesman was carefully scrutinized for its meaning in Bohemia. Beneš did not conceal his disappointment over "what seemed to be a growing tendency on the part of the British government to avoid any reference to the dissolution of Austria–Hungary".

But the Czech leader had to realize that Britain was in a difficult

---

[99] *Hansard, loc.cit.*
[100] Beneš, *War Memoirs*, pp.188–97.
[101] *F.O.* 371/2864, No. 207241/134254 of 26 Oct.
[102] *Ibid.*, No. 207244 of 26 Oct.

position at that stage of the war, when victory was still far out of reach. So Clerk had to content himself with acknowledging Britain's great obligation to the Czechoslovak organization and Hardinge's minute on Clerk's memorandum gives proof of the sceptical attitude of the Foreign Office towards the Czech demands:

> It would be difficult to give more than an expression of sympathy with Czech aspirations on the basis of self-government of minor nationalities. The geographical position of Bohemia is an almost unsurmountable obstacle.

The reservations against Beneš became even greater when Lord St. Cyres, attache to the British legation in Berne, sent in a memorandum on the "split parties in Bohemia".[103] He distinguished between Imperialist Austrians, 'Old Czechs' who were satisfied with trialism, and 'Young Czechs' who wanted to break away from the Monarchy. Although the report stressed that the latter were the most numerous, the mere mention of loyalist Conservative groups was sufficient to undermine the standing of the exiles and Beneš's friends in the Department of Information were at pains to affirm the unity of the Czechs.[104]

There was no reason for the British government to support the claim for Czech independence, as long as no material gains came from such a commitment. The material profit was then offered in the form of the Czechoslovak brigade, which received formal recognition from the French on 16 December 1917. The French sponsorship of the Czech army was due to the precarious situation on the South Eastern front in Russia and Rumania, where reinforcements of any kind were desperately needed. In view of the state of disorganisation of the Russian army and its doubtful value for some time to come, the British War Office agreed with the French General Staff that their proposals for a "Serbo-Czech" army deserved encouragement and support. Balfour concurred despite the fact that by promoting this project the Allied governments "would be assuming thereby a specific responsibility towards Czech aspirations".[105]

The outbreak of the Bolshevik revolution and the collapse of the Ukrainian front made the Franco-British plans in this area null and void. French diplomatic and military circles immediately thought of utilizing the Czechs as the nucleus of local resistance against the Maximalists.[106] But the Czechoslovak National Council in Paris was

---

[103] Rumbold's telegram of 27 Oct. 1917, *ibid.*

[104] When Cecil expressed his doubts over the truth of Beneš's assertions, Seton-Watson sent an answer to Rumbold contradicting his report (*Ibid.*, 19 Nov.).

[105] *Min.Aff.Etr., Autriche-Hongrie, Combattants Tchèques,* communication of the British Embassy of 19 Nov. 1917.

[106] *Ibid.*, Barrère to Pichon, 8 Dec. 1917.

opposed to the idea of interfering in the internal affairs of Russia. They wanted their army to be transported to the Western front, hoping that the Czech soldiers could make an impressive enough contribution there to induce at least the French government to recognize their efforts politically. The Czechs could rely upon the fact that the French were most inclined to encourage the formation of a cordon sanitaire of small East European nation states between Germany and Russia in the hope that those new states would take the place of the latter in an alliance to contain Germany in the future.[107] This preoccupation with the German "menace" was shared by the British. However, they were neither directly threatened by its geographical proximity nor had they therefore premeditated a plan of a policy with a view to a future Europe without the Habsburg Monarchy. The British did not yet possess enough confidence in the capacity of the Slav nationalities to allot them a permanent role in the post-war settlement.

In any case, the eventual political status of the Czechoslovaks remained a matter to be decided at a time when the general situation of the war could be judged with greater foresight. The immediate problem was to make appropriate use of the limited man-power available. At the insistence of Masaryk, Foch finally approved of the transfer of the Czech legion to Europe.[108] The British military planners did not respond favourably to this decision. They regarded it as highly improbable that tonnage could be provided to transport the Czechs to Europe and told the Foreign Office that "it would seem far wiser to allow them to remain in Russia, where their presence might be of importance".[109] The British generals though in terms of supplementing a Japanese intervention by the Czech forces on the spot. The chief purpose was not to depose the Bolsheviks but to re-establish the Eastern front which was considered vital for the safety of the British Empire, because it barred the Germans from penetrating into the British spheres of influence in the Near East.

But since the Czech army was a French creation, their consent was regarded as imperative by the British and so Clemenceau could successfully insist upon their transport to the Western front. At the Abbeville conference on 2 May 1918 the British had to accept taking care of the shipping, which after all gave them a lever to protract the actual execution of the inter-Allied decision. Thus the British politicians were given time to try to find ways and means to reverse the solution they did not want. The Foreign Secretary regarded the policy of the S.W.C. as "absurd" and the policy of the British remained "to

---

[107] *Ibid.*, 15 Feb. 1918.

[108] General Spears to W.O., 24 Feb. 1918, summarized in "Precis of Intelligence regarding Czech Troops", Milner papers, box 118.

[109] War Office memorandum of 30 Mar. 1918 ("Czech Troops in Russia"), *F.O.* 371/3323, No. 57780/f.50420.

keep the Czechs in Russia, if possible, and if the French were persuaded to agree".[110]

While the further destiny of the Czech troops was not yet determined, their political representatives tried to profit from the sudden Allied attention to their legionaries. After the recent events which had indicated that the British scruples against engaging in a policy of disrupting the Habsburg Empire had diminished, if not completely vanished, the Czech National Council considered it appropriate to improve its political position in Britain. Therefore Beneš came to London with the aim of negotiating with the British over the recognition of the National Council "as an outward sign that the British government was in agreement with our war aims".[111] Beneš was aware of the guarded British attitude concerning their general policy towards Austria–Hungary and in particular the aspirations for independence of her subject races. But he could point out that France had already committed herself in the direction desired by the Czechs and appealed for a common Entente policy, on which the British were always intent in questions of great importance.

The proposals for a convention were drafted by Milan Štefanik, a Slovak who was responsible for the military organization of the Czechoslovaks. He demanded that the British government recognized the Czech army "under the authority of the National Council" and gave moral and material support to it, for which they would get a powerful propaganda argument in turn. His endeavours were supported by Steed and Delmé-Radcliffe, who submitted the request through the D.M.I. explaining the advantages for the military development at the front and the impression on the Slav peoples inside the Monarchy.[112] The importance of full recognition was also pressed upon the London Chancery by Colonel Glanville of the propaganda committee in Italy, who recommended the recognition "of a Czecho-Slovak state" (!), whose present position he described as equal to that of Belgium and Serbia.[113]

The request for the recognition of the National Council with many features of a government created an unprecedented situation in international relations. The Foreign Office was thus inclined not to act without the consent of the other Allies. As to the Italians, their Minister of Foreign Affairs immediately explained that, despite the Italo-Czech military agreement which had just been signed, he was opposed to Italy recognizing Czechoslovak independence, because it was not opportune for reasons of Italian domestic policy "publicly to emphasize what

---

[110] *Ibid.* Minutes by Balfour on No. 79525 and Gregory on No. 93398.
[111] Beneš, *War Memoirs*, p.373.
[112] *F.O.* 371/3135, No. 75654/f.64427 of 26 Apr. 1918.
[113] *Ibid.*, No. 82126.

would be tantamount to the recognition of the dismemberment of the Austrian Empire".[114]

The Foreign Office was also hesitant to execute what amounted to a death sentence on the Monarchy. In H. G. Nicolson's opinion a recognition in the form suggested by Delmé-Radcliffe would go far to meet the Czech wishes and Hardinge felt convinced that the British had already gone far enough.[115] The question facing the Foreign Office was whether Britain should go beyond the inter-Allied declaration which was just being drafted for the Versailles meeting. "To do so", Nicolson realized, "would of course cut our last hope of preventing Austria and Hungary from capitulating to Berlin".[116] He did not think that there was much hope left to forestall the subjugation of the Monarchy to Germany's *Mitteleuropa* construction, but Nicolson's reluctance to see Germany's challenge counteracted by an increase of Britain's war obligations reflected the general feeling in Whitehall at that critical stage of the war. Even the P.I.D. did not champion the adoption of the Czech programme as an integral part of the Allied war aims, though Namier urged that some measure be taken to acknowledge the Czech movement, which was in his view entitled to some form of encouragement for its persistent and active opposition to the "Germanic Powers". Now the British needed to have no more scruples about sparing the Monarchy:

> As far as Austria and the Habsburgs are concerned, events have proved that if any hopes have been entertained in the past, they rested on most slender foundations and that now no chance whatsoever remains of detaching Austria–Hungary from Germany. Therefore absolutely nothing is to be gained by a soft handling of Austria.[117]

The British intentions to utilize the Czechoslovak forces in Russia as a vanguard for an intervention would make it soon inevitable to comply with the political aspirations of the National Council. This interdependence between a British recognition and a Czechoslovak approval of the British designs in Siberia marked the interviews Beneš had with the leading British statesmen in the middle of May. It then transpired that the British were not just concerned with renewing the Eastern front but also with checking the advance of Bolshevism towards the Far East.[118] Nevertheless Benes had no objections to a Czech participation in this enterprise as long as he was assured that it would be really effective and would not involve the Czechs in taking sides in a Russian civil war and

---

[114] *Ibid.*, No. 80031 (Rodd's telegram of 5 May).
[115] Minutes on No. 84727.
[116] Minute on Delmé-Radcliffe's report of 19 May. *F.O.* 371/3135, No. 90542.
[117] *F.O.* 371/3135, No. 89425 of 18 May.
[118] Beneš, *War Memoirs*, pp.374–75.

was accompanied by a declaration in favour of Czechoslovak aspirations.

The Czech leader perfectly anticipated the British anxiety to avoid binding commitments. He did not ask for any promises obliging the British to guarantee the future status of the Czechoslovaks. He rather pleaded for an emphatic acknowledgment of the Czechs and the Slovaks "as a nationality with just claims to independence".[119] Cecil found this a very acceptable solution and was authorized by the War Cabinet to address a letter to the London representative of the National Council "which, while giving the measure of recognition desired, would not commit the Government to any increased war obligations".[120] The document, which was communicated in its final form on 3 June, granted the Czechs the same measure of recognition that had been given by France and Italy and emphasized that the British government recognized the Council "as the supreme organ of the Czechoslovak movement in Allied countries".[121] The new alliance between Britain and the Czechs was ostensibly manifested by the Prince of Wales's visit to Italy, where two Czech companies formed part of his special guard of honour. This unusual display of patronage for the Czechs caused no little alarm in Vienna.[122] It had now become evident that British policy was turning against the Habsburg Empire.

The impulse to this switch of a long-standing attitude was solely due to the British obsession with the necessity of relieving the pressure of the German onslaught by a diversion in the East. The French regarded this strategy as mistaken and warned the C.I.G.S. not to count upon the co-operation of the Czechs in Russia. Cecil tried to change Clemenceau's opinion over the Czechs by reporting Beneš's willingness to place the legion entirely at the Allies' disposal, but the French Premier did not yet give up his resistance. He preferred the Czech soldiers at the Western front to the Americans and also expected a greater reward from their employment there in view of the political provocation of the Habsburg position in Bohemia.[123] For Balfour this political effect had already been achieved by the Czechs in Italy, but since the British did not want to force their French allies to abandon their point of view the illusory agreement on the shipping of the Czechs to Western Europe was once more confirmed.[124]

The escape from the Franco-British deadlock was finally provided by the Czechs in Russia themselves, who became involved in a brawl with

---

[119] Cecil's memorandum of a conversation with Beneš on 15 May, *F.O.* 371/3443, No. 89880.

[120] *WC* 418 of 24 May, *Cab.* 23/6.

[121] The document is reproduced in full in Beneš, *War Memoirs*, p.376.

[122] Cf. the abusive article in the *Neue Freie Presse* of 6 June.

[123] The Cecil–Clemenceau corrce. is filed in *F.O.* 371/3443, F.89411, Nos. 89881 & 93804 of 18 and 22 May. For quotations from the duplicates in the Milner papers cf. R. H. Ullman, *Intervention and the War*, London 1961, pp.169–71, and Zeman, *op.cit.*, pp.213–14.

[124] *I.C.* 63, *Cab.* 28/3, 28 May.

Magyar prisoners fighting on the Bolshevik side. The notorious incident at Chelyabinsk and the ensuing hostility between the Czechs and the Bolsheviks was seized upon by the British advocates of intervention, once the full proportion of the event had been realized. Then R. Bruce Lockhart, the semi-official British representative with the Soviet government, advised his superiors in London to make immediate use of the presence of the Czechs in Russia.[125] All intelligence information now indicated that the Czechs were prepared to fight the Bolsheviks in spite of previous information to the contrary.[126] The Czech example, if followed by the other subject races, opened up new perspectives for the whole Russian policy. Delmé-Radcliffe was stimulated to sketch out "a Slav Austria serving as a bridge to Russia. The example of the Freed Nations", he predicted, "would be an inspiration to the Russians and direct means would thus be provided to enable the Allies to assist in the reorganisation of Russia".[127]

These were pipe dreams for the present when the Czechs were in danger of being destroyed by the Bolsheviks in collaboration with the Germans.[128] London was seriously concerned over their fate. The Czechs were now regarded as Allies, who had to be saved if it was possible. Moreover, they had become a "providential weapon", as Clerk termed it, which after being saved from destruction could then be used for the interests of the British Empire.[129] Since it was not clear that they were unlikely ever to get to Archangel for embarkation, the French acquiesced in their "self-defensive" actions in Russia.[130]

France and Britain alone were too weak to undertake the task of intervention and needed American assistance, which had been refused hitherto. At last the entente had found a forceful argument to persuade Wilson to intervene in Siberia. A clever tactician like Lloyd George quickly grasped that "a highly educated democratic people" like the Czechs were the key to the position.[131] Such a large Slav force could counterbalance the Japanese and overcome all Anglo-Saxon fears of a yellow intervention and render feasible a joint Allied control in Siberia.

The President remained opposed to intervention as such but felt obliged to help the Czechs in their plight.[132] While the intervention never transcended the stage of a half-hearted engagement, the Czechoslovaks, from their original role as a tool of devious British machinations, emerged as the real profiteers of the Russian adventure. The

---

[125] Lockhart's tel. of 2 June, rec. 14 inst., *F.O.* 371/3323, No. 106181.
[126] *W.O.* 106/681 (12 June).
[127] *Ibid.*, 824 (21 June).
[128] *F.O.* 371/3286, No. 114921/f.6.
[129] *F.O.* 371/3324, No. 112629.
[130] Telegram by Derby of 26 June, reported in *I.W.C.* 21, *Cab.* 23/41.
[131] Telegram for Reading, 18 July, *B.M. Add. MSS.* 49692.
[132] *Ibid.*, Reading to Balfour, 13 July. Cf. Ullman, *op.cit.*, p.213 and G. Kennan, *The Decision to Intervene*, Princeton 1958, pp.391–95.

reward for the Czech military organization was further exhibited by the presentation of the colours to the Czech army in France, which was accompanied by a declaration of the French Government promising them "to fulfill your aspirations for independence within the historical frontiers of your territories".[133]

The event was inaugurated by an emphatic speech by Poincaré and in turn Balfour sent a letter to Pichon associating the British government with the speech by the French President.[134] Though the main purpose of this communication was to help the Yugoslavs, it was taken by Beneš as another sign of the new British policy towards Austria–Hungary. He therefore set out to exploit the favourable atmosphere by attempting to induce the British government to give the National Council an even greater measure of recognition. After the second battle of the Marne had ended successfully for the Allies, this request for a clarification and reassurance of the position of British policy towards the subject races was now also supported by a wider political spectrum in Britain. In Parliament, for instance, the Irish Nationalist Dillon interpreted the Versailles declaration as implying the "obliteration" of Austria–Hungary and displayed his personal understanding for such a decision, while suggesting a definite statement by the Prime Minister.[135]

Since the tide of the war had perceptibly turned in favour of the Allies, Beneš could hope to get more concessions from the British when he came to London at the end of July. In his conversations with Balfour, Cecil and Drummond he tried to appeal to their Anglo-Saxon mentality, when he submitted his arguments in word and writing. Thus he put particular emphasis upon "the special service" rendered by the Czech legion in Russia for the security of the British Empire in view of securing the route to India from Germany's grip.[136] Beneš claimed that the National Council could only guarantee to control the legionaries in Siberia if it was endowed with the desired political authority by the Entente, and he asked for "real sovereignty as a State" for the National Council.

This novel request was generally regarded as premature in the Foreign Office. The P.I.D. warned against prejudging forthcoming events in the Monarchy by the recognition of a government before the people themselves could freely express their own will.[137] H. G. Nicolson thought the Czechs did not qualify more for a *de facto* recognition than

---

[133] Cit. Beneš, *War Memoirs*, p.383.
[134] The Council was allowed to publish this letter, which appeared in *La Nation Tchèque*, 15 Aug. 1918.
[135] *Hansard*, 5th ser., cix, 769–10 (1 Aug.).
[136] *F.O.* 371/3135, No. 127473/f.64427 of 26 July.
[137] Cf. the minute by Namier on No. 127473 and the summary by Kennard on No. 142344, *F.O.* 371/3136.

the Sinn Fein. They should not be treated differently from the Poles and the Yugoslavs, a view to which Balfour subscribed.[138] Hardinge was only prepared to grant the Czech demand, "if one were convinced that the equal recognition of a Czech government in France would provoke a revolution in Bohemia".[139] Cecil, whom Beneš later praised for his idealism, thought it worth considering the granting of full recognition, if that would have prevented the Austrian military authorities from executing recaptured Czech prisoners as traitors, and Balfour was also inclined to recognize them "on grounds of humanity", if it really helped to "save the lives".[140] On the other hand, he did not recommend it from a diplomatic point of view, although he admitted that he would be a good deal influenced by Beneš's arguments, however carefully he listened to this biased witness.

In principle, the British were then willing to give in to Beneš's claims. Only the word "sovereign" in his draft was not swallowed. But it was finally acknowledged that the Czechoslovaks deserved a better treatment than the Poles and Yugoslavs. Cecil found it "foolish, if we allow international pedantries to injure our relations with the Czechs", and – contrary to Balfour – held the view that Britain need not consult her allies over the matter. So he recommended the acceptance of the draft of the National Council with the omission of the reference to "sovereignty" and some other slight modifications.[141]

Britain was thus going to recognize the Czechoslovaks as an Allied nation and in the final clause of the declaration as drafted by Cecil and approved by Balfour "Great Britain also recognized the right of the Czechoslovak National Council to exercise supreme authority over (its) belligerent army".[142] In addition to avoiding any reference to "sovereignty", "State", or "Government", the British were not prepared to recognize the National Council as an interim government. It was Steed who improved the situation by suggesting the legally noncommittal formula "present 'trustee' of the future Czecho-Slovak government", which was then inserted in the final version of 9 August.[143]

The declaration was followed by the drafting of a convention to secure the participation of the Czechs at inter-Allied conferences.[144] This was important, because the British declaration had been silent over the "historical rights" of the Czechoslovaks as expressed in the French manifesto of 29 June. But the clauses of the convention gave the Czechs an opportunity to claim their *desiderata* on an official level. Here

---

[138] Minute on No. 127473, *F.O.* 371/3135.
[139] *Ibid.*
[140] Minutes on No. 132422, *F.O.* 371/3136.
[141] Minutes of 2 Aug., No. 135135, *ibid.*
[142] No. 132422.
[143] *Through Thirty Years*, ii, p.232.
[144] *F.O.* 371/3136, Nos. 142344 & 148362 of 17 and 29 Aug.

lay the significance of the convention, which gave the National Council an international status for participation at the Peace Conference.

The recognition also meant that the British could "no longer think of the preservation of Austria–Hungary in her integrity", as Masaryk noted with satisfaction. However, the Czech leader himself did not visualize the complete disappearance of the Monarchy and believed that she would "vegetate as a sort of small Byzantine empire".[145] It seems that it was for such reasons that the British recognition was so carefully worded. On the one hand it was "consistent with the dismemberment of Austria", as Cecil concluded, but on the other hand it left him and his fellow policymakers in London under the illusion that their hands were still not bound as to the final settlement of the Austro-Hungarian question.[146]

The decisive importance of the British recognition was best reflected by the reaction of the Austrian government, which issued an official protest against it.[147]

On request Masaryk forwarded a copy of the British declaration to the State Department, where Lansing was surprised over the British move, fearing that the Central Powers might retaliate by a similar recognition of Ireland, Egypt and India. In fact, Vienna considered organizing a *pendant* to the Congress of Oppressed Nationalities for the peoples of the British Empire, but the idea was turned down by Berlin.[148]

Once the British had taken the risk, Wilson saw no need to stand back behind the Anglo-Saxon ally and on 2 September the United States recognized the Czecho-Slovak National Council as a *"de facto belligerent government"*.[149] America and Britain alike had finally complied with the wishes of the Czechoslovak emigrés. The offer of an anti-Bolshevik alternative to the Habsburgs in the East had won the enthusiasm of the Allied statesmen.[150] Together with Germany's military collapse in the West it provided the ground on which they felt safe to condemn the Habsburg Monarchy to its fall.

4. The Desire for Yugoslav Union

The only Allied power which remained opposed to the recognition of the Czechoslovaks was Italy. The Italians wanted to prevent a precedent for the Yugoslav question, which was bound to be raised in the

145 *Ibid.*, No. 161521 of 4 Sept.
146 *Ibid.*, No. 152102, minute of 2 Sept.
147 Scott, *op.cit.*, p.373 (17 Aug.).
148 Mamatey, *op.cit.*, p.304. Without the knowledge of the *Ballhausplatz* plan the author wrongly concludes that "recognizing the British 'oppressed nationalities' never seems to have entered the heads of Austrian and German statesmen" (*ibid.*, p.305). But cf. H.H.St.A., *Generalia*, ix, 7.
149 *Ibid.*, p.309.
150 A. J. P. Taylor, *The Habsburg Monarchy*, Peregrine reprint, Harmondsworth 1964, pp.264–65.

wake of the discussions with the Czechs. Ever since the Versailles declaration the South Slavs felt neglected by the Allies. Their concern was appreciated in London but out of loyalty to the Italian ally the British government did not feel entitled to meet the demands of the Yugoslavs, disregarding the fact that the approval of an independent Czechoslovak state made the formation of a united South Slav state appear inevitable.

The South Slavs had been supported during the whole of the war by the anti-Habsburg circle, which was now exerting its influence on the Foreign Office and urged a declaration that would counter the sneers of the Viennese press over the frigidity of the Versailles declaration.[151]

Among the traditionalists of the Foreign Office it was felt unnecessary to follow the same policy of recognition for the Yugoslavs as had been done for the Czechs. The former were not regarded as forming a distinct state, but expected to be merely assimilated into Serbia.[152] However, the Foreign Office was ready to give the Yugoslavs at least some public encouragement. This was done with Poincaré's speech to the Czech troops on 29 June, when the address of the French President was amended on British initiative to include a phrase explicitly alluding to "the other nationalities of Slav origin".[153] The initiative for this unusual interest in the South Slav problem had come from Hardinge, who had been impressed by a report from Captain Temperley, a historian from the War Office, who outlined convincingly that the Yugoslavs preferred independence to autonomy.[154] The Yugoslavs who were content with autonomy within the Habsburg monarchy were dismissed by Steed:

> I believe that their number is small and their importance still smaller, but you must not forget that for tactical reasons it is often necessary for Yugoslav deputies in Austria to qualify their demands for unity by adding 'within the framework of the Monarchy'.[155]

An immediate motive for Britain to promote the Yugoslav cause was the threat of the Piave offensive. To avoid a further discouragement of the South Slavs it was regarded as vital to demonstrate sympathy with their aims. Conversely, the Yugoslavs were aware that they had to make a contribution to the Allied war effort comparable to that of the Czechs if they desired the same political success. The French, warmly supported by the British, suggested the incorporation of South Slav prisoners in the Serbian army to undermine the morale of the Habsburg subjects of the same race. But the Italians merely accepted the

---

[151] *F.O.* 371/3135, No. 114845. Cf. *Neue Freie Presse* of 11 June.
[152] *Ibid.*
[153] *Ibid.*, No. 115851.
[154] *Ibid.*, No. 116831 of 28 June.
[155] Steed to McClure, 9 May, Steed papers.

inclusion of Yugoslav prisoners of the Serbian race, that is, orthodox Bosnian Serbs.[156] In vain did Steed appeal to Orlando that the propaganda against Austria should not be obstructed "by tendencies not completely conformist with the spirit of the Rome Congress".[157] While the Italian Premier could be expected to agree to modifications of the Treaty of London and be content with what Italy could claim on ethnological grounds together with reasonable frontier guarantees, Sonnino's reservations against a united South Slav state were very outspoken. He expressed severe doubts as to whether it was possible to constitute a permanent buffer state keeping Germany off the Mediterranean through the Yugoslavs alone. The Italian Foreign Minister painted the picture of this new state, which remote from the major Allies, was bound to gravitate towards Germany in the long run and to co-operate with her in the fields of economy and commerce, which would then give Germany the opportunity to exercise influence in the Mediterranean.[158] Soon afterwards a more convincing aspect was raised in Sonnino's argumentation. He was extremely concerned at the possible incorporation of the Austrian Germans into Germany, which he regarded as inevitable after the break-up of Austria–Hungary and the detachment of the Slav races from the Monarchy, and Rodd's deputy Erskine believed that the mere prospect of a direct border between Italy and a future Germany was "the real secret of Sonnino's reluctance to encourage the idea of the complete independence of the Jugo-Slavs".[159]

The British Cabinet and Foreign Office, however, had already made up their minds in favour of a Yugoslav state. On 25 July Balfour made a speech at Mansion House, in which he called the Yugoslav case a "test of Allied sincerity", and left little doubt that the full Yugoslav programme had the support of the British government.[160] This public commitment was welcomed by the *New Europe*,[161] as a sign that the policy of the Rome Congress had become "an integral part of British policy".

In mid-September the Italian official attitude became more promising for the Yugoslavs, whose aims were found "in accordance with the principle for which the Allies were fighting".[162] This sounded consonant with the British policy towards the Yugoslavs but in practice it was not. Steed, for instance, hoped in vain that the hour of birth of the Yugoslav legion had come. Sonnino did not relent and had a new

[156] *Cab.* 28/4, I.C. 71, 4 July.
[157] Steed to Orlando, 24 June, Steed papers.
[158] *Cab.* 23/43, 14 Aug.
[159] *F.O.* 371/3136, No. 152437 of 1 Sept.
[160] Cit. Hanak, *op.cit.*, p.263.
[161] *New Europe*, 1 Aug.
[162] *F.O.* 371/2137, No. 158233.

excuse: The Yugoslavs had to give proof of their capacity and national unity, before their case could be approved.[163] Discordance between the Pan-Serbs and the Croat Federalists was rekindled by Pašić's insistence on Serbia's "right to liberate" her South Slav brethren. The Serb Premier encountered the stern opposition of Steed to his hegemonial plans, whereas Balfour – contrary to the account of Steed – would have been satisfied with the inclusion of a couple of ministers of the London Committee into the Serb Cabinet.[164] But Pašić denied the representative character of the Yugoslav Committee in London. When its chairman Trumbić submitted a draft for the recognition of the Yugoslavs, Balfour assured its author of his warmest sympathy, but the British did not want to act over the head of their Serbian ally. They still hoped for an agreement between the two sides before making any declaration.[165] Such a unified South Slav representation would also have facilitated the British position in relation to the Italian claims.

British sympathies lay clearly on the side of the "relatively advanced Slavs of Croatia", of whom Cecil thought that they would "never consent to be 'bossed' by the bands of dishonest and murderous intriguers which constitute the backbone of the Serbian Government".[166] Finally, Drummond suggested that Britain should take the liberty to act in the direction desired by Trumbić.[167] But then it was too late. The revolution in the Monarchy and the end of the war had transformed the situation. Thus the question of Yugoslav union and independence was decided by the South Slav peoples themselves, before the British had come to any decision in their favour. Since the Yugoslav problem was an international one, British diplomacy did not possess the freedom of action of recognizing in advance and thereby promoting the formation of the new state as was the case with Czechoslovakia. Yugoslavia, despite all the British sympathy for it, had never become a declared British war aim. Its emergence on the eve of the war was, however, consistent with British policy towards Austro-Hungarian affairs and sealed the fate of the Kingdom of Hungary.

---

[163] *Ibid.*, No. 161039 of 19 Sept.
[164] *Ibid.*, No. 171759; cf. *Through Thirty Years*, ii, pp.235–39.
[165] *F.O.* 371/3137, No. 176415 of 22 Oct. (minute by Graham).
[166] *Ibid.*, minute by Cecil on No. 172539 of 14 Oct.
[167] *Ibid.*, No. 172915 of 14 Oct.

CHAPTER VII

Defeat and Dissolution

The military turn of the tide in favour of the Allies, which furthered the British decision to comply with the requests made by the representatives of the subject nationalities, had a corresponding effect upon the British attitude towards the Austro-Hungarian government. The latter's new Foreign Secretary Count Burián, provoked by a speech of Milner's of 8 June, gave an interview to the *Fremdenblatt* in which he refuted the notion that Austria was a victim of Germany. Laying stress on the unity of the Central Powers, he pointed out that their war aims were "very far from those which their opponents ascribe" to them. Burián implied that a peace could still be concluded on the basis of the *status quo ante*.[1]

Far from attaining such a general compromise there was, however, not even any desire left within the British government and Foreign Office to try once again to come to a separate peace with Austria. When the *Reichspost* reported on 8 June that the British Legation in Stockholm had stated that the object of the Entente was to detach Austria from Germany by sacrificing Italian claims, Hardinge dismissed it as a fabrication.[2] Such rumours were primarily spread by the Austrians with the intention of keeping up the spirits of their local subjects by making them believe that prominent representatives of the Entente were still willing to discuss terms of peace on the basis of the preservation of the integrity of Austria–Hungary. Finally the internal situation forced the Austrian government to undertake a last military offensive to prove the viability of the Empire. While this independent Austrian action ·annoyed the Germans, who resented any dissipation of the Central Powers' final effort, it did not help to emancipate the Habsburg Monarchy from Berlin, where the position of the Austrian Emperor

---

[1] *The Times* of 19 June.
[2] *F.O.* 371/3134, No. 104586/f.13977 of 11 June.

245

had been "hopelessly weakened by the divulgation of his letter to Prince Sixtus".[3]

With Austria desperately struggling on both the diplomatic and the war fronts, her enemies were driven to make the final decision about her fate. The inter-Allied debate was revived by the Italian apprehensions of yet another attack by the Austrians on their front. But Lord Cavan, who commanded the British divisions in Italy, was rather sceptical about the Italian suggestion of an Allied offensive. He admitted that the Austrian morale was low and would be shaken even more, if the Allies reached Trent or got near it. In Cavan's opinion it was possible to enter Austria but not to penetrate her and the mountainous front always implied imponderables making it uncertain whether an overwhelming disaster could be inflicted. Faced with this military opinion in the Imperial War Cabinet Prime Minister Hughes of Australia pointed out the political importance of getting some hold on Austrian territory before the Peace Conference.[4] His argument was typical of the widespread view at the time that the war would end with neither side being completely beaten and at the mercy of the victors, who were supposed to be unable to impose their will on the defeated in all territorial matters without having actually conquered them with their armies.

The renewal of the strategic discussion was followed with particular interest by the Prime Minister. Lloyd George had always been a strong adherent of the idea of an attack on the other front, which he would have liked to use as a lever for obtaining a separate peace with the Habsburgs. After the Clemenceau revelations Lloyd George also seemed to have given up all hope of such a diplomatic solution. Nevertheless he did not discard a military advance particularly directed against the Austrians. His Austrian policy was still guided by the desire to hasten the defeat of Germany. At the end of July 1918 Lloyd George showed himself very much impressed by "a sure source under the obligation of secrecy" according to which the Allies ought to have followed up the recent Italian victory over the Austrians.[5] The informant whom the Prime Minister considered to be well placed to judge had reported that the state of Austria was "critical in the extreme". An advance on the vital Austro-Italian front might have been the way to turn the flank of Germany, because, so the writer contended,

> Austria was 'a tale that was told' and a doomed Empire whose subject peoples would either obtain autonomy under the aegis of the Allies or remain in servitude under German oppression.[6]

---

[3] Minute by Hardinge on Rumbold's telegram of 26 June, *ibid.*, No. 115623.
[4] Committee of Prime Ministers, 23 July, *Cab.* 23/44, *I.W.C.* 26a.
[5] *Ibid.*, I.W.C. 27a, 31 July.
[6] *Ibid.*

By paying regard to evidence pointing in the above direction the Prime Minister must have been convinced that the fate of the Austrian Empire was sealed. This feeling was now gradually spreading within the upper echelons of British policymakers. While the Prime Minister still preferred to rely on what seems to have been a secret diplomatic channel, other members of his government listened more and more to the arguments expounded by the P.I.D., which just then had prepared a long memorandum on the Austrian situation.[7] Its general gist was anti-Habsburg, too, but with different conclusions as to the military action to take. The P.I.D. argued that things were so bad in Austria that it would be better not to take any action which might bring the various sections in the Empire together against the common Italian foe, for the Slavs would probably prefer to remain under Austrian rule rather than to pass on to that of Italy, a prospect which would become more likely once the Italians had set foot on Istrian territory. Lord Robert Cecil did not personally share this view and believed in the efficacy of a severe blow at Austria.[8] He thought that such a military policy would ease the way to pursue Britain's chief objects in the war, namely "to obtain such a settlement as will prevent any repetition of the events of the last four years".[9]

As to Germany, the means to achieve this aim was simply defined as the extirpation of what was called Prussian militarism. Concerning Austria Cecil admitted that the problem was more complicated, for she by herself would not be a serious danger to peace.

> It is only in alliance with Germany that she becomes formidable. On the other hand the defeat of Austria is a step towards the defeat of Germany, and all the problems connected with the Austrian nationalities should be considered, as far as we are concerned, from that point of view in the first instance.[10]

This basic motivation had in fact led the British to embark on a policy that encouraged the subject nationalities, since by stirring up internal trouble in the Monarchy they would not only weaken her but also indirectly weaken Germany. Thus Britain had supported the Czechs (and the Poles) and was more or less committed to the Yugoslavs by endorsing their claim to independence and Cecil felt that "in the case of the Czechs at any rate we have unquestionably received full value for our endorsement". On the other hand he confessed that it seemed very doubtful to him "whether a new Europe with two or three additional Slav states will really be more peaceful than the old Europe". Cecil agreed that there would have been much to say for some kind of Central

---

[7] *F.O.* 371/4350.
[8] *Cab.* 23/44, *I.W.C.* 29a, 8 Aug.
[9] Memorandum of 7 Aug., Cecil papers, *B.M. Add. MSS.* 51105.
[10] *Ibid.*

European Confederation headed by Austria if that had been possible. But he was optimistic that a strong Yugoslav state, a liberated Bohemia and an independent Poland might form "a real barrier against German expansionism provided that they could be induced to cooperate for this object". Another consequence Cecil took into account as the probable result of a complete break-up of Austria–Hungary was that Hungary would give up the dual partnership with Vienna and that the German provinces of Austria would then be absorbed in the German Empire. But Cecil regarded such a reconstruction as less formidable than the present conditions under which Germany could also command the services of a great mass of non-Germanic peoples.

As far as the Italian claims were concerned he could go no further than to hope that Britain would no longer be bound to support the full Italian demand as laid down in the treaty of 1915. This hope was, however, merely founded upon the fact that many Italians themselves did not support the maximum demand and Cecil had to concede that Britain was still pledged to these promises. Without a practical solution in sight Cecil contented himself with giving his personal opinion on what he considered justifiable: accordingly, Italy should not be entitled to more than the "recovery" of the Trentino, free access to the port of Trieste and at the very most some strategic positions on the other side of the Adriatic.

The minimum aims therefore had to be the "independence *or* autonomy of the Slav population" and some rearrangement of the Italian frontiers as above indicated. The immediate conclusion derived from this political conception was in any case that it was advisable to adopt a military policy that aimed ruthlessly at shaking the foundations of Austria–Hungary,

> hoping either to secure her retirement from the war – in which case the settlement of her relations to the Slavs might be left for the settlement at the general peace – or to bring about her destruction as a military force, in which case we should probably have to take our chance as to the result of the complete break-up of the Austrian Empire and the setting up of a number of new Slav States.

Cecil clearly tended to assume the final collapse of the Empire as being highly probable if not yet inevitable. But behind such careful judgments there was still a certain measure of doubt as to whether the Empire would suddenly disappear from the European scene. Such reservations were particularly strong within the War Office, which tried to provide the politicians with an impartial estimate,[11] in which considerable evidence of decline and weakness was compiled, but it was

---

[11] Notes on the situation in Austria–Hungary, No. III, Aug. 1918, *W.O.* M.I. 3(B), filed in *F.O.* 371/3134.

stated that unrest and discord were "normal" conditions and that the racial and social differences were only leading "almost to disruption". So far one could not say more than that the situation was "growing steadily worse". The War Office saw three different lines of reaction open to the Austrian government: firstly, she could completely depend on Germany; secondly, she could enter a devolution towards a very loose community of federal states; and thirdly the Crown could attempt some sort of *rapprochement* with the Social Democrats so as to satisfy the social needs of their subject masses.

It was among these masses that there was still support for the dynasty throughout all component nationalities. This was the mainstay of the Empire's solidity and unity. Signs of such a "faint feeling of solidarity" became evident from the statements of prisoners and even deserters coming from the different parts of the Empire and were especially strong among the uneducated masses. Consequently the Czech and South Slav parties, believing in their salvation outside of the Monarchy by depending on the Entente, tried to overcome this obstacle of ignorance among their people by gradually "educating" them to be prepared for an eventual international Peace Conference. Until the masses were mobilized by the intellectual elite of the subject nationalities the Habsburg regime could cling to this final sheet-anchor and the War Office therefore came to the conclusion that it was "still premature to argue that the unrest and the demoralization (were) the last struggles of a perishing Empire".

This detailed and careful analysis by the War Office intelligence certainly was a powerful argument for the C.I.G.S. not to be persuaded to launch an offensive from which the collapse of the Empire was to be expected. It rather suggested that the ramshackle Empire would hold out for some time and dampen hopes of a revolutionary avalanche sweeping the Monarchy. But it did not reverse the decision of the government to opt for a policy at the end of which there would have to come about the dissolution of the Habsburg Empire.

After Cecil's venture in this direction this line was taken with greater competence and determination by the Foreign Secretary himself in his survey of foreign policy before the Imperial War Cabinet on 13 August.[12] With regard to Central Europe he pointed out that the issue on the threshold of the whole question was that of Austria–Hungary whose status Balfour now considered to be "more or less decided". With Allied victory in sight Balfour rhetorically confronted the two alternative solutions: the dismemberment of the Habsburg Empire into ethnological units or the preservation of it in a modified form within roughly the same frontiers. He acknowledged the historical perfor-

---

[12] *I.W.C.* 30, *Cab.* 23/42; shorthand notes *Cab.* 23/43; cf. also H. I. Nelson, *op.cit.*, pp.43–44.

mance of her function in the balance of European powers and "if there was the slightest hope that a renovated Austria or an Austria at all would be a counterpoise to Germany in Central Europe, it really would be worthwhile seeing whether we could not keep her and alter her. "But since the conclusion of a military treaty with Germany following the Emperor's visit to Spa, Austria was entirely dependent on Germany and Balfour found it impossible to see her play the part which in traditional British interest he would have liked her to resume. While the prospect of an emancipated Austria had been moved further and further away from the ground of reality, "the whole movement, almost unconsciously, but quite steadily, (had) been going or drifting in the direction of giving autonomy, real independence, if possible" to the Poles, Czecho-Slovaks, and Yugoslavs. It was obvious that once these subject races were liberated, the Magyars would part from the Germans, too. This would then leave the Austro-Germans alone and prone to join their fellow-countrymen in the German *Reich*. Balfour did not share the fears of those who regarded the union of the German-Austrians with Germany as a disaster, because it added to the strength of the *Reich*. After all their number did not exceed eleven million and quite a few of them were scattered, partly outside the Austrian half of the Dual Monarchy. Moreover, their anti-Prussian attitude might even have a beneficial influence on the Prussian element in Germany which possibly would not even like their inclusion. However the Austro-German relationship was to be settled, Balfour was convinced

> that it would be in the interest of the world that Austria should be broken up into its constituent elements rather than that the population of 51 to 52 million . . . should be bound to its other central neighbour, forming an immense addition both economically and from the point of view of man-power.

Balfour had to admit that the execution of such a policy involved a number of problems when it came to frontier-drawing. The worst specimen was Bohemia, for which Balfour was "inclined to feel the most respect" and prepared "to throw ethnology to the winds". As regards the Yugoslavs he did not see any problems in setting up a homogeneous state and he discounted the argument of religious diversity, which was raised in the Cabinet, by pointing out that it did not play an important part at Corfu.

The only member of the Imperial War Cabinet to challenge Balfour's point of view was General Smuts, who wondered "whether it was a good thing for the world" to break up Austria. At least this should not be a war aim. It would be a different matter if it was accomplished in the revolution which Smuts expected to follow the war. Smuts had no doubts that Austria was "in the most desperate condition" and asked his colleagues to consider a large-scale attack against her from Italy, thereby trying "really to finish Austria". "Austria is getting ripe, the pear will not fall so long as we keep shaking another tree", Smuts concluded metaphorically.[13] Lloyd George himself seemed now convinced that this would inevitably happen sooner or later. He thought that Austria was "in a very rickety condition" and would be worn down.[14]

The despair of Austria–Hungary became all-apparent when on 14 September Burián issued a public appeal to all belligerents for confidential conversations on peace to be held in a neutral country.[15] In London the Austrian "olive branch" was received with suspicion. Lloyd George gave his opinion on the Austrian overture at a meeting with press editors on the next day.[16] He said that he had reason to believe that Germany and Turkey were closely identified with and approved of these proposals. The Austrians were suspected of acting in Germany's interest by trying to win sympathy in Allied and neutral countries. They did not seem to expect that their offer would be accepted, but they wanted merely to gain time for the Germans to reorganize their armies. The Prime Minister was anxious not to play into the enemy's hands and suggested consultations with the other Allies. Balfour struck the same note at the Guildhall on 30 September when he called the note "a cynical effort to split the Allies".[17] The Foreign Secretary was asked by Sir Eric Geddes of the Admiralty, who had talked the matter over with the Prime Minister, whether the question of some reply to the peace note did not lend itself to the opening of talks with Austria. If it could be demonstrated to Austria that only her alliance with Germany prevented peace, as Geddes suggested, Austria might eventually break with Germany.[18] But the British left it to the Americans to convey an official reply and Wilson's retort was very brusque. It needed the surrender of Bulgaria on 25 September to force the Austrians (as well as Germany) to ask Washington for an armistice.[19] This was done in the hope that one could take Wilson's previous declarations, especially the Fourteen Points, and literally employ him as a mediator with the Entente, thus avoiding a direct acceptance of their demands, to which America was not pledged by treaty. The Allies, knowing that time was working for them inside

---

[13] *Ibid.*

[14] *I.W.C.* 32, 15 Aug., *ibid.*

[15] Text in Scott, *op.cit.*, pp.386–89.

[16] Lloyd George papers, F/8/2/16, memorandum of 15 Sept.

[17] Scott, *op.cit.*, p.395; Lloyd George to Balfour, 16 Sept., *F.O.* 800/200.

[18] Geddes to Balfour, 15 Sept. and memorandum of 17 inst., *F.O.* 800/200.

[19] Scott, *op.cit.*, p.418, contains the text of the Austrian note of 7 October which was almost identical with the German note.

the Monarchy, pursued a policy of deliberate delay.[20]

The Austrian Foreign Office also undertook some last minute attempts to come into diplomatic contact with Britain and France. On 8 October Mensdorff sent a letter to Sir William Tyrrell, in which he contended that the talks between him and Smuts had proved that the British and Austrian concepts of a future settlement did not differ greatly from each other. Mensdorff was still convinced, or at least expressed the conviction that there were no genuine differences between Britain and Austria, which could therefore cooperate for a settlement at the Peace Conference. Mensdorff explained that the official Austrian peace offer had been sent to Wilson, because the President had formulated "a precise programme". This made him the most suitable addressee for the note which ought to be carefully considered by the British Government as well.[21] But the Foreign Office could see no useful purpose in answering Mensdorff's letter and although the Prime Minister requested a translation of it, nothing came of it. It only underlined the prevalent feeling that the Austro-Hungarian government was desperate. This also applies to their next move, the visit of the younger Count Andrassy to Switzerland. There he forwarded a memorandum, which proposed to "accept the Wilsonian principles without altering the international status of Austria–Hungary".[22] Britain was asked to help the Monarchy survive in her own interest, because she would then have a friend in the Danube valley instead of a *poussière d'états*.

Before this document arrived in London, it was overtaken by events. On 15 October *The Times* published the proclamation of the Yugoslav Club in Vienna. The corollary drawn by Headlam-Morley was that no peace negotiations should be begun with the Austrian government. Since Wilson was the addressee of the Austrian peace request, a British warning was sent to Washington pointing out

> that in the opinion of the British government the position of Austria–Hungary is completely different from Germany and that the British government will not be prepared to negotiate with the government of Austria–Hungary regarding peace terms as they apply to the Slavonic peoples and districts of the Empire.[23]

In this situation the publication of the imperial manifesto on 16

---

[20] "I remember", said Namier to I. Berlin, "the day in 1918 when the Emperor Karl sued for peace. I said to Headlam-Morley: 'wait'. Headlam-Morley said to Balfour: 'Wait'. Lloyd George said to Wilson: 'Wait'. And while they all waited, the Austro-Hungarian Empire disintegrated. I may say that I pulled it to pieces with my own hands." Cit. I. Berlin, "Lewis Namier: A Personal Impression", in *A Century of Conflict, op.cit.*, p.224.

[21] *F.O.* 371/3444, No. 170636/f.157260. Cf. also B. Krizman, "Austro-Hungarian Diplomacy before the Collapse of the Empire", in *Journal of Contemporary History*, IV, p.202.

[22] *F.O.* 371/3437, No. 176260/f.7 1973.

[23] *F.O.* 371/3444, No. 173441/f.156260.

October, which announced the establishment of a federal state, could not improve the fate of Austria. Apart from the fact that its regulations applied to Cisleithania only and satisfied neither the ruling nor the subject nationalities, the Emperor's last dramatic but futile act was completely disregarded by the Allied statesmen and derided in the British press.[24]

On the same day Wilson had already confided to Wiseman that he would make a speech saying that two changes had been made since his fourteen points speech, namely the recognition of the Czechoslovaks and the Yugoslavs, whose claims he felt obliged to support.[25] When on 19 October Wilson replied publicly that mere autonomy for the Czechoslovaks and the Yugoslavs was no longer an adequate basis for peace,[26] Austrian diplomacy was without further resources. On 28 October Andrássy, who had meanwhile become the last Foreign Minister of the Habsburg Monarchy, had to ask the United States for an immediate armistice. While this was negotiated in the Supreme War Council at Versailles, Austria–Hungary crumbled into its disparate elements which proclaimed their independence.

There was no doubt that the iron hand of Germany over Austria had relaxed, although Sir Valentine Chirol in a letter to *The Times* published on 30 October suggested that even now Austria might be acting in concert with Germany in order to secure an armistice as a breathing space. The danger feared by Chirol and some others was that Austria–Hungary might succeed in securing terms of some leniency and that Germany might ultimately profit from them. But matters had gone much too far. When the victorious advance of the Italians and their Allies forced the Austro-Hungarian army to capitulate on 3 November, the Empire in whose name they surrendered had already ceased to exist. The exact future of its successors was still uncertain. To avoid any prejudgment of the final settlement in Central and South East Europe the armistice offered by the Allies was restricted to purely military and naval terms. Thus it was in no sense a pledge of any particular peace terms which remained a matter for the Peace Conference.[27]

The Habsburg Monarchy had been the original basis upon which German hegemony in Central Europe was founded. From the outbreak of the war, when the subject nationalities had begun to voice their demands, the Habsburg regime relied upon the efficiency of the German army for the maintenance of the Empire. There remains the question of whether its fate was inevitable. Was the Habsburg Monar-

[24] Cf. *The Times* of 19 Oct., *Spectator*, 26 Oct., *New Europe*, 24 Oct.
[25] *F.O.* 371/3444, No. 174313 of 18 Oct.
[26] Mamatey, *op.cit.*, pp.333–34.
[27] Cf. L. S. Amery, *My Political Life*, London, ii, 1953, p.170. For the text of the armistice with Austria–Hungary cf. H. Rudin, *Armistice 1918*, New Haven 1944, pp.407–09.

chy doomed to break up under the strain of the war or could it have been saved by a drastic change of policy, in making a separate peace with the Allies in defiance of Germany and by simultaneously reconstituting the Empire in accordance with the claims of all its nationalities? The answer must be in the negative, because there were too many obstacles on the road to reconstruction. It was the weakness of Austria–Hungary that she found herself altogether harrassed by internal difficulties, exigencies of the war (and the mistrust of her own ally).

Any constitutional improvement would have been short of the ideal aspirations of the fringe nationalities in Galicia, Transylvania, and the Trentino. But whereas these might have been just indispensable, the major questions of the Czechoslovaks and the Yugoslavs had to be solved within the framework of the Empire. It would have needed the overthrow of the Dual system at the cost of the Magyar ascendancy, for their extreme subjugation of the Croats, the Slovaks, and the Rumanians had become unbearable for these nationalities. Since the Magyars could not be expected to favour a renunciation of their rights which would have reduced their position to insignificance, the initiative had to come from the dynasty with the support of the German Austrian progressive forces. But the Emperor, however sincere his personal motives might have been, found no means of extracting himself from the traditionalist exponents of the Dualist principle. It seems that such a step would have been beyond the very nature of the Monarchy,

> for the Hapsburg could never have broken with the vested interests and all the forces of Conservatism in Church and State: he could never have headed a revolution. The impossibility of concluding a separate peace, apart from the military problem of disentangling the Austro-Hungarian from the German armies directly followed from the impossibility of reconstructing the Empire. For only on condition of such a reconstruction could the Allies have come to terms without repudiating the ideals for which they were fighting. Thus the Hapsburg Empire stood self-condemned. Trapped in its own antiquated system of national and social tyranny, it could not, even to escape destruction, right the wrong of its being.[28]

---

[28] *Round Table*, No. xxxiii, Dec. 1918.

EPILOGUE

Problems of a Permanent Settlement

By the end of 1918 the cornerstones of the Habsburg Monarchy had crumbled to pieces. Now the victors of the war had to search for the rightful successors with whom they could negotiate a future settlement in South East Central Europe. In all parts of the former Monarchy the Austro-Hungarian government had been replaced by separate institutions of the various nations and the Allies were confronted with the existence of six independent governments. Thus the legal partition of the Empire was a *fait accompli* and the Entente powers, faced with declarations of independence by the National Assemblies of each of the new nations, had to acknowledge the existence of new independent states.

But keen observers of developments in Central Europe were aware that it was not sufficient to simply release the new nations from Habsburg domination. For the advocates of the subject races their liberation was only the first step towards a European peace, which had to be followed by a policy of reconstruction, which would satisfy the essential requirements of peace in Central Europe. Therefore people with political foresight laid stress upon the necessity for co-operation between the successors of the Habsburg Monarchy. So the *New Europe*, once the foremost aim of the destruction of the Habsburg Empire had been achieved, insisted upon the need for the formation of a "new Central European Commonwealth" which was to comprise the formerly oppressed peoples within the Monarchy.[1]

This quest for a federal union between the successors of the Habsburgs rested upon the fear that each component part on its own would not be really capable of an independent existence either from the economic or the defence point of view. The old *mot*, "if Austria did not exist, it would be necessary to invent her", served to sum up the new problem:

---

[1] *New Europe* of 5 Sept. 1918.

A whole family of new States must be called into being. Some provisions must be made for their economic relations with each other; for the hard fact will begin to emerge that the Austro-Hungarian Empire, like its Roman predecessor provided for real needs, which must now be met in some other way. It did not survive so long merely to support Hapsburg pretensions.[2]

While the problem of the Italian and Rumanian *irredenta* would be solved by their inclusion in already existing mother states, there were two theoretical alternative possibilities of a solution for the Slavonic nations. They could either form a Slav Confederation among themselves or re-federate themselves under different provisions with the Germans and the Magyars. It was the former solution which the *New Europe* had in mind, assuming that the Austro-Germans would join Germany. The Magyars, as the main culprits for misrule in the Monarchy, were probably expected to be associated with their neighbour after a period of penitence.

This concept for a reconstruction was not as simple as it sounded. There were geographical and ethnological factors which prevented a "clean" division into states which would have been viable on their own. This had always been the argument of those who warned of the Balkanization of Central Europe and had advised against a complete dismemberment of the Habsburg Monarchy. In wartime they had pleaded for a federal solution under the Habsburg dynasty. Now they raised their voices for the creation of a "new Austria" or a Danubian Confederation.[3] This seemed the most rational policy for the treatment of minorities and trade communications. But a Confederation without the former German nucleus implied severe difficulties. It would add to the numerical strength of post-war Germany, which might then become more powerful and consolidated than ever before. Should the German Austrians be included inside the *Reich*, the wishes of the *Sudeten* in Bohemia could be expected to go in the same direction, which would immediately have endangered the viability of the centrepiece of the new system.

It was the presence of a large German element in the future Czechoslovak state that led an exponent of British imperial thinking like L. S. Amery to believe that an independent Bohemia

> could only command the patriotic interest of the German element, if it was practically loosely linked up with German Austria and Germany, just as South Africa can only enlist the unanimous patriotism of its population of both white races if it remains in the British Commonwealth.[4]

---

[2] *Round Table*, No. xxxiii (Dec. 1918).
[3] Cf. *Nation* of 26 Oct., 2 and 9 Nov. 1918.
[4] *F.O.* 371/3136, No. 177223/f.64427 of 26 Oct. 1918.

It would therefore be "almost inevitable in the long run" to conceive a solution that excluded the close co-operation of a new federal union with Germany. The new confederacy need not again be dominated by the Germans and the Magyars, but Amery was convinced

> that 'Middle Europe' is an inevitable and necessary outcome of this war whatever the actual issue of the struggle or the terms of peace imposed by the victors.

In Amery's view the main danger confronting Europe was no longer the German menace but the wave of Bolshevism, which threatened the small nations, which were faced with enormous social problems. In view of this new struggle in the wake of the war, the perspective for a British policy towards the former subject nationalities had changed and the chaotic situation demanded a solution that promised political and social stability:

> For the purposes of the war we have rightly backed up Czecho-slovakia, Yugoslavia and every anti-German and anti-Austrian movement we could find. But for the purpose of a lasting settlement we must regulate the satisfaction of these national aspirations by the need of creating or re-creating a larger supernational unity in Central and South East Europe.

Amery's suggestions were received favourably in the Foreign Office by Cecil who agreed that "unless we can induce the small states we are setting up to federate with one another the last state of Europe may well be worse than the first".[5] A detailed consideration of the paper was left by Cecil to the War Department with the "skilled" technical assistance of the P.I.D. In turn H. G. Nicolson and L. B. Namier reviewed the possibilities of a federal solution.[6] They came to the conclusion that an Austrian federation including the Germans of Austria was neither in the interest of the Slav nations nor to the advantage of the Allies, whose difficulties in restoring a balance against Germany after the Russian collapse would be further increased. In any federation centring round Vienna, the Germans were expected to take up a leading position, because they could count upon the support of Germany. It was therefore clear to the Foreign Office peace planners

> that the constitution of a Danubian federation with German Austria for a centre is clearly contrary to our interests, and in the long run would merely amount to a resurrection of Austria under a new name.[7]

---

[5] Minute by Cecil, *ibid*.
[6] Commentary of 7 Nov., *ibid*.
[7] *F.O.* 371/4355, P.I.D. memorandum compiled under the supervision of R. Paget, dated 29 Nov.

To avoid the rebirth of *Mitteleuropa* the Foreign Office suggested the liberation of "economic routes and outlets in such a way as will draw the trade of Central Europe to the Mediterranean while at the same time laying the foundation for a Customs Union".[8] The Czechs themselves had conveyed their determination not to enter into any close connection with German Austria and also urged the Allies to prevent the German Austrians from joining Germany. This problem of an *Anschluss* was given considerable thought in Britain and even King George V was struck by suggestions that the Entente would have an obvious interest in preventing a union between German-speaking Austria and Germany.[9] The Foreign Secretary and his staff were equally concerned but could see no way how to oppose the union between the Germans of Austria and their kinsmen in the *Reich*. "To do so would violate one of the cardinal principles for which the Allies have been fighting", Balfour replied to the King.[10] He hoped that an *Anschluss* could also have a salutary effect, because it would strengthen the South German element in Germany. The P.I.D. also thought that the inclusion of the Austrian Germans might not turn out to be altogether disadvantageous to the balance inside Germany as well as the position in Central Europe, because "it would prevent the German '*Ostmark*' on the Danube from ever reconstituting a federation under German leadership".[11]

The concern over the prospect of an enlarged Germany through the incorporation of the Austrian Germans was even stronger in France, from where the British heard suggestions for the maintenance of the old Austria–Hungary in a reformed shape. But from a British point of view this was out of the question:

> We have pledged ourselves to the entire independence of too many of Austria–Hungary's constituent elements to make it practicable.[12]

The only thing that the British and their allies should supervise and influence was the correctness of the frontier-drawing. In this respect they had to make clear to them

> that the doctrine of self-determination, not being merely an excuse for anti-German map-making, overwhelming reasons will have to be adduced for any infringement of that principle whomever this may concern.[13]

Such expected rivalry could be controlled by a League of Nations, if this

---

[8] *Ibid.*, for further extracts of the memorandum cf. Nelson, *op.cit.*, pp.101–04.
[9] *F.O.* 800/200, Stamfordham to Balfour, 9 Nov.
[10] Balfour's reply, *ibid.*, 11 Nov.
[11] *F.O.* 371/4355 (memorandum of 29 Nov.).
[12] P.I.D. Memorandum by J. Bailey of 28 Nov., *F.O.* 371/4354.
[13] Notes by L. B. Namier on Amery's paper, *loc.cit.*

institution was really going to be an impartial arbiter to secure the application of certain principles and not a sham organization that would sanction the sufferings of the enemies in all doubtful cases. On the other hand the British were careful not to claim the right of the League to interfere in the internal affairs of a sovereign state, for if that was laid down as a fundamental principle, it would bring the British into difficulties about Ireland or the French in Canada. There remained, however, the possibility of only admitting some nations to the family of the states on condition that they would not claim the full and equal status of the former states. This was envisaged by the intellectual begetters of the League, who thought in terms of a trustee-ship for the nationalities cut off from the Russian and the Turkish Empires.

In the cases of Poland, Czechoslovakia, and Yugoslavia these nations were found sufficiently capable to be recognized as independent states of the usual type. But it was hoped that as the successor to the Habsburg Monarchy, the League of Nations would "directly and without power of delegation watch over the relations *inter se* of the new independent states arising from the break-up (of this Empire)".[14]

The new nations could not be expected to achieve true freedom through diplomacy or even through war. All that the Allied statesmen could do with their military success was to remove from their shoulders the Habsburg domination. But with the break-up of the Habsburg Monarchy and the setting up of a number of small states the national problem of Central Europe was not yet solved. Their British sympathizers would have to exert all their influence to help them overcome the problems of independent existence. Here Great Britain, more than any other of the Allied Powers, could inspire the building of a new union on the ruins of the Habsburg Monarchy by the example of the British Commonwealth.[15]

With the vital artery of the Danube as a bond for an economic union around which the disintegrated parts of the Habsburg Monarchy could crystallize there was the hope that a stable and peaceful settlement could be achieved in South East Central Europe. The foundations had been laid by the removal of the Dual system of the Habsburg Empire as a major result of the war. The British contribution to this effect had not been small and it remained to be seen whether Britain was prepared to share the responsibility of finding a better substitute for the "ram-shackle Empire".

---

[14] J. C. Smuts, *Suggestions for a Future League of Peace*, London 1918, p.12.
[15] *New Europe*, 14 Nov. 1918.

BIBLIOGRAPHY

(A) Manuscript Sources

I RECORDS OF GOVERNMENT DEPARTMENTS

1. Austria (*Haus-Hof- und Staatsarchiv*, Vienna):
Krieg geh. XLVII/3 (P.A.I. 503–505): Verhandlungen mit Deutschland.
Krieg geh. XLVII/13 (P.A.I. 524) Verhandlungen über Friedensbedingungen, Nov. 1916–1918.
Krieg 25a (P.A.I. 951) Angebliche und wirkliche Friedensverhandlungen.
Krieg 25s (P.A.I. 956) Friedenssondierungen seitens Italiens.
Krieg 25w (P.A.I. 956) Friedenssondierungen in der Schweiz.
Krieg 25/27 (P.A.I. 963) Friedenssondierungen seitens Englands.
Kabinett des Ministers IIn (P.A.I. 619) Reisen, Personalia (Czernin).
Botschaft Berlin (P.A. III 173–175) Preussen, Weisungen und Varia.
Generalia IX, 7: Nationalitätenkongress in Rom.

2. Germany (*Auswärtiges Amt*, Bonn):
Weltkrieg 23 geh. Friedensstimmungen und Aktionen zur Vermittlung des Friedens, vols. 22–60.
Weltkrieg Grosses Hauptquartier, Österreich-Ungarn, Nr. 23, vols. 1–4.
Österreich 86 Nr. 1: Das österreichische Kaiserhaus, vols. 21–23.
Österreich 86 Nr. 2: Österreichische Staatsmänner, vols. 20–25.
Österreich 95: Beziehungen Österreichs zu Deutschland, vols. 22–24.
Österreich 95 geh.: Beziehungen Österreichs zu Deutschland, vols. 4–5.
Deutschland 135 Nr. 6 geh.: Botschaft in Wien, vol. 1.

Bibliography

3. France (*Archives du Ministère des Affaires Etrangères*, Paris):
Autriche-Hongrie: Mouvement National Tchèque.
               Combattants Tchèques (Cartons 310–311).
               Les Yougoslaves (Carton 313).
Conférences internationales, Dec. 1916–Mar. 1918 (Carton 369).

4. Great Britain (*Public Record Office*, London):
Cabinet Office:
    Cab. 1/25–27, Miscellaneous Records.
    Cab. 21/77, 88, Registered Files.
    Cab. 23/1–6, Cabinet Minutes.
            13–14, 'A' Minutes.
            44, Minutes with I.W.C. References.
    Cab. 24/1–5 Cabinet Memoranda, G.-Papers.
            6–72 Cabinet Memoranda, GT.-Papers.
    Cab. 25/119–22 Supreme War Council.
    Cab. 27/7–8 Cabinet Committees.
    Cab. 28/1–5 Allied Conferences.
    Cab. 37/160–162 Cabinet Papers, 1916.
    Cab. 41/35/25.
    Cab. 42/2/1, 2.

Foreign Office, General Correspondence, Political (371):
    Austria–Hungary: 1898–1900, 2241, 2602, 2862–64, 3133–39.
    Balkans: 1900–05, 2242–2280, 2603–34, 2865–95, 3140–60.
    France: 1983–84, 2360–66, 2675–78, 3212–21.
    Germany: 1992, 2367–68, 2678–80, 3222–27.
    Italy: 2008–09, 2374–80, 2684–87, 3228–33.
    Russia: 2095–2096, 2245–2457, 2995–3020, 3284–3350.
    America: 2846–52, 3108–34, 3483–93.
    War (general): 2138–47, 2503–10, 3075–86, 3434–51.
    Miscellaneous General Files: 3474–75.
    P.I.D. Files: 4357–69.

Confidential Print
Austria 465.
War (General) 438.

Embassy Correspondence
United States (115).
France (146), Italy (170), Russia (181), Switzerland (192), Serbia
    (260), Rumania (770).

War Office, Directorates of Military Operations
and Intelligence (106).
308 General War Policy and Situation Reports.

310–15 General Staff Appreciation and Memoranda for the War
Cabinet.
373 Austria.
678–98 Czechoslovakia.
746–856 Italy.

II PRIVATE PAPERS:

H.H.St.A., Vienna
Baernreither diary.
Mensdorff papers and diary.
Public Record Office
Arthur Nicolson papers, F.O. 800/373–77.
Balfour papers, F.O. 800/199–200.
Cromer papers, F.O. 633/23–24.
British Museum
Balfour papers, Add.MSS. 49692–797.
Cecil papers, Add.MSS. 51073–51105.
Walburga Paget papers, Add.MSS. 51238–40/1.
C. P. Scott papers, Add.MSS. 50901–09.
Beaverbrook Library, London
Lloyd George papers.
Times Archives, London
Steed papers.
School of Slavonic and East European Studies, London
Seton-Watson papers (Selected letters by courtesy of H. Seton-
Watson).
Bodleian Library, Oxford
Asquith papers, MSS. 1–18, 19–35, 46–63, 83–133, 136–140.
Milner papers, boxes 108, 118, 124–25, 210–11, 280, 301.
Scottish Record Office, Edinburgh
Lothian papers (Philip Kerr).

(B) Printed Sources

I PRIMARY SOURCES
1. Published Documents
Berliner Monatshefte zur Kriegsschuldfrage, xv (1938), pp.401–19: "Die
Friedensgespräche der Grafen Mensdorff und Revertera im
Dezember 1917 und Februar 1918 nach ihren Berichten an den
Grafen Czernin." (anonymous publication from H.H.St.A.).

L'Allemagne et les problèmes de la paix pendant la première guerre mondiale. Documents extraits des archives de l'office allemand des affaires etrangères. eds. A. Scherer and J. Grunewald, 2 vols., Paris 1962–66.

British Documents on the Origin of the War, 1898–1914, ed. G. P. Gooch and H. Temperley, vols. v-xi., London 1926ff.

Die Deutschen Dokumente zum Kriegsausbruch, ed. Auswärtiges Amt., 2 vols., Berlin 1919.

Documents Diplomatiques Français, 1871–1914, ed. Commission de Publication des Documents Relatifs aux Origines de la Guerre de 1914, 3rd ser., vols. i-xi, Paris 1929ff.

Documenti Diplomatici Italiani, ed. Commissione per la Pubblicazione del Documenti Diplomatici, 5th ser., 1914–1918, vol. i, Rome 1954.

Die Grosse Politik der Europäischen Kabinette, 1871–1914, ed. J. Lepsius, et al., Berlin 1924ff.

Hansard's Parliamentary Debates. House of Commons, 5th ser., vols. 93–111.

Die Internationalen Beziehungen im Zeitalter des Imperialismus. Dokumente aus den Archiven der Zarischen und der Provisorischen Regierung. Ger. ed. O. Hoetzsh, Berlin 1936.

The Lansing Papers, ed. U.S. Department of State, Washington 1939.

Österreich-Ungarns Aussenpolitik. Von der bosnischen Krise 1908 bis zum Kriegsausbruch 1914, Diplomatische Aktenstücke des Österreich-ungarischen Ministeriums des Äusseren, ed. L. Bittner et al., 8 vols., Vienna 1930.

Österreich-Ungarns letzter Krieg, 1914–1918. ed. Österreichisches Bundesministerium f. Heerwesen. vols. i-vii, Vienna 1938.

Official German Documents relating to the World War (Reichstag Inquiry Commission), 2 vols., New York 1923.

Official Statements of War Aims and Peace Proposals, December 1916 to November 1918, ed. J. B. Scott, Washington 1921.

Papers Relating to the Foreign Relations of the United States. The World War 1917–1918. ed. U.S. Department of State, Washington 1933.

Protokolle des Gemeinsamen Ministerrats der österreich-ungarischen Monarchie (1914–1918). ed. M. Komjáthy, Budapest 1966.

Report on the 16th Annual Conference of the Labour Party, London 1917.

Report on the 17th Annual Conference of the Labour Party, London 1918.

2. Contemporary Newspapers and Periodicals

Call	*Fremdenblatt*	*Quarterly Review*
Cambridge Magazine	*Manchester Guardian*	*Round Table*
Common Sense	*Nation*	*Saturday Review*
Contemporary Review	*National Review*	*Spectator*
Daily Telegraph	*La Nation Tchèque*	*The Times*
Edinburgh Review	*Neue Freie Presse*	*Westminster Gazette*
	New Europe	

3. Contemporary Publications, Diaries, Letters, Memoirs

Acton, Lord, *Essays on Church and State*, London repr. 1952.

Amery, L. S., *My Political Life*, London 1953.

Andrássy, J., *Diplomatie und Weltkrieg*, Berlin 1920.

Baernreither, J., *Der Verfall des Habsburger Reiches und die Deutschen*, Vienna 1938.

Beneš, E., *Souvenirs de guerre et de révolution*, Paris 1928.

Blake, R. (ed.), *The Private Papers of Douglas Haig*, London 1952.

Buchanan, G., *My Mission to Russia*, London 1923.

Burián, S., *Austria in Dissolution*, London 1931.

Buxton, Ch. and N., *The War and the Balkans*, London 1915.

Calwell, C. E., *Field Marshal Sir Henry Wilson: His Life and His Diaries*, London 1927.

Cambon, P., *Correspondence, 1870–1924*, vol. iii, Paris 1946.

Cecil, R., *All the Way*, London 1949.

Chapman Huston, D., *The Lost Historian. A Memoir of Sir Sidney Low*, London 1936.

Charles-Roux, F., *Souvenirs Diplomatiques*, Paris 1947.

Chéradame, A., *L'Allemagne, la France et la question d'Autriche*, Paris 1902.

Cole, M. I. (ed.), *Beatrice Webb's Diaries, 1912–1924*, London 1952.

Czernin, O., *Im Weltkriege*, Berlin 1919.

Fellner, F. (ed.), *Schicksalsjahre Österreichs. Das Politische Tagebuch Joseph Redlichs, 1908–1919*, Vienna 1954.

Foerster, F. W., *Erlebte Weltgeschichte*, Nuremberg 1953.

Funder, F., *Vom Gestern zum Heute*, Vienna 1952.

Grey, E., *Twenty-Five Years*, London 1925.

Hancock, W. K. and Poel, J. van der, *Selections from the Smuts Papers*, vol. iii, Cambridge 1966.

Hankey, M., *The Supreme Command*, London 1961.

Hardinge, Ch., *Old Diplomacy*, London 1947.

Henderson, A., *The Aims of Labour*, London 1918.

Károlyi, M., *Fighting the World*, New York 1925.

Laroche, J., *Au Quai d'Orsay avec Briand et Poincaré*, Paris 1957.

Lennox, A. G. (ed.), *Diary of Lord Bertie of Thame*, London 1925.

Lloyd George, D., *War Memoirs*, London (2) 19 (Quoted by its title).

Malagodi, O., *Conversazioni della guerra*, Milan 1960.

Masaryk, T. G., *The Making of a State*, London 1927.

Namier, L. B., *Avenues of History*, London 1952.

—— *Vanished Supremacies*, Peregrine rep., Harmondsworth 1962.

Orlando, V. E., *Memorie*, Milan 1960.

Paléologue, M., *La Russie des Tsars pendant la Grande Guerre*, Paris 1921/2.

Poincaré, R., *Au service de la France*, vol. ix, Paris 1933.

Polzer-Hoditz, A., *Kaiser Karl*, Vienna 1929.

Ribot, A. jr., *Journal d'Alexandre Ribot*, Paris 1938.

Ribot, A., *Lettres à un ami*, Paris 1926.
Riddell, G., *War Diary*, London 1933.
Robertson, W., *From Private to Field-Marshal*, London 1921.
Rodd, R., *Memoirs*, vol. iii, London 1935.
Seton-Watson, R. W., *The Future of Austria–Hungary*, London 1913.
—— et al., *War and Democracy*, London 1914.
Seymour, Ch. (ed.), *The Intimate Papers of Colonel House*, vol. iii, Boston 1938.
Smuts, J. C., *The League of Nations: A Practical Suggestion*, London 1918.
Steed, H. W., *The Hapsburg Monarchy*, London 1913.
—— *Through Thirty Years*, London 1924 (quoted by its title).
Toynbee, A., *Nationality and the War*, London 1915.
—— *The New Europe*, London 1915.
Trubetzkoi, G., *Russland als Grossmacht*, Stuttgart, 2nd ed., 1917.
Werkmann, A., *Aus der Aktenmappe seines Kabinettschefs*, Vienna 1922.
Woolf, L., *International Government*, London 1916.
Worsfold, W. B., *The Empire on the Anvil*, London 1916.
The War Aims of the British People. Statement of the Labour Party, London 1918.

II SECONDARY SOURCES
1. Books

Amiguet, Ph., *La vie du prince Sixte de Bourbon*, Paris 1934.
Auerbach, B., *L'Autriche et la Hongrie pendant la guerre*, Paris 1925.
Benedikt, H., *Die Friedensaktion der Meinlgruppe*, Vienna 1962.
Bohanifać, A. F. and Mihanović, L. S., eds., *The Croatian Nation*, Chicago 1955.
Bradley, J., *Allied Intervention in Russia, 1917–1920*, London 1968.
Bréal, A., *Philippe Berthelot*, Paris 1937.
Briggs, M., *George D. Herron and the European Settlement*, Stanford 1932.
Brook-Shepherd, G., *The Last Habsburg*, London 1969.
Butler, J. R. M., *Lord Lothian (Philip Kerr)*, London 1960.
Charles-Roux, F., *La paix des empires centraux*, Paris 1947.
Conwell-Evans, T. P., *Foreign Policy from a Back Bench*, London 1932.
Crankshaw, E., *The Fall of the House of Habsburg*, London 1963.
Dallin, A., et al., *Russian Diplomacy and Eastern Europe, 1914–1917*, New York 1963.
Dugdale, E. T. S., *Maurice de Bunsen*, London 1934.
Engel-Janosi, F., *Die Friedensgespräche Graf Nikolaus Reverteras mit Comte Abel Armand, 1917–1918*, Graz 1965.
Erickson, J., *Panslavism*, London 1964.
Feis, H., *Europe, the World's Banker*, repr., New York, 1965.
Fester, R., *Die Politik Kaiser Karls und der Wendepunkt des Krieges*, Munich 1925.

Fischer, F., *Griff nach der Weltmacht*, Düsseldorf, 3rd ed., 1964. Quotations from the English Edition, *Germany's Aims in the First World War*, London 1967.

Forster, K., *The Failures of Peace*, Washington 1941.

Franz, G., *Erzherzog Franz Ferdinand und die Pläne zur Reform der Habsburger Monarchie*, Brünn 1943.

Gilbert, M. (ed.), *A Century of Conflict*, London 1961.

Glaise-Horstenau, E., *Die Katastrophe*, Vienna 1929.

Gollin, A., *Proconsul in Politics*, London 1964.

Gottlieb, W., *Studies in Secret Diplomacy during the First World War*, London 1964.

Guinn, P., *British Strategy and Politics*, 1914–1918, London 1965.

Hammond, J., *C. P. Scott of the Manchester Guardian*, London 1934.

Hanak, H., *Great Britain and Austria–Hungary during the First World War. A Study in the Formation of Public Opinion*, Oxford 1962.

Hancock, W. K., *Smuts*, Vol. I: *The Sanguine Years*, London 1962.

Hodža, M., *Federation in Central Europe*, London 1942.

Hoeglinger, F., *Ministerpräsident Heinrich Clam-Martinic*, Vienna 1964.

Hopwood, F., *"Interalliance Diplomacy: Count Czernin and Germany, 1916–1918"*, (Stamford Univ., Ph.D. thesis).

Jászi, O., *The Dissolution of the Habsburg Monarchy*, Chicago (2) 1961.

Jones, Th., *Lloyd George*, Cambridge, Mass., 1957.

Kann, R. A., *Die Sixtus affaire*, Munich 1966.

Kennan, G. F., *The Decision to Intervene*, Princeton 1958.

—— *Russia Leaves the War*, Princeton 1956.

Klein, F. (ed.), *Österreich-Ungarn in der Weltpolitik*, Berlin 1966.

Kiszling, R., *Erzherzog Franz Ferdinand von Österreich-Este*, Graz 1953.

Křižek, J., *Die wirtschaftlichen Grundzüge des österreich-ungarischen Imperialismus in der Vorkriegszeit*, Prague 1963.

Kybal, V., *Les origines diplomatiques de l'état tchécoslovaque*, Prague 1929.

Launay, J. de, *Secrets diplomatiques, 1914–1918*, Brussels 1963.

Link, A. S., *Wilson*, vol. v., Princeton 1966.

Lorenz, R., *Kaiser Karl und der Untergang der Donaumonarchie*, Graz 1959.

Macartney, C. A., *The Habsburg Empire 1790–1918*, London 1968.

Macartney, C. A. and Palmer, A. W., *Independent Eastern Europe*, London 1962.

Mamatey, V. S., *The United States and East Central Europe*, Princeton 1957.

Manteyer, G., *Austria's Peace Offer*, London 1920.

May, A., *The Passing of the Hapsburg Monarchy*, Philadelphia 1966.

Mayer, A. J., *Wilson vs. Lenin, Origins of the New Diplomacy*, Cleveland 1964.

Martin, L. W., *Peace without Victory*, New Haven 1964.

McBriar, A. M., *Fabian Socialism in English Politics*, Cambridge 1962.

Meckling, I., *Die Aussenpolitik des Grafen Czernin*, Munich 1969.
Nelson, H. I., *Land and Power*, London 1963.
Newton, P., *Lord Lansdowne*, London 1929.
Nicolson, H., *King George V*, London 1952.
Nowak, K., *Der Sturz der Mittelmächte*, Munich 1921.
Ostović, P., *The Truth about Yugoslavia*, New York 1957.
Pingaud, A., *Histoire diplomatique de la France pendant la Grande Guerre*, vol. iii, Paris 1940.
Přibram, A. F., *Great Britain and Austria–Hungary, 1908–1914*, London 1951.
—— *Austrian Foreign Policy, 1908–1918*, London 1923.
Pound, R. and Harmsworth, G., *Northcliffe*, London 1959.
Ritter, G. A., *Staatskunst und Kriegshandwerk*, vols. iii, iv, Munich 1966–68.
Renouvin, P., *La crise européene et la première guerre mondiale*, Paris (4) 1962.
Rothwell, V. H., *British War Aims and Peace Diplomacy, 1914–1918*, Oxford 1971.
Rudin, H., *Armistice 1918*, New Haven 1944.
Rumpler, H., *Die Kriegsziele Österreich-Ungarns auf dem Balkan, 1915/1916*, Graz 1965.
Seton-Watson, R. W., *Masaryk in England*, Cambridge 1943.
Singer, L., *Czernin*, Graz 1966.
Slice, A. van der, *International Labour, Diplomacy and Peace, 1914–1919*, Philadelphia 1941.
Steglich, W., *Die Friedenspolitik der Mittelmächte, 1917–1918*, Wiesbaden 1964.
Suarez, G., *Briand*, iv, Paris 1940.
Swanwick, H. M., *Builders of Peace*, London 1924.
Taylor, A. J. P., *Politics in Wartime*, London 1964.
—— *The Trouble Makers*, London 1964.
—— *The Habsburg Monarchy*, Peregrine repr. Harmondsworth 1964.
Toscano, M., *Gli accordi di San Giovanni di Mooriano*, Milan 1936.
Trevelyan, G. M., *Grey of Fallodon*, London 1937.
Ullman, R. H., *Intervention and the War*, London 1961.
Valiani, L., *La dissoluzione dell'Austria–Ungheria*, Milan 1966.
Willert, A., *The Road to Safety*, London.
Woodward, L., *Britain and the First World War*, London 1966.
Young, E., *Arthur James Balfour*, London 1963.
Zeman, Z. A. B., *The Break-up of the Habsburg Empire*, London 1961.
—— *A Diplomatic History of the First World War*, London 1971.
The History of The Times, vols. ii, iv, London 1952.

2. Articles

Appuhn, Ch., "Les négotiations austro-allemands du printemps de 1917", *Revue d'histoire du première guerre mondiale*, xiii, 1935.

Barrère, C., "Souvenirs diplomatiques", *Revue des Deux Mondes* (R.D.M.), 15 Apr. 1938.

Bridge, F. R., "The British Declaration of War on Austria–Hungary in 1914", *Slavonic and East European Review*, xlvii, 1969. (S.E.E.R.)

Baumont, M., "L'Italie et la guerre", *R.D.M.*, 1 Sept. 1964.

Brunauer, E., "Peace Proposals of December, 1916–January, 1917", *Journal of Modern History*, iv, 1932 (J.M.H.)

Bradley, J., "The Allies and the Czechoslovak Revolt against the Bolsheviks in 1918", *S.E.E.R.*, xliii, 1964/65.

Craig, G., "The World War I Alliance of the Central Powers in Retrospect", *J.M.R.*, xxxvii, 1965.

Epstein, K., "The Development of German–Austrian War Aims in the Spring of 1917", *Journal of Central European Affairs* (J.C.E.A.), xvii, 1957.

Ferro, M., "La Politique des nationalités du gouvernement provisoire russe", *Cahiers du Monde russe et soviétique*, 1961.

Fest, W. B., "British War Aims and German Peace Feelers during the First World War (December 1916–November 1918)", *Historical Journal*, xv, 1972.

Fester, R., "Die Sonderfriedensaktion des Prinzen Sixtus von Bourbon-Parma und die Legende des italienischen Fühlers", *Berliner Monatshefte*, xv, 1937.

Hanak, H., "The New Europe, 1916–1920", *S.E.E.R.*, 1961.

—— "The Government, the Foreign Office and Austria–Hungary, 1914–1918", *ibid.*, xlvii, 1969.

—— "A Lost Cause: The English Radicals and the Habsburg Empire, 1914–1918", *J.C.E.A.*, xxiii, 1963.

Hölzle, E., "Das Experiment des Friedens im ersten Weltkrieg", *Geschichte in Wissenschaft und Unterricht*, xiii, 1962.

Joll, J., "The End of Dynamic Diplomacy", *The Listener*, 23 June 1966.

Kann, R. A., "Count Ottokar Czernin and Archduke Francis Ferdinand", *J.C.E.A.*, xvi, 1956.

Kernek, S., "The British Government's Reaction to President Wilson's 'Peace' Note of December 1916", *Historical Journal*, xiii, 1970.

Kohn, H., "The Viability of the Habsburg Monarchy", *Slavic Review*, xxii, 1963.

Krizman, B., "Austro–Hungarian Diplomacy before the Collapse of the Empire", *Journal of Contemporary History* (J.C.H.), iv, 1968.

Lehmann, H., "Österreiche-Ungarns Belgienpolitik im ersten Weltkrieg", *Historische Zeitschrift*, cxcii, 1961.

Lowe, C. J., "Britain and the Italian Intervention, 1914–1915", *Historical Journal*, xii, 1969.

Mamatey, V. S., "The United States and the Dissolution of Austria–Hungary", *J.C.E.A.*, x, 1950.

—— "The Recognition of the Czechoslovak National Council", *ibid.*, xiii, 1953.

May, A., "Woodrow Wilson and Austria–Hungary to the End of 1917", *Festschrift f.H. Benedikt*, Vienna 1957.

Pingaud, A., "L'Entente et la Roumanie on 1915", *R.D.M.*, May 1930.

Pinon, R., "Clemenceau et l'Autriche", *Revue politique et parlementaire*, cxciv, 1948.

Renouvin, P., "Les tentatives de paix et le gouvernement français en 1917", *R.D.M.*, 1964.

Sepić, D., "The Question of Yugoslav Union in 1918", *J.C.H.*, iii, 1968.

Sixte de Bourbon-Parma, "Austria's Peace Offer: Afterthoughts", *Dublin Review*, clxx, 1922.

—— "Quinze ans d'après", *La Revue de Paris*, xxxix, 1932.

Sweet, P., "Germany, Austria–Hungary and Mitteleuropa", *Festschrift f.H. Benedikt*, Vienna 1957.

Valiani, L., "Italian–Austro–Hungarian Negotiations 1914–1915", *J.C.H.*, 1966.

—— "Documenti francesi sull'Italia e il movimento jugoslavo", *Rivista Storica Italiana*, lxxx, 1968.

—— "Documenti tedeschi ed inglesi sui tentativi di pace fra l'Intesa e l'Austria–Ungheria", *ibid.*

Addenda

Addenda

Ara, A., *L'Austria–Ungheria nella politica americana durante la prima guerra mondiale*, Rome 1973.

Bridge, F.R., *Great Britain and Austria–Hungary 1906–14*, London 1972.

Calder, K. J., *Britain and the Origins of the New Europe 1914–1918*, Cambridge 1976.

Raabe, J., *Beiträge zur Geschichte der diplomatischen Beziehungen zwischen Frankreich und Österreich-Ungarn, 1908–1912*, Vienna 1971.

Schuster, P., *Henry Wickham Steed und die Habsburgermonarchie*, Vienna 1970.

INDEX